DEC Networks and Architectures

DEC Networks and Architectures

Carl Malamud

Intertext Publications
McGraw-Hill Book Company

New York St. Louis San Francisco Auckland Bogotá
Hamburg London Madrid Mexico Milan Montreal
New Delhi Panama Paris São Paulo
Singapore Sidney Tokyo Toronto

Library of Congress Catalog Card Number 88-83063

10 9 8 7 6 5 4 3 2

TK
5105.5
,M357
1989

64958

ISBN 0-07-039822-4

Intertext Publications/Multiscience Press, Inc.
One Lincoln Plaza
New York, NY 10023

McGraw-Hill Book Company
1221 Avenue of the Americas
New York, NY 10020

Contents

To
Rita and Nate Malamud

Trademarks

PostScript is a trademark of Adobe Systems, Inc.

AlisaTalk is a trademark of Alisa Systems.

Alliant is a trademark of Alliant.

Linotronic is a registered trademark of Allied Linotype Co.

PDS, Dimension, and Unix are registered trademarks of American Telephone & Telegraph Corporation.

Macintosh, AppleTalk, Apple IIE, and CL/1 are trademarks of Apple Computer, Inc.

Boston Business Computing is a trademark of Boston Business Computing, Inc.

IDM 500 is a trademark of Britton Lee, Inc.

Chipcom and Ethermodem is a trademark of Chipcom Corp.

Kermit is copyright 1985, Trustees of Columbia University.

COMPAQ is a registered trademark of Compaq Computer Corporation.

Convex is a trademark of Convex Computer Corp.

Cullinet is a registered trademark and IDMS is a trademark of Cullinet Software Inc.

Cray is a trademark of Cray Research, Inc.

ALL-IN-1, BI Bus, CI Bus, CIT, CTERM, DAP, DDCMP, DEC, DECconnect, DECMUXII, DECNA, DECnet, DECnet-DOS, DECnet Router, DECnet/RSX, DECnet-Ultrix, DECserver, DECnet/SNA Gateway, DECnet-VMS, DECOM, DECSA, DECServer, DECtalk, DECwindows, DECworld, DELNI, DELUA, DEMPR, DEMSA, DEQNA, DEREP, DESTA, DMB32, DNA, DNS, DQS, DSRI, DSV11, Easynet, EDE, EDE-W, ELK, EMA, EtherNIM, H4000, HSC, LAN Bridge 100, LAN Traffic Monitor, LAT, LAVC, LPS40, mail-11, MAILbus, Message Router, METROWAVE Bridge, MicroVAX, MOP, MSCP, MUXserver, NMCC/DECnet Monitor, NSP, OSAK, P/FM, PDP, Q-Bus, Rally, RBMS, RD53, Rdb, RMS, RSM, SA482,

Acknowledgments

Many individuals and companies have been particularly helpful in the production of this book. They have provided information on their products, photographs, access to facilities and a host of other invaluable services to me. I would like to particularly thank Carolyn Mathews of Digital Equipment Corporation without whom this book would not have been produced.

I was also greatly aided by many of the product and consultant relations managers at DEC, including Chris Gannon, Bill Gassman, Bob McCauley and the Easynet staff, Judy Finman, Bill Kenda, Randy Messer, and Joyce Townsend. I am particularly grateful to the many members of the DEC Network and Communications Group who provided me with briefings and reviews of drafts of the manuscript.

Much of the material for this book was initially presented in seminars. I am especially appreciative of all that I learned from my students in the course of teaching the seminars. Two other seminar instructors, Uyless Black of the Information Engineering Institute, and Dennis Linnell of Gate Technology, provided valuable feedback, both in the review of the book and in many technical discussions in the past.

Nancy Groves of Sun Microsystems, Tom Baffico of Adobe Systems, Margaret Epperheimer of 3COM, Guy Van Buskirk of Vitalink and Jay Dombrowski of the San Diego Supercomputer Center also provided valuable information. Harry Saal and George Comstock of Network General were especially generous in providing access to their facilities.

As I'm not an expert on every subject (and have no desire to be an expert in many subjects), I would like to acknowledge the help that several books written by prominent industry experts played in some of the overview sections. Specifically, I would like to thank Adobe Systems, Uyless Black, Douglas Comer, Adrian Nye and William Stallings for their well thought out treatment of a variety of topics.

Preface

This book presents one view of the world. It's a survey of how to connect computers and other devices together to form a large, coherent network. The book focuses on DEC computers, but the focus is on how to use DEC computers in combination with a wide variety of other resources.

Part 1 is an introduction to networks and architectures. This introductory chapter provides a first glimpse of many of the concepts found throughout the book.

Part 2 begins with a survey of the architectures that DEC has developed to connect computers together. Several different architectures coexist to provide different types of functionality in the network. The Digital Network Architecture is the primary architecture used for DECnet products. Specialized architectures are used for Clusters, the Local Area Transport, and maintenance operations.

Part 3 shows how the DEC architectures are implemented into networks. Local area networks and wide area networks are considered in turn. The final chapter discusses how the DECnet software is implemented and managed.

Part 4 discusses a variety of other networking architectures. SNA and TCP/IP provide connections to the IBM, government, and Unix computing environments. OSI is discussed in great detail because of its central role in DNA Phase V.

Part 5 of the book is a discussion of two very sophisticated protocols that are used to provide a full-featured graphics user interface in a networked environment. The X Windows System and Postscript allow the full power of the underlying network to be used in a workstation environment.

An understanding of the different architectures and their implementation provides a valuable perspective for those who use networks. This book tries to provide a survey of the options available and some of their implications. As such it provides a starting point. Suggestions for further reading accompany each chapter for those desiring a more in-depth examination of selected topics.

Part

1

Introduction

1

Introduction: Networks and Architectures

This is a book about networks and architectures. An architecture, like a building architecture, is a plan. If each of the components of an architecture is built according to the plan, they will work together. Simply put, a computer architecture is a way of making many individual components work together as a system.

Network architectures are just one of many different kinds of architectures. A computer, such as a VAX, has an architecture. The architecture details how the components of a CPU will function. Disk drives might also have an architecture. DEC's Digital Storage Architecture details how disk drives and disk controllers work together.

The network architecture begins with a complete computer system and says how these computers will communicate. The computer doesn't have to be a general-purpose machine like a VAX, however. Dedicated computers, known as servers, also play a part in distributed network architectures like those discussed in this book.

A distributed network means that different computers on the network specialize in different tasks. One computer, known as a terminal server, might specialize in communicating with terminals. Another computer, known as a print server, might specialize in laser printing services. Finally, a general-purpose computer like a VAX would specialize in computation such as a database management system. All of these computers work together in a transparent fashion. How they work together is the subject of this book.

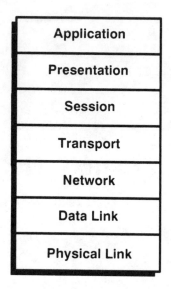

Application
Presentation
Session
Transport
Network
Data Link
Physical Link

Fig. 1-1   ISO reference model.

Layered Architectures: The ISO Reference Model

A computer network is a complex system. The goal of the architecture is to hide that complexity from the user of the network. The user wants services—printing, computation, remote access to data, remote access to systems, messaging, or any of the other myriad services available in a modern computer network.

The goal is thus a transparent network. Once the architecture is in place and implemented, the network should fade into the background. A user can ask for data without knowing its location. The fact that a network goes and gets the data should be irrelevant to the user. The user is more interested in the semantics of the data—what it means and what to do with it. The procedural aspects of the data should be hidden.

This transparent access to network services is accomplished by dividing the tasks of the network into a series of layers. Each layer accomplishes a specific set of tasks, which are then offered as a service to the user of that layer. How those tasks are accomplished are hidden from the service user. The service provider transparently accomplishes the given task.

The International Standards Organization (ISO) reference model is the most widely accepted layered architecture for a computer network. Figure 1-1 shows the different layers in the ISO reference model. There are two characteristics to this model:

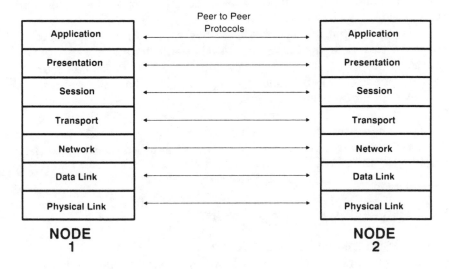

Fig. 1-2 Peer-to-peer communications.

■ Each layer communicates with its peer on another node using a
protocol.
■ Each layer presents a rigorously defined set of services to the layer
on top of it.

This is a layered architecture in that each layer has a specific set of
tasks that it accomplishes. That layer then presents a set of services
to the node on top. For example, the network layer is responsible for
getting data to another node on the network. The service it presents
to the transport layer is the delivery of data to a node.

Once data gets to a node, the transport layer is responsible for
delivering that data to a specific user. The transport layer thus performs the service of delivery of data to a user. The transport layer
will use the services of the network layer to get the data to the next
node. Figure 1-2 illustrates these peer to peer protocols.

Peer-to-peer protocols are used to communicate between one instance of a layer and another instance on another node. A peer-to
peer-protocol for the transport layer would indicate that the following
information was meant for a specific user. Following the user address,
known as a header, is a set of data.

The transport layer would take the incoming message, strip off the header, and then hand the user data off to the user of the transport service.

Likewise, when the transport service has prepared a message, consisting of a header and data, it hands that information down to the network layer. The network layer treats the whole message as user data and appends its own header to the message. That header would indicate which node of the network it goes to.

At the receiving end, the network layer would strip off the network header and hand the data up to the transport layer. The transport layer would strip off the transport header and hand the data up to the session layer, and so on.

Lower Layers: Networks and Subnetworks

The bottom of three layers of the ISO reference model are the lower layer services. These deliver data from one node on the network to another. To the user of the network layer, the topology of that network is masked.

At the bottom of the architecture is the physical layer of a network. The responsibility of the physical layer is to transmit a series of bits over a wire. The fact that the bits may eventually go to different nodes or to different users is not the concern of this layer.

The data link layer uses that service to send frames of data across a subnetwork. A frame consists of several bytes of data with a header. The header indicates the address of the receiving node. As can be seen, it is possible for several nodes to all access the same physical medium. It is the responsibility of the data link layer to deliver data to the appropriate user of the medium.

An example of a combination of data link and physical layers is the Ethernet local area network (LAN) standard. Ethernet allows up to 1024 nodes to share a single logical wire. The term "logical wire" indicates that the actual physical topology may consist of several segments of wire connected together. To the user of the Ethernet, however, all nodes look as though they are on one piece of wire and are directly accessible.

Ethernet is an example of a subnetwork. A subnetwork allows data to be delivered directly to any node connected to the subnetwork. No routing decisions need be made. The header is added to the data and it is sent out. The subnetwork sends the data along to its destination.

Other subnetwork technologies examined in this book are X.25 and ISDN. They allow data to be delivered in a wide area environment. Both X.25 and ISDN are connection oriented subnetwork services,

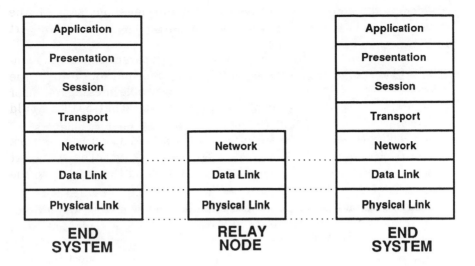

Fig. 1-3 Intermediate and end nodes.

meaning that the user must first set up a virtual circuit to their destination. How to get to that destination, however, is masked from the user.

The network layer is responsible for interconnecting subnetworks together and making routing decisions. If data must go through several different subnetworks, the network must decide which subnetwork is on the path to the eventual destination.

A packet may go through several intermediate nodes before it reaches its eventual destination. The network layer is responsible for finding each of the nodes along a path to the end destination. The network layer is also responsible for adapting to changes in the topology of the network. Users of the network service do not concern themselves with the fact that a packet may go through intermediate nodes.

Figure 1-3 illustrates how intermediate nodes serve as a relay. A packet goes down the protocol stack, then back up the protocol stack at the intermediate node. Only when the packet reaches its final destination does it go up to the peer transport layer entity.

While the topology of a subnetwork is hidden from the network architecture, the topology at the network layer is quite important. Update messages are periodically sent between all the different routing nodes on the network to keep them informed of any changes in the topology. A change in the topology might be a new subnetwork or a new node or the failure of an existing component.

Upper Layers: Users and Services

Once data has gone through the network layer, the topology of the underlying network is hidden from users. The next two layers are responsible for farming out a stream of data to different users.

The transport layer is responsible for providing reliable end to end communications. This is accomplished by assigning a logical circuit to each user of the transport layer. All data received is tagged with the number of this logical circuit. The transport layer is able to multiplex data from many different users and present a single stream-oriented interface to the network layer.

In addition to the multiplexing function, the transport layer is responsible for reliable communications. All data received is broken up into packets and sent down to the network layer. Each packet is numbered. At the destination end, the transport layer examines each packet received to see if any are missing. If they are, it sends a message to its peer transport entity at the source end and requests retransmission of that particular packet.

The user of the transport layer is thus assured of reliable end to end communications. The next layer, the session layer, is the interface to the operating system. When a new connection request is received, it is up to the session layer to validate that request. If the request is allowed, the session layer then activates the required service.

Services are the real aim of the network. Services can include remote data access, remote printing, network-based electronic mail, Videotex, and a host of other functions. A service is performed by two applications communicating with each other.

For two applications to communicate with each other, they have to agree on a common representation for data. Even a simple concept such as an integer is represented in different ways on different vendor's machines.

More complex objects, such as a file or a document or a graphic image, are also represented in different ways. It is the responsibility of the presentation layer to represent information in a machine-independent fashion.

While the presentation layer is concerned with the representation of information, the application layer is responsible for the semantics of that information. The command "send a mail message" is an example of a semantic construct. How that mail message is represented would then be the responsibility of the presentation layer.

Multiple Architectures in Networks

The abstract concepts in the ISO reference model have been implemented into a variety of specific architectures. Some of the architectures are general-purpose architectures meant to address a variety of needs. IBM's System Network Architecture (SNA) or DEC's Digital Network Architecture (DNA) are two examples of general purpose architectures.

Other architectures are specialized. DEC's Local Area Transport Architecture, for example, only deals with how terminal servers talk to hosts on an Ethernet. The purpose of this book is twofold:

- To illustrate the different architectures and their different functions
- To show how the architectures are implemented in various physical media, on different hardware platforms, and in different software packages

The book begins by talking about DEC network architectures. Next, it will talk about how to implement those architectures. In Part 4, a variety of other architectures are presented.

Digital Network Architecture

There are several DEC architectures. The most general network architecture is the Digital Network Architecture. DECnet consists of a series of DEC products that conform to the DNA architecture specifications. Figure 1-4 shows the layers of the DNA protocol stack.

DNA is able to use three different subnetwork technologies. The Digital Data Communications Message Protocol is an example of a traditional data link protocol. DDCMP is used to form a point-to-point link between two computers. The physical medium used by DDCMP could be a simple RS-232-C cable or could consist of a satellite, microwave, or other wide area communications link.

Another subnetwork technology is Ethernet. Ethernet consists of data and physical link protocols. To the DNA routing layer, the Ethernet topology looks like a single wire with many nodes on it. As we will see in the local area network chapter, this topology can actually be quite complex.

Ethernet is used by many other architectures. An important characteristic of Ethernet is that many users can coexist on the medium. The DNA routing layer is one of those users, but TCP/IP or LAT or other architectures will also be present on the same data link.

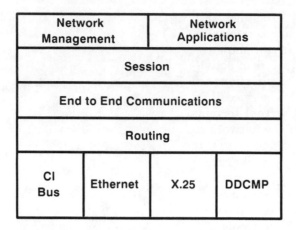

Fig. 1-4   Digital Network Architecture.

A third subnetwork technology supported by DNA is the X.25 standard. X.25 is a packet-switched data communications architecture. Again, DNA may share X.25 facilities with other users.

The routing layer of DNA, which corresponds to the ISO network layer, is responsible for taking packets of data and deciding which data link the packet should travel on. A DNA network can have a highly complex topology with up to 63,000 computers. The responsibility of the routing layer is to know what that topology is and to stay abreast of any changes in the topology caused by node or line failures.

The next two layers of DNA are the end-to-end communications and session layers. End-to-end communications is identical to the ISO transport layer. The session provides several important functions. First, it validates incoming connection requests. Second, it activates the appropriate service for a user. If a connection request comes in for an interactive log-in, for example, the session layer would activate the virtual terminal service.

Third, the session layer provides a node name to address mapping service. Nodes, to users, have names like "MYVAX" or "GRAPHICS" or "DATABASE." The session layer turns those logical names into DECnet addresses.

Services in DNA fall into two categories:

- Network management services
- Network applications

Network management services are a set of programs and protocols used to manage the network. These services use the facilities of the network to exchange data on the current state of nodes, lines, and other network components. A variety of different user interfaces are present that can show the status of the network or historical utilization or indicators of activity.

Network applications are the real reason we have this network. Applications are services that users will see. An example of an application is the virtual terminal service. This service allows any user on any node of the network to log into any other node on the network.

The role of the virtual terminal service is to mask the remote access from software packages. To the software package, there is no distinction between a remote user and a local user. This means that the software does not have to be rewritten because of remote access.

Other services allow remote access to data on the network. The Data Access Protocols (DAP) are a set of services that allow a user to access any file on the network, subject to security restrictions. Other data access protocols, such as the Distributed File Service, allow data on the network to appear as though it were local. Files anywhere on the network appear as though they were on the local disk drive. DFS provides a network-transparent access to data. This means that no matter which node a user logs onto, that user will always see the same files.

Many other services will be examined in this book. Several message-handling protocols in DNA allow mail messages to be exchanged. Other protocols have been defined for Videotex and for computer conferencing.

Other DEC architectures

DNA services have the important characteristic of functioning on any node of a DECnet. The nodes can be remote using wide area networking links. Because of the general nature of the Digital Network Architecture, there are instances where performance is sacrificed for flexibility.

Several other special-purpose architectures are meant to address highly specific functions. An example of this is the Maintenance Operations Protocol shown in Figure 1-5. Most services in DNA have to go through the protocol stack, including the session, end-to-end communications, and routing layers. MOP is a direct user of the data link layers, usually the Ethernet.

Because MOP uses the Ethernet directly, it is a very simple protocol. This simple protocol can be implemented in a node's read- only memory (ROM), whereas DNA is too complex to fit into the limited space available in ROM. MOP is thus used when a node is turned on

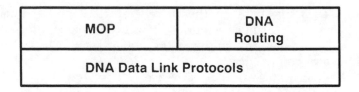

Fig. 1-5   MOP and the DNA routing layer.

as a protocol for fetching an operating system over the network. MOP allows for diskless nodes.

Diskless nodes save money because expensive disk drives do not have to be furnished for specialized equipment. Diskless nodes also simplify system administration because software is stored in a central location. A device that uses the MOP protocols is a MicroVAX 2000. The MicroVAX 2000 is a general-purpose VAX computer, without a disk drive. The VMS operating system is stored on another system and downline loaded when the MicroVAX is turned on.

Other diskless nodes are special-purpose computers. A terminal server is a dedicated computer that does nothing but handle terminal traffic. When a terminal server is initialized, it uses the MOP protocols to broadcast an appeal for help over the Ethernet. A VAX would then send the terminal server its operating system. DEC uses the MOP protocols for terminal servers, print servers, communications servers, SNA gateways, and many other specialized devices.

Another special purpose architecture is the Local Area Transport Architecture (LAT). Figure 1-6 shows the LAT protocol stack. LAT is used exclusively on an Ethernet and provides an efficient method of sending terminal traffic to a host.

LAT is able to use a single Ethernet packet to send data for many different users to the same host. LAT establishes a virtual circuit to that host, then puts many slots of data into each packet. Notice that both the DNA routing layer and LAT may coexist on a single Ethernet.

LAT has many other features oriented toward terminal applications. For example, every host that is able to accept LAT traffic periodically broadcasts the availability of a service that it offers. Several nodes can offer the same service. Each node that offers a service also periodically broadcasts a service rating. The terminal server is able to connect a user to the node with the best service rating.

A third architecture is the System Communications Architecture, also known as VAX Clusters. Figure 1-7 shows the SCA protocol stack. VAX Clusters allow several nodes to be joined into a closely coupled network. The System Communication Services is somewhat

LAT Slot Layer	DNA Transport
LAT Virtual Circuit	DNA Routing
Ethernet	

Fig. 1-6 Local Area Transport Architecture.

equivalent to the DNA routing layer—both offer internode communications services.

SCA is able to use two different data link layers. Ethernet has a bandwidth of 10 million bits per second (mbps). The Computer Interconnect bus operates at 70 mbps. The CI bus is used to connect large VAX systems and a special-purpose computer called the Hierarchical Storage Controller (HSC). The HSC is used to connect high performance disk drives to a very intelligent disk controller.

The main purpose of the cluster is to allow multiple computers to share disk drives at high speeds. The CI bus cluster provides memory-to-memory throughput rates between a VAX and an HSC of 2 megabytes per second (Mbps).

A Local Area VAX Cluster (LAVC) provides the same functionality, but over the Ethernet. HSC controllers cannot be connected to the Ethernet, so a general purpose VAX must provide disk services.

In either the LAVC or CI bus environment, clusters offer a unified security and management domain for multiple VAX systems. They also offer highly concurrent access to data, using distributed lock and file managers. This entire cluster is managed with an application called the Cluster Manager.

While DNA provides access to data, the cluster does the same service in a tightly coupled fashion. The cluster is thus limited to 42 nodes but provides higher performance and functionality. DNA provides lower performance but allows access to data anywhere on the DECnet, which can have up to 63,000 nodes.

On a single Ethernet, it is not unusual to see DECnet, clusters, and the Local Area Transport Architecture all providing services. The services vary in performance, functionality, and flexibility. The purpose of Part 2 of this book is to show the three major architectures and their components. Part 3 will illustrate how the architectures are implemented.

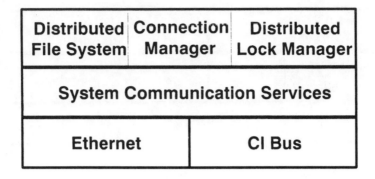

Fig. 1-7   System Communications Architecture (SCA).

TCP/IP and SNA

Part 4 discusses other network architectures, beginning with TCP/IP and SNA. TCP/IP is an architecture used in a heterogeneous environment consisting of many different vendors' equipment. An addition to the TCP/IP protocol stack is the Network File System, developed by Sun Microsystems. Figure 1-8 shows the TCP/IP and NFS protocol stacks.

TCP/IP is actually layers 3 and 4 of the ISO reference model. TCP/IP is able to use several subnetwork technologies, including Ethernet and token ring LANs. In addition, TCP/IP frequently uses X.25 for wide area networking links.

The Internet Protocols allow the different subnetworks to be connected together. IP thus operates at layer 3 of the ISO reference model. Two different transport layer protocols are offered. The Transmission Control Protocol (TCP) provides reliable end-to-end communications. An alternate transport mechanism is the User Datagram Protocol (UDP). UDP is more efficient than TCP but does not guarantee that data will be delivered. It is up to the user of UDP to discover that a particular packet, or datagram, was delivered out of sequence or not delivered.

Built on top of the basic TCP/IP protocol suite are three applications. TELNET provides a virtual terminal service. The File Transfer Protocol (FTP) allows files to be copied from one node to another. The Simple Mail Transfer Protocol (SMTP) allows mail messages to be exchanged.

All three of these basic services are direct users of the transport layer. This has several drawbacks. First, there is no general mechanism for interprocess communication over the network. This is a func-

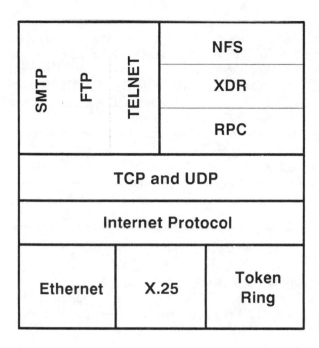

Fig. 1-8   TCP/IP and the Network File System.

tion usually found in the session layer. Second, there is no provision for different types of nodes to exchange data in a node-independent fashion. Each application must provide for data representation. This is usually a function of the presentation layer.

Sun Microsystems developed a set of protocols that are referred to as the Network File System. Although NFS could be implemented on other transport mechanisms, it is usually implemented on top of TCP/IP. Over 250 vendors have NFS licenses and implementations.

NFS begins by adding a Remote Procedure Call (RPC) mechanism on top of the transport layer. RPC allows a process on one node to communicate with a process on another node. RPC thus extends the memory of a single system to allow function calls over a network.

The External Data Representation (XDR) is a presentation layer protocol. XDR consists of a series of filters that translate node-specific data representation into a machine-independent representation. XDR defines filters for simple data types such as integers and characters but also defines mechanisms for filtering complex data structures, such as packed arrays.

The Network File System is an application that uses the services of XDR, RPC, and the TCP/IP protocol stack. NFS allows a file system on a remote node to appear as though it were local. A similar service is offered in DNA as the Distributed File Service. Both services will be described in this book, and the reader will notice both similarities and differences between the two implementations.

The Systems Network Architecture (SNA) is yet another general-purpose network architecture, used for connecting IBM computers together. The SNA chapter of this book will describe different methods for interconnecting SNA and DNA environments together. DEC provides a high level of interconnectivity to SNA environments.

Open architectures: OSI and DECnet/OSI

The last general-purpose network architecture that will be described is Open Systems Interconnect (OSI). OSI is an implementation of the ISO reference model. OSI is important for a variety of reasons.

First, OSI is an open networking environment. The protocol specifications are very specific and were arrived at over many years by international standards committees. Because they are open standards, many different vendors will be able to write to them. OSI offers the capability of both high functionality and a heterogeneous networking environment.

Second, DEC is adopting OSI for Phase V of the Digital Network Architecture. DECnet Phase V is known as DECnet/OSI. The DNA architecture described in Part 2 of this book will thus be gradually supplanted by the services and protocols described in Part 4.

Third, OSI looks like it will work. The standards committees built OSI on top of existing technologies. In particular, existing subnetworking technologies are incorporated by reference into the OSI protocol stack. Figure 1-9 shows this protocol stack.

The logical link control is a subnetwork access procedure that works with different local area network technologies. Specifically, the Logical link control is able to send data out over Ethernet, token ring, and token bus networks.

Another subnetwork technology is the Integrated Services Digital Network (ISDN). ISDN is described in Chapter 7 of this book. ISDN allows transparent access to high-bandwidth wide area data links. Other subnetworks are X.25 for packet switching and X.21 for circuit switching applications.

Since different subnetworks offer different levels of functionality, the network layer of OSI is split into two pieces. The subnetwork dependent convergence functions are used to supplement the services

File Transfer Access and Management	Remote Data Access	Virtual Terminal	Job Transfer and Manipulation

COMMON APPLICATION SERVICE ELEMENTS

PRESENTATION LAYER

SESSION LAYER

TRANSPORT LAYER

SUBNETWORK INDEPENDENT CONVERGENCE FUNCTIONS

SUBNETWORK DEPENDENT CONVERGENCE FUNCTIONS

X.21 CIRCUIT SWITCHING	ISDN	X.25 PACKET SWITCHING	LOGICAL LINK CONTROL		
			TOKEN RING	CSMA/CD	TOKEN BUS

Fig. 1-9 Open Systems Interconnect.

of the subnetwork and to provide any subnetwork-dependent services. For example, in X.25 a virtual circuit must first be established before a packet can be sent. Establishing that virtual circuit would be a subnetwork-dependent convergence function for X.25.

The upper sublayer of the network layer provides the packet forwarding function. This function accepts a packet from one subnetwork and forwards it over another. The user of the network layer sees only end-to-end communication.

There are many different applications in the OSI model. The applications layer, like the network layer, is split into two pieces. The lower sublayer, the Common Application Service Elements (CASE) are used to provide common services needed by all application entities. This sublayer allows an association between two entities to be formed.

The services built on top of CASE range from file access (FTAM) to database access (the Remote Data Access Protocols). The Job Transfer and Manipulation (JTM) service allows a work order to be sent to many different nodes and jobs to be executed. A virtual terminal service allows many different kinds of terminal to log into different nodes of an OSI network. Chapter 12 describes a variety of these OSI services.

Architectures and implementations

While much of this book describes architectures, there is a strong focus on how those architectures are implemented into networks. Part 3, in particular, is focused on this question. Chapter 6 looks at Local area networks and Chapter 7 looks at wide area networks. Chapter 8 looks at the implementation of DNA on different operating systems and how different user interfaces are used to manage a multi-architecture network.

In addition to Part 3, the rest of the book also examines how these networks are implemented. The chapters on TCP/IP and SNA, for example, look at a variety of hardware and software products used to connect to the architectures.

It is important to remember that an architecture is a theory. The theory says that all equipment that conforms to the architecture will work together. Implementations of architectures are reality. Reality means that different vendors may have different versions of the architecture or different levels of performance. This book looks at many of these implementation issues, but it is important to remember that implementations change rapidly. The last section of this chapter makes a few suggestions on how to find and compare different products that implement these architectures.

Services

The real purpose of a network is a service. We don't buy Ethernet cable to send packets of data between two nodes. We buy Ethernet cable because we want to send electronic mail or transfer files or log into a remote node. Throughout the book, a variety of applications are examined. Three particularly important types of applications are:

■ File and data access

- Messaging systems
- Windows and workstations

File and data access

File and data access are one of the main reasons for installing a network. Many different protocols, such as the Distributed File Service in DNA and the Network File System, are meant to address this issue.

Distributed data access can range from simple file copies to more sophisticated protocols that offer highly concurrent access to individual records in files. The following chapters describe data access protocols:

Protocol	Architecture	Chapter
Data Access Protocol	DNA	3
Distributed File Service	DNA	3
Clusters	SCA	5
Network File Service	NFS	9
DSR	DNA	10
FTAM	OSI	12

Messaging systems

Chapter 14 has an extensive discussion of the X.400 protocols. X.400 is an OSI application that defines a message-handling system. DEC networks have always provided extensive message-handling capabilities. Following the general discussion of X.400, there is a discussion of an important DEC architecture known as MAILBUS.

MAILbus is a message-handling architecture that is able to work with many different message-handling systems and user interfaces. Gateways exist to X.400 message-handling environments, the TCP/IP SMTP system, and the IBM SNADS and PROFS office automation environments. Other gateways exist to public electronic mail providers such as MCI Mail.

MAILbus, as its name implies, allows many different forms of mail messages to be exchanged. A single user interface, such as All-In-One, is able to send mail messages to a variety of different environments. In fact, through MCI Mail and Western Union's Easylink, electronic mail can be printed out and delivered as a telegram or letter to users who have never seen a computer.

Windows and Workstations

Part 5 of this book has an extensive discussion of an important new set of protocols aimed at allowing many different computers to provide services to a single bit-mapped workstation. The X Windows System is a set of protocols developed at the Massachusetts Institute of Technology to allow programs to share a workstation. X has been adopted by DEC as part of their DECwindows environment.

DECwindows also includes standards for a common look and feel. With many different applications accessible over a network, there is a danger in overwhelming a user with many different styles of operation. A common look and feel allows a user to interact with each computer program the same way. This means, for example, that menus always function the same way or that a HELP is always activated the same way.

The last chapter of this book describes the PostScript imaging system. X allows different programs to coordinate their access to a common workstation display. PostScript is an imaging system used to construct and manipulate bit maps. PostScript is device independent, which means that the information on a user's screen will look exactly the same when it is printed. PostScript is an especially powerful imaging system with graphics capabilities that allow application programmers to exploit the power of modern workstations.

The network provides transparent access to data and computing resource. The windowing system coordinates these different programs on the user's screen. PostScript allows the user's screen to stop looking like an extension of a dumb terminal. PostScript allows the user interface to move toward a more sophisticated presentation style.

What to do after you read this book

This book is an introduction to a very complex world. Its purpose is to give the reader a flavor for the different architectures and implementations that can be used with DEC computers. Serious readers should continue their research in a number of ways.

First, readers should continue doing research on topics of interest. Each chapter of the book covers a fairly complex area. Suggestions for further reading are included for a more in-depth examination of topics.

Some of these suggestions are DEC manuals or architectures specifications. Others are textbooks or other standard reference materials in the field.

Second, readers should investigate specific products and implementations. Throughout the book, specific examples are cited that illustrate some of the features available. These products are cited for illustration and not as a recommendation for purchase. The field changes too quickly to be that specific.

Readers who are investigating purchase of products should consult the trade press and trade shows to find out which vendors are producing products. These sources can help narrow a vast field down to a few potential choices. Then, those vendors should be called in to present technical details about their product set. While it is tempting to quickly select the one "best" product, it is worth remembering that it is highly unlikely that a single vendor is the obvious choice for all situations. If that were the case, other vendors would have been attracted to this market niche!

This book should thus be used as a method of gaining some perspective on how computers can be connected together and what they can do once they are connected together. By understanding this view the reader can begin to evaluate the many different products and features and see how they fit into this framework. It's important to remember, however, that this is one view of the world, and there are many other valid views.

Part

2

DEC Architectures

2

DNA Lower-Layer Protocols

Overview of Lower-Layer Protocols

The lowest layer of a network, the physical layer, is concerned with transmitting a bit of information from one node to another. The fact that this bit may continue on over another wire at a later point does not yet concern us. Nor does the question of the use of the bit concern us: the fact that this bit may be used for a user's terminal session and another bit is part of a file transfer is not yet of importance.

The wire connecting the two nodes is known as the physical medium. The role of the physical layer is to take a stream of bits on one node and send them to the node at the other end of the wire.

The actual type of wire that is used depends on the use that will be made of the physical layer. An RS-232-C cable might be an appropriate physical link for a terminal to a computer. In this case, both the terminal and the computer are considered to be nodes and the RS-232-C serial cable is the physical link. This is known as a point-to-point link because there is one node at each end of the wire.

Another type of physical media is a coax cable. While an RS-232-C cable is limited to a transmission rate of 19,000 bps, a piece of coax can easily accommodate rates of 10 mbps. The coax cable can also be 500 meters (m) long instead of the 76 m limit of the RS-232 cable because of the electrical and insulating characteristics of the medium.

Another distinguishing factor of the coax is that many nodes can be simultaneously connected to the same wire. As many as 100 nodes can be connected to a single piece of coax.

Needless to say, the increased performance and flexibility of the coax is offset by the increased cost of not only the cable but of the devices used to connect the cable to a node. While a simple $20 controller port can handle an RS-232-C physical connection, it usually takes a separate computer to monitor a piece of coax.

Physical links are not necessarily a single piece of wire. Two modems communicating over a phone line are considered to be a physical link. This is because the goal of transmitting a stream of bits from one node to another is still met. Other types of physical links include very high bandwidth microwave and satellite links.

Moving a bit from one end of a physical link to the other end is in itself not very interesting. For one thing, there is no way of labeling each bit to signify what it is for. For this reason there is added a data link layer to use a physical link and manage its resources. This provides a more efficient use of the physical link by moving blocks of bits.

A typical data link layer takes data and groups it into separate frames of information. A frame is a message, complete with an address and contents (the data to be transmited). A frame might be as large as 1500 bytes or as small as 1 byte. By grouping data into frames, the data link layer is able to append an integrity check to the data being transmitted. The data link layer at the receiving end is able to use the integrity check to examine the data and make sure that it was correctly received.

A parity check is a very simple example of this type of integrity check imposed by a data link layer. On most RS-232-C connections, characters are represented by 7 bits of information. Different bit patterns represent different bits. A parity check adds an eighth bit to the data and sends all 8 bits to the remote node.

When the remote node receives the data, it separates it into the 7 bits and the parity check. An example of a simple parity check is to flip the value of the parity bit for every 1 bit contained in the original data. If a character was represented by the bit pattern 1000000, the parity bit would be flipped once and would be a 1. The transmitted data would be 10000001. If the bit pattern was 1100000, the parity bit would flip twice to 0, so the transmitted data would be 11000000.

More sophisticated integrity checks can also be added by the data link layer to detect any errors induced during transmission. Sometimes the data link layer precedes the data with a length indicator. The receiving end then knows how much data to expect. At the end of the data may be a more sophisticated integrity check such as a frame check sequence.

Once a packet of data has been successfully sent over a data link, it is passed up to a routing layer module. This module is responsible for determining where the packet is destined. Two people communicating over a network may have to go through several data links to reach their destination. For example, a piece of data may be sent over an Ethernet to a VAX, which forwards it over a 56 kbps leased line to another VAX, which in turn sends it over another Ethernet to its eventual destination.

The physical layer is not considered in detail in this chapter. Specific physical layer support is more properly dealt with in Part 3 of this book on network implementation.

DDCMP Data Link Protocols

DDCMP is an example of a data link protocol that manages the use of an underlying physical medium. The data link layer thus provides a point to point link between two nodes on the network. The question of taking a piece of information and sending over a series of different data links is the responsibility of the user of the data link service, in this case the DNA Phase IV routing protocol.

DDCMP is a fairly versatile set of protocols and is able to send data out over either asynchronous or synchronous links. An asynchronous link can be considered to be a mini-synchronous link—each packet of data consists of a single byte of data. Asynchronous have more over-head because timing and signalling needs to be adjusted for each byte instead of for a frame.

DDCMP is also able to operate over either serial or parallel lines. A parallel line sends individual bits down different wires, whereas a serial line sends the bits serially down a single wire.

There are three major components to a DDCMP module:

- Framing is the process of taking data and preparing it for transmission.
- Link management manages half duplex or multipoint links.
- Message exchange is the actual transfer of data.

The framing component of a DDCMP module monitors the media and locates the beginning and end of a message. This occurs at three levels. First, the module must locate each bit on the network. This is known as bit synchronization. Next, the process of byte synchronization groups data into 8-bit quantities. The final level is message synchronization, which groups bytes into frames.

Byte synchronization is done through the use of a special 8-bit pattern called the synchronization byte. After that has been received, the DDCMP module begins counting bits. Every 8 bits is considered a byte. Needless to say, eventually the framing component can get out of sequence. Usually, a sync byte is sent for each message. On an asynchronous link, there is no need for a synchronization byte since the start-stop nature of the link provides this function.

The last level of synchronization is message synchronization. Once byte synchronization is achieved, the DDCMP module searches for one of three message start bytes. Message types can be:

- numbered data messages
- control messages
- maintenance messages

The normal type of message is a numbered data message that carries user data over the link. The first piece of data following the start of header (SOH), or message start byte, is a count field that tells how long the message is. Because the data is counted, any bit pattern can be included in the user data. If the user data happens to have piece of data equivalent to a start of message or byte synchronization pattern in it, this will not effect the transmission of the data. Only after the specified number of bytes has been received does the DDCMP module begin looking for unique patterns such as the sync byte.

Also in the frame header are a series of link control flags. These tell the receiving end whether another message will abut this one or, failing that, that the receiving end should resync after this message. The link control flags also control which nodes on a multipoint link control are involved in this particular packet transmission.

The frame header for a numbered data message also contains a sequence number. The receiving end must acknowledge the receipt of each packet by number. This can be somewhat inefficient if each packet must be acknowledged, so there are two techniques allowed to prevent the acknowledgment of each and every packet.

Pipelining means that several packets may be sent. When an acknowledgment is received, the acknowledgment signifies receipt of that packet and all lower numbered packets. Thus, an ACK3 signifies receipt of packets one, two, and three.

The second technique for increasing efficiency is to piggyback the acknowledgment on a user data packet. One of the fields in the numbered data message header is for a response number. If that field is present, it signifies an acknowledgment for that message number. Of course, if no user data is to be sent, the acknowledgment cannot piggyback and must travel in its own separate packet. Figure 2-1 illustrates a piggybacked ACK.

Another type of message used in DDCMP is the control message. This is an unnumbered message used to transmit channel control in-

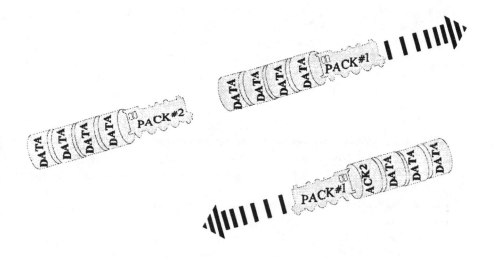

Fig. 2-1 Piggybacked acknowledgment in DDCMP.

formation in a multipoint link. It is also used to transmit status information and for initialization of a new link between two protocol modules.

An acknowledgment message is also a form of a DDCMP control message. It is used when no user data is going in that direction and an ACK is required. A negative acknowledgment has the same format but also includes a reason indicator. A negative acknowledgment can be generated because the transmission media has corrupted the data, either the header or the user data. Another reason for a NAK is problems with the computer interface, such as all buffers being currently in use.

The last message type is the maintenance message. This is only used in offline mode to test a link. It is similar to the data message but does not include any retransmit, error recovery, or other mechanisms.

Link management

Link management is the second component of a DDCMP module. It is only necessary where the flow of data must be controlled, as in the case of either a multipoint or a half-duplex line. A full-duplex line does not need this function.

A half-duplex line is under the control of the data sender. The receiver may not send data until it has received permission. On a half-duplex line, the sending node sends a selection flag when it has completed sending data. This instructs the receiving end to enter the transmit mode.

In a full-duplex environment, either node may send at any time. A full-duplex environment requires more resources because each node must monitor an incoming and outgoing signal simultaneously. Full-duplex environments thus require more buffer space but offer higher performance.

Multipoint links are a special case in DDCMP. One station, the control station, is the master of the line. A selection flag is used to assign temporary control of the line to a tributary that has data to send. The control station polls the tributaries periodically to determine if one desires temporary control of the line.

Message exchange

The third component of a DDCMP module is the message exchange component. Once data has been framed, it is handed off to the message exchange component. This is where acknowledgment numbers are actually inserted into the frame header.

Each message sent by the message exchange component has a message number. Each message must have a positive acknowledgment, or ACK. If a negative acknowledgment is received, the message is resent. Each message also has a timer associated with it. If the timer expires, this is accepted as a negative acknowledgment of the message.

Time-out values must be set in a way that take into account the number of messages that are pipelined, propagation delay, and processing delays at the recipient nodes. It is important that a time-out value is not short so that a NAK is implied even though the message was correctly received. Typically, transmission of a packet might take a few milliseconds. A time-out value is usually a few seconds.

When a timer expires, it is possible the ACK was lost in transmission and the data actually arrived. Rather than resend the entire data packet, a Reply to Message Number (REP) packet is sent. This has two effects. First, it requires an acknowledgment of the REP message, which implies an ACK for the original data message. Second, it forces the timer to be reset and the two nodes to synchronize their message numbering.

If a timer expires several times, it is logical to assume that the link is down. After a user-set number of timer failures, the DDCMP module notifies the user of the line failure. Typically, the user of the DDCMP service is a DNA routing module.

One of the DDCMP issues is the amount of processing done at the operating system level and the amount that can be built into a hardware controller. In the case of asynchronous DDCMP, all processing is done in the DDCMP module. The data is then sent to the asynchronous device driver. Another user of that asynchronous device driver might be a terminal services manager. On a VMS node, a particular hardware port may dynamically change from terminal mode into asynchronous DECnet mode.

Multipoint links are supported in DDCMP. Another way to have multiple nodes share the same physical medium is the Ethernet data link protocol. Because DDCMP uses a polling mechanism, it is not optimal for large numbers of nodes sharing the same physical medium, when each needs a short response time. In these cases, Ethernet is a more suitable data link.

DDCMP, unlike Ethernet, does not support any kind of broadcast or multicasting facility. On multipoint lines, there may only be one control station. That control station must remain fixed and cannot float among the multiple tributaries.

Ethernet Data Link Protocols

DDCMP as a data link protocol has two significant drawbacks. First, it is relatively slow. As will be seen in the wide area network chapter, DDCMP links are usually 19 to 56 thousand bits per second (kbps). Occasionally, T1 speeds of 1.544 megabits per second (mbps) may be obtained.

The second disadvantage of DDCMP is that it is essentially a point-to-point data link mechanism. This works fine in a wide area network (WAN) scenario but is not a very efficient way to allow hundreds of workstations to communicate with each other. DDCMP is thus used to provide point to point links over long distances. Another protocol is needed to support the high-speed networking capabilities of a local area network.

Ethernet provides an alternative data link mechanism to connect nodes together. Two nodes may be able to communicate over both a DDCMP connection and an Ethernet connection. Which of the two alternatives to use for sending a particular data message is the responsibility of the routing layer of DNA. As with DDCMP, all we are concerned with is how to get some data from one node to another. The eventual destination or eventual use of that data does not yet interest us.

Ethernet connects many nodes at a speed of 10 mbps. Up to 1024 nodes may be part of a single Ethernet. Ethernet looks to the user of this data link service like 1024 separate wires with 1024 nodes connected to them.

Conceptually, Ethernet looks like a single logical wire, known as a bus. In reality, the physical configuration may consist of many different segments connected together using a set of configuration rules. The different physical configuration options are the subject of the local area network implementation chapter.

Ethernet is one of several different techniques for connecting large numbers of nodes. It happens to be the principal method advocated by DEC. Other alternatives to Ethernet, such as the token ring or the token bus, will be discussed in subsequent chapters.

Because Ethernet is incorporated into the DNA, this is a convenient place to introduce it. Later chapters contain more information on Ethernet in other architectures and on the physical configuration of an Ethernet network. DNA happens to use Ethernet as a way of making two DECnet nodes communicate with each other. In this case, the user of the Ethernet service is the DNA routing layer.

Other users of the Ethernet include other networking architectures (See Figure 2-2). Two DEC networking architectures, for example, are able to use the services of the Ethernet. The Local Area Transport Architecture is a set of protocols that allow terminals to use an Ethernet to efficiently communicate with a host. As will be seen, both DNA traffic (host to host) and LAT traffic (terminal to host) can share the services of the Ethernet, just as different kinds of businesses can all share the services of the phone network.

Another DEC-developed user of the Ethernet service is the System Communication Architecture that is used for VAX Clusters. While DNA is a very general purpose architecture for many nodes, the SCA is a special purpose architecture that allows just a few nodes to participate in a closely coupled environment.

It is not unusual to see a single VAX computer speaking three different languages. The first language is DNA, which is used to transmit electronic mail, remote file transfers, and remote log-in to anywhere on the network. The VAX computer thus has a set of software for speaking DNA, which ultimately requires the service of Ethernet, DDCMP, or other data link layers to transfer data to another node.

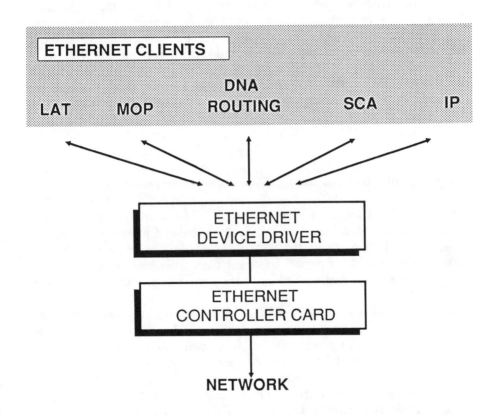

Fig. 2-2   Multiple Ethernet clients.

The second language that the VAX speaks is LAT, which is used to communicate with terminals connected to a special-purpose computer called a terminal server. This LAT software also requires the services of the Ethernet. As you can see, the Ethernet is a general-purpose service provider.

The third client might be the System Communication Architecture (SCA), otherwise known as a VAX Cluster. The cluster allows many different computers to share a single disk drive. Since the disk drive is an expensive peripheral, VAX Clusters allow a single high-performance disk drive to be shared among many users. Other clients of the Ethernet may include non-DEC architectures such as TCP/IP or XNS.

There are thus four different architectures that will use the services of the Ethernet: TCP/IP, LAT, SCA, and DNA. Three other chapters discuss increasing levels of complexity of Ethernet implementation. The local area network chapter discusses how to configure a basic Ethernet, consisting of multiple segments and repeaters. The wide area network chapter will discuss how to extend these Ethernet systems over wide areas. Finally, the chapter on OSI lower layer protocols provides a more general abstract model of how Ethernet works with other types of media to provide internetworking capabilities.

CSMA/CD media access control

Several different methods allow many nodes to share one logical piece of cable. Ethernet is based on a technique called Carrier Sense Multiple Access/Collision Detect (CSMA/CD). This is known as a Media Access Control or MAC Protocol because it controls how different nodes gain access to the media. Other MAC protocols are token rings and token buses.

The "Multiple Access" part of CSMA/CD means that every node connected to the Ethernet is able to access the media. There is no master node which polls and gives permission to speak, as we saw in the case of DDCMP multipoint links. Every node can access the media at any time.

"Carrier Sense" means that the nodes have the ability to sense if another node is currently transmitting data. If another node is currently transmitting, the Ethernet node knows enough to refrain from sending at the same time. A node can only send 1500 bytes of data at one time, so a single node is unable to monopolize the media.

The fact that each node can send packets out means that occasionally two nodes will transmit at the same time. This happens when both nodes monitor the network and start sending at exactly the same time. This is known as a collision. The collision is identical to two people talking at the same time—they may feel better, but they have exchanged no information.

A collision results in what can be described as a situation of somewhat controlled anarchy. Each node involved in the collision stops sending and then waits for a random period of time. Needless to say, that random period of time is different for each node. At the end of this time, the node then listens again to the media to see if it is available.

Ethernet Version 2.0

Ethernet was originally developed by DEC, Intel, and Xerox. This original specification is currently in its second revision. Subsequent to the original Ethernet work by the three developers, the question of LANs was considered by the IEEE. The IEEE generalized this model to provide support for a more general LAN architecture.

Each Ethernet station has a physical address that is assigned when the device is shipped from the manufacturer. Xerox administers addresses to ensure that each device is unique. Each device monitors the Ethernet and listens for any frames that are addressed to it. It is possible for the network administrator to replace the globally administered address shipped with the hardware with a local address determined locally.

In addition to the specific physical address, a station monitors the Ethernet for two other kinds of addresses. A broadcast address is automatically picked up by every station on the Ethernet. A multicast address is picked up by a subset of stations on the network.

Different users of the Ethernet will all make use of multicast address. Later in this book we will examine several DEC-defined multicasts, including ones for a DNA Load Assistance in the MOP protocols, routing layer control messages, LAT service broadcasts, and System Communications Architecture broadcasts for nodes attempting to join a Local Area VAX Cluster.

The interface that different users of the Ethernet use is called a portal. The portal database contains a list of protocol types and multicast addresses that are destined for that particular user of the Ethernet. Each node on the Ethernet monitors the medium for all packets containing the broadcast address or any of the local and multicast addresses that are registered in the portal database. The Ethernet takes each of these packets received, strips off any header information, and then passes the data up to the service user.

IEEE 802.3 LANs

The original Intel/DEC/Xerox specification for the Ethernet was taken over by the IEEE standards committees and extended. DECnet supports both versions of Ethernets. While there are a few minor electrical differences between the two specifications, the differences are negligible for all but the makers of transceivers.

The major extension provided by the IEEE committees has been to generalize the standard to support a variety of different local area network technologies. This was done by splitting the data link layer into sublayers.

The original Ethernet CSMA/CD access techniques are part of the lower sublayer, called the media access control. In addition to CSMA/CD LANs, the IEEE specifications support other MAC layers such as the token ring or token bus access methods.

The upper sublayer is called the logical link control (LLC). This sublayer provides a single interface to the users of the local area network. This allows a single routing layer to utilize different kinds of LAN technologies. Thus, the IEEE protocols allow several users to use a single data link layer mechanism. Each of the users sends packets of information to the LLC sublayer. Underneath the LLC sublayer a variety of different MAC sublayers can reside. The LLC sublayer functions as a simplifying mechanism that allows multiple users to use multiple LAN technologies using a common packet format.

There is a slight difference in the packet formats between an IEEE CSMA/CD MAC layer and the original Ethernet packet. In Ethernet, a type indicator follows the source and destination addresses. The type indicator has been moved out of the MAC layer in the IEEE format and a length indicator immediately follows the source and destination address.

The two formats have been made compatible using a simple trick. The length of a packet in both instances is between 46 and 1500 bytes long. To avoid a conflict, type indicators do not fall within this range. By examining the third field of an incoming packet, the Ethernet controller board is able to immediately distinguish between the two types of formats.

The type indicators in the original Ethernet have been replaced with a logical link control header which is embedded inside of the MAC packet header and contains a source and destination address. This format allows more flexibility for further expansion than the single type field in the original specification.

There are three classes of logical link controls. Present LAN implementations use LLC class 1, which is simply a datagram service. This means that the LLC service consists of accepting a single packet of data and sending it out over the network. No error recovery or virtual connections are provided.

The LLC standards include two further classes that will be used to provide increased functionality at the LAN layer. LLC class 2 provides a connection-oriented service at this layer of the network. In DNA Phase IV, it is the responsibility of a higher layer of the network to provide this functionality. Embedding a connection-oriented service into lower layers of the network has the advantage of allowing much of the connection-oriented functionality to be provided in dedicated hardware controllers instead of in the main memory of the system.

The third LLC class provides a connectionless service like the first LLC class. However, LLC class 3 provides an acknowledgment for the receipt of the packet. In LLC class 1 operations, if a packet does not reach its destination, it will be the responsibility of a higher layer of the network to discover the error and provide some form of recovery.

Routing

The data link layer provides an ability to connect two nodes on the same wire. In the case of Ethernet, there are actually many nodes sharing the same wire. However, the Ethernet module masks this multiaccess nature of the media and provides a virtual point-to-point link. Likewise, multipoint DDCMP links also look like a series of virtual point-to-point links because the DDCMP module masks the process of polling and granting access to selected nodes.

The routing layer is responsible for taking a packet from data link and deciding which data link to send the packet back out on. The routing layer thus takes a series of data links and forwards a packet from the source to the destination. In this case, the destination could be separated from the source by many hops (individual instances of a datalink).

The routing layer thus masks the topology of the network from the users of the routing service. Higher layers of the network are able to assume that they can talk directly to their destination. At this point, we are still not concerned with what the data is going to be used for or who the user of the data is. This functionality will provided by yet another module.

A byte of data destined for data transmission has now been twice packetized. First, the routing layer receives data and puts a routing layer header on it. All of this information is then considered to be "user data" for the data link layer. The data link layer puts its own packet header on the information.

Figure 2-3 shows some data being transmitted on an Ethernet with both Ethernet (data link) and routing headers on it. Normally, the data on the Ethernet consists of a series of bits. A tool called a network analyzer is used to observe Ethernet packets and translate the control information into high level indicators.

This book makes extensive use of screen dumps of this sort to illustrate various networking protocols. The particular product used is the Sniffer, made by Network General. This network analyzer consists of a special purpose portable computer, usually either a Compaq

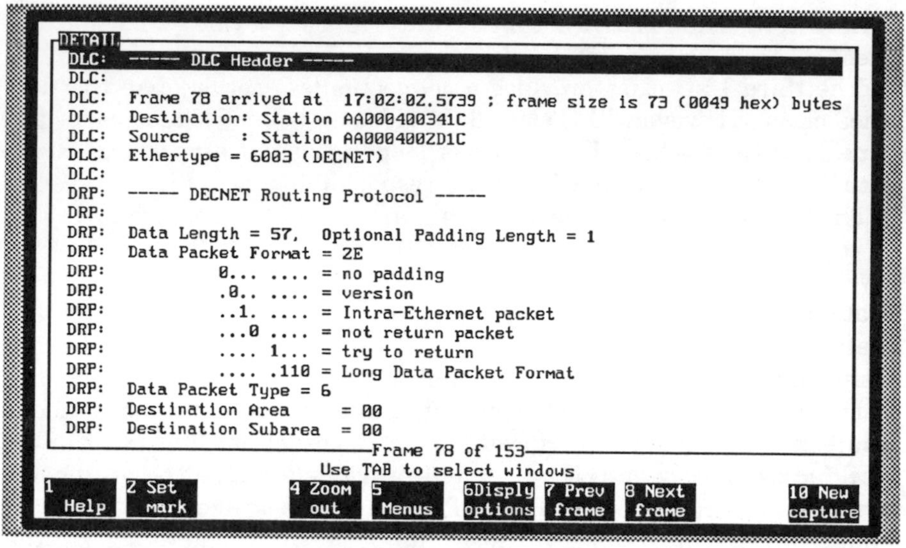

```
┌─DETAIL┬──────────────────────────────────────────────────────────┐
│  DLC: ───── DLC Header ─────                                      │
│  DLC:                                                             │
│  DLC:  Frame 78 arrived at  17:02:02.5739 ; frame size is 73 (0049 hex) bytes
│  DLC:  Destination: Station AA000400341C                         │
│  DLC:  Source     : Station AA000400ZD1C                         │
│  DLC:  Ethertype = 6003 (DECNET)                                 │
│  DLC:                                                             │
│  DRP: ───── DECNET Routing Protocol ─────                        │
│  DRP:                                                             │
│  DRP:  Data Length = 57,  Optional Padding Length = 1            │
│  DRP:  Data Packet Format = 2E                                   │
│  DRP:          0... .... = no padding                            │
│  DRP:          .0.. .... = version                               │
│  DRP:          ..1. .... = Intra-Ethernet packet                 │
│  DRP:          ...0 .... = not return packet                     │
│  DRP:          .... 1... = try to return                         │
│  DRP:          .... .110 = Long Data Packet Format               │
│  DRP:  Data Packet Type = 6                                      │
│  DRP:  Destination Area    = 00                                  │
│  DRP:  Destination Subarea = 00                                  │
│                    ──────Frame 78 of 153──────                   │
│                     Use TAB to select windows                    │
├──────────────────────────────────────────────────────────────────┤
│ 1       2 Set        4 Zoom  5        6Disply 7 Prev  8 Next      10 New │
│  Help    mark         out     Menus   options  frame   frame      capture│
└──────────────────────────────────────────────────────────────────┘
```

Courtesy of Network General

Fig. 2-3   An Ethernet packet delivering routing info.

or a Toshiba 3200. The Sniffer also has special-purpose software for analyzing and managing data as well as network adapters. While these examples use an Ethernet controller to observe Ethernet, the same basic hardware can also observe other LAN technologies such as token rings.

Data links between individual nodes on a network are subject to failure, as are individual systems in the network. Because this is a fairly common occurrence, the routing layer has to be able to adapt to changes in the network topology. If one line goes down in the network, the routing layer is able to take an individual packet and send it over an alternative route. Only if no routes are available is the user of the routing service notified of a network error. Otherwise, the dynamic topology of the network is transparent to the upper layers.

An important concept in DNA Phase IV routing is that the routing layer provides adaptive routing only for topographical failures. A particular path is designated as the best path to a particular end destination. Only if that line goes down is an alternative route found.

To illustrate this concept of adaptive routing for topographical changes, imagine that there are two lines to a particular node. A 56 kbps line is considered to be the best path. There is also an alternate path consisting of a 9600 bps line. Even if the 56 kbps line is nearing saturation, all traffic is pumped down that path and the 9600 bps line remains idle with respect to this particular source and destination combination.

As will be seen, path splitting is a special exception to this rule. If there are two lines that have equal costs, as determined by the routing decision algorithm, packets will be distributed between the two lines in a round-robin fashion. Note that this still does not account for actual traffic on the two lines—it is not adaptive routing based on actual loads on the system.

The routing module has four major functions. The primary function, of course, is routing. The initialization function sets up a data link layer and connects to adjacent nodes. Congestion control is a function that prevents a node from flooding the network with packets. Packet lifetime control, the last function, destroys packets that have already visited too many nodes.

There are several things that the routing layer does not accomplish. The DNA routing layer does not provide for different classes of traffic. The next layer up, the end communication layer, has some limited capabilities to prioritize traffic through the use of other-data logical links. The routing layer itself does not have any capability to distinguish among different priorities of delivery.

The routing layer also does not react to the amount of traffic on a line. It does dynamic routing, but only for topographical failure. Once a particular routing path has been determined to be the least-cost path, it is used for all packets regardless of congestion. If multiple paths of equal cost exist, the routing layer is able to distribute packets among the different routes in a round-robin fashion.

Types of nodes in a network

A DECnet has two types of nodes. A routing node, typically a VMS system or a dedicated router consisting of special hardware and software, is able to provide routing services to other nodes on the network for route-through traffic.

An end node is a full member of the DECnet and can send and receive traffic. An end node, however, is unable to provide routing services for other members of the DECnet. Implementations of DECnet under Ultrix and on MS-DOS are examples of end nodes. Third party clones of DECnet, such as those that run on the Apple Macintosh, are also end node implementations. Needless to say, it is significantly easier to implement an end node version of DECnet than it is to implement a full routing version.

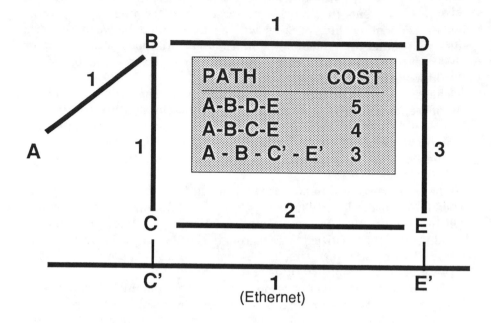

Fig. 2-4   DNA routing layer cost calculation.

Routing Decisions

The actual routing decision is the most complicated component of the routing layer. There are four separate processes involved in the routing component:

- the decision process,
- topology updates,
- forwarding of packets, and
- receiving packets.

The decision on which path to pick in a network is a function of the cost of different routing paths. Each link between two nodes is considered to be one hop. Every node on an Ethernet is one node away from every other node on the Ethernet. Every hop on the network is assigned a cost. Figure 2-4 illustrates a routing topology with a least-cost path calculation.

Each time a packet is received from an adjacent node, the receiving node must decide how to forward the packet. Based on the least cost path, the node is able to decide which adjacent node should next receive the packet. Note that each node along the delivery path reexecutes the decision process.

Costs are assigned by the network manager. These numbers are arbitrary. Usually, the cost figures have some relationship to the bandwidth of the media. A 56 kbps link would have a lower cost than a 9.6 kbps link. Another factor used in assigning costs is the number of nodes sharing a broadcast circuit. If 1000 nodes share an Ethernet that circuit should have a higher cost than another Ethernet that has only 3 nodes on it.

A routing node continually monitors the circuits that are directly attached to it. If the node detects a circuit failure, it must notify other routing nodes on the network of that failure so they may update their routing databases.

Notification of other nodes is done through a routing control message. This message contains path cost and path length for all destinations. A level 1 router would send a routing control message to all adjacent routing nodes within its home area. A level 2 router would send a routing control message to all adjacent level 2 routers. The concept of different levels of routing is discussed in the next section.

To stop routing control messages from flooding the network there is a parameter called the rate control frequency timer, which sets the minimum time period before another routing message can be sent. This timer is usually set at 1 second.

Routing control messages on an Ethernet are sent via a multicast address. All routers on the Ethernet enable receipt of this multicast address as part of the data link initialization process. It is important that there are not an excessive number of routers on an Ethernet, if there are, they will flood the network with routing control messages.

An Ethernet has special routing algorithms because of the broadcast nature of the media. There may be several routers on an Ethernet. Each of these nodes sends routing control messages to each other. When a new router joins the Ethernet, it sends a **NEWROUTER** message out. If the number of routers has not exceeded the predetermined number, each routing node updates their tables.

On the Ethernet, one node is known as the designated router. This node periodically sends messages to all end nodes on the network informing them of its address. End nodes each have a limited cache, containing the destination of other nodes that are on the Ethernet. If the end node attempts to communicate with another node not in the cache or not on the Ethernet, it sends the packet to the designated router. Figure 2-5 illustrates a **HELLO** packet from a new router on the Ethernet.

```
┌─DETAIL────────────────────────────────────────────────────────────┐
│ DRP:  ───── DECNET Routing Protocol ─────                          │
│ DRP:                                                               │
│ DRP:  Data length = 41                                            │
│ DRP:  Control Packet Format = 0B                                  │
│ DRP:              0... .... = no padding                          │
│ DRP:              .000 .... = reserved                            │
│ DRP:              .... 101. = Ethernet Router Hello Message       │
│ DRP:              .... ...1 = Control Packet Format               │
│ DRP:  Control Packet Type = 05                                    │
│ DRP:  Version Number  = 02                                        │
│ DRP:  ECO Number      = 00                                        │
│ DRP:  User ECO Number = 00                                        │
│ DRP:  ID of Transmitting Node = 7.47                              │
│ DRP:       Information = 01                                        │
│ DRP:         0... .... = reserved                                 │
│ DRP:         .0.. .... = not blocking request                     │
│ DRP:         ..0. .... = multicast traffic accepted              │
│ DRP:         ...0 .... = verification ok                          │
│ DRP:         .... 0... = do not reject                            │
│ DRP:         .... .0.. = no verification required                │
│ DRP:         .... ..01 = level 2 router                           │
│ DRP:  Receive Block Size  = 1498                                  │
│ DRP:  Router's priority   = 64                                    │
│ DRP:  Area (reserved)     = 0                                     │
│ DRP:  Hello timer (seconds) = 15                                 │
│ DRP:  MPD (reserved)      = 15                                    │
│ DRP:  E-List length = 22                                          │
│ DRP:  Ethernet Name, reserved = 00000000000000                   │
│ DRP:  Router/State length = 14                                   │
│ DRP:                                                              │
│ DRP:  Router ID = 7.45                                            │
│ DRP:  Priority and State = C0                                     │
│ DRP:         1... .... = State known 2-way                        │
│ DRP:         .100 0000 = Router's priority                        │
│ DRP:                                                              │
│ DRP:  Router ID = 7.46                                            │
│ DRP:  Priority and State = C0                                     │
│ DRP:         1... .... = State known 2-way                        │
│ DRP:         .100 0000 = Router's priority                        │
│ DRP:                                                              │
│                            ─Frame 118 of 153─                     │
│                       Use TAB to select windows                   │
│ ┌1      ┌2 Set   ┌4 Zoom ┌5      ┌6Disply┌7 Prev ┌8 Next          │
│ │ Help  │ mark   │ out   │ Menus │options│ frame │ frame          │
└────────────────────────────────────────────────────────────────────┘
```

Courtesy of Network General

Fig. 2-5   A router HELLO message on Ethernet.

Areas

The process of continually updating dynamic routing tables becomes
increasingly difficult as the number of nodes increases. In order to
maintain the efficiency of the routing module, DECnet limits this
process to groups of 1024 nodes. For large customers, this provides a
severe limitation to their ability to provide one common network. Included in this group of large customers is DEC, which has an internal
network of well over 30,000 nodes.

To provide large networks, DECnet segments nodes into areas. A single area has up to 1024 nodes and provides the full adaptive routing algorithms. In addition, up to 63 areas can be connected together to form a multiarea DECnet.

Routers that provide functionality within an area are known as level 1 routers. Routing between areas is provided by level 2 routers. The level 2 routing scheme consists of a series of static links between different areas. Figure 2-6 illustrates a DNA topology that has two areas.

Level 1 routers are not required to know about different areas in the network. When they receive a packet destined for another area, they forward that packet to the nearest level 2 router. The level II router then forwards the packet to its peer level 2 router in the destination area. That level 2 router hands it off to a level 1 router which delivers it to its eventual destination.

Levels 1 and 2 thus provide a hierarchical routing scheme. One set of routing decisions is made for level 2 routing and then a further series of decisions are made by the level 1 routers. Level 2 routing allows the establishment of very large networks.

Even a network of 63,000 nodes has proved to be a limitation. DEC, for example, has pushed the limits of Phase IV networks because of the large growth of the internal EasyNet system. For this reason, among others, DECnet Phase IV is being supplanted by Phase V. Phase V has an address space of 20 bytes instead of the 20 bit Phase IV address space. This allows networks consisting of up to 10^{48} nodes, enough to hold even DEC for a few years. DECnet Phase V is considered in more detail in Part 4 of this book in the chapters on Open Systems Interconnect.

Congestion and lifetime control

Congestion control is an important part of the routing process. If the network is already congested, it is important not to send more packets out onto the already scarce bandwidth. The routing layer will arbitrarily destroy packets under certain types of congestion. It is up to the end-to-end communications layer to detect that a packet was not received and to resend it.

At first glance, it seems wasteful to have a routing layer throw out a packet rather than buffer it for future transmission. The reasoning behind this design decision is that a congestion problem is a transient phenomenon. Usually there is either a node or circuit failure or there is a temporary high load on a particular route. If the load is high, one

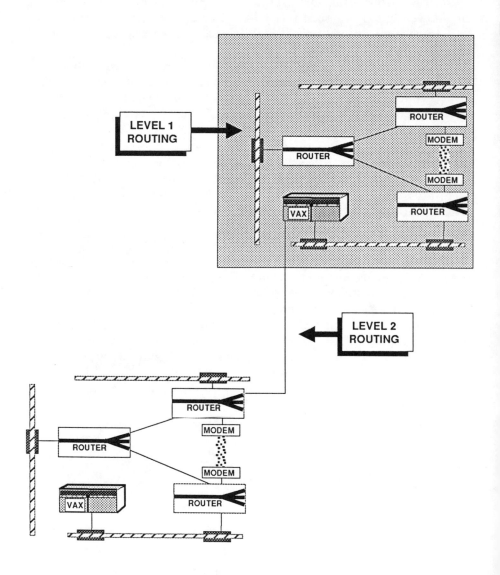

Fig. 2-6   Inter-area routing in DNA.

can expect that situation to change shortly. If the load remains exces-
sively high, the network manager needs to reconfigure the network.

If there is a node or circuit failure, there will shortly be a routing
control message sent which will be transmitted throughout the area or

among areas. In either case, by the time the source end communication layer has noticed the lack of acknowledgment of a particular segment, routing control messages will have propagated throughout the network and the packet will be sent via an alternative route.

There are several kinds of congestion control used in a DNA network. First, there is a limit on the number of packets that can be queued at any one time for transmission. This queue limit is a function of the number of routing layer buffers available and the number of active output circuits. All packets, whether local or route-through, above this are discarded.

A second kind of congestion control is the originating packet limiter. The routing module is able to distinguish between local and route-through packets. The originating packet limiter ensures that a certain percentage of routing resources is always available for route-through traffic. This means that under certain conditions, route-through packets are accepted while local packets are rejected. This is because the network already has a substantial investment in the route-through packet. Again, it is assumed that this condition is a transient one and that resources will become available shortly and the local packet will then be transmitted.

A third kind of congestion control is a flusher. Any packets intended for an adjacent node that has failed are flushed. It will be the responsibility of the sending end communications layer to resend those packets after a time-out period. The queue of packets intended for the failed node (or failed circuit) could have originated from a wide variety of nodes in the network. Rather than require the local routing layer to notify each of these different nodes that a particular packet was not sent, a single routing control message is sent network wide.

Summary

The first three layers allow a node on the network to send a packet of information to any other node on the DECnet. The data link and physical layers together are concerned with delivering information between a pair of nodes. Using multiple access media, such as the Ethernet, many nodes can actually be connected to a single piece of physical wire. The data link layer, however, makes this look like a series of virtual wires between each of the nodes connected to the Ethernet.

The routing layer takes these series of point-to-point links, whether real or virtual, and combines them into a large network. The function of the routing layer is thus to decide which combinations of individual data links form a path to a particular destination. This path may consist of combinations of satellite links, microwave, dedicated tele-phone lines, or Ethernets. Users of the network layer are unaware of this network topology and can thus focus exclusively on the tasks they wish to accomplish, such as file transfer, without worrying about the underlying topology of the network.

We will see that several sophisticated services are built on top of this underlying network service. The first user of the network will be the transport layer of the network. The transport layer takes an un-derlying network connection and allows many users, such as file transfer users or virtual terminal service users, to share the network service. The transport layer thus provides a way of using one network for multiple users. Upper layers will then allow those individual users to perform their tasks.

For Further Reading

Black, *Computer Networks, Protocols, Standards and Interfaces*, Pren-tice Hall, Englewood Cliffs, N.J., 1987.

——, *Data Communications and Distributed Networks*, 2d. ed., Pren-tice Hall, Englewood Cliffs, N.J., 1987.

DEC, Intel, Xerox, "The Ethernet: A Local Area Network, Data Link Layer and Physical Layer Specifications," version 2.0, AA-K759B-TK, November 1982.

Digital Equipment Corporation, "DECnet Phase IV General Descrip-tion," AA-N149A-TC, May 1982.

——, "DECnet Phase IV Routing Layer Functional Specification," AA-X435A-TK, December 1983.

——, "The Ethernet, A Local Area Network Data Link Layer and Physical Layer Specifications," version 2.0, Digital, Intel, Xerox, AA-K759B-TK, November 1982.

Lauck, et al., "Digital Network Architecture Overview," *Digital Techni-cal Journal*, No. 3, September 1986, p. 10.

McNamara, *Technical Aspects of Data Communication*, 3d ed., Digital Press, Maynard, Mass., 1988.

3

DNA Upper-Layer Protocols

Overview of Upper Layer Protocols

The network services, or lower layers, of DNA provide a service of delivering data from one node on the network to another node. The upper-layer services take this data and deliver it to particular users of the network.

The bridge between the network services and the upper-layer services, such as data access, is provided by the transport and session layers. In DNA Phase IV, the transport layer is known as the end-to-end communications layer and uses a set of protocols called the Network Services Protocol (NSP). The function of NSP is to form a series of logical links between users. NSP thus serves as a form of multiplexer which takes many different users and delivers a single stream of data to the network services. Each packet of data is delivered by the network services and then demultiplexed at the destination.

The session layer forms a bridge to the services of DNA. While NSP is responsible for delivering data to end user services, it is the responsibility of the session layer to determine if that end user exists and to validate access in the context of the security domain of the operating system. The session control layer is also responsible for mapping a logical DECnet node name composed of an alphanumeric string into a DECnet address consisting of an area and node designation.

The upper layers of DNA perform a variety of functions. The two primary Phase IV services are remote log-in and remote data access. The CTERM protocols provide a remote log-in service by taking a validated logical link and supplementing it by managing the particular characteristics of a terminal session. The Data Access Protocols are a separate set of protocols used to access remote data, including individual records in a file and attributes of a file such as the size or security attributes.

A variety of other services are also available in DECnet. For example, two different mail delivery protocols exist. The mail-11 protocols are used for traditional VMS mail delivery services. A more modern set of protocols centered around the mailbus architecture are also available. Message handling systems are considered in more detail in the OSI upper layers chapter.

Another service is a videotex service. This allows remote access to data in a VTX "info base" located anywhere in the network. Several other services have been built on top of the network that are not considered in detail in this book. For example, a bulletin board service based on the VAXnotes software is available. As will be seen in the discussion of the session control functions, it is quite simple to build network-based services in DECnet. This is because services such as DAP and the session control databases allow the network to function as a simple extension of the individual node.

Network Services Protocol

The Network Services Protocol of the end-to-end communications layer is closely coupled with the session layer protocols. NSP provides a logical link service to the session layer. Together, they take data that the routing layer has delivered to the proper node and deliver it to the proper user on that node.

The basic NSP concept is a logical link that connects two session control modules. The session control modules turn the logical link into a session, which is then used between two higher layer services, such as a virtual terminal session. Figures 3-1 and 3-2 shows NSP traffic on an Ethernet.

There are four major NSP functions:

- Establishing and destroying logical links
- Error control
- Flow control
- Segmentation and reassembly of messages

When a session layer module requests a logical link, it submits a CONNECT-XMT message to the NSP module. The NSP module submits it to the routing layer, which delivers it to the target NSP module. The target NSP module sends the source NSP module an acknow-

```
SUMMRY—Delta T—DST————SRC—
    5   3.2827  7.45          +7.52           NSP CTRL Connect Confirm  D
    6   0.0049  7.52          +7.45           NSP DATA Link        D=1413 S
    7   0.0024  7.45          +7.52           NSP DATA Link        D=0C39 S
    8   0.0047  7.52          +7.45           NSP ACK  0th-Data    D=1413 S
    9   0.0064  7.52          +7.45           NSP DATA Begin-End   D=1413 S
   10   0.0590  7.45          +7.52           NSP ACK  Data        D=0C39 S
   11   0.0300  7.45          +7.52           NSP DATA Begin-End   D=0C39 S
   12   0.0041  7.52          +7.45           NSP ACK  Data        D=1413 S
   13   0.0061  7.52          +7.45           NSP DATA Begin-End   D=1413 S

DETAIL
NSP:  ----- Network Services Protocol -----
NSP:
NSP:  Message Identifier = 28
NSP:           0... .... = Non-extensible field
NSP:           .010 .... = Connect Confirm Message
NSP:           .... 10.. = Control Message
NSP:           .... ..00 = always zero
NSP:  Type    = 2 (Control Message)
NSP:  Sub-type = 2 (Connect Confirm Message)
                          -Frame 5 of 153-
                      Use TAB to select windows
1         2 Set              4 Zoom  5        6Disply 7 Prev  8 Next          10 New
  Help    mark                 in    Menus   options frame   frame           capture
```

Courtesy of Network General

Fig. 3-1 NSP traffic on an Ethernet.

```
DETAIL
NSP:  ----- Network Services Protocol -----
NSP:
NSP:  Message Identifier = 10
NSP:           0... .... = Non-extensible field
NSP:           .001 .... = Link Service Message
NSP:           .... 00.. = Data Message
NSP:           .... ..00 = always zero
NSP:  Type    = 0 (Data Message)
NSP:  Sub-type = 1 (Link Service Message)
NSP:  Logical Link Destination = 1413
NSP:  Logical Link Source    = 0C39
NSP:  Link Acknowledgment Number
NSP:     Acknowledge Qualifier      = ACK
NSP:     Message Number Acknowledged = 0
NSP:  Link Segment Number = 1
NSP:  Link Service Flags = 00
NSP:           .... 00.. = data/message request count
NSP:           .... ..00 = no change
NSP:  Message Credit = 0
NSP:
                          -Frame 6 of 153-
                      Use TAB to select windows
1         2 Set              4 Zoom  5        6Disply 7 Prev  8 Next          10 New
  Help    mark                out    Menus   options frame   frame           capture
```

Courtesy of Network General

Fig. 3-2 An NSP packet.

ledgment that it has received the request. It then notifies the session control module, which can ACCEPT or REJECT the request. When the target session control module accepts a session request, it notifies the target NSP module, which sends back a connect confirm message.

Sometimes, a connect request is received on a node that has no resources available for new logical links. The NSP module is able to reject this request without notifying the session control module of the incoming request.

Within a logical link, there are two data subchannels. The normal data subchannel is used for data passed in from higher-level modules. The other-data subchannel is used for interrupts and other out-of-band signaling. The function of the other-data subchannel is to move an interrupt signal to the head of the transport layer queue. Since the routing layer has no prioritization capabilities, this does not result in the routing layer delivering the data more quickly. However, it does bypass any data in the transport layer queues.

Within each subchannel, messages are numbered sequentially. Each message sent must be acknowledged or the sending NSP module will retransmit the message. Pipelining allows the receiving NSP to acknowledge several messages by acknowledging receipt of the highest-numbered message. The receiving NSP module can only wait, however, for a period of time that is less than the sending node's time-out factor.

NSP flow control

There are several flow control mechanisms that are available within the NSP modules. When a logical link is being formed, the NSP module at each end tells the other side what type of flow control to use when sending it data. Three options are no flow control, segment flow control, and session control message flow control.

Segment flow control is accomplished by sending a request count parameter. The sending NSP may only have that number of messages outstanding. It looks at the highest-numbered message segment that has been acknowledged, adds the request count parameter, and then sends messages segments until it reaches that sequence number.

Session control flow control operates the same way, but instead of using individual message segments, the request count parameter refers to the entire message. The NSP module thus looks for the highest acknowledged end-of-message segment and adds the request count parameter to it.

Since a logical link is full duplex, each side of an NSP logical link may request different flow control mechanisms. A large VAX connected to a PC might have a session. The VAX, as a data receiver with a large buffer space, might request either no flow control or segment flow control with a large request count parameter. The PC would have very few restraints on the amount of data it can send. On the other hand, the PC as a data-receiving NSP module would probably request a fairly small request count parameter.

In addition to the normal flow control, either end of a session may also use an On/Off control mechanism. The data-receiving module requests that no further messages be sent until an ON message is transmitted.

The other-data subchannel uses a message-based flow control mechanism. When a logical link is established, there is an implicit request count parameter of one. This means that an interrupt message must be acknowledged before a second one is sent.

One of the prime functions of the NSP module is segmentation and reassembly of messages received from the session control module. A single segment is limited by the size of data that the network services, or routing, layer can accept. NSP takes data from a session control buffer, breaks it into segments, and submits each individual segment to the routing layer.

NSP components

An NSP process has three types of components: databases, buffer pools, and modules. Figure 3-3 illustrates the structure of an NSP process. Note that these are functional components. The division of functionality in an architecture helps show what a particular layer is supposed to accomplish. Often, several components are combined into a single process. Any NSP implementation that can receive a call and submit the proper messages to a routing layer is considered a valid NSP implementation.

There are four databases used by NSP:

- The NSP internal database
- The reserved port database
- The session control database
- The node database

The first two databases are used internally by NSP to manage itself. The NSP internal database contains information and parameters used in the internal management of the NSP module. An example of a parameter would be the maximum number of logical links allowed on this node.

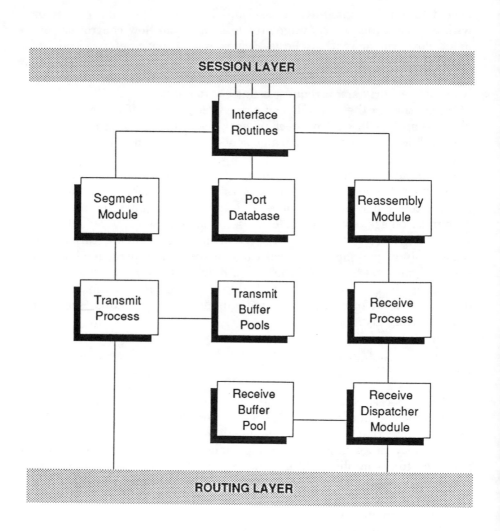

Fig. 3-3 NSP modules.

A port in NSP is equivalent to the Ethernet concept of a portal. Both refer to a particular registered user of the service. Normally, the user of the end-to-end communications layer is the session control layer. The reserved port database contains a list of resources that NSP modules use for exchanging control messages that are not mapped into any session control port.

The other two databases can be thought of as interfaces to other layers. The session control port database is an interface to the session control layer. When the NSP module sets up a logical link, it allocates one of the available ports to the session control layer. When the logical link is destroyed, the NSP module frees the port and returns it to the database. The node database contains information on each of the nodes with which a logical link is established, including traffic usage counters and estimates of the round-trip communications delay.

Buffers are how data is exchanged with other modules in the Digital Network Architecture. A receive buffer pool contains data received from the routing layer. An event buffer pool is used to queue events that are then put into an event queue (another type of buffer) for processing by the network management layer.

NSP modules

Several types of modules operate within the confines of the larger NSP module. The interface routines intercept all calls from session control and provide a unified calling environment. If a message is to be transmitted, it is sent to a segmentation module, which breaks the message up into segments of appropriate size. The transmit buffer pool is used as a queue to the routing layer. The transmit process polls the routing layer to determine when transmission of certain buffers has been completed.

The receive dispatcher module also works with the routing layer. It polls the routing layer for received messages and then dispatches them to the appropriate receive processes. Each logical link has its own processes, which manage the logical link state. The receive process sends data up to be reassembled, which in turn is sent up to the session control layer.

Session Control Layer

When a session control receives a logical link request from an end user on the local node, it must first identify the destination address. In addition to the required name mapping database, some DECnet nodes also contain an alias database which allows users to specify additional names for destination addresses. Figure 3-4 illustrates the relation of the session control database to the operating system and the lower layers of the network.

The session control module must then format a connect request that will be passed to the destination session control module. This information might contain a user name and password. Other times, the connect data will not specify this information, and the module will

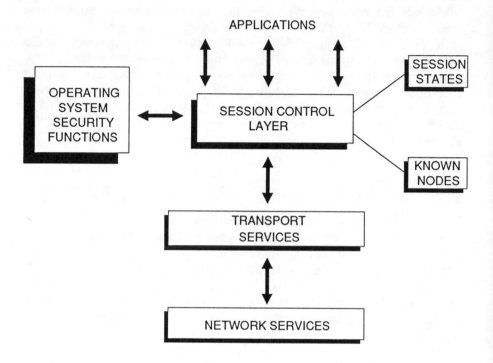

Fig. 3-4 Session layer functions.

attempt to use default accounts on the destination node, if that node has those enabled.

The session control module passes the connect request to the network services layer. If an outgoing timer has been enabled, the timer is started. The module waits for a packet with this logical link identifier to be received from the network services layer indicating that the destination session control module has accepted or rejected the request. If the timer was set and no reply was received, a rejection is assumed.

Upon receiving an incoming request, the destination network services module notifies the session control module of the incoming logical link address and passes a buffer containing the connect data. The session control module parses the connect data and validates the access control information. It then either identifies, creates, or activates the destination end user and passes connection information to the end user processes, attempting to parse the source address into a logical node name. If the node name is not contained in the mapping database, the end user layer is notified that an unknown node is communicating.

Once a session has been established, the two session control modules act as a conduit for data for the upper-layer services. If an end user instructs the session control module to disconnect or abort, the module passes a 2-byte disconnect code and up to 16 bytes of disconnect data to the network services.

The session control layer can log two types of events in an event log for the network management layer. Changes in node state are logged along with any access control failures. Most systems also log success log-in attempts in the normal operating system accounting file. Figure 3-5 illustrates a session control connection request.

Session control databases

The session control layer has two databases that are used during network operation. These are:

- A node name mapping table
- A session state database

The node name mapping table translates logical addresses into the 20-bit DECnet address. One of the problems in a large Phase IV network is updating the session control database on all nodes of the network. Even though a node is reachable at the routing layer, users of network services need the logical name. It is much easier to ask for FILESER-VER::FILE.DAT than it is to remember that FILESERVER has a DECnet address of 2.136.

Phase V of DECnet will expand the session control layer to include a distributed naming service. New nodes or services entering the network can register themselves with the DNS. If an unknown node name is received from an end user, the session control layer will be able to query DNS as to the validity of that name.

The second database kept by the session control layer is a state database. A particular session control module can be operating in one of four different modes. When the module is off, there are no logical links operational. In SHUT state, the module keeps existing logical links in operation but will not accept new requests from either another session control module or from an end user process. RESTRICTED is like the SHUT state but does accept new logical links from users with sufficient levels of privilege. On is the state for normal operation.

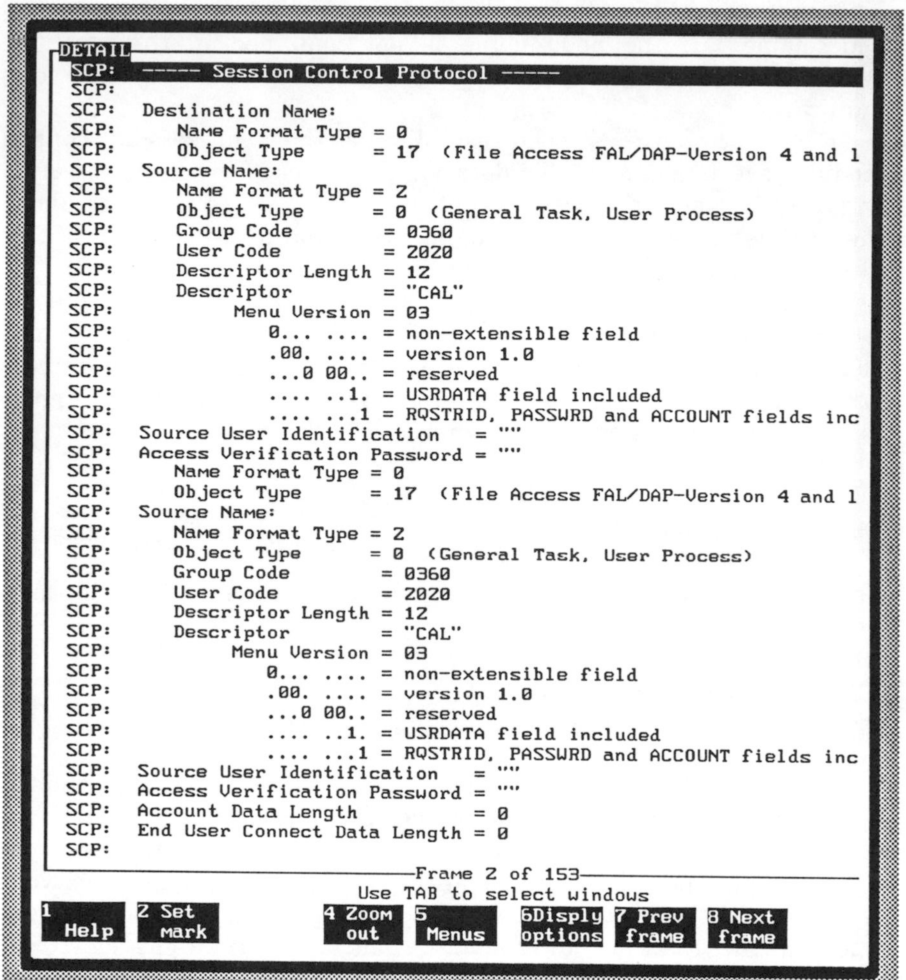

```
┌DETAIL────────────────────────────────────────────────────────┐
│SCP:  ----- Session Control Protocol -----                     │
│SCP:                                                            │
│SCP:  Destination Name:                                        │
│SCP:     Name Format Type = 0                                  │
│SCP:     Object Type      = 17  (File Access FAL/DAP-Version 4 and 1│
│SCP:  Source Name:                                             │
│SCP:     Name Format Type = 2                                  │
│SCP:     Object Type      = 0  (General Task, User Process)    │
│SCP:     Group Code       = 0360                               │
│SCP:     User Code        = 2020                               │
│SCP:     Descriptor Length = 12                                │
│SCP:     Descriptor       = "CAL"                              │
│SCP:         Menu Version = 03                                 │
│SCP:         0... .... = non-extensible field                 │
│SCP:         .00. .... = version 1.0                           │
│SCP:         ...0 00.. = reserved                              │
│SCP:         .... ..1. = USRDATA field included                │
│SCP:         .... ...1 = RQSTRID, PASSWRD and ACCOUNT fields inc│
│SCP:  Source User Identification   = ""                        │
│SCP:  Access Verification Password = ""                        │
│SCP:     Name Format Type = 0                                  │
│SCP:     Object Type      = 17  (File Access FAL/DAP-Version 4 and 1│
│SCP:  Source Name:                                             │
│SCP:     Name Format Type = 2                                  │
│SCP:     Object Type      = 0  (General Task, User Process)    │
│SCP:     Group Code       = 0360                               │
│SCP:     User Code        = 2020                               │
│SCP:     Descriptor Length = 12                                │
│SCP:     Descriptor       = "CAL"                              │
│SCP:         Menu Version = 03                                 │
│SCP:         0... .... = non-extensible field                 │
│SCP:         .00. .... = version 1.0                           │
│SCP:         ...0 00.. = reserved                              │
│SCP:         .... ..1. = USRDATA field included                │
│SCP:         .... ...1 = RQSTRID, PASSWRD and ACCOUNT fields inc│
│SCP:  Source User Identification   = ""                        │
│SCP:  Access Verification Password = ""                        │
│SCP:  Account Data Length       = 0                            │
│SCP:  End User Connect Data Length = 0                         │
│SCP:                                                            │
│                        ─────Frame 2 of 153─────               │
│                        Use TAB to select windows              │
│ ┌1──────┐┌2 Set──┐  ┌4 Zoom─┐┌5──────┐┌6Disply┐┌7 Prev─┐┌8 Next─┐│
│ │ Help  ││ mark  │  │ out   ││ Menus ││options││ frame ││ frame ││
│ └───────┘└───────┘  └───────┘└───────┘└───────┘└───────┘└───────┘│
└────────────────────────────────────────────────────────────────┘
```

Courtesy of Network General

Fig. 3-5   A session control packet.

The state database can also contain default connection timers. When an incoming request is received, the session control module passes that request to an upper-layer process. Normally, this upper-layer process is under no time constraint to accept or reject the request. By setting a timer, the network manager allows the session control module to assume a request has been rejected upon expiration of the timer.

```
NCP>show known object


Known Object Volatile Summary as of 15-JUN-1988 10:54:10

   Object   Number  File/PID                    User Id        Password

   $MOM        0
   $NICONFIG   0
   DNZIN       0    0000008E
   TASK        0
   FAL        17    FAL.EXE
   HLD        18
   NML        19    NML.EXE
   REMACP     23    00000089
   MIRROR     25
   EVL        26    00000088
   MAIL       27    MAIL.EXE
   PHONE      29    PHONE.EXE
   NOTES      33    NOTES$SERVER.EXE            NOTES$SERVER
   CTERM      42    00000089
   UPM        51    UPM.EXE
   DTR        63
NCP>
```

Courtesy of Digital Equipment Corporation

Fig. 3-6   Registered objects in a session database.

DNA objects

A connect request from an end user process usually contains an object type to indicate the type of service required to the destination session control module (See Figure 3-6). An object type 4, for example, is for the CTERM protocols in the virtual terminal service. An object type 17 is for the Data Access Protocol. An object type 0 is for non-registered object types, which must be further specified by the requesting end user. In VMS, for example, the user would specify the destination task as:

NODE::"task=taskname.com"

This is equivalent to an object type 0 call for a user-written program called **TASKNAME.COM**. In this case, the destination VMS would look either in the requesting user has a proxy log-in or would look in a default area for object type 0 execution to see if **TASKNAME.COM** exists.

If the end user in VMS had wished to specify an account to run the task in, the syntax would have been:

NODE"username password"::"task=taskname.com"

In many networks, there is a default area for FAL access as well as for object type 0 execution. If these two default areas are the same, it is possible to copy a file to a remote node, then have it executed at the remote node, and the results copied back. This provides an easy way to either steal or borrow CPU cycles.

Virtual Terminal Service

The virtual terminal (VT) service is one of two ways to allow a remote terminal to access a host system. The Local Area Transport protocols are an alternative service that provides similar functionality. Both services allow a host to treat all terminals, remote or local, in the same way. The LAT protocols are a non-DECnet set of protocols that interface directly with the Ethernet. LAT is more efficient than the DECnet virtual terminal service but is limited only to use on Ethernet devices. The DECnet VT service, on the other hand, is able to operate over any DECnet configuration.

The virtual terminal service consists of two sublayers. The terminal communication module establishes a data stream between two nodes on the network. This module can be thought of as an extension of the session control layer in that it binds two terminal services managers together into a session.

The command terminal module is the upper sublayer of the virtual terminal service. The command terminal protocols provide the actual I/O exchange between a host and a terminal. The virtual terminal service is usually referred to as CTERM after the command terminal module. This is in contrast to LAT-based services.

To establish a terminal session there are two nodes involved. The server is the local node that actually has the terminal connected. The host node is the remote node to which the user wishes to connect. The terminal communication module allows the host node to treat all terminals as though they were local. This allows software to function effectively across a network, irrespective of the location of the users. Figure 3-7 illustrates CTERM traffic on an Ethernet.

There may be several nodes in between the host and the server in a virtual terminal connection. The VT process on the server side constructs messages. These messages are sent down to the network services layers. These layers may route the message through many different nodes. Eventually, the message is received by the network services layer at the host node which sends it up to the host virtual terminal modules. This is in contrast to the LAT protocols, which only work with nodes that are one hop away from each other on the Ethernet.

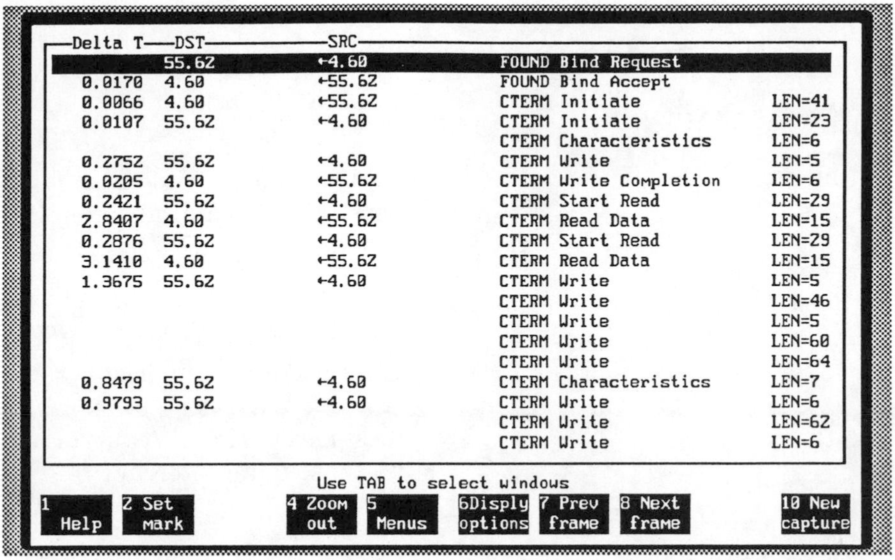

```
 ─Delta T──DST─────────SRC─
              55.62      ←4.60             FOUND Bind Request
    0.0170   4.60       ←55.62             FOUND Bind Accept
    0.0066   4.60       ←55.62             CTERM Initiate          LEN=41
    0.0107   55.62      ←4.60              CTERM Initiate          LEN=23
                                           CTERM Characteristics   LEN=6
    0.2752   55.62      ←4.60              CTERM Write             LEN=5
    0.0205   4.60       ←55.62             CTERM Write Completion  LEN=6
    0.2421   55.62      ←4.60              CTERM Start Read        LEN=29
    2.8407   4.60       ←55.62             CTERM Read Data         LEN=15
    0.2876   55.62      ←4.60              CTERM Start Read        LEN=29
    3.1410   4.60       ←55.62             CTERM Read Data         LEN=15
    1.3675   55.62      ←4.60              CTERM Write             LEN=5
                                           CTERM Write             LEN=46
                                           CTERM Write             LEN=5
                                           CTERM Write             LEN=60
                                           CTERM Write             LEN=64
    0.8479   55.62      ←4.60              CTERM Characteristics   LEN=7
    0.9793   55.62      ←4.60              CTERM Write             LEN=6
                                           CTERM Write             LEN=62
                                           CTERM Write             LEN=6

                        Use TAB to select windows
  1       2 Set        4 Zoom  5         6Disply 7 Prev  8 Next        10 New
   Help     mark         out    Menus     options  frame   frame       capture
```

Fig. 3-7   CTERM traffic on an Ethernet.

The terminal communication module first begins by binding two sessions together. It then notifies the remote module to enter a particular mode. The only mode currently defined is the CTERM module. Users could define their own modes, to be used on other kinds of terminals such as non-VT100-type terminals. Finally, the terminal communication module dispatches a series of data messages. These messages contain CTERM commands. Figure 3-8 illustrates some CTERM commands and their function.

The CTERM module is used to carry out the actual terminal functions. The CTERM modules recognize standard VT-style escape sequences, which are a superset of the ANSI standard. CTERM modules can read and set terminal device characteristics. Like local terminals, the CTERM module is able to read and write to a device concurrently. This includes support for a type-ahead buffer, so the user may type in characters even though the program on the host has not yet issued a read request.

Data Access Protocols

DAP is a language used to access data across the network. It uses a session established at the lower layers of DNA and then provides additional functionality for the specific purpose of data access (as opposed

Command Terminal Protocol Messages

Message Type	Function
Initiate	Verify protocol version numbers and other initialization information.
Read	Issues a read request to the server terminal manager. Carries the data to the host system. Can also send unread messages to cancel requests (in response to an interrupt request)
Out-of-band	Carries out-of-band data such as interrupt requests.
Write	Writes data to terminal and receives a confirmation that the write completed successfully.
Characteristics	Reads and sets terminal characteristics. For example, can dynamically change terminal type from ANSI to VT100.
Buffers	Can check status of input and type-ahead buffers.

Fig. 3-8   CTERM messages.

to remote log-in, Videotex, or other network services). DAP allows users to get files from remote input and store them on a remote output device. Multiple data streams can share a common data link, allowing for the use of wild cards and other similar operations. DAP is significant for an early file access protocol in its ability to provide random access to a wide variety of different file structures. Figure 3-9 illustrates the use of DAP to access directory information across a DECnet.

```
$ dir/full cats::*.*

Directory CATS::SYS$COMMON:[DECNET]

ATLANTA$PRINT.DAT;1          File ID:   None
Size:            38/38       Owner:     [376,376]
Created:   13-NOV-1987 08:08 Revised:   13-NOV-1987 08:08 (1)
Expires:   <None specified>  Backup:    29-MAY-1988 07:07
File organization:  Sequential
File attributes:    Allocation: 38, Extend: 0, Global buffer count: 0
                    Version limit: 0
Record format:      Variable length
Record attributes:  Carriage return carriage control
Journaling enabled: None
File protection:    System:RWED, Owner:RWED, Group:RE, World:
Access Cntrl List:  None

ATLANTA$PRINT.MAP;1          File ID:   None
Size:             6/6        Owner:     [376,376]
Created:   14-DEC-1987 10:36 Revised:   14-DEC-1987 10:36 (1)
Expires:   <None specified>  Backup:    29-MAY-1988 07:07
File organization:  Sequential
File attributes:    Allocation: 6, Extend: 0, Global buffer count: 0
```

Courtesy of Digital Equipment Corporation

Fig. 3-9   Using DAP to access directory information.

DAP is being gradually supplanted by the Phase V Distributed File System and by other remote data access mechanisms such as the Local Area VAX Cluster. The File Transfer Access Management (FTAM) pieces of OSI are also an alternative to the DAP protocols. DAP protocols still provide higher performance than DFS and other complex protocol suites over low-speed dial-up lines. In high-bandwidth environments, the LAVC and DFS mechanisms can provide up to 5 times the performance of the DAP protocols. Obviously, a key element of the DAP protocols is their longevity, which means that a large number of applications have been coded to take advantage of them.

A DAP session consists of a series of messages exchanged between the DAP server and the DAP client. Each message consists of an operator (or packet header) and an operand (or packet data). The operator can consist of up to seven fields. Operand structure depends on the command chosen. Figure 3-10 illustrates a series of DAP messages over an Ethernet link.

The operator begins with a type field. These type fields can be DAP defined or user extensions. The next field consists of a series of flags which indicate if the next five parameters in the operator are present

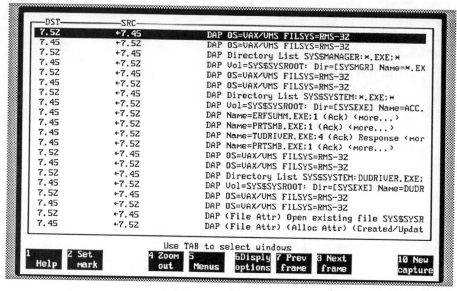

Courtesy of Network General

Fig. 3-10 DAP traffic on an Ethernet link.

or missing. This field also contains a MORE bit which signals the presence of more data in subsequent packets that form one segment.

A stream ID field is used when a single user transmits multiple streams of data. This does not mean that multiple users can share one logical link. This is because each DAP session must run in the authorization context of the remote user to prevent unauthorized access to information.

Two length fields are available. If a single-length field is used, up to 256 bytes can be contained in a message. If the second-length field is used, between 256 and 64,000 bytes can be contained in a message. If an acknowledgment is sent, it often consists simply of a type field and nothing else. This 1-byte acknowledgment helps increase the efficiency of DAP data transfers.

The last two fields in the operator are the bit count and system-specific fields. A bit count field is used when the last byte of a data message has some unused bits in it. The system-specific environment is used only in homogeneous environments, such as one VAX RMS file system talking to another VAX RMS file system. If a DAP message containing system-specific fields is received in a heterogenous environment, it causes a fatal error and termination of the session.

It is possible to multiplex several DAP messages into a single session control buffer. If this option is used, length fields are required. The length fields enable the DAP process to demultiplex a single data message into each of the logical data streams.

Configuration messages

To begin a DAP session, configuration messages are exchanged between the two systems. This message establishes the maximum buffer sizes, operating system type, and file system type. The configuration field also contains a system capability bit map that has an exhaustive list of different capabilities. When each of these bits is set, it indicates that the system has that capability. Figure 3-11 illustrates a DAP configuration message.

After a configuration message, the session usually exchanges access and attribute messages. An access message establishes the type of access requested, and an attribute message defines the type of data in the file or the type of data needed.

The access message specifies a file name and the type of access requested. Access types can be used to open a file or a create a file. Users can also specify management functions needed, such as renaming or erasing a file. Finally, a special type of access is a directory list, which will return a list of file names.

The access message also specifies what to do in the case of errors. It is possible for users to proceed upon encountering I/O errors or to return a fatal error message. The user can also specify that status messages be sent when data is accessed.

A special type of access is the go/no-go option. When a user specifies that they want to delete a file, and that file has a wild card in it, it is possible that the operation will refer to several different files. With the go/no-go option, the name of each file accessed is returned to the requesting process. The requesting process can then indicate continuation of the operation with a RESUME flag in a CONTROL message. Alternatively, the user can issue a SKIP flag in a control message to move to the next file. Figure 3-12 illustrates a data access message using the DAP protocols.

A further function in the access message is the type of access level that the user will be requesting of the file. This allows the specification of reads, writes, deletes, updates, or to perform block I/O. The process can also specify the type of shared access it is willing to accommodate—the ability of other users to read, write, delete, update, or perform other operations. The combination of the two types of access

```
┌DETAIL
 DAP:  ───── Data Access Protocol ─────
 DAP:
 DAP:  Code = 1 (Configuration)
 DAP:  Buffer Size        = 1060
 DAP:  Operating System Type = VAX/VMS
 DAP:  File System Version  = RMS-32
 DAP:  DAP Version Number          = 7
 DAP:  DAP ECO Number              = 0
 DAP:  DAP User Number             = 0
 DAP:  DAP Software Version Number       = 5
 DAP:  DAP User Software Version Number = 0
 DAP:  Generic System Capabilities:
 DAP:    File preallocation
 DAP:    Sequential file organization
 DAP:    Relative file organization
 DAP:    Single keyed indexed file organization
 DAP:    Sequential file transfer
 DAP:    Random access by record number
 DAP:    Random access by Virtual Block Number
 DAP:    Random access by key
 DAP:    Random access by Record File Address (RFA)
 DAP:    Multi-key indexed file organization
 DAP:    Switching access code
 DAP:    Append to file access
 DAP:    Command file submission and/or execution as in Access Messa
 DAP:    Status return
 DAP:    Blocking of DAP messages up to response
 DAP:    Use of 2 byte operand length in DAP message header
 DAP:    Status return
 DAP:    Blocking of DAP messages up to response
 DAP:    Use of 2 byte operand length in DAP message header
 DAP:    The file checksum option
 DAP:    Key Definition Extended Attributes Message
 DAP:    Allocation Extended Attributes Message
 DAP:    Summary Extended Attributes Message
 DAP:    Directory list
 DAP:    Date and Time Extended Attributes Message
 DAP:    File Protection Extended Attributes Message
 DAP:    Spooling, specified by bit 20 of FOP field
 DAP:    Command file submission, specified by bit 21 of FOP field
 DAP:    File deletion, specified by bit 22 of FOP field
 DAP:    Sequential record access
 DAP:    File rename operation
 DAP:    Wildcard operation
 DAP:    Name message
 DAP:    Supports change of date and time on close
 DAP:    Supports change of protection on close
 DAP:
                         ─Frame 9 of 153─
                     Use TAB to select windows
 ┌─────┐┌────────┐  ┌──────┐┌───────┐┌────────┐┌───────┐┌───────┐
 │1    ││2 Set   │  │4 Zoom││5      ││6Display││7 Prev ││8 Next │
 │Help ││  mark  │  │  out ││ Menus ││options ││ frame ││ frame │
 └─────┘└────────┘  └──────┘└───────┘└────────┘└───────┘└───────┘
```

Courtesy of Network General

Fig. 3-11   A DAP configuration message.

can then be translated into a VMS lock. The clusters chapter of this book has a discussion of VMS lock compatibility tables.

The last function of the access message is to indicate the types of attributes the user is interested in retrieving for this particular access.

```
┌─DETAIL┐
│ DAP: ----- Data Access Protocol -----
│ DAP:
│ DAP:   Code = 2 (Attributes)  Operand Length = 11
│ DAP:   Attribute Data Type:   ASCII Data
│ DAP:   Attribute of File being Accessed = FB$SEQ;  Sequential
│ DAP:   Attribute Record Format      = FB$VAR;  Variable-length re
│ DAP:   Record Attribute Type:
│ DAP:     FB$CR;  Records have an implied LF/CR envelope
│ DAP:   File Record Length (bytes)   = 0
│ DAP:   File Operation Attribute Type:
│ DAP:     FB$SQO; Sequential access only
│ DAP:
│ DAP:   Code = 3 (Access)
│ DAP:   Access Function = $OPEN;   Open existing file
│ DAP:   Access Options Type:
│ DAP:     I/O errors are non-fatal
│ DAP:     A 16-bit checksum is generated by the transmitting and rece
│ DAP:   File Name Specification = "SYS$SYSROOT:[SYSEXE]DUDRIVER.EXE;5"
│ DAP:   File Access Type:
│ DAP:     FB$GET; Get access
│ DAP:     FB$SQO; Sequential access only
│ DAP:
│ DAP:   Code = 3 (Access)
│ DAP:   Access Function = $OPEN;   Open existing file
│ DAP:   Access Options Type:
│ DAP:     I/O errors are non-fatal
│ DAP:     A 16-bit checksum is generated by the transmitting and rece
│ DAP:   File Name Specification = "SYS$SYSROOT:[SYSEXE]DUDRIVER.EXE;5"
│ DAP:   File Access Type:
│ DAP:     FB$GET; Get access
│ DAP:     FB$BRO; Support switching between block and record I/O
│ DAP:   Shared File Access Type:
│ DAP:     FB$GET; Get access
│ DAP:   Display File Access Type:
│ DAP:     Main Attributes message
│ DAP:     Allocation Main Attributes message
│ DAP:     Date and Time Attributes message
│ DAP:     File Protection Attributes message
│ DAP:     Name message containing resultant file specification
│ DAP:
└──────────────────────Frame 103 of 153─────────────────────────
                  Use TAB to select windows
 ┌─┐ ┌────┐     ┌────┐ ┌─────┐  ┌──────┐ ┌──────┐ ┌──────┐
 │1│ │2 Set│    │4 Zoom│ │5    │  │6Disply│ │7 Prev│ │8 Next│
 │Help│ │mark│  │out  │ │Menus│  │options│ │frame │ │frame │
 └─┘ └────┘     └────┘ └─────┘  └──────┘ └──────┘ └──────┘
```

Fig. 3-12 DAP data access message.

The user can request any combination of summary data, file protection, access control information, date and time created, or other information typically available in a VMS environment.

An attribute message would be returned in response to an access message. In the case of a directory listing, the operation may end after the last attribute message is received. In the case of a data access operation, the attribute message may be followed by several data transfer messages.

Attribute messages describe, in great detail, the structure of the file. The type of data can be left undefined or can specify ASCII, EBCDIC, compressed, or other options. Files can be organized as sequential, hashed, or indexed in various ways. The record format can be specified as fixed, variable length, or a single stream of ASCII data.

Other attributes of a file include a series of file access options. This allows a user to specify that a file be rewound when it is opened or closed. The user can also specify that contiguous space is needed for a file or that a particular file is locked. Several file operations are meant to address a magnetic tape environment.

Other file access options deal with concurrency issues. Files can be signaled as locked, and users can signal that they are willing to wait for a currently locked file. Waiting for a currently locked file is analogous to the asynchronous system trap (AST) locking option in a single system or clustered environment. As can be seen, DAP maps most single-system file operations into a networked environment.

A final set of file access options determines the disposition of a file at the end of a session. The end of the session could be a normal DAP termination or the result of a node or network failure. Temporary files can be deleted upon closure or can be spooled to a line printer. A file can even be submitted as a command file when it gets closed.

The last set of attributes for a file is the device characteristics. This list includes support for mailboxes, real-time devices, and network devices. Devices can be signaled as mounted or allocated, terminal or file oriented, sharable or spooled.

Control messages and data access

Once the access and attributes are established, the user can perform a series of control operations on the file. These allow the user to delete data, request blocks of data, or set and release locks. Commands are provided to flush all data through the protocol stack to ensure that there are no outstanding messages. Control messages also are used to control the position within a file—the user process can issue commands to move forward or backward within the file or to find a particular record in a random access file.

The actual transfer is done via a data message. The data in this message is totally transparent and can consist of binary data, although there's no guarantee that the receiving system will know what to do with that data. A PC can use DAP to bring a VAX-executable image to the PC disk. This does not mean that the VAX program will run very effectively on the PC operating system.

Several other messages allow the extension of certain types of attributes. The date-time attribute extension message is used to transfer the date and time that a file was created, modified, or last accessed. Key definition attribute extension messages are used to define keys on remote files. Protection and access control attributes allow remote manipulation of a file's security attributes.

DAP operation

The DAP exchange begins with the link being set up by passing authorization information down to the session control layer. The session control layer may accept a user ID, a password, or an account identification. The remote session process will then activate a DAP-speaking process to run in the user's authorization context. DNA can include a default account for users that do not furnish access information.

On a VAX running VMS, the processing of providing files to remote users is accomplished with a File Access Listener (FAL). The FAL is a DAP-speaking process that negotiates with the local instance of the Record Management Services (RMS). The DAP-speaking process transfers the data across the network. The local user then sees the data as though it were furnished locally. This is because the RMS services shield the user from the location of the data. Figure 3-13 illustrates the relationship of RMS to File Access Listeners on remote nodes.

Original DAP implementations required a separate DAP-speaking process for each file accessed. Needless to say, wild-card operations on files became highly inefficient. Current implementations of DAP are multithreaded, allowing a single user the ability to access multiple files. The stream ID function allows data and attribute messages to apply to a particular file.

During normal operation, a status message is returned with each message sent. During the data transfer process, it is possible to omit success status messages until after the completion of the file transfer process.

When errors occur in I/O processing, the remote DAP-speaking process typically suspends processing and sends a warning status message to the user process. The user then can send a control message to indicate whether to resume data transfer or to terminate the access. These options can also be set in the initial access configuration messages.

Data transfer operations can operate either on sequential or direct access files. In a sequential file retrieval, a single GET control mes-

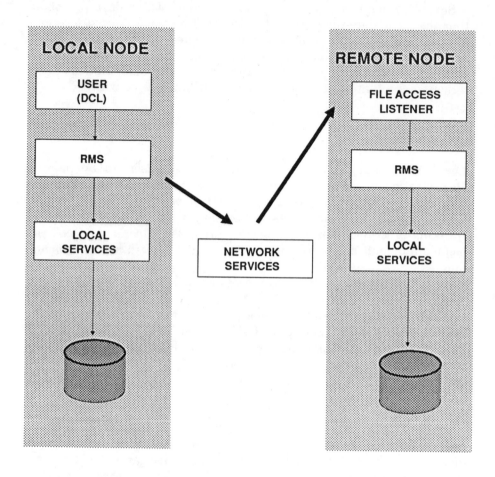

Fig. 3-13 File access listeners.

sage is issued. This is followed by the transmission of all records in the file without further DAP messages. It is the responsibility of the lower layers of the network to perform flow control during this phase. Streaming of data across the network stops when an end-of-file or error occurs. It is also possible for the receiving process to abort the transfer.

Aborting the transfer is done by sending an access complete message. The process that issued the access complete may still receive a considerable amount of data if the network has a large store of buffers.

Sending a sequential file to a remote location is very similar to getting one. A single PUT control message is issued, followed by a series of data transfer messages. The system that is storing the file continues to accept data until it receives an access complete message.

Record level access proceeds in a more complex manner. For each record accessed, the user submits a CONTROL message which contains a GET command along with a key value. This is followed by the return of the desired record. The issuing program issues another control message and receives the next record of data. The meaning of the key depends on the type of access that was requested—a key value has a different meaning for the different structures of random access files.

Accessing directory information is done by first issuing a directory list command. This may contain a series for wild cards in the file name field of the access message. A directory list access command results in a whole slew of return messages. The return message begins by issuing a name message, which contains a volume or device name. This is followed by a second name message which contains the directory specification. Next, a third name message contains the name of the first file. This is followed by a series of attributes of that file, depending on the ones that were requested in the access message. Then, the next file name is transmitted, followed by another set of attribute messages. At the end of the process, an access complete message is sent.

DAP is a highly sophisticated file access mechanism, considering the age of the protocol. It specifies a great number of different options that are used to access most VMS file systems and other file systems used on the other DEC operating systems. In a sense, DAP hardcodes the different options available by making long lists and exchanging long configuration messages.

A series of more modern approaches are available and are discussed later in this book. The OSI FTAM protocols, for example, build a virtual model of a file store. This virtual model is then encoded in a variety of presentation contexts which allow dissimilar systems to exchange data. The definition of the format for that data transfer can be negotiated using a combination of presentation layer facilities. This allows a wider variety of systems to interconnect.

The Data Access Protocol is the original Phase IV service used for the exchange of data across the network. The Distributed System Services, discussed later, are gradually supplanting the use of DAP-based services.

DAP is a protocol used by two cooperating processes to define the exchange of data. The NSP protocols together with the session control layer allow the exchange of messages. These messages, however, contain no semantic information on the type of data. DAP builds on top of these lower-layer services to add more complex concepts such as indexed data or file protection codes.

On a VAX system, all requests for data are typically intercepted by the Record Management Services (RMS). If the request is for local data, RMS uses a QIO system call to request data from the local device driver. That local device can be a locally attached disk or even a disk attached to an HSC controller in a cluster.

If the requested data is not local, RMS redirects the call, still using a QIO system service, to the network. The remote session control layer receives the request for data and activates a File Access Listener. A FAL is a DAP-speaking process which cooperates with the local instance of the Record Management Services. The FAL process acts as an agent for remote nodes to deliver data.

The exchange of data using the DAP protocols can be fairly complex. The procedure begins with the exchange of a set of configuration messages. These messages establish the parameters of the DAP session, such as buffer sizes, file system type, and operating system type.

Following the basic configuration, the DAP-speaking processes can exchange information about the attributes of files being accessed. This information may include file organization, device characteristics (tape, disk, etc.), and the format or data records.

The originating DAP process can then request a certain type of access to a file. This access could be read, write, or delete. This is followed by a data exchange phase. The DAP protocols include provisions for the establishment of a data stream, status messages, and data stream termination.

The DAP protocols also include several provisions for more complex information about files. Key definitions of remote files can be requested and data can be accessed at the record level by index values. This record level access makes the DAP protocols more than a simple file server.

Usually, the DAP protocols are used in the Record Management Services. It is possible to write user programs that access DAP directly through the Network File Access Routines. A Network File Transfer utility is also available, an interactive utility used to access DAP-speaking processes.

Distributed Naming Service

The Distributed Naming Service is a lookup service that separates the logical name of an entity from its physical location. This is the same service that is provided with VMS logical names but is extended into a distributed network environment. Sets of names, called directories, can be located in multiple locations on the network. When a host or user encounters a need for a service, it is able to contact a nameserver to find out who is providing that service.

DNS is a service that will be used at two levels of the network. At the session layer, DNS replaces the need for a local node database that contains translations of node names to DNA addresses. In a Phase IV network, adding a new node to the network meant updating the local databases of every node that would need to access the new node. In Phase V implementations, a new node registers itself with DNS and all other nodes on the network are thus made aware of its presence.

The second use of DNS is by upper-layer services. DNS can be used by a message-handling system to provide locations of electronic mail users. Another use is to provide transparent access to files located throughout the network.

Each type of name, such as file name or node name, is stored in a directory. A directory may have child directory entries to add further structure to the definition of a type of service.

At the bottom of a directory tree is a series of object. Each object has a name and a set of attributes. The session layer node name directory, for example, would have an object named Nodename with an attribute called DNA Address.

A special type of name is called a soft link. This is a pointer to an object someplace else in the directory service. An object name must be unique—it can be stored in only one place in the directory structure. Soft links allow an object to be referred to by multiple names or aliases. Figure 3-14 illustrates a DNS namespace.

The namespace is the collection of all directories. A network usually has only one namespace. It is possible for development or transition purposes to have dual namespaces, but each namespace is totally distinct. The namespace has a namespace unique identifier (NSUID). Usually, a nickname for the namespace is defined on each node in the form of a logical name.

Each name in the namespace has internal and external representations. An internal representation of the name is provided for program-to-program communication, as in the case of client programs, protocols, and databases.

An external representation is used for the user interface. The external representation consists of the NSUID (or a nickname which is translated into the NSUID) plus a list of simple names that together uniquely identify the object. Each name (representing a directory, child directory, object, or soft name) is concatenated together. For example, the namespace DEC might have a directory representing files,

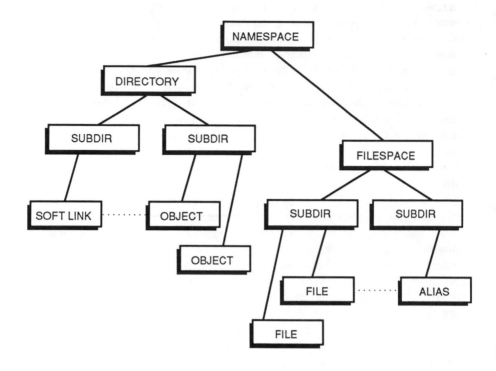

Fig. 3-14   A DNS namespace.

which has subdirectories which has individual files in it. This might
be represented by the syntax:

DEC:FILES.MY_SUBDIRECTORY.FILE1

The complete list of the hierarchy provides a unique name. Note
that there might be multiple instances of **FILE1**, but only one may
exist in the subdirectory **MY_SUBDIRECTORY**. Names in DNS are case
sensitive. If a space or a period is contained in an object name, it
must be delimited by double quotes.

Object attributes

All names in the namespace have a series of attributes. Global attributes are present in all kinds of entities including objects, directories, soft links, and child directories. Each type of entity, such as an

object, also has a series of class-specific attributes. An attribute can be single valued or can consist of a multivalued attribute set.

Global attributes include a unique ID for each object and an update time stamp which signals when this entity was last modified. All objects also include an Access Control Set. The Access Control Set is a multivalued attribute which consists of a set of Authorization Entities.

Objects have a type-specific attribute called object class. Two predefined object classes are the clearinghouse and the group. Clearinghouse objects are lists of collections of nameservers. The nameserver thus uses its database to manage itself.

A second predefined class is the group. The group consists of a list of single objects or other groups of objects. A program operation Test-Group can test one of these objects to detect loops in groups. A loop would occur when a group object has itself as one of its own members.

Directories also have a series of type-specific attributes. The Replicas attribute contains a set of clearinghouse objects. This attribute specifies all clearinghouses that participate in providing a name service for this particular directory. The AllUpTo attribute is a date up to which all updates and modifications to this directory are guaranteed to have been applied.

Replicas and Partitions

The namespace has two important characteristics. It is partitioned, meaning that different directories of a namespace can be stored on different nameservers, and it is partially replicated, meaning that a particular directory may reside in several different locations.

A clearinghouse is a particular set of directories located on a nameserver. A nameserver may actually have several different clearinghouses that it manages. If a clearinghouse is inactive, it is unable to service client requests. Active clearinghouses are available to provide the name service.

Replicas of directories may be located at several different clearinghouses. A replica is an instance of a particular directory at a particular clearinghouse. One of the replicas is considered the master; others are secondary replicas. Both master and secondary replicas can accept updates. The single instance of the master is used to provide certain overhead functions that don't need to be duplicated. Other replicas may be designated as read-only replicas.

It is important to understand that a nameserver does not guarantee the accuracy of the results it provides. This loose consistency guarantee is because updates may be made in several places and must propagate through the namespace. At any one point a query to dif-

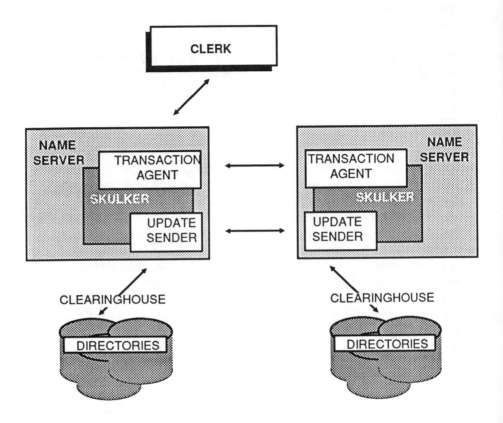

Fig. 3-15   DNS modules.

ferent nameservers may result in different answers. Over time, the
different replicas are guaranteed to converge.

A special process called a skulker is responsible for providing the
convergence among replicas. A skulk runs in the background and can
be configured to run at different time intervals depending on the criti-
cal nature of the particular directory it is updating. A skulk can also
be manually initiated by a client. Figure 3-15 shows the different
modules of a DNS implementation.

The skulk begins by forming a virtual ring. Each replica of the
directory has a pointer to one other replica. Together, all of the

replicas form a ring. If the ring cannot be formed, two different skulks have been initiated at the same time. It is important that all instances of the directory contain the same information so only one skulk can run at a time.

Once the ring has been closed, the skulker on the initiating node goes to every master and secondary replica and gathers all updates that have been made since the last skulk. These are applied to the local clearinghouse, then propagated to the other replicas. Finally, the AllUpTo pointer is updated on every replica as of the time of the beginning of the skulk.

While the skulk works in the background, there are several other processes that form part of the nameserving environment. A clerk runs on every machine on the network. The clerk makes the name service available to client programs, such as the DNA Phase V session layer or a distributed file system. In order to improve performance, a clerk maintains a cache of recently accessed entries.

Each clerk is responsible for knowing about the existence of at least one nameserver. Clerks send solicitations to learn about the existence of a nameserver. Servers also periodically send out service advertisements to signal their availability.

A clerk interacts with a transaction agent. The agent is responsible for accessing clearinghouses on behalf of the clerk and performs entity creations, updates, deletes, and lookups on the local clearinghouse. The transaction agent also coordinates directory operations and communicates with other servers using a special directory maintenance protocol.

When an update is made, the transaction agent notifies an update module. The update module is responsible for notifying the update listeners on other nodes that instances of the relevant directory have been changed. The update listener on each node then performs the updates as needed.

Update modules work in conjunction with the skulker. The update module handles immediate updates while the skulker handles deferred updates and provides a higher degree of consistency checks. Note that the update modules are multithreaded and can handle multiple conversations with other update modules throughout the network.

Update senders make known the presence of a new clearinghouse. A clearinghouse name is an object in a directory that is replicated at every node, so the new clearinghouse is created on one node and the update sender notifies listeners on every other node. Since the presence of this type of high-level namespace information is important, this particular directory has an attribute which indicates that other nodes have a persistent need to know about updates. When a new clearinghouse is added, all other nodes are informed about this new collection of replicas.

Security in the namespace is maintained through a series of Authorization Entries. These entries can apply to individuals or to groups. Groups can consist of other groups.

Each particular entity has flags for read, write, delete, test, or control over that entity. Control is the ability to change the attributes such as access control. Entities can also have propagation control, which determines how to propagate access control to lower layers in the namespace.

Distributed File System

The Distributed File System is an application similar to the DAP protocols discussed earlier. Because DFS is more modern than DAP, it provides a significantly higher degree of performance with an equivalent level of functionality. DFS allows a foreign file to appear to the user as though it were local. Thus, rather than referring to a local file **DISK1:FILENAME**, the user can refer to a file **DFS1:FILENAME.**

DFS differs from the DAP services in that users do not have to know the location of the information they are looking for. In the DAP protocols, users must specify a filename in the syntax

NODENAME::DEVICE_NAME:FILENAME.

DFS allows users to strip off one level of the name, the node, and refer to all files as though they were local. DFS also allows files in multiple locations to appear as though they resided on the one DFS device. DFS, like the NFS services discussed in the TCP/IP chapter, allows the user to treat the network as one transperant file system. If a network administrator moves the files, DNS allows the user to remain unaware of the change in physical location.

DFS has some similarities to VAX Clusters and the distributed file system that is part of that architecture. They both provide transparent access to files. The cluster file system, however, is limited to members of the cluster. This is because the cluster provides a high degree of concurrency to users, including write sharing on files. DFS requires that a write lock on a file be exclusive, but is not limited to members of the cluster.

DFS takes a local system and makes it available to the network. This is done by designating a particular portion of the local file system as an access point. An access point can be a device name, a directory name, or a subdirectory name. The DFS server informs a DNS nameserver of the existence of an access point and maps it to its node name.

Once an access point is defined, it becomes a virtual file system for access on remote nodes. A local node then mounts that access point to make it part of a virtual local file system. Note that this virtual local file system may consist of local files, files available through a cluster environment, files available through DAP protocols, and files available through the DFS service. The Record Management Services is able to determine the type of file referred to and notify the appropriate service provider. In the case of a local file, the service provider is a local class driver which is able to accept QIO requests to read and write data. In the case of the DFS services, the service provider is the DFS entity which also accepts QIO requests.

Servers are able to accept requests for normal file operations, including reading and writing blocks of data. File management operations include the ability to create, open, and close. Directory operations include lookups, creation, and deletion. Finally, file management operations such as allocating blocks to the file or reading or changing the file header are also available.

The DFS is a connection-oriented service, unlike the Network File System. A logical link is maintained at the end of an operation and only deleted after a fairly long time-out period. This reduces the overhead in accessing data by not requiring the creation of a logical link.

A connection-oriented service has the potential disadvantage of causing the file system (RMS) to return errors when the service provider is temporarily unavailable. Rather than immediately returning an error message to the user program, the DFS is able to retry the operation. Up to five retries, each one occurring every 15 seconds, can occur before an error message is sent to the user.

A special feature of the DFS is when a remote file system actually belongs to a cluster. Several nodes of the cluster could potentially provide access to data through the second level of distributed files, the cluster file system. If a mount operation to a member of a cluster fails, the DFS client is able to immediately try another cluster member and remount the file system.

Security in the DFS environment is a function of the security scheme on the server. Users are authenticated through the use of proxy accounts. It is fairly important that the user space consist of a flat namespace. That is, no two users should share the same name. Otherwise, the security system may fail.

DFS is restricted to exclusive locking at the file level and shared read access. If a user attempts to lock a file at a lower level (remember—this is a transparent file, so a program could easily issue this request), the DFS server automatically provides an exclusive lock.

Special-purpose files, such as installed files in VMS or swapping and paging files, are unavailable in a DFS environment.

Distributed Queuing Service

A related utility to DFS is the Distributed Queuing Service. This service makes remote printers available across the network. The printer can be located on an Ethernet, as in the case of the LPS40 or on a host. Additionally the print queue may be on a particular host, but the actual printer may be available via a LAT connection to a terminal server.

DQS is not really a printing utility. Its function is to take a job from one queue and place it in another one. This mechanism could thus work on other queue types such as batch queues. Batch queues are not included in DQS for security and accounting reasons.

DQS examines each queue and looks for jobs and resubmits them on the target queue. Queues can be daisy chained together. The notification facility makes sure that the original submitter of the job is notified of completion or abortion.

A symbiont is a process which accepts information from a queue and moves it over to a printer. Symbiosis is the process of bringing two worlds together and the VMS symbiont brings disk-based data over to the world of printer-based data. DQS operates in a flexible manner because VMS separates the function of queue management from processing the items on a queue.

The link between queues and symbionts is provided by a VMS system level process called JOB_CONTROL. This process takes the top item off a queue and then calls a program to run. For batch queues, the program to run is the job on the top of the queue. For print jobs, the JOB_CONTROL calls the symbiont.

Since any symbiont can be tied to a queue, the DQS service is compatible with the various types of printer drivers, including those written by users. DQS is also used to pass application-specific flags through to the symbiont. A symbiont for an LPS40, for example, might accept a variety of flags from DQS and then use a new DNA logical link to request access to the LPS40 located on the Ethernet.

User-written symbionts may at first glance seem a waste of programming resources. To make the need for this facility more apparent, imagine 6000 students all enrolled in an Introduction to PL/1 class. It is a law of nature that a substantial portion of those students will decide to print out their executable images to see what they look like. What they look like is a lot of pages on the floor. A user-written symbiont could very easily decline to process those types of files. More

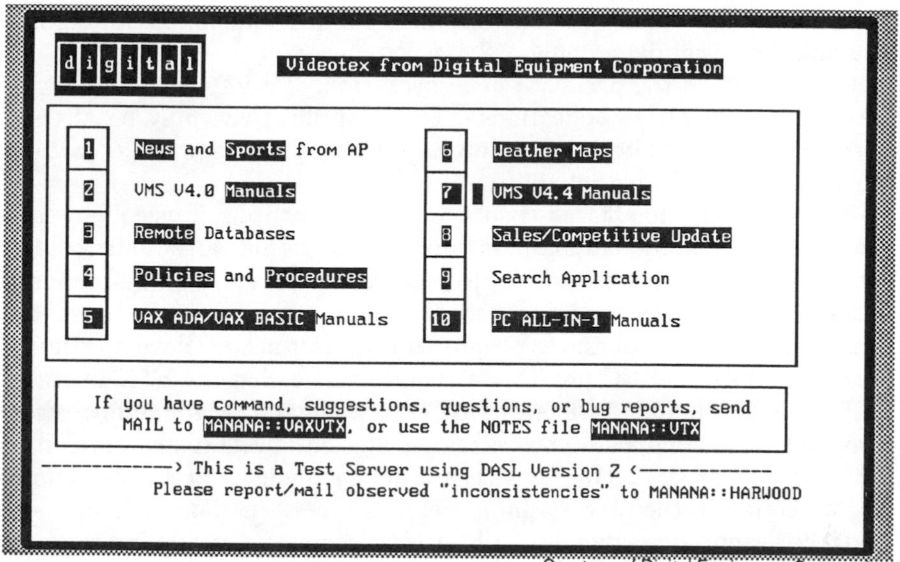

Courtesy of Digital Equipment Corporation

Fig. 3-16 VTX Videotex software.

sophisticated uses are for devices with complicated setups, such as plotters.

Videotex

Videotex is an interactive system which allows a user to download several pages of information to a local terminal (or local node acting as a videotex terminal) and then peruse these pages at his leisure. DEC's VTX product is compatible with the CCITT F.300 standards for videotex systems. Videotex systems provide the user with interactive access to information. That information is distributed transparently in the network and is accessed using a consistent, hierarchical menu structure. Figure 3-16 illustrates the main screen for DEC's VTX software.

A variety of different terminals are supported, including the Prestel terminals and French Minitel series. Also supported are the DEC VT series, the IBM 3270 terminals, and the DECtalk voice output system. A user of a VT-series terminal can use a local node to buffer pages and thus appear as a multipage videotex terminal to the system.

A VTX infobase consists of multiple pages of information that are structured in a hierarchical fashion. DEC uses this system internally for distributing pages of manuals to sales staff. Each of the pages can consist of mixed text and graphics and a request for data can lead to multiple pages of data.

In addition to the database of information, the VTX system can include links to other applications. These applications may be already written and complete in themselves, or they can be written to take advantage of VTX-like capabilities.

A VTX environment has two types of users. End users, or subscribers, access the infobase or applications that are linked to it. These users may access VTX through X.25 networks, from SNA environments, or from anywhere on a DECnet.

Information providers are people who maintain and develop the information bases. DEC provides a special tool called the VTX Infobase Structure Tool and Assister (VISTA) which allows the information provider to develop a storyboard layout and build menu structures.

The VTX server is able to access both an infobase and applications that are tied to the server. Infobases are stored in RMS files and are thus accessed using the RMS file access services. If the information requested is not locally maintained, the VTX server is able to contact other VTX servers to find the information.

Foreign applications are tied into remote applications using an interface library called the External Link Interface (ELK), which is a protocol library for accessing servers over DECnets. This requires the user to manage all context for a user session. ELK is able to accept keywords from a VTX server and deliver them to the application. The application delivers a series of pages, which are delivered to the VTX server, which then forwards them to the user.

The VTX Application Service (VAS) builds on top of ELK to provide additional functionality. VAS is able to collect user responses, make flow control decisions, and display pages for users. VAS is built on a request-response protocol and is able to accept remote connections from applications over DNA, SNA, and X.25. Because VAS uses multiple simultaneous contexts, it is used for applications with multiple request and response users.

ELK-based programs are often used to provide information to the update servers, which in turn add the information the infobase. If the ELK application is located on a remote node, it needs to use a remote update server link module. This allows the VTX update modules to be extended over the DECnet facilities.

The terminal-specific modules are used to provide concentrator support for X.29 virtual devices and for 3270 class terminals.

Summary

The DNA Phase IV services discussed in this chapter provide a full-featured set of network capabilities. They make the network look like a simple extension of the individual node. Remote files appear local, either through DAP protocols or with the distributed file service. Remote nodes can be logged into using the CTERM protocols.

DNA Phase IV began in 1980 and at the time was widely considered to be the most modern commercial network software available. Despite its functionality, DNA Phase IV has several limitations that have led to other architectures. The Local Area Transport Architecture, for example, deals with the potential inefficiencies of CTERM in handling large amounts of nodes in the Ethernet environment.

Another architecture, the System Communication Architecture, supplements DNA by allowing highly concurrent, highly efficient access to data in a VAX Cluster. While DFS and DAP function well in a full DECnet, their generality leads to some decrease in potential performance. SCA, by contrast, is able to work very efficiently, but only with a limited number of nodes.

The next chapters of this book consider these alternative DEC-developed architectures in detail. After the architectures are presented, Part 3 describes how these various architectures are implemented into actual networks. Local area networks are first considered, followed by wide area networks. Then, the question of implementing DNA on particular operating systems and managing the network is considered.

For Further Reading

Benson et al., "VTX and VALU—Software Productivity Tools for Distributed Applications Development," *Digital Technical Journal*, February 1988, vol. 1, no. 6, p. 80.

Digital Equipment Corporation, "DNA Data Access Protocol Functional Specification," version 5.6.0, AA-K177A-TK

——, "DECnet-DNA NSP Functional Specification," version 4.0, AA-X439A-TK.

4

Direct Ethernet Clients:
LAT and MOP

Overview of LAT and MOP Protocols

The DNA protocol stack provides a general layered network service that is able to adapt to a variety of different network topologies. In a local area network environment, however, the DNA protocol stack can introduce needless overhead. This is particularly true in the case of the CTERM protocols, which require each character to be sent in a separate packet. While this is efficient for wide area networking scenarios, it does not function well in a LAN environment.

The Local Area Transport architecture is meant to address a very specific problem of terminals communicating to hosts over an Ethernet. Because of its limited scope, the LAT architecture is able to bypass the session, transport, and routing layers and make direct use of the Ethernet. The LAT architecture multiplexes user data headed for the same destination into a single packet. The LAT architecture also off-loads much of the terminal services management function from the host, freeing up CPU cycles for other types of computation.

Another direct Ethernet client is the Maintenance Operations Protocol (MOP). One purpose of these protocols is to downline load operating systems into a remote device that does not have any mass storage facilities. Since DNA is a fairly complicated set of software modules, it is unreasonable to expect that the diskless node has the capability to make DNA requests. Instead, the MOP protocols are used, which consist of a very simple set of services that can be built into the read-only memory of a device. As will be seen, although MOP is technically part of the DNA architecture, it operates in a different fashion from DNA services examined previously.

MOP is used for a large number of different devices by DEC. Diskless VAXs are one example of a device that uses MOP. General-purpose servers, such as terminal or communications servers, also use the MOP protocols. In all three cases, the operating system for the device is kept on a Phase IV host on the Ethernet. When the diskless device is initialized, the first thing it does is broadcast a request for an operating system on the Ethernet. A Phase IV host then responds by downline loading the operating system to the device. Once the device is initialized, it uses another architecture such as LAT or DNA to perform further network functions.

Local Area Transport Architecture

Terminal servers are important in a VAX Cluster because one of the goals is to allow a user on a given terminal to access any one of several hosts. DEC originally wanted to put terminal servers directly onto a CI bus cluster. CI bus hardware was expensive enough to make DEC look for an Ethernet-based solution. The search for a cheaper link was also the impetus for the Ethernet-based Local Area VAX Clusters (LAVC).

The DECnet CTERM protocols would provide one possible solution for terminal access. Terminal servers would just be dedicated DECnet nodes, much like the Ethernet-based DECnet Router. CTERM could rapidly saturate an Ethernet because every character is sent in a separate packet. Because an Ethernet packet must have at least 46 bytes of data and because echoing means that each character typed uses two packets, CTERM is not an efficient solution.

The other solution is to use a system that is similar to the public X.25 networks. Rather than send each character off in a packet, multiple characters (possibly from multiple users) are saved and sent off together. In X.25, this is the function of the X.3 Packet Assembler/Disassembler (PAD). For terminals on an Ethernet, DEC LAT protocols perform a similar multiplexing function.

Local Area Transport protocols

There are two layers to the LAT architecture. A virtual circuit layer provides a link to all hosts that the terminal server is communicating to. Establishment of a virtual circuit takes only one message ex-

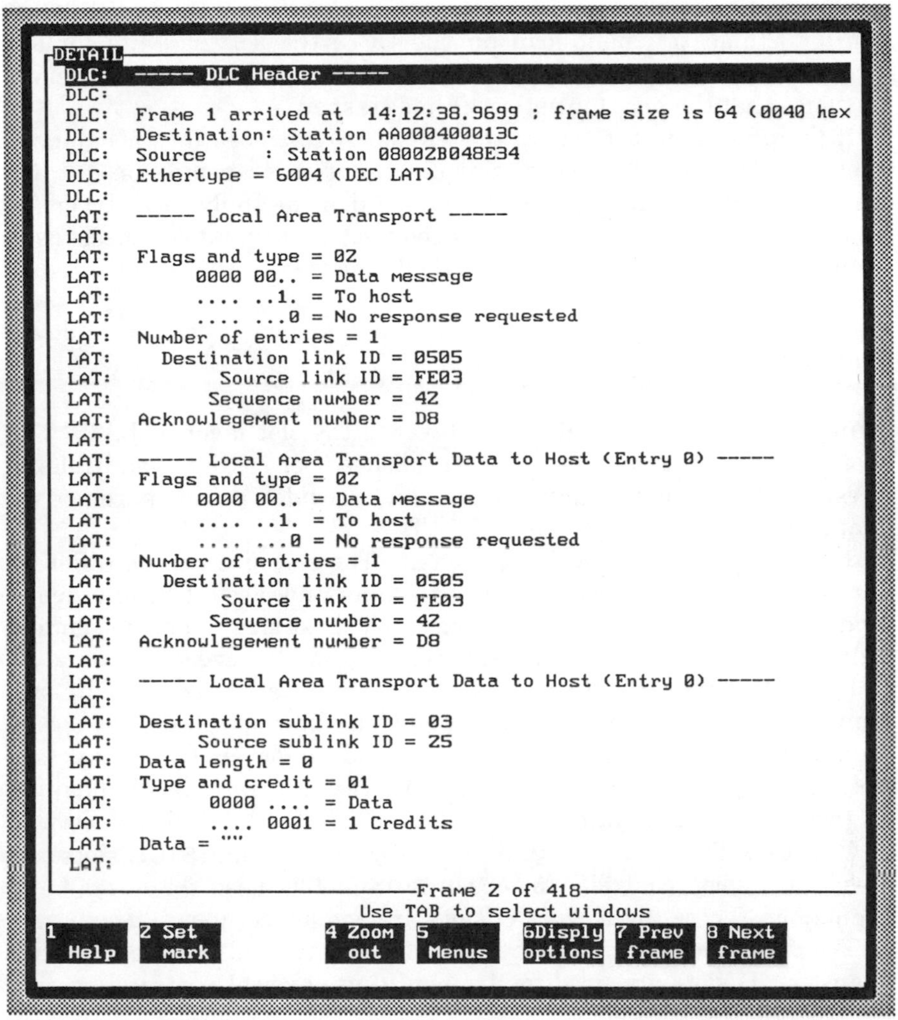

```
┌─DETAIL─────────────────────────────────────────────────────────────────
│ DLC: ───── DLC Header ─────
│ DLC:
│ DLC: Frame 1 arrived at  14:12:38.9699 ; frame size is 64 (0040 hex
│ DLC: Destination: Station AA000400013C
│ DLC: Source     : Station 08002B048E34
│ DLC: Ethertype = 6004 (DEC LAT)
│ DLC:
│ LAT: ───── Local Area Transport ─────
│ LAT:
│ LAT: Flags and type = 02
│ LAT:      0000 00.. = Data message
│ LAT:      .... ..1. = To host
│ LAT:      .... ...0 = No response requested
│ LAT: Number of entries = 1
│ LAT:    Destination link ID = 0505
│ LAT:         Source link ID = FE03
│ LAT:         Sequence number = 42
│ LAT: Acknowlegement number = D8
│ LAT:
│ LAT: ───── Local Area Transport Data to Host (Entry 0) ─────
│ LAT: Flags and type = 02
│ LAT:      0000 00.. = Data message
│ LAT:      .... ..1. = To host
│ LAT:      .... ...0 = No response requested
│ LAT: Number of entries = 1
│ LAT:    Destination link ID = 0505
│ LAT:         Source link ID = FE03
│ LAT:         Sequence number = 42
│ LAT: Acknowlegement number = D8
│ LAT:
│ LAT: ───── Local Area Transport Data to Host (Entry 0) ─────
│ LAT:
│ LAT: Destination sublink ID = 03
│ LAT:       Source sublink ID = 25
│ LAT: Data length = 0
│ LAT: Type and credit = 01
│ LAT:      0000 .... = Data
│ LAT:      .... 0001 = 1 Credits
│ LAT: Data = ""
│ LAT:
│─────────────────────────Frame 2 of 418─────────────────────────
│                    Use TAB to select windows
│ 1        2 Set            4 Zoom  5         6Disply 7 Prev  8 Next
│  Help     mark             out     Menus    options  frame   frame
```

Courtesy of Network General

Fig. 4-1 LAT data packet.

change. The virtual circuit layer provides a data transport service for the slot layer. By default, every 80 milliseconds (ms) the virtual circuit layer sends off a packet. This parameter can be adjusted by the network manager to be 30 milliseconds or greater. Studies have shown that a good touch typist begins to have problems if the echo delay is greater than 100 ms. Figure 4-1 shows LAT data on an Ethernet.

If a virtual circuit packet is not acknowledged within the circuit timer parameter, (usually 80 ms), the server assumes that there is a problem. Rather than compound an existing network saturation problem or a high transient load on the CPU, the server waits for approximately 1 second. After a user-set number of retries, the server assumes that the host (or network) has crashed.

If there is no data to send, the virtual circuit goes into a balanced mode. This means that either side can reinitiate transmission if it has data to send. In the normal unbalanced mode, only the server initiates the data exchange. In balanced mode, a KEEPALIVE message is sent every 20 seconds. Otherwise, no data is sent.

Slot layer

Built on top of the virtual circuit layer is the slot layer of LAT. The slot layer has three functions. It establishes user sessions, multiplexes sessions over a virtual circuit layer, and provides a transparent data transfer access service to users of LAT.

The maximum slot size is 255 bytes. The slot size can be different for each side of a connection. The terminal side would have a typist and would only need a small slot size. The host side might be sending full screens of data and could thus use a larger slot size.

Between the terminal server and the host, LAT uses a credit system. Each side of a session is independent, allowing full duplex operation at the slot layer even though the underlying virtual circuit is a request-response system. Each side in a session can typically have up to two credits outstanding.

LAT uses five different kinds of slots. START and STOP slots are used for session control. An ATTENTION slot is used for out-of-band signalling. These three types of slots are not subject to credit limits.

The other two slot types are A and B slots. A slots are used for data transfer. B slots are used for transmitting physical port and session characteristics.

A single packet at the virtual circuit layer can contain several slots. By combining several characters per user in a slot and several users in a virtual circuit packet, the LAT architecture multiplexes data between the terminal server and a particular host.

Service advertisements

In addition to virtual circuit and session-related messages, LAT also has a third kind of message called a service advertisement. Every host willing to accept terminal sessions is a service provider. All service providers multicast the availability of their service and a current

```
DETAIL
DLC: ----- DLC Header -----
DLC:
DLC: Frame 10 arrived at  08:00:17.5723 ; frame size is 153 (0099 h
DLC: Destination: Functional address 09002B00000F
DLC: Source     : Station 08002B001391
DLC: Ethertype = 6004 (DEC LAT)
DLC:
LAT: ----- Local Area Transport -----
LAT:
LAT: Flags and type = 28
LAT:      0010 10.. = Service message
LAT:      .... ..0. = From host
LAT:      .... ...0 = No response requested
LAT: Server circuit timer = 8 ms
LAT: Highest supported protocol version = 5
LAT: Lowest supported protocol version = 5
LAT:          Current protocol version = 5
LAT:              Current protocol ECO = 0
LAT: Message ID = 135
LAT: Change flags = 00
LAT:      .... ...0 = No node groups have changed
LAT:      .... ..0. = Node descriptor hasn't changed
LAT:      .... .0.. = No service names have changed
LAT:      .... 0... = No service ratings have changed
LAT:      ...0 .... = No service descriptors have changed
LAT:      ..0. .... = No service classes have changed
LAT:      .0.. .... = Unused
LAT:      0... .... = No other parameters have changed
LAT: Receive frame size = 1518 bytes
LAT: Multicast timer = 30 seconds
LAT: Host status = 00
LAT:      0000 000. = Unused
LAT:      .... ...0 = Host is accepting new sessions
LAT: Node groups:
LAT:
LAT:    Node group length = 32 bytes
LAT:    Group byte 0, Groups enabled: 0
LAT: Node name = "SRIKL"
LAT: Node description = "KL.SRI.COM, TOPS-20 Monitor 6.1(16230)"
LAT: Service descriptors:
LAT: Multicast timer = 30 seconds
LAT: Host status = 00
LAT:      0000 000. = Unused
LAT:      .... ...0 = Host is accepting new sessions
LAT: Node groups:
LAT:
LAT:    Node group length = 32 bytes
LAT:    Group byte 0, Groups enabled: 0
LAT: Node name = "SRIKL"
LAT: Node description = "KL.SRI.COM, TOPS-20 Monitor 6.1(16230)"
LAT: Service descriptors:
LAT:    Number of service descriptors = 1
LAT: Service descriptor 0:
LAT:    Rating = 1
LAT:    Service name = "SRIKL"
LAT:    Service description = "KL.SRI.COM, TOPS-20 Monitor 6.1(16230
LAT: Service classes:
LAT:    Number of service classes = 1
LAT:    Service 0 = 1 (Remote terminal service)
LAT:
-------------------------Frame 10 of 111-------------------------
               Use TAB to select windows
1       2 Set          4 Zoom  5        6Disply 7 Prev  8 Next
Help    mark           out     Menus    options frame   frame
```

Fig. 4-2 A LAT service advertisement.

service rating every 60 seconds. Figure 4-2 illustrates a LAT service advertisement.

A node might provide multiple types of services. Thus a machine could be a member of a cluster and thus offer a CLUSTER service. That node might also have some special-purpose graphics software not available on the rest of the cluster and could broadcast the availability of a GRAPHIC service.

When a user makes a service request and there are multiple providers of that service, the terminal server logs the user on to the node with the best service rating. On a VMS system, the LTDRIVER process uses four factors to calculate a service rating, including the most recent CPU idle time, the CPU type, the amount of memory, and the number of interactive slots left.

Service ratings provide a fairly sophisticated form of load balancing. The system manager is also allowed to set a static service rating for a node. This can be used to allow a "hot" backup service. Normally, users are logged onto a production system which has a high service rating. A backup node is given a lower service rating. If the production system crashes, the backup node becomes the offerer of the service.

Service providers can be assigned a LAT group code. This can be used to partition an Ethernet into several different environments. Users would only see the services that pertain to their group.

Reverse LAT

A reverse LAT capability allows a terminal server to provide services instead of just using them. This is typical in three situations:

- Connection of modems
- Connection of non-LAT hosts
- Connection of printers

Modems on a terminal server can be dial-in or dial-out. Dial-in modems are just an extension of the terminal. Dial-out modems, however, are used by the host as a peripheral device. Often, a set of modems need to be offered in a rotary. The rotary allows the host to refer to modems as a generic service and the service provider, in this case the terminal service, to log the user onto the first available modem.

Often, there is a need to connect a user of the DECnet to a foreign host. One solution to this connectivity problem is to have both hosts on DECnet, TCP/IP, or some other network architecture in common with both systems. If there is no common networking solution, however, a possible solution is to use a reverse LAT capability with the foreign host.

Most systems provide support for asynchronous terminals. The reverse LAT solution entails connecting an RS-232 cable from the asynchronous ports on the host to ports on the terminal server. Users wishing to connect to the foreign host then request a service, which connects them to the appropriate port of the terminal server, which in turn passes the user through to the foreign host as though they were a directly attached terminal.

Asynchronous printers are a third use of the reverse LAT function. Print queues are logically connected from the host to the terminal server port with the printer. Multiple systems can share one printer, although only one host can have a virtual connection active with a particular printer at one time. It is also possible to define a printer service which consists of several printers configured in a rotary.

Host transparency

To the host, the incoming session from a terminal server consists of a virtual terminal port. The terminal class driver deals with this virtual port just like it would a locally connected terminal. Each session gets a unique slot number and all data for that session is identified by that slot number.

LAT, CTERM, and other network-based virtual terminal protocols allow a host to treat all incoming sessions the same way. This is important because it means that individual pieces of software do not have to first determine if the session is remote or local. DEC accomplishes this on a VMS system by using a two-level device driver. When software sends data, it sends it to a terminal class driver. The class driver is used for all terminal applications. Figure 4-3 illustrates the two level device driver.

The terminal class driver, in turn, hands off the data to a particular device driver based on the type of connection. For a LAT server, the host sends the data down to a LAT driver. If the session is a CTERM process, it sends the data to the CTERM driver, which in turn hands it down to the lower layers of the network stack. If the terminal is locally connected, the terminal class driver hands the data down to a physical device driver.

The LAT architecture is able to off-load a significant portion of host overhead for terminal services management. There are two kinds of directly connected devices, those that use direct memory access (DMA) and those that use a character interrupt scheme. Under heavy loads,

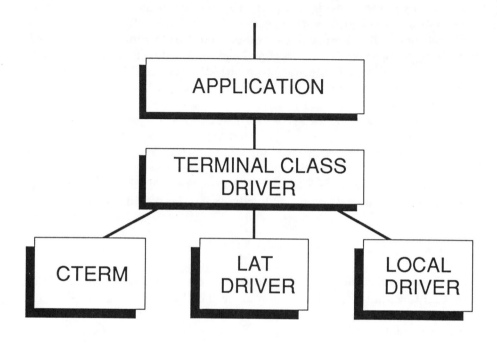

Fig. 4-3 Two-level terminal driver.

LAT provides better performance than either type of asynchronous communications controller.

Under very light loads, a non-DMA character interrupt system provides better performance. A DMA controller on the system requires polling and is thus inefficient with a very sporadic load. With a bigger load, the DMA controller becomes more efficient because the increased number of interrupts helps justify the polling overhead. With a large number of users, the LAT architecture is significantly more efficient than either DMA or character interrupt devices.

Although LAT servers are best when there are multiple sessions over one virtual session, its use is also frequently justified in single-node implementations. This is frequently the case when a PC with an Ethernet controller uses the LAT protocols instead of DECnet to provide access to a host. Services such as load balancing are provided and LAT can provide block transfer of data coming back from the host, in contrast to the asynchronous nature of the CTERM protocols.

LAT drivers exist for VMS, RSX, Ultrix, and even the Tops 20 operating systems. LAT terminal servers are available from DEC and a few third-party providers such as Emulex. LAT implementations for PCs are available from DEC, Polygon, and other companies. PC LAT implementations are a supplement to DECnet/DOS in that they allow the user to choose among multiple service types.

Maintenance Operations Protocol

The Maintenance Operations Protocol (MOP) is technically part of the Digital Network Architecture. However, most maintenance functions cannot assume the presence of the other portions of the network, such as a routing layer or session control module. MOP thus works directly with the data link layers and bypasses the rest of the networking protocol stack. In this sense, MOP cannot be considered to have the same status within DNA that the other layers do.

MOP is used in conjunction with other protocols on the network. MOP might be used for downline loading an operating system. After that, the network management protocols (NICE) are used to exchange management data, and the DNA protocols are used for exchanging higher-level information (See Figure 4-4).

There are three major functions provided by the MOP protocols. A communications test function is used to see if a data link layer is operative. A system console function is used to provide console tasks, such as a remote operator function. Finally, a load-dump function is used to transfer directly to and from remote processor memory.

MOP is a high-performance, low-overhead client of the data link layer. It assumes minimal processing power on remote systems. In many cases, the MOP client is a diskless CPU that is using MOP to boot itself over the network. MOP is able to work with both DDCMP and Ethernet data links. The CI bus can also be used as a data link layer.

MOP operates in a client/server mode. Requesters are the clients in the relationship and they control the MOP operation. Servers may be known, or in the case of the Ethernet, a general appeal for help may be broadcast. A server will then volunteer to service the request.

The data link layer is assumed to provide two types of services: framing and error checking. In the case of Ethernet, there is only minimal error checking. Both DDCMP and the CI bus provide packet acknowledgment. Since Ethernet is relatively error free, there is really no need for the type of checking done in a DDCMP environment.

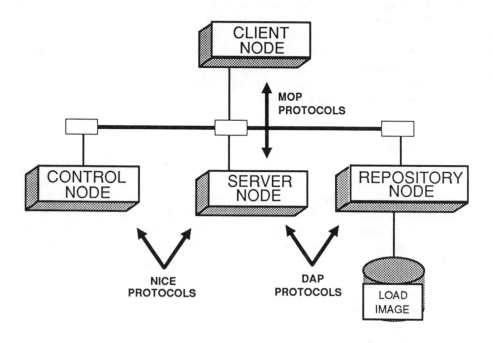

Fig. 4-4   MOP and other DNA protocols.

Remote booting

The typical use of MOP is for booting a diskless node. This can be a router, a MicroVAX, an SNA gateway, or any of a variety of different servers on an Ethernet. This can also include a VAX connected to an HSC controller on a CI bus. Remote boot operations can also be used on a dedicated DDCMP line.

Since the device requesting the remote boot may have no disk drives, the MOP protocols are built into read-only memory (ROM). The node transmits a request load service message. In the case of the Ethernet, this requires another node to volunteer assistance. The requesting node not only requests the service but specifies the type of file that it is requesting. The server then checks to see that this is a valid load request before volunteering assistance.

The load operation typically occurs in several stages. The primary loader in ROM is able to request that a secondary loader be put into memory starting at a certain memory address. Usually, the secondary loader is able to request that a tertiary loader is put into memory at another address. Finally, the tertiary loader requests that the operating system itself is loaded.

Remote console function

The remote console function is used to control nodes on a network. Typically, low-level operations must be done only on the console of a system. Thus, requesting that a frozen system reboot itself is usually accomplished by executing a special key sequence that gives the user access to low-level functions on the CPU, bypassing the operating system. The remote console function allows these operations to be performed remotely. The remote console function allows a single operator to manage multiple remote devices, such as MicroVAXs or terminal services. Figure 4-5 illustrates the remote console function.

The user (i.e., the Network Control Program) first requests that it become the console for a remote system. There can only be one console active on a system at one time. All requests to reserve the console to a remote system or for remote boots are subject to a 4-byte verification check by the target system before they are honored.

In addition to forcing a remote boot, the console function can be used to perform two other functions. The system ID and type can be requested. This includes the type of communications device, such as an Ethernet controller. It also includes the type of processor, such as a communications server.

Finally, the console can be used to read a variety of low level counters. For example, the console can request the number of send failures and the failure reasons from an Ethernet controller. Failure reasons might include a frame that was too long, excessive collisions, or block check errors.

Summary

The Local Area Transport mechanism provides an efficient method to connect terminals to an Ethernet via a terminal server. The CTERM protocols provide another capability to perform the same function. In addition, there are several other alternatives for connecting terminals to hosts that will be examined.

Two of the other alternatives are to use X.25 or TCP/IP to connect terminals to hosts. Since a terminal cannot be connected to a network, in both cases a terminal server is used to connect to the net-

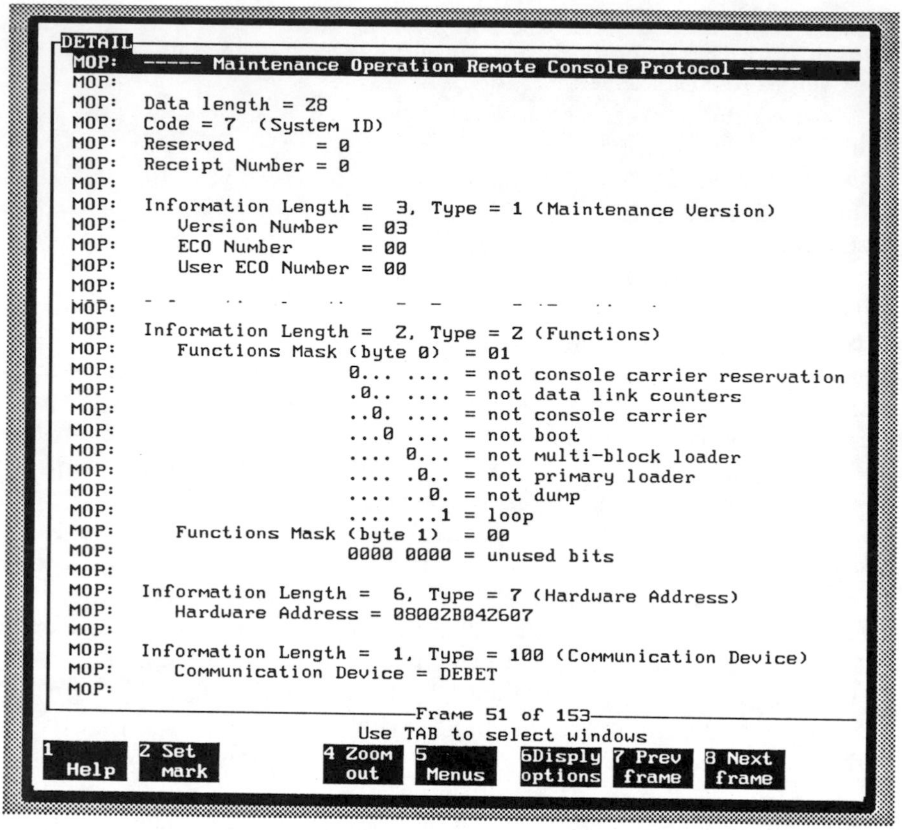

```
┌─DETAIL──────────────────────────────────────────────────────────┐
│ MOP:   ───── Maintenance Operation Remote Console Protocol ───── │
│ MOP:                                                             │
│ MOP:   Data length = 28                                         │
│ MOP:   Code = 7  (System ID)                                    │
│ MOP:   Reserved      = 0                                        │
│ MOP:   Receipt Number = 0                                       │
│ MOP:                                                             │
│ MOP:   Information Length =  3, Type = 1 (Maintenance Version)  │
│ MOP:       Version Number  = 03                                 │
│ MOP:       ECO Number      = 00                                 │
│ MOP:       User ECO Number = 00                                 │
│ MOP:                                                             │
│ MOP:   -  -    ..    . .     _   _      _ .─   .. .              │
│ MOP:   Information Length =  2, Type = 2 (Functions)            │
│ MOP:       Functions Mask (byte 0)  = 01                        │
│ MOP:                       0... .... = not console carrier reservation │
│ MOP:                       .0.. .... = not data link counters  │
│ MOP:                       ..0. .... = not console carrier      │
│ MOP:                       ...0 .... = not boot                 │
│ MOP:                       .... 0... = not multi-block loader   │
│ MOP:                       .... .0.. = not primary loader       │
│ MOP:                       .... ..0. = not dump                 │
│ MOP:                       .... ...1 = loop                     │
│ MOP:       Functions Mask (byte 1)  = 00                        │
│ MOP:                       0000 0000 = unused bits              │
│ MOP:                                                             │
│ MOP:   Information Length =  6, Type = 7 (Hardware Address)     │
│ MOP:       Hardware Address = 0800ZB04Z607                      │
│ MOP:                                                             │
│ MOP:   Information Length =  1, Type = 100 (Communication Device) │
│ MOP:       Communication Device = DEBET                         │
│ MOP:                                                             │
│ ───────────────────────────Frame 51 of 153──────────────────── │
│                        Use TAB to select windows                │
│ ┌─┐   ┌─────┐    ┌─────┐┌─┐     ┌──────┐┌──────┐┌──────┐        │
│ │1│   │2 Set│    │4 Zoom│5│     │6Disply││7 Prev││8 Next│        │
│ │Help│ │ mark│   │ out ││Menus││options││frame ││frame │        │
│ └─┘   └─────┘    └─────┘└─┘     └──────┘└──────┘└──────┘        │
└─────────────────────────────────────────────────────────────────┘
```

Courtesy of Network General

Fig. 4-5   A MOP packet on Ethernet.

work. In the case of TCP/IP, the terminal server functions much like any other computer using the TCP/IP protocols.

For X.25, a special set of LAT-like protocols are used with an X.3 Packet Assembler/Disassembler (PAD). The PAD buffers characters typed in and then sends off the packet when it is full, a time-out counter expires, or certain special characters are encountered. A special character might be a carriage return or function key.

LAT differs from other packet-oriented transport services in several respects. It uses a request-response connection management rather than the usual symmetric connection. Message exchange is timer based rather than event driven. Finally, service availability can be multicast.

In addition to network-oriented methods of connecting terminals, it is important to consider other alternatives such as the use of a PBX. In this scenario, the network is not used to connect terminals. Instead, the network is used for machine-to-machine communications. The PBX provides a separate front-end network for connecting the user device to a particular host.

A third alternative is to move from terminals which cannot be part of a network to intelligent user workstations. A PC with DECnet/DOS is an example of such an approach. Another approach is to use the X Windows System protocol discussed in the last part of this book as a way of connecting bit-mapped graphics workstations to various compute servers on the network.

The MOP protocols, like LAT, are also direct users of the Ethernet. A terminal server from DEC will use both sets of protocols. MOP is used to initialize the device and downline load the terminal server software. Included in the software that is downline loaded are the software modules that process the LAT protocols.

For Further Reading

Digital Equipment Corporation, "DECnet Phase IV Maintenance Operations Functional Specification," AA-X436A-TK, December 1983.

Mann et al., "Terminal Servers on Ethernet Local Area Networks," *Digital Technical Journal*, vol. 1, no. 3, September 1986, p. 73.

5

Clusters

Overview of Clusters

Clusters are a cross between a parallel processor and a network. Like a single system, a cluster shares a common file system and has high-speed communication between processors. Like the network, there are multiple instances of the operating system and a system of inter-process communication instead of the shared memory of the parallel processor. Figure 5-1 shows the characteristics that clusters have in common with networks and parallel processors.

There are two kinds of clusters. A CI Cluster uses a very high-speed network at the physical and data link layers. This CI bus operates at 70 mbps, in contrast to the 10 mbps of the Ethernet. A Local Area VAX Cluster (LAVC) uses the Ethernet as the data link layer. Both types of clusters use the System Communication Architecture and have the same functionality.

Nodes in a cluster consist of either a VAX or an HSC controller. The HSC controller is a special purpose computer that has up to 32 disk drives connected to it. An LAVC has only VAX systems, while the CI bus can have a combination of VAXs and HSC controllers.

There are three primary benefits to a cluster. First, there is high availability. Disk drives can be volume shadowed and dual ported in case of either disk or controller failure. Multiple VAX systems can access file systems providing a degree of fault tolerance in case of processor failure.

The second benefit is modularity. Disk drives, controllers, and processors can be independently upgraded. A cluster can have the

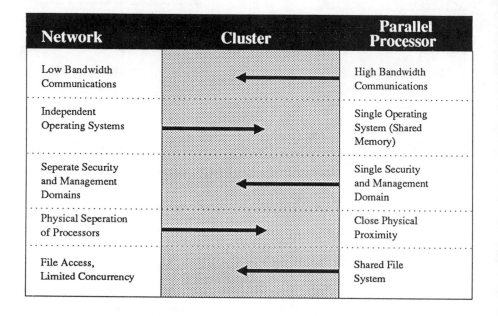

Network	Cluster	Parallel Processor
Low Bandwidth Communications		High Bandwidth Communications
Independent Operating Systems		Single Operating System (Shared Memory)
Seperate Security and Management Domains		Single Security and Management Domain
Physical Seperation of Processors		Close Physical Proximity
File Access, Limited Concurrency		Shared File System

Figure 5-1   Networks, clusters, and parallel processors.

processing power of one VAX 11/780 or can be as powerful as hundreds of 11/780s using a cluster of 8840s. The LAT architecture for terminal servers makes this look like one big computer through the mechanism of service providers. Each member of the VAX Cluster provides the same service, and the terminal server logs the next user onto the service provider with the highest service rating.

Finally, clusters provide a very high-performance method of data sharing. The file system is transparent to users. In the case of the CI bus clusters, throughput for data access can be as high as two Mbps. Even with the Ethernet-based LAVC, file access is 10 times faster than the older Decnet DAP protocols. This high-performance file system is coupled with a relatively efficient distributed lock manager to provide full concurrency in the distributed file system.

Although an LAVC-based file system is faster than a DECnet, it is still not as fast as a local file system. Usually, an LAVC would be used for applications that are fairly compute intensive. A CAD/CAM system, for example, would fetch a diagram and then an engineer would work for a long period of time on that diagram. An LAVC would allow the engineer to use a diskless workstation. The worksta-

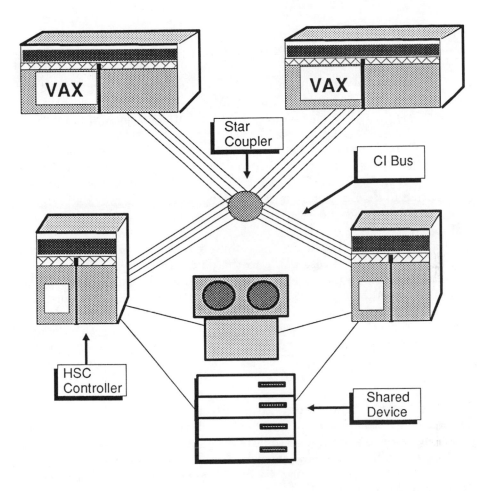

Fig. 5-2 CI bus hardware components.

tion is obviously cheaper because of the lack of a disk, but it also avoids many system management problems associated with distributed backup over a network.

CI bus hardware

The CI Bus is a 70 mbps bus which connects nodes of a cluster using a star configuration. The star coupler is a passive device which can accommodate up to 24 nodes. A node is any device that has a CI controller, which means a VAX with a BI bus or Unibus, or a Hierarchical Storage Controller (HSC). Figure 5-2 illustrates the component of a CI bus Cluster.

Connecting individual nodes to the star coupler are four pieces of coax cable, up to 45 meters (m) in length. The four cables provide separate send and receive paths, with dual paths for each function.

The HSC is a PDP-11-based system that functions as a Digital Storage Architecture-compatible disk controller. Because it is also a stand-alone computer, the HSC can service requests from multiple VAX systems. The HSC70 can have up to 32 tape and disk drives connected to it. Burst speeds of 3.25 Mbps can be accommodated from any one drive and the HSC has an internal data bandwidth of 13.3 Mbps.

Individual disk drives can be connected to two HSC controllers. This provides dual access paths to the data. In many configurations, disk drives use volume shadowing so that every change to one copy of the data is automatically reflected on a mirrored volume on another disk pack. Dual ports and volume shadowing together provide a degree of fault tolerance against either HSC or disk failure. Dual copies of the data also increase retrieval speed. Since volume shadowing takes place on the HSC controller, it requires little intervention from a host CPU. Figures 5-3 and 5-4 show an HSC controller and a star coupler.

User access to the cluster is usually through some form of data switch that attempts to balance the load among multiple CPUs all offering the same service. This could be a simple data switch with a rotary capability. The switch picks the next available line and connects the user to it. Because the lines are interleaved, this provides a form of load balancing.

The LAT protocols used by terminal servers provide a more sophisticated way of performing load balancing. All members of the cluster periodically broadcast the availability of a service type along with a service rating. The service rating is a function of idle CPU time and the number of available log-in slots. The terminal server evaluates each connect request by a user and connects it to the service provider with the best service rating at that time.

Because the cluster forms a common system from the users point of view, it also makes sense to create the same unified system from the point of view of the system manager. Clusters allow a common security and management domain, as well as a common monitoring interface. Figure 5-5 illustrates the use of the VMS monitor utility on multiple cluster nodes.

Courtesy of Digital Equipment Corporation

Fig. 5-3   HSC 70 and 50 storage controllers.

System Communication Architecture

The System Communication Architecture is a different networking architecture from the Digital Network Architectures.   In most cases,
both DNA and SCA will be used together.   Often, the Local Area
Transport Architecture (LAT) will also be used.   It is possible to have
all three networks share the same Ethernet.

The SCA has two main layers.   The System Communication Services (SCS) provide a software layer for internode communication.
SCS can be though of as providing a transport layer akin to the NSP
protocols in the DNA architecture.

System Communication Services provides for three types of services.
A datagram is an unacknowledged packet up to 576 bytes long.   This
is used by upper-layer services that provide their own guarantees of
delivery.   Most disk read and write operations are transmitted in the
form of datagrams.

Messages are up to 112 bytes long and are always acknowledged.
Messages are used, among other things, for SCS control information.

Courtesy of Digital Equipment Corporation

Fig. 5-4   A star coupler.

Acknowledgment is immediate as the CI port retains control of the bus long enough to send the reply back.

Block data transfer is used for transfer of information greater than 4000 bytes. This is a guaranteed delivery of information from the memory of one node to the memory of another. For long transfers, this method can achieve throughput of 2 Mbps on the CI bus. The CI port has direct memory access and thus requires very few CPU interrupts for fairly extensive data transfer operations.

Below the SCS is a data link layer, consisting either of a CI bus or an Ethernet. A routing layer is not present because all nodes are always one hop away from each other. The physical media depend on the data link protocol used. For the CI bus, only a coax cable is supported. For an LAVC, Ethernet supports five types of media including broadband, baseband, ThinWire, twisted pair, and optical fiber.

Above the SCS layer are a variety of service providers. These service providers are programs on each node of the cluster that communicate with each other over virtual circuits provided by the SCS. An example of a service provider is the connection manager, which detects

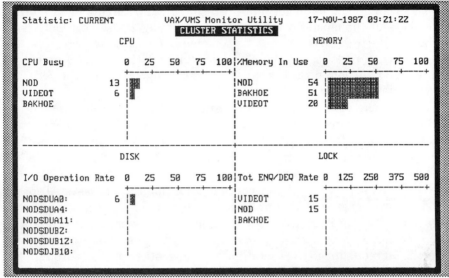

```
Statistic: CURRENT          VAX/VMS Monitor Utility    17-NOV-1987 09:21:22
                              CLUSTER STATISTICS
                    CPU                    |             MEMORY

 CPU Busy          0   25   50   75  100|%Memory In Use  0   25   50   75  100
                   +----+----+----+----+ |               +----+----+----+----+
 NOD          13 |▓                      |NOD        54 |▓▓▓▓▓▓▓▓▓▓
 VIDEOT        6 |▓                      |BAKHOE     51 |▓▓▓▓▓▓▓▓▓
 BAKHOE          |                       |VIDEOT     20 |▓▓▓▓
                 |                       |              |
                 |                       |              |
                 |                       |              |
 ----------------|-----------------------|--------------|----------------------
                    DISK                  |             LOCK

 I/O Operation Rate  0  25  50  75  100|Tot ENQ/DEQ Rate 0  125  250  375  500
                     +----+----+----+----+ |              +----+----+----+----+
 NOD$DUA0:        6 |▓                      |VIDEOT     15 |
 NOD$DUA4:          |                       |NOD        15 |
 NOD$DUA11:         |                       |BAKHOE        |
 NOD$DUB2:          |                       |              |
 NOD$DUB12:         |                       |              |
 NOD$DJB10:         |                       |              |
```

Courtesy of Digital Equipment Corporation

Fig. 5-5   Monitoring multiple cluster nodes.

state transitions in the cluster configuration. Another service provider
is a distributed file system that allows multiple nodes to all request
I/O services from multiple HSC controllers.

Every node in a cluster has a special service provider known as the
SCS$DIRECTORY. This application keeps a list of all services offered
within the cluster. Thus, a file system wishing to know the cluster
address of all disk servers (**MSCP$DISK**) would consult the **SCS$DIREC-
TORY** for that information.

Connection Management

Each member of a cluster has a service provider called the connection
manager. Together the connection managers ensure that the cluster
does not become partitioned. A partitioned cluster means one device
participates in two different clusters. An HSC controller might be
part of two different systems. Since the lock manager on each cluster
is in charge of synchronizing all access to data, two different lock
managers mean that there is a very real possibility of data corruption.

The connection manager maintains a virtual circuit to all other members of the cluster. The connection manager also regularly polls other nodes to keep a current list of members. A state transition occurs when a node leaves the cluster (a virtual circuit fails) or enters the cluster (a new node is connected). During transition periods, all cluster processing stops.

In the case of a virtual circuit failure, it may be some temporary problem. Before declaring a cluster transition, the connection manager waits for a system-manager-set period of time to elapse. If the time-out period elapses, a coordinator node is elected to guide the members through the transition period.

The coordinator proposes a configuration for the cluster. All other nodes must agree with this proposed configuration. If no agreement is reached, the coordinator backs out. Another node can then attempt to become coordinator with its proposed configuration. Once a configuration is agreed upon, the coordinator leads other nodes through the process of rebuilding the distributed lock space.

Because cluster processing does stop during transition periods, the cluster cannot be considered to be fault tolerant in the sense of computers such as those made by Tandem. Cluster reformation time can take several minutes in some configurations.

Distributed Lock Manager

The lock manager in VMS is implemented independently of the file system. This allows other systems, such as database management software, to implement their own types of locks.

Locking is performed on a hierarchical resource tree. A lock on a higher part of the tree applies to all lower parts of the tree. A disk volume might consist of the top of the tree. The next level of the tree would be an individual file. A page of data would be a lower level and an individual record would be a leaf node on the resource tree.

One of the key questions in designing a file system is locking granularity. Since locks consume resources and take time to obtain, it is more efficient to lock large amounts of data for any one application. However, this reduces the concurrency of the system by making that data unavailable to other users.

A database vendor might wish to synchronize access to data at the table level or the tuple level (the equivalent of a record). Some DBMS vendors also provide locking at the page level. Each page may contain several tuples of data. Keeping the file system independent with the lock allows implementation of systems with different levels of locking granularity.

In VMS, the lock manager uses the same code for single-node operation as is used for a distributed cluster environment. Software systems, such as the file system, issue ENQUEUE and DEQUEUE calls to the lock manager. An ENQUEUE call queues a lock request. A DEQUEUE call releases the lock on a resource.

The call to the lock manager can be of two different types: request-response or AST. A request-response call is either granted or denied at the time it is processsed. The other option is to set an asynchronous system trap (AST). If the resource is unavailable, the request is queued and the calling process is notified when the resource becomes available.

When requesting a lock, the calling process can also request a blocking AST. This means that the process is notified when some other process wants the resources in some way that is incompatible with the present lock. A blocking AST allows the process with the lock to avoid constant calls to the lock manager. While holding locks with a blocking AST may be optimal during periods of low use, during periods of high use many systems switch back to the request-response protocol.

The lock manager defines a variety of different kinds of locks in terms of their compatibility with other forms of locks. Each particular lock has no set definition, but a suggested meaning is supplied and is usually used for file-oriented applications. Figure 5-6 shows the lock compatibility table and its suggested interpretations.

Applications may frequently start out with one type of lock and then decide they need another. A user reads a record of data and then later may decide to update it. Rather than releasing existing locks, the lock system allows a user to convert a lock to a different type. A convert operation may be denied if an incompatible lock on the resource already exists, or the request may be queued and an AST requested.

In a cluster, the lock manager is distributed across the different VMS nodes in the cluster. Distributing the lock manager reduces the overhead on any one node and frequently allows the node that wants to use a resource to perform local locking rather than generating SCS messages.

Each resource, such as a disk volume, has a resource manager. Requests for locks on the resource, whether issued locally or from another node, must be directed to this resource manager. If the request for the lock came from another node, it also keeps track of locks it has obtained.

Because resource managers may change, the locking system also provides a directory service. The connection manager keeps a list of all nodes in the cluster and the resources they provide directories for. If a node wants a lock, it first finds the location of the directory service. It then asks the directory node who is managing the resource. If no node is managing the resource, the directory tells the requesting node to manage the resource itself. Figure 5-7 shows the three messages needed to obtain a lock.

During a cluster transition, the lock space is rebuilt. This means that all systems release all foreign locks. The locks are then reacquired one by one. During this rebuild process, a different resource manager may be appointed. The possibility of a new resource manager means that lock management functions do not eventually all migrate to the oldest member of the cluster.

One potential problem in a lock manager is deadlock. Deadlock, often called a "deadly embrace," arises when two processes are each waiting for each other to finish a certain task. Deadlock detection is fairly expensive and is only initiated after a time-out period. If deadlock is detected, a victim is arbitrarily selected to break the embrace.

Deadlock can happen easily when many locks at the bottom of a resource tree are converted to a higher-level lock. For example, if a

LOCK COMPATABILITY TABLE

		CURRENT LOCK					
		NL	CR	CW	PR	PW	EX
REQUESTED LOCK	NL	Y	Y	Y	Y	Y	Y
	CR	Y	Y	Y	Y	Y	N
	CW	Y	Y	Y	N	N	N
	PR	Y	Y	N	Y	N	N
	PW	Y	Y	N	N	N	N
	EX	Y	N	N	N	N	N

SUGGESTED INTERPRETATION:

NL   Null Lock
CR   Shared Read
CW   Shared Write
PR   Protected Read
PW   Protected Write
EX   Exclusive Lock

Fig. 5-6   VMS lock types.

process acquires a dozen record-level locks, it may decide to try to convert those dozen locks into a single table-level lock.

Another conversion is from shared to exclusive locks. Two processes may both have concurrent read locks on a piece of data. Process A may then request that it be granted an exclusive lock on the resource. An EX lock is incompatible with process B's existing CR lock. Process A therefore queues its convert request. Process B also requests an EX lock, which is incompatible with process A's CR lock. Each process ends up waiting for the other to finish.

The second kind of deadlock is also a deadly embrace, but in this case two different resource managers are involved. This is a much more difficult situation to address. After the possibility of a convert deadlock is ruled out, the system begins looking at all locks held by other processes that the time-out process is waiting for. The deadlock detection code then tries to trace their locks back to the first process.

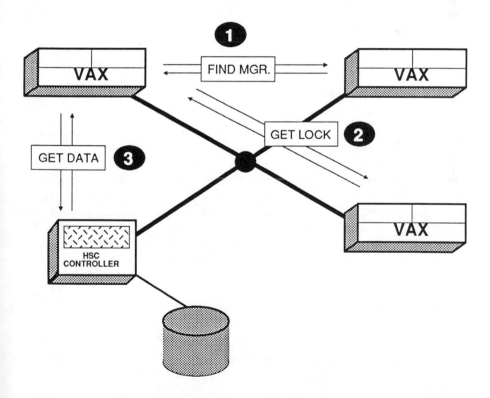

Fig. 5-7 Finding and locking a resource.

CLUSTER LOCK PERFORMANCE

(Source: Digital Technical Journal, Number 5, September 1987, p. 40)

	LOCAL LOCK	REMOTE LOCK		
		LOCAL CPU	REMOTE CPU	ELAPSED TIME
VAX 11/780 CI Bus Cluster	.6	2.7	1.5	3.9
MicroVAX II Ethernet Cluster	.7	6.0	4.8	8.1

All times in milliseconds.

Times are for one ENQ (Lock) and one DEQ (Unlock) Operation.

Fig. 5-8 Lock performance data.

It is interesting that both DEC and IBM use the same algorithm, independently arrived at, to detect this form of deadlock.

Performance of the lock manager does add a significant amount of overhead in a clustered environment because of the extra trips that are taken over the CI bus or Ethernet to gain permission to lock a resource. Often, this increase in lock-time performance is more than offset by being able to share a high-performance disk drive and controller over multiple nodes. Figure 5-8 shows the difference in performance between a local and remote locking operation.

Distributed File System

Most of the synchronization issues that must be resolved for a file system are dealt with in the lock manager. The file system under VMS can thus operate without regard to the clustered environment. Implementation of file management functions, such as security, space allocations, and other issues are done using an Extended QIO Processor (XQP) which is present on VMS nodes.

Devices that are cluster accessible use the Mass Storage Control Protocol (MSCP), a message-oriented set of protocols for access to data. The message-based system allows multiple hosts to queue data requests on a single controller. More traditional register-oriented controllers allow several processes on one node to access data because that one node was able to queue and synchronize the requests. An MSCP-based device takes over that function from the host system.

XQP makes extensive use of locks for synchronization purposes. For example, a volume synchronization lock is taken out when a volume is mounted. When a particular instance of an XQP needs to allocate more space for a file, a protected write (PW) lock is requested. This allows other XQP processes to continue their read operations, but they would not be able to simultaneously allocate the same space to another file.

Locks are also used at the file level to provide synchronization. Any user attempting to open, close, extend, delete, or otherwise affect a file is issued a PW lock on that file. This ensures that file operations occur in a serial fashion.

In VMS, a series of five different caches are used to reduce the I/O operations associated with file management by almost 75 percent. For example, a file control block list contains the attributes of all open files and recently referenced directories. An extent cache holds copies of free disk space and is used for quick allocation of new space. A quota cache eliminates much of the overhead associated with quota management.

A significant issue in cache management is the possibility of cached data becoming out of date because of an operation performed by another node in the cluster. Associated with each lock is a 16-byte space called a value block. This value block is a way of passing information between different lock users.

When a resource is changed, the file system updates the value block. Often, a node will release its locks but continue to cache data. To check the validity of this cached data, the node can request a lock at the appropriate level. When the lock is granted, the XQP compares the value block on the new lock with the value block associated with the cached data. If the values are different, the XQP knows that the cached data was not valid.

Distributed Queuing Systems

In a cluster, the user is usually not aware of what node they are logged onto, especially if they use the LAT services to request a generic type of service. Printers and batch queues, however, are associated with a particular node on the cluster. Since the user does not usually care on which node a print or batch job is executed, the dis-

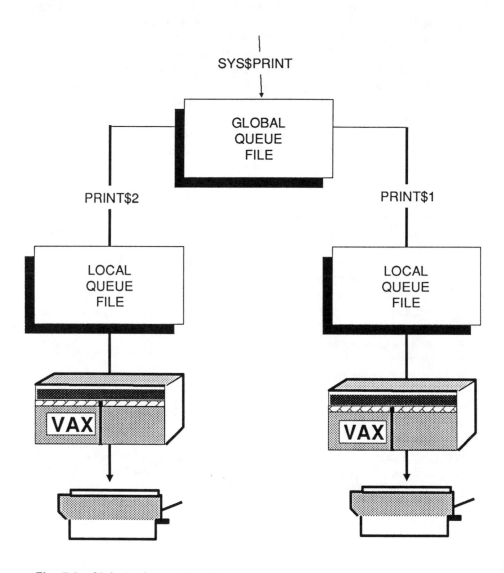

Fig. 5-9 Global print and batch queues.

tributed queuing systems provide a generic resource controller, which farms out work to specific print or batch queues.

Print and batch queues both operate the same way. An input file is placed in a designated subdirectory and the job is put into a queue with a particular priority. When the queue controller decides to process that particular file, it sends it either to a printer or as a process to be computed. Upon completion, the user is optionally notified. Figure 5-9 shows the queueing mechanism.

A queue is first initialized on the local machine. Next, a cluster-wide queue controller file is created. Finally, individual queues are joined to the cluster-wide queue.

Local Area VAX Clusters

Local Area VAX Clusters have the same functionality as a CI bus system, with three important performance-related differences. First, the CI bus which operates at 70 mbps is replaced by an Ethernet which operates at 10 mbps. Secondly, the System Communications Services is implemented in software on the MicroVAX instead of the CI controller as it is for a CI bus. This means that the CPU must perform tasks previously off-loaded to a controller.

Finally, the HSC controller is replaced by a MicroVAX, which performs these functions in software instead of in a dedicated processor. This MicroVAX is known as the boot member of the LAVC. A combination of the CI bus and the Ethernet, known as a Mixed Interconnect Cluster, does allow an Ethernet-based VAX to access the services of an HSC controller.

An LAVC is usually used for compute-intensive applications such as CAD/CAM, some integrated office automation environments, or desktop publishing. Usually, though not always, members of an LAVC are VAXstations and make intensive use of graphics for the user interface and the display of data.

LAVCs replace the function of the CI port with a port emulator. This is a software process that emulates the SCS interface on a CI port. The software then reformats the information for transmission on the Ethernet.

Although the Ethernet and the CI bus both operate at the data link layer, there are important differences between the two. Ethernet does not have the capability to send different kinds of messages, nor does it provide for automatic acknowledgment of data. Of course, there is also a significant difference in performance between the two media. The port emulator must therefore mask these differences from higher-level processes that use SCS, such as an MSCP server or a connection manager. Figure 5-10 illustrates data access in an LAVC environment.

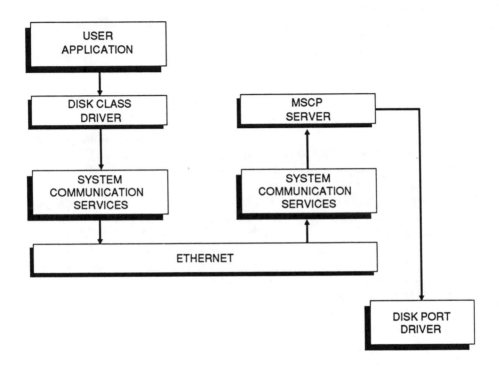

Fig. 5-10 Data access in an LAVC.

Boot nodes

There are two kinds of nodes in an LAVC that operate in a sort of client/server relationship. A boot node provides management functions and has a disk drive with the cluster common files. Satellite nodes are clients of the boot node and use it for disk drives, printers, and distributed batch processing. Figure 5-11 shows boot and satellite nodes on an Ethernet.

A boot node can require substantial disk space and CPU resources in a large cluster. A boot node must be at least a MicroVAX II with

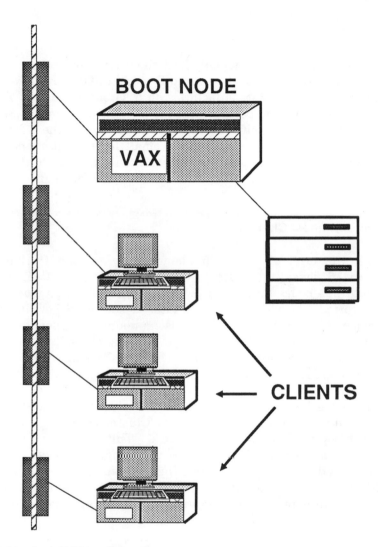

Fig. 5-11 An LAVC configuration.

150 Mbytes of storage. This boot node can only service three satellite nodes, and they would probably need local disk drives for paging and swapping. A cluster can have two boot nodes to reduce the bottleneck at a single CPU (usually at the Ethernet controller) and also to provide some fault tolerance.

Satellite nodes

Satellite nodes in a cluster usually boot themselves over the network, using the DNA Maintenance Operation Protocol (MOP). It is thus possible to have no mass storage facilities on a satellite node. If a diskless node is used, it is important that the node have at least 4 Mbytes of memory to avoid excessive paging and swapping over the Ethernet.

Often, a satellite node might have a small laser printer and a 70-Mbyte local disk drive for local storage. It would then go to the client node for access to larger mass storage facilities and faster printers.

Mixed Interconnect Clusters

Although the original cluster implementation on the CI bus was limited to 16 nodes, the Systems Communications Architecture permits up to 224 nodes in a cluster. The original LAVC announcement only supported 13 nodes, which was later raised to 26. With the announcement of VMS version 5, DEC also announced support for Mixed Interconnect Clusters. This allows up to 42 members in a cluster, of which up to 24 can be on a CI bus. These limits can be expected to gradually increase as DEC continues to gain experience with VAX Clusters.

Some studies have shown that it is actually quicker for a MicroVAX II to get data over a Mixed Interconnect Cluster than to go to a local drive such as an RD53 Winchester disk. This is because the HSC controllers and associated disk drives are so much quicker that the intermediate time spent on transmitting data through the CI Bus and the Ethernet plus all the intervening software layers is recovered. It is important to note that these results are highly application dependent.

Availability and Performance

In a Local Area VAX Cluster the limiting factor is usually the ability of the boot node to process both CI port emulation code and MSCP server code. With a fast CPU, the next bottleneck becomes the speed of the Ethernet controller. The next bottleneck is Ethernet saturation, reached at the rate of roughly 100 typical I/O requests per second.

A common configuration is to use an Ethernet bridge to segment the members of an LAVC from other members of the larger network. The bridge allows connectivity to a backbone network but keeps local traffic on the work area network. When there is extensive I/O activity on the LAVC, a segmented Ethernet allows the work group to degrade its local performance without affecting the rest of the network.

Two types of issues seem to limit the performance of a cluster. First, locking is considerably slower in a cluster environment than with local locking. If the directory node is not known and there is an existing resource manager, it takes four messages to receive a lock. Even if the resource manager is known, such as in the case of a convert operation, it still takes two messages to receive a lock. The bandwidth of even a CI bus is significantly slower than that needed for a local lock operation within main memory.

The most significant performance implication of clusters seems to be in cluster reformation time. The rebuilding of a lock space and establishing the connection managers can take seconds and or even minutes to accomplish. This is a significant processing pause in a busy environment. For this reason, a cluster is known as a high availability instead of a fault-tolerant computing environment.

With enough resources, losing one node in a cluster will not result in re-forming the cluster. This means that the lapse in service can be minimized. Of course, the node cannot immediately rejoin the cluster or cluster processing would have to stop so a new cluster could be formed. Thus, in a fairly stable environment, reforming clusters does not become a major issue.

Census Bureau Clustering Case Study

An interesting example of the use of clusters can be found in the Census Automated Processing System (CAPS) used by the U.S. Census Bureau to manage data it collects. CAPS consists of a series of clusters located throughout the country. The initial VAX Cluster was installed in Suitland, Maryland.

The cluster itself consists of two VAX 8700 processors connected to four HSC70 controllers. Fourteen of DEC's SA482 disk clusters are connected to the HSC processors for a total of 35 gigabytes of disk space.

It is important to distinguish a disk cluster from a VAX Cluster. The disk cluster allows multiple disk drives to share a set of independent parallel spindles. In a normal disk drive, a single spindle provides access to the data. With multiple spindles, if one is busy, the other can access the disk drive to get the data. While an individual spindle on the SA482 has an average access time of 32 ms, the combination of multiple spindles provides average access times in the range of 20 ms.

Both of the VAX 8700 processors are connected to an Ethernet that is used to provide front-end access. Local user workstations consist of over 200 VT220 terminals as well as 80 VAXmates. The VAXmate is DEC's PC/AT compatible system.

Most of the data entry operations in CAPS are performed at another facility located in Jeffersonville, Indiana. Those users are connected to VT220 terminals, which are in turn connected to terminal servers. This configuration is linked to Maryland with a leased line on an extended Ethernet.

The main purpose of the CAPS system is to process incoming census data, such as the agricultural, economic, and decennial censuses. For the economic and agricultural censuses alone, over 7 million forms are processed in Indiana.

Data is stored in a relational database using DEC's Rdb software. Once the initial data is entered, workers in Maryland are able to perform a variety of validity checks to verify the data-entry operation. Data that is flagged as suspect is returned to Indiana for verification against the original paper forms. Over 60 different databases are maintained on the cluster for the different forms of data.

The CAPS cluster in Maryland is the first phase. The eventual configuration consists of over 450 MicroVAX systems located around the country. In addition, a series of clusters will be located in field offices and at the headquarters site.

The Maryland cluster illustrates how VAX Clusters can provide a modular upgrade path. Disk drives can be added separately from HSC controllers, which can in turn be added independently of new VAX processors. Needless to say, the modular upgrade path does not alleviate the need for a balanced configuration.

Summary

Clusters provide a very important alternative to buying (or making) larger and larger systems. Important resources such as file systems and lock managers are shared in a coordinated fashion. Clusters do not provide shared memory such as a VAX 8840 would have with four CPUs, all having access to shared memory. The cluster instead functions like a conventional network, complete with a multilayered architecture.

The most important benefit of clustering is a distributed file system that has full concurrency control. Most other file systems, such as DEC's Distributed File Service and the Network File System do not have a limit on the number of nodes participating. However, this has been achieved at the expense of the locking services available. It is important to remember that the distinction between clusters and other distributed file systems is beginning to fade as higher-speed data link mechanisms and distributed lock managers become available.

The SCA architecture provides a complimentary set of services to DECnet. DECnet provides access to all nodes in a network, but this generality is at the expense of control and performance. The cluster environment provides a common management and security domain, but for a limited number of nodes. Clusters allow concurrent access to data with full locking capabilities.

The LAVC environment uses the same architecture as a CI bus system, but at a significantly reduced level of performance. The Ethernet provides a raw bandwidth of 10 mbps as compared to the 70 mbps of the CI bus. In addition, the SCS internode communications functions are performed in software on the LAVC, whereas these functions are built into the CI controller on larger clusters.

Because of the difference in performance, the LAVC is used for very different purposes than the large machine clusters. Large clusters are typically used by many users who desire rapid access to data in a transactions processing environment. The LAVC, by contrast, is typically used by a few users on VAXstations. The applications of the LAVC are centered around graphics-intensive operations such as CAD/CAM or desktop publishing. The LAVC environment is used for infrequent access to large amounts of data.

Note that these differences in cluster use are based solely on performance. The functionality of the systems is the same, and there is no reason why an LAVC could not be used for small transactions processing environments.

Mixed Interconnect Clusters provide an important blending of the two capabilities. Because both the Ethernet and the CI Bus data link can be mixed in a common cluster, both VAXstations and large VAXs can share a common file system and a common management domain. Care should be taken, however, that node failures on the LAVC portion of the Mixed Interconnect Cluster do not result in a state transition that stops processing for interactive users of the larger systems.

For Further Reading

Balkovich, et al., "VAXcluster Availability Modeling, *Digital Technical Journal*," vol. 1, no. 5, September 1987, p. 69.

Digital Equipment Corporation, "VAXcluster Systems Handbook," order no. EB-28858-46.

——, "VMS Local Area VAXcluster Manual," order no. AA-JP20C-TE.

——, " VMS Local Area VAXcluster Manual," AA-JP20C-TE, June 1987.

Duffy, "The System Communication Architecture," *Digital Technical Journal*, vol. 1, no. 5, September 1987, p. 22.

Fox and Ywoskus, "Local Area VAXcluster Systems," *Digital Technical Journal*, vol. 1, no. 5, September 1987, p. 56.

Goldstein, "The Design and Implementation of a Distributed File System," *Digital Technical Journal*, vol. 1, no. 5, September 1987, p. 45.

Insight Magazine (Census Example), vol. 8, no. 5, June 1986.

Kronenberg, et al., "The VAXcluster Concept: An Overview of a Distributed System," *Digital Technical Journal*, vol. 1, no. 5, September 1987, p. 7.

——, " VAXclusters: A Closely-coupled Distributed System," *ACM Transactions on Computer Systems*, vol. 4, no. 2. May 1986: pp. 130–146.

Park, et al., "System Level Performance of VAX 8974 and 8978 System," *Digital Technical Journal*, vol. 1, no. 5, September 1987, p. 80.

Snaman and Thiel, "The VAX/VMS Distributed Lock Manager," *Digital Technical Journal*, vol. 1, no. 5, September, 1987, p. 29.

Part

3

DEC Networks

6

Local Area Networks

Overview of Local Area Networks

To the routing layer of DNA or the LAT processes, an Ethernet appears as a single logical bus. This means that every node on the Ethernet is adjacent to every other node and thus does not involve any routing decisions. In reality, the configuration of this logical bus can be quite complicated.

Ethernets can be implemented with a variety of physical media. Traditional coax cable, known as baseband, can be up to 500 m long with 100 nodes connected on it. Another type of coax cable, known as ThinWire, allows up to 30 nodes to be connected to a cable up to 185 m long. Other Ethernet implementations might use broadband technology, fiber optic, or twisted pair wires. Each of these instances of a physical medium corresponds to a single-segment Ethernet.

Multiple segments, possibly consisting of different physical media, can be connected together with repeaters. A repeater takes every bit on a single segment, retimes and reamplifies it, and rebroadcasts it on another segment. Repeaters can be remote repeaters, allowing two segments to be separated by up to 1000 m of fiber optic cable. These multiple segments constitute a single Ethernet.

An extended Ethernet allows multiple Ethernets to be connected together. Each of those Ethernets might be in itself a complex topology of mixed media and multiple segments connected with repeaters. The extended Ethernet consists of a series of Ethernets connected together with a bridge. While a repeater sends every bit over each segment, the bridge is able to determine if a packet of data needs to be forwarded on the second Ethernet. The bridge thus allows connectivity while still segmenting the networks.

Connected to the Ethernet are a series of servers. Obviously a server can be a VAX or MicroVAX computer. Often, different VAXs are dedicated to different tasks such as database, graphics, document processing, or CAD/CAM. Another type of server might be a VAXstation that serves as the user interface. All of these different forms of computers are able to communicate at high speeds to form a coherent, cooperative network.

Single-Segment Ethernets

The basic Ethernet configuration consists of a segment of coax cable with up to 100 nodes on it. The segment can be up to 500 m long and is known as baseband or ThickWire. Connected to the Ethernet media is a transceiver. DEC's H4000 transceiver is typical of most Ethernet transceivers. A vampire tap is used to make the connection to the media without cutting the cable. Figure 6-1 illustrates a basic configuration on an Ethernet. Figure 6-2 shows an H4000 transceiver.

Ethernet is a broadcast media. Each node is able to send signals onto the cable. Those signals then propagate the length of the cable as a broadcast. In order to detect a collision, the Ethernet is terminated on both ends. This absorbs the signal and allows nodes to detect any collisions with their original broadcast.

Each host on the Ethernet has an Ethernet controller. These controllers are built into special-purpose devices such as terminal servers. For PCs, VAXs, and Macintosh systems, Ethernet controllers are either an add-on peripheral or are built into the system.

A controller needs to be compatible with the bus of the system it is going on. Thus, an Ethernet controller on a VAX 11/780 would need to be Unibus compatible, while a controller on a VAX 8800 would need to be BI bus compatible. The Ethernet controller joins other communications controllers on the host, such as asynchronous communications controllers for connecting terminals.

A transceiver cable connects the transceiver to the Ethernet controller card. There are two grades of transceiver cable: low loss (BNE3x) and high loss (BNE4x). Low-loss cables can be up to 50 m long. High-loss cables are cheaper, smaller, and more flexible but can only be 12.5 m long.

Although a transceiver cable can be 50 m long, some of this length can be used up by the Ethernet controller. This is because a controller has an internal cabling equivalency. DEC recommends allowing 10 m

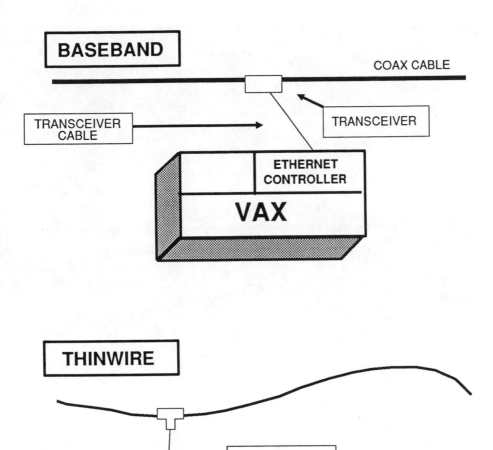

Fig. 6-1 Connecting hosts to coax media.

of low loss and 2.5 m of high loss as an internal cabling equivalency for most controllers.

Transceivers on a segment of baseband are spaced apart in multiples of 2.5 m. Most baseband cables have a colored ring to show where these positions occur. The reason for the spacing restriction is

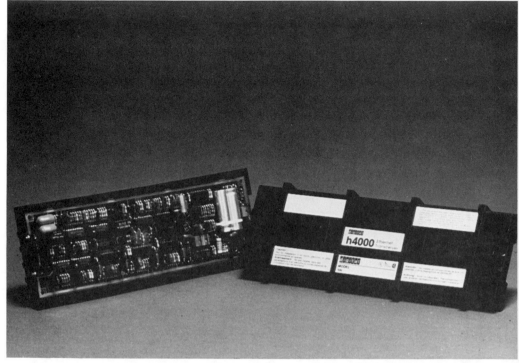

Courtesy of Digital Equipment Corporation

Fig. 6-2   H4000 transceiver.

that each transceiver introduces a certain amount of noise on the cable. By spacing the intervals at 2.5 m (or multiples thereof), the waves of noise generated by each of the transceivers cancel each other out. A second form of limitation on transceivers is that there can only be 100 transceivers on a single segment of baseband.

A special form of transceiver is the multiport transceiver. DEC markets a multiport transceiver under the name of DEC Local Network Interconnect (DELNI). Up to eight individual Ethernet hosts can be connected to a single DELNI. The DELNI can operate in local mode which is commonly known as "Ethernet in a Can." This is because the DELNI takes the place of the Ethernet coax cable. Figure 6-3 shows a configuration of nodes on a DELNI.

In global mode, the DELNI is connected to the baseband segment using a transceiver cable and a transceiver. This means that eight devices that are close to each other don't have to use up eight transceivers on the baseband with the required 2.5 m separation between each node.

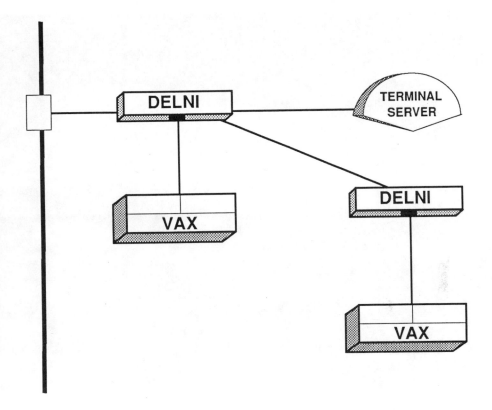

Fig. 6-3 Multiport transceivers.

Each node on a global DELNI needs to be within 45 m of the transceiver that connects the DELNI to the baseband. This means that the transceiver cable connecting the node to the DELNI plus the transceiver cable connecting the DELNI to the baseband must equal 45 m or less. The "missing" 5 m is because the DELNI is equivalent to 5 m of transceiver cable, just as some Ethernet controllers are equivalent to 10 m of cable.

In a machine room environment, it is not uncommon to cascade two levels of DELNIs. This means that eight DELNIs are connected to a ninth DELNI. Up to 64 hosts can thus be connected without laying any coax cable, as long as each node is within 50 m of the top-level DELNI.

Many organizations use Ethernet only as a method of connecting machine-room hosts together. A separate front-end network is used to allow PCs and terminals access to the machine room environment.

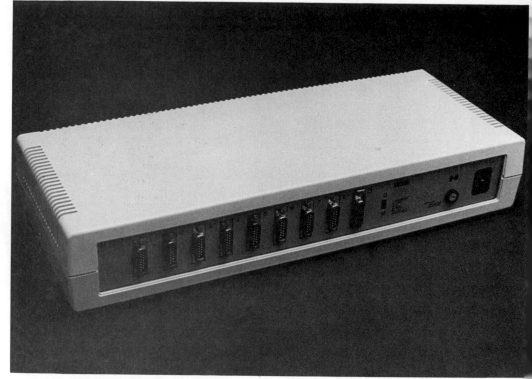

Courtesy of Digital Equipment Corporation

Fig. 6-4   DEC's multiport transceiver (DELNI).

This front-end network might be a data PBX. For these organizations, it is not necessary to lay cable and the DELNI is an appropriate solution for an Ethernet because they can be rack mounted with other communications equipment in the machine room. Figure 6-4 shows a DELNI.

ThinWire coax segments

The baseband Ethernet media has several advantages. Its nonintrusive tapping method means new nodes can be added to the network without disrupting service. Baseband is also fairly resistant to electromagnetic interference. On the other hand, it is fairly expensive and hard to handle.

An alternative form of Ethernet cable is based on RG58, a thinner grade of coax known as Cheapernet or ThinWire. A single segment of

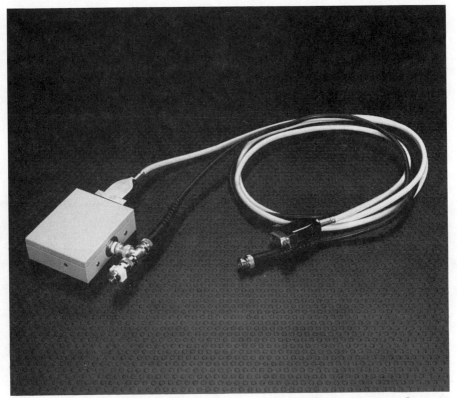

Courtesy of Digital Equipment Corporation

Fig. 6-5 DESTA ThinWire transceiver.

ThinWire can only be 185 m long and can have a maximum of 30 nodes on it.

A different kind of transceiver is used for ThinWire connections. DEC sells one known as a DEC Station Adapter or DESTA. As with other ThinWire transceivers, these require that the cable be physically cut. The DESTA is then put in between the two segments. If a node is the last one on a segment, it puts a special terminator on the other side of the DESTA. Figure 6-5 shows a DESTA.

Connecting the DESTA to the Ethernet controller is a standard transceiver cable. Usually, this is high-loss (but low-cost) cable. The length of the transceiver cable is restricted to a few feet.

One problem with the DESTA is that if the DESTA is removed, there is an unterminated Ethernet. This disrupts service for every node on the ThinWire segment. The baseband segment, by contrast, has no problem if a node is removed because of the nonintrusive tapping method.

The problem of the unterminated ThinWire is not necessarily a hypothetical one. Most ThinWire nodes are personal workstations. When a user wants to move the workstation, the DESTA often seems to be the logical place to make the disconnection. The network manager may wish to invest in a supply of "high voltage" or "radioactive" stickers to place on the DESTAs in such areas.

Broadband segments

Broadband is based on the Community Antenna TV technology (CATV) used in cable TV systems. This CATV technology is meant to be hung on telephone cables and is thus highly resistant to salt, spray, and bird droppings. Each piece of CATV cable has a bandwidth of 300 to 400 megahertz (MHz). This tremendous bandwidth means that broadband can serve the purposes of a number of communications technologies, including Ethernet, voice, and video.

Broadband is often used as a backbone system between buildings in a campus-like environment. Because it is highly resistant to noise, it is also used in laboratories, factories, and electrically noisy offices.

The topology of a broadband Ethernet is like a tree. At the head of the tree is a head end. Nodes send and receive at different frequencies on broadband systems. Nodes send data to the head end on a "reverse band." The head end sends data back to the device on a "forward band." The head end translates sending to receiving frequencies. A third frequency, known as the "guard band," is used to separate the two data frequencies.

Nodes connecting to broadband systems can use the same Ethernet controller and transceiver cable. The transceiver is no longer an H4000 transceiver, however. Instead, a broadband modem is used to connect to the medium. It is called a modem because broadband is analog in contrast to the digital baseband medium.

Broadband modems use particular frequencies on the CATV cable. Because of that, broadband modems on a single segment must all come from the same manufacturer. Chipcom Ethermodems and DEC DECOM modems are two examples of broadband modems.

It is also possible to have dual CATV broadband cables. In this case, send and receive signals occupy different cables. The modem must be able to connect to a dual-cable broadband.

Broadband has the significant advantage over ThickWire (the traditional coax medium) of allowing segments to be 10 to 12 miles long. It is thus ideal in an extended local area environment. Many sites are using fiber as an alternative to broadband. This is because fiber has a potential bandwidth of many gigabits, while broadband systems are more limited.

Fiber segments

Fiber is used in many organizations in a similar role to broadband—as a backbone cabling system. Fiber is also used as a wide area backbone because of its tremendous potential bandwidth of gigabits per second. Because fiber does not oxidize as copper does, it is becoming the wide area backbone for many organizations. DEC, for example, has an extensive fiber optic network linking their Massachusetts and New Hampshire facilities together (see the case study in the next chapter for more information).

Fiber is used in three different scenarios for LAN technologies. Most often, fiber is used as a method of connecting bridges or repeaters together. The fiber in this case is not used to connect nodes to the Ethernet, only to connect separate segments of Ethernets together.

The second use of fiber is as a backbone environment. In this case, fiber actually forms part of an Ethernet segment but has very few hosts connected to it. The LattisNet example in the next section is an example of using fiber as a backbone network.

The third option is to actually connect hosts to the fiber. This is usually done in an environment with security constraints because it is harder to attach to a piece of fiber and remain undetected than it is to a ThickWire segment that can accept a vampire tap without interrupting service.

Twisted pair segments

Ethernet implementations using twisted pair wiring are quite attractive because many organizations have excess twisted pair already in place for their phone system. In some instances, these wires can be cannibalized to provide Ethernet access and eliminating the need to lay more cable.

Twisted pair has several advantages over more traditional Ethernet media. First, it can provide a transition to the four-wire ISDN physical interface. Second, it is lighter, more flexible, and smaller than coax cable. Twisted pair can be used in Ethernet as well as token ring networking schemes, allowing the network manager the flexibility to change LAN technologies.

On the other hand, coax can be used for longer distances because of its greater insulation. A limitation of twisted pair is that wires cannot be placed directly next to those used for phone systems. This is because when a telephone rings, a high volt signal is transmitted down the wire. This limits the situations in which unshielded twisted pair can be used.

Most implementations of twisted pair Ethernet still use coax cable or fiber as a backbone. The twisted pair wiring is attached onto a segment of coax using a device called a BALUN (balanced-unbalanced) adapter. This device has an RJ11 or RJ45 connector for the twisted pair and a standard BNC connector for the ThinWire. The device converts the 60- to 90-ohm coax impedance to the 120- to 140-ohm impedance of the twisted pair.

The coax segment of the BALUN is then connected to some form of concentrator. In the case of DEC, this is usually a single port of the DEMPR. A single segment of twisted pair in this configuration can be up to 70 m long. At the node end of the connection, the twisted pair is once again converted into ThinWire to connect to the DESTA, which in turn connects to the Ethernet controller.

Another vendor that has been prominent in the twisted pair Ethernet market is SynOptics Communications. Their LattisNet uses a combination of fiber and twisted pair. Nodes are connected to concentrators using twisted pair. Fiber is then used to connect concentrators together. A segment of twisted pair is able to go up to 360 feet (ft) before it has to join a local concentrator.

Concentrators in LattisNet can be either local or global. A global concentrator is the same as a local except that it has the capability to have other concentrators connected to it, while the local concentrator can only accept connections from hosts. Global concentrators may in turn be in a hierarchical configuration (a "super" global concentrator).

Local concentrators can have three or eight host modules depending on the model. A typical host module is the twisted pair module which can accept up to eight twisted pair connectors while a fiber module can accept up to four fiber optic connections.

Each local concentrator also includes a power supply module and a terminator module. The terminator module uses fiber to connect to a global concentrator. The global concentrator includes a retiming module which retimes and amplifies signals before transmitting them back down the tree.

The entire LattisNet is considered to be a single segment of Ethernet. It is thus possible to use one of the twisted pair ports and connect that to a BALUN, which is connected to one side of an Ethernet repeater. That repeater in turn would be connected to another Ethernet segment, such as a baseband segment.

The advantage of twisted pair is that many sites already have two unused pairs of wire going into each office. For example, many sites adopted the AT&T Premises Distribution System (PDS) which specifies that each office should have four pairs of wires. Since most phone systems only use two pairs for each telephone unit, a LattisNet or twisted pair network can plug right in without laying cable.

It is important to recognize the convenience of not having to lay cable. In many organizations, facilities maintenance is an entirely different group from data communications. Often, this relationship can deteriorate if the data communications staff insists on tearing up the building when the building staff is busy concentrating on allocating parking spaces. If the wire is already there, it means one less department to contend with. Of course, the voice wiring may be "owned" by a separate department, but that is another issue!

Comparison of different media

A particular set of computers can be wired together using any one of the media discussed. Usually, each type of media fits a special purpose. Broadband and fiber, for example, are usually used as an Ethernet backbone. In a campus environment, this media would be used to connect multiple buildings together.

Baseband or ThickWire is also used as a form of backbone. Often, this medium is used in the machine room and to connect various floors of a building together. It is not uncommon to see broadband used to connect buildings together and baseband used to connect floors together. ThinWire and twisted pair are usually used as a local distribution method. User workstations, such as MicroVAXs, terminal servers, PCs, and Macintoshes are often connected to either type of media.

Repeaters are used to connect these different types of media together into a single multisegment Ethernet. An alternative to connecting segments with a repeater is to use a bridge or a router. While the repeater operates at the physical layer of the network, bridges and routers operate at the next two layers. This allows some forms of filtering and control over cross-segment traffic, but at the expense of performance. In a wide area environment, repeaters are not a viable option and bridges and routers are used to form connections.

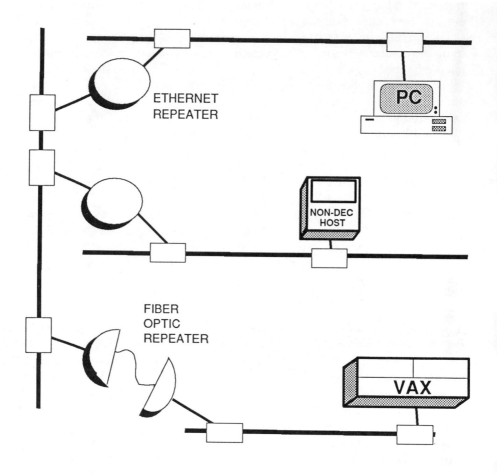

Fig. 6-6   Ethernet repeaters.

Repeaters: Multisegment Ethernets

The limits of a single-segment Ethernet may be reached because of either distance limitations or because the number of nodes has reached the maximum. As previously discussed, a single baseband segment can only have 100 transceivers on it and can be only 500 meters long, while a single ThinWire segment can only have 30 nodes and be 185 meters long.

A repeater retimes and reamplifies the signal on an Ethernet and allows multiple segments to be tied together.   The basic rule for repeaters is that there can be only two repeaters in the path between

Courtesy of Digital Equipment Corporation

Fig. 6-7   DEREP Ethernet repeater.

any two nodes on the Ethernet. This two repeater rule has been expanded to four repeaters by the IEEE. DEC supports only two-repeater configurations to minimize the delay introduced into configurations with many repeaters. Figure 6-6 shows a basic repeater configuration.

The two repeater rule means that a multisegment Ethernet usually consists of a backbone with segments fanning out from it. This might mean a backbone down the elevator shaft of a building and then segments on each floor. Alternatively, it might mean a backbone between buildings and then a single segment per building.

The basic DEC repeater is the DEREP. A DEREP connects two separate baseband segments together. Since the DEREP is connected to two segments, it needs two transceivers and two transceiver cables. Each transceiver cable can be 50 m long, so the individual segments can be as much as 100 m apart.

A remote repeater consists of two DEREP units. Each one is connected to a single baseband segment. In between the two DEREP units can be as much as 1000 m of fiber optic cable. Between any two

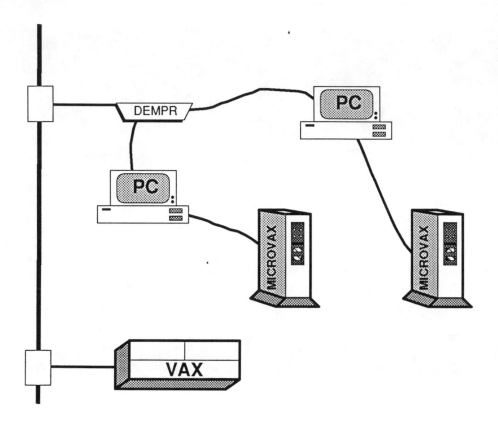

Fig. 6-8 Multiport repeaters.

nodes on the Ethernet, there can be only 1000 m of fiber optic cable. This could be split between two sets of remote repeaters or can all be used on a single remote DEREP. Figure 6-7 shows a photo of a DEC DEREP repeater.

Fiber as a way of connecting Ethernet segments will be seen again in the discussion of extended Ethernets later in this chapter. In that type of configuration, fiber optic is used to connect separate Ethernets into an extended Ethernet. Repeaters connect multiple segments into a single Ethernet. It is important not to confuse the 1000-m repeater rule with configuration guidelines for extended Ethernets.

The maximum separation of two nodes on a baseband Ethernet can be calculated as 2800 m:

- Three 500-m coax segments
- Six 50-m transceiver cables
- One thousand m of fiber

The total amount of cable on this subnetwork could be much greater than 2800 m. The rule only serves to limit the total distance between any two nodes and not the total amount of cable.

ThinWire segments are connected together using a multiport repeater. DEC's DEMPR allows up to eight segments of ThinWire to be connected together. A single segment of ThinWire can have 30 connections on it, and the DEMPR counts as 1. This means that up to 8 times 29, or 232, nodes can be put on a single DEMPR (See Figure 6-8).

The DEMPR can function as a stand-alone unit in an exclusively ThinWire network. The DEMPR can also connect to a segment of baseband. Since the DEMPR is a repeater, it counts against the two-repeater limit between any two nodes on the Ethernet.

The DEMPR is frequently used as a wiring concentrator in a cluster of offices. Baseband is used as a backbone between floors, and the ThinWire segments are connected to the backbone using a DEMPR. Optionally, the DEMPR can be connected to a DELNI, which in turn is connected to the backbone. This configuration is often used when a single floor has a combination of terminal servers and DEMPR ports on it, all connected to the DELNI.

Both the DELNI and the DEMPR add delay to the Ethernet as they must both receive and rebroadcast all signals. If a network consists of a baseband backbone, with ThinWire segments connected by a combination of DEMPR and DELNI, the backbone can only be 300 m long.

Extended Ethernets

There are several reasons that the limits of a single Ethernet may be reached. The most obvious is that the 1024 node-limit has been reached. Another limitation is that because of restrictions on segment sizes and the numbers of repeaters, a distance limitation has been reached. Thirdly, the number of nodes may be less than 1024, but they may be saturating the media. A final reason is administrative—finance may not be willing to have accounting in charge of "their" network.

Multiple Ethernets can be connected together into an extended Ethernet. An extended Ethernet looks like a single piece of cable to the Ethernet user—for example a DNA routing layer. All nodes on this extended Ethernet appear as though they were connected to a single piece of logical cable. Figure 6-9 shows two Ethernets connected together into an extended Ethernet.

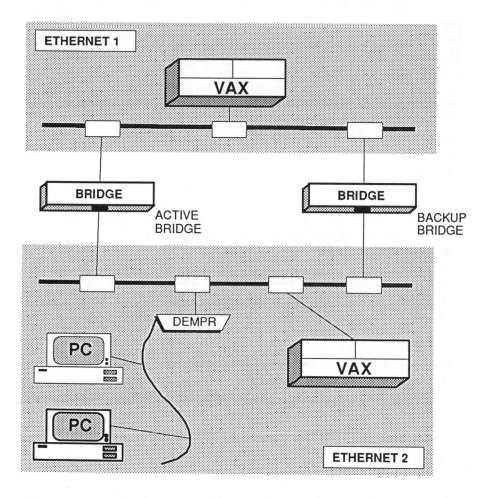

Fig. 6-9   Basic bridge configuration.

A bridge is used to connect the separate Ethernets; this is a device connected to two separate Ethernets and belongs to each one. The bridge listens to the packets on each Ethernet. If the packet is local to the Ethernet it is heard on, the bridge ignores it. If the packet has a remote Ethernet address on it, the bridge forwards the packet onto the second Ethernet and rebroadcasts it.

It is important to remember that each of the two Ethernets combined together could be in themselves a fairly complex topology. The rules for an individual Ethernet on distance, node, and repeater limits still apply. For simplicity, the diagrams in this book show individual-segment Ethernets connected together using bridges. Each of these individual Ethernets could instead be a multiple-segment network.

Although it is possible to have an infinite number of bridges in an extended Ethernet, each bridge adds processing time for filtering and forwarding packets. This is crucial in timer-based protocols like LAT, which expect to receive an ACK on a packet within 80 milliseconds.

A bridge adds a little over 1 ms to the longest path delay time on an extended LAN. DEC recommends no more than eight bridges in the path between any two Ethernets to keep the total path delay under 10 ms in time-critical applications like LAT or LAVC traffic.

Automatic learning

Bridges quickly learn the addresses of all Ethernets that lie to either side of them. This allows the bridge to build up a forwarding database and increases the forwarding rate and prevents excessive rebroadcasting of packets. The forwarding database can have up to 8000 entries in it, enough for most applications.

When a packet is sent, the bridge knows that the source address it hears lies in that direction. It is possible that the destination address is either in that direction or on the other side of the bridge. When the bridge encounters an unknown destination, it forwards the packet. Eventually, the node that receives the packet will send a reply. That reply will have the unknown node as the source. See Figure 6-10 for an illustration of this process.

In this way, the bridge is able to learn about the existence of previously unknown nodes and update the forwarding database.

The question of which packet to forward is a crucial one for the bridge. Each node on each Ethernet has an address. When a bridge powers up, it begins by listening to each network and builds up a list of addresses. This prevents the bridge from sending a packet back out on the same Ethernet and flooding the network with duplicate packets.

There is an extremely high probability that a packet sent will generate an acknowledgment from the target node or will be followed by another packet from the source. A two address cache will thus provide the forwarding rule for up to 60 percent of the packets the bridge must forward.

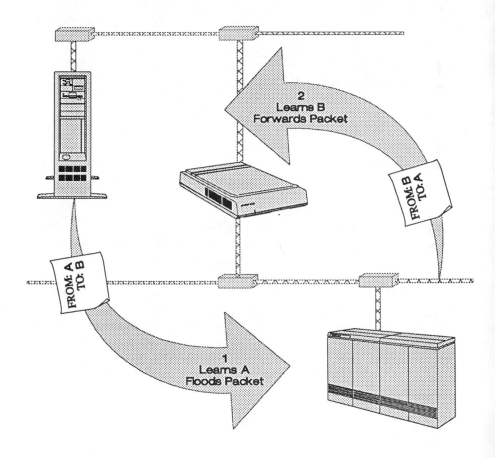

Fig. 6-10   Bridge learning algorithm.

Spanning tree algorithm

An important consideration on an extended Ethernet is that the bridges should not form a loop. Suppose a series of four Ethernets. Ethernets A and B are connected by a single bridge. Ethernets B and C are connected by dual bridges. Ethernets C and D are connected with a single bridge. Figure 6-11 illustrates this configuration.

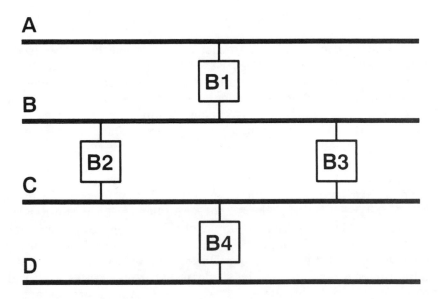

Fig. 6-11 Chernobyl effect example.

Now suppose that a new node is added to Ethernet A. It immediately transmits a packet with an address on D. Bridge B2 hears the packet broadcast, recognizes the address as not being local, and rebroadcasts it out on Ethernet C. Bridge B3 hears this packet on Ethernet C and sends it back to Ethernet B. In the case of a broadcast address, this pattern can quickly generate a tremendous amount of cyclical traffic out of one packet—known as the "Chernobyl effect" by some.

To prohibit this type of a loop, bridges begin by configuring themselves as a spanning tree. This means there is only one path to a particular Ethernet from a given point, as opposed to a more general mesh topology. Several vendors, including Digital, Vitalink, and Chipcom use the same spanning tree algorithm, allowing different brands of bridges to mixed in a single extended Ethernet.

If there are two bridges connecting a pair of Ethernets, some bridge implementations, including DEC's, allow one of the bridges enters a hot backup state. The backup bridge periodically monitors the Ethernet to listen for the status message of the active bridge. If it is not received after a time-out period, the backup bridge takes over.

Multicast addresses and filtering

Rebroadcasting packets with multicast addresses can have potentially disastrous effects on an extended Ethernet. A single broadcast message asking for help (i.e., the location of a nameserver) could generate a large number of responses, particularly if the response to the multicast is another multicast message requiring further assistance. This same phenomenon can occur on a single Ethernet, but the number of nodes in an extended Ethernet can compound the seriousness of the problem.

Some bridges, such as those made by Vitalink, allow the manager to filter out certain types of traffic. Usually, multicast messages are one of the first types of traffic filtered out. Another option is to filter out whole protocol families. For example, the San Diego Supercomputer Center has a series of bridges that link it to the academic network at the University of California at San Diego. The bridge is used to filter out the protocol families used by students and thus creates a firewall around the center. Researchers that use the same protocols as the Center have their packets forwarded as normal.

Types of bridges

Several types of bridges are available. The LAN Bridge 100 is DEC's basic bridge. It connects via transceiver cables to two separate Ethernets. The two Ethernets can thus be up to 100 m apart. Usually, both Ethernets terminate in a common wiring closet and separation of the networks is not an issue.

A remote bridge combines the DEREP repeater with the LAN Bridge 100. A DEREP is connected to one Ethernet and the bridge is connected to a second one. The bridge and the repeater can be connected by up to 500 m of fiber optic cable. In addition to the 500 m, this configuration can use anything that is left over from the 1000 m limit of fiber optic cables connecting repeaters in the network. Thus, if no fiber repeaters are used, the bridge-repeater combination can be separated by up to 1500 m of fiber. Figure 6-12 illustrates the different types of bridges.

Two bridges can also be connected by fiber. If a bridge is located on each end of the connection, up to 3000 m of fiber can be used. Since a bridge is more expensive than a repeater, this configuration costs more than the bridge-repeater configuration.

Fiber links are used to connect separate buildings together into either a multisegment Ethernet or an extended Ethernet, depending

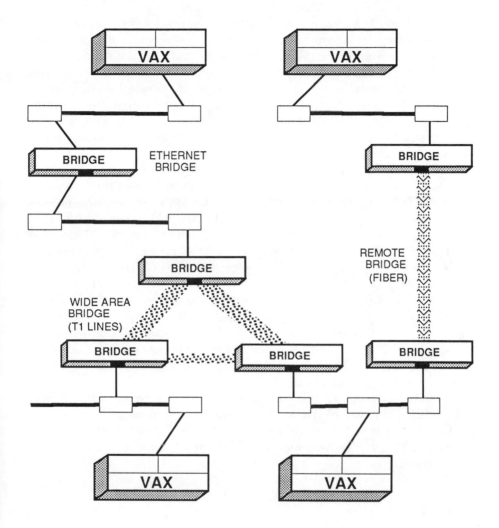

Fig. 6-12   Three types of Ethernet bridges.

on whether bridges or repeaters are used. Unfortunately, it is not always easy to secure permission to tear up the corporate parking lot to lay the fiber. While computers are a key corporate resource, most network managers will soon find that computers are low in priority when compared to parking spaces.

A solution to this situation is the use of a microwave link between buildings. The microwave link is combined with a LAN Bridge 100 to form DEC's METROWAVE Bridge solution. This uses microwave equipment made by M/A-Com, Inc. This solution only works if there is a line-of-site link between the buildings that is 4.5 miles or less.

The limiting factor in the extended Ethernet is the ability of the bridge to monitor two separate Ethernets and then rebroadcast the packet. A high level of traffic destinated for the other Ethernet can saturate the bridge buffer space and lead to undelivered traffic. Since Ethernet does not assure delivery of data, the transport layer would eventually detect that it had not received a segment and ask for retransmission. The retransmission can lead to an increase in the amount of traffic on an already saturated bridge.

Buffer overflows are not usually a problem for local and fiber bridges. These devices are often able to filter packets and forward them as fast as any incoming traffic. The LAN Bridge 100, for example, can filter packets at a rate of 24,200 packets per second, and can forward packets at rates of 13,000 packets per second. Wide area bridges, discussed in the next chapter, have significantly lower packet-forwarding rates because of the lower bandwidth of the connections involved.

Bridges tend to be used in two kinds of situations. One is to isolate a work group, often consisting of diskless nodes that do all I/O operations over the Ethernet. The other is to connect two separately administered, often very large, networks together. Often the networks are connected together using bridges that support a common carrier link over fairly long distances.

Often, it is not really necessary to have a bridge between two Ethernets. If the amount of traffic is relatively small or occurs only in off-peak hours, a router connected to two different Ethernets is a possible solution. This router can be a MicroVAX or VAX configured as a DNA routing node.

Servers

In the arcane study of economics, there is an even more arcane principle that states that global optimization within a single system will not produce a locally optimal solution for any part of that system. This principle can be easily applied to computers. A single VAX cannot be optimized for multiple types of applications. This is because a single application has a set of operating characteristics, such as the dynamic nature of memory requirements or the pattern of user input. A VAX, especially with the VMS operating system, has a great number of parameters that allow the system to be tuned to a particular set of operating characteristics. Tuning for any one application will thus not be optimal for other applications.

The solution to the problem of global optimization is to distribute processing on special-purpose computers. An obvious example is the problem of terminal users. When terminals are connected directly to a VAX, a great deal of VAX CPU cycles are spent echoing characters onto user screens, polling for user input, and other maintenance tasks. This means that the VAX CPU cycles are unavailable for the intended purpose, such as inverting matrices or making hyphenation decisions.

DECnet and other architectures such as LAT provide a layer of transparency allowing multiple computers to cooperate to produce services for users. Servers are dedicated computers that participate in these networking protocols and are optimized for a particular task. This doesn't mean that the hardware manufacturer had to modify circuit boards for particular functions. A general-purpose computer, such as a MicroVAX II, can easily be tuned for specific types of functions and become a dedicated server.

Terminal servers

Terminal servers use the LAT architecture that was previously discussed in Chapter 4. The LAT architecture is a set of protocols that are optimized for transmitting many relatively short packets over an Ethernet. Because all nodes are on the Ethernet, there is no need for a routing layer. Transport and session functions are all folded into the general-purpose LAT architecture.

Terminal servers are devices that implement the LAT architecture. It should be noted that LAT is not the only way to provide this service over the network—other terminal servers have been designed to use TCP/IP or XNS protocols. LAT just happens to have been developed by DEC, so DEC terminal servers use it.

The DECserver 200 is a low-cost terminal server with eight ports. A special version of the DECserver 200 has modem control, allowing the terminal server to terminate a session when the user hangs up the phone from a remote site. Without modem control, the session stays in place, including a virtual circuit to a host. The next user that is connected to that modem port is automatically passed through to an existing session on a host without having to log in. Needless to say, this is not optimal from a security standpoint.

The DECserver 500 is a server that can be configured with up to 128 ports. The server can have up to eight interface cards. A CXY08 interface card has eight RS-232-C ports on it. If all eight of the slots

Courtesy of Digital Equipment Corporation

Fig 6-13   DECserver 500 with two slots open.

Courtesy of Digital Equipment Corporation

Fig. 6-14   Assembled DECserver 500.

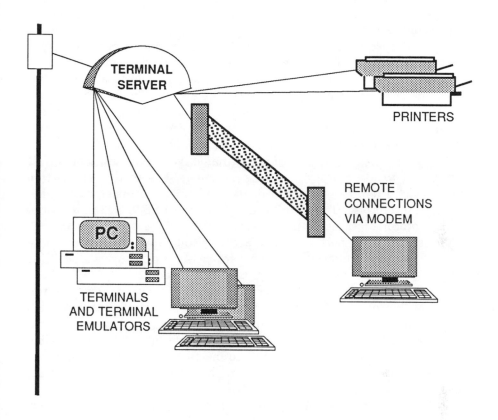

TERMINAL
SERVER

PRINTERS

REMOTE
CONNECTIONS
VIA MODEM

TERMINALS
AND TERMINAL
EMULATORS

PC

Fig. 6-15 Different devices on a terminal server.

on the server are filled with CXY08 cards, the server can accommodate 64 ports. Figures 6-13 and 6-14 show a DECserver 500 with different line cards.

A second interface card is the CXA16. This consists of 16 DEC423 ports per card. If all cards on the DECserver are CXA16s, the server has 128 ports on it. A third interface card is the CXB16 which consists of 16 RS-422-A ports. All three types of interface cards can be mixed on the same server.

Each port on the terminal server is in one of four modes. First, the port can be disabled. Second, it can be in local mode, meaning that the initiating user of a session will be a locally connected terminal (or a modem). The third connection option is remote, meaning that the user will come from a LAT host. An example of this is attaching a printer to the port in which case the remote user will be a special print symbiont.

The last port configuration option is dynamic and is able to flip between local and remote modes. This option is used when a modem is attached to the terminal server. The modem is able to accept either incoming or outgoing calls. Incoming calls are local mode—the session is initiated from the port side of the server. Outgoing calls are remote—the session initiated from the Ethernet side of the server. Figure 6-15 shows the different uses of a terminal server.

When a printer is used on the terminal server, there must be a host configured to use this printer. Users queue jobs to this supporting host, which then uses a special print symbiont to transfer data using the LAT protocols. This is different from the LPS40 which uses the DNA protocols to transmit print data.

The server print port is able to accept print requests from multiple hosts. Only one connection can be active simultaneously. Incoming connect requests from hosts are queued at the server.

When users connect to the terminal server, they are usually unaware of the concept of ports. Instead, they look for services they wish to connect to. When they log onto a terminal server, they are given a list of all services they are authorized to know about. It is possible that the LAT server can make the connection to the service but that the user does not have an account on that system and is refused access.

Services are usually VAX systems. If the service is a VAX Cluster, the user is logged onto the cluster node that has the best service rating. It is also possible to have nonclustered nodes all offering the same service. An example is configuring several small MicroVAX systems as dial-out service providers.

In order to offer a service, the host must provide LAT support. Because of that, terminal server users are unable to connect directly to a DECnet X.25 Gateway, a DECnet Router, or a DECnet SNA Gateway. That is because these nodes all speak DNA and not LAT. The services of an intermediary host that speaks both languages must be employed.

Other services may be offered by the terminal server itself. These services are advertised just like host-based services and become part of the directory listing on each terminal server. A host may consist of a single port, or a group of ports all offering the same service and configured as a rotary.

Another use of remote mode is to allow the VMS host to get access to external resources. One example of this is dial-out access. A

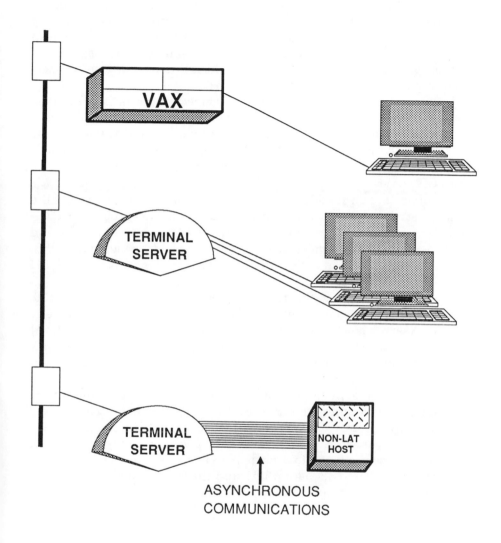

Fig. 6-16 Using terminal servers for foreign hosts.

second use is to configure the ports for reverse LAT capability. If a host is on the network but does not support DNA (or some other common Ethernet protocol such as TCP/IP or XNS), the VAX and the foreign host do not share a common language.

Most hosts are able to accept asynchronous terminal access. Reverse LAT capabilities mean that the asynchronous ports on the foreign host are all connected to terminal server ports. The LAT host is then able to set up a connection to that terminal server port, which is then passed through to the host as though it were a local connection. Figure 6-16 illustrates this configuration.

The use of terminal server ports to connect to hosts is a common way to integrate dissimilar networking environments. If one terminal server speaks one language (say TCP/IP) and another server speaks LAT, the Ethernet consists of two dissimilar environments. The LAT hosts can speak to the LAT servers, and the TCP hosts can speak to the TCP servers.

By connecting an RS-232 cable between a port on each server, there is at least the ability to log into a remote system. From there, file transfer protocols such as Kermit can be used to pass data back and forth. While this provides a minimum level of connectivity, it of course does not provide the full functionality of network-based file transfer protocols.

A special instance of the terminal server is the MUXserver 100. This device is designed to support remote access to terminal servers. The MUXserver is a combination of the DECserver 100 and the DFM Series multiplexers. The remote user configures a DECMUX II with up to eight lines and then uses a leased line or a null modem to connect to the MUXserver.

If the MUXserver is not optimal, because of the 16 port limitation, for example, it is quite simple to configure a similar system. Users can configure a rotary of ports on a DECserver 500 for incoming calls. A multiplexer, made by DEC or by another vendor, is then connected to each of those ports and to a modem. The modem connects to a peer modem over a leased or dial-up line and the remote modem is in turn connected to another multiplexer.

Print servers

Print services in a LAN environment are usually accomplished in three different ways. First, individual workstations or hosts may have printers attached to them. Each individual node is responsible for managing the queue on its own printer. With the Distributed Queuing Service discussed in Chapter 2, it is possible to integrate all these separate queues into a common printing environment.

The other two methods of providing printing services are through dedicated print servers and by attaching printers to a terminal server.

Attaching a printer to a terminal server was discussed previously and uses the remote port configuration option of the terminal server.

A dedicated print server attaches to the Ethernet, just as a terminal server or a host does. The server thus off-loads much of the print management tasks from host computers and allows an expensive high-speed laser printer to be shared among many users. DEC's LPS40 is a 40-page-per-minute laser printer. The LPS40 includes an Ethernet controller and DNA software. Like other servers, it requires a Phase IV host for downloading the initial software. The MOP protocols are used for the initial downline load operation.

The supporting host has a copy of the VAX PrintServer 40 Supporting Host Software. There can be only one host active for each laser printer, although a single host can manage multiple LPS printers. The Supporting Host Software consists of two pieces. The downloadable image is used to initialize the printer. The second software component is management software. The management software is used to activate and deactivate functions such as new job acceptance by the printer, to abort jobs, and to control event logging. Event logging includes the numbers of copies printed by job.

A variety of status commands is also provided by the management function. Unprivileged users can query the print server status and characteristics. They can also, see which jobs are currently queued and the characteristics of currently active jobs.

Hosts that wish to use the services of the LPS40 each need to have installed PrintServer 40 Client Software. This includes a print symbiont which is able to accept requests from multiple queues. The client software also includes software that can establish a DNA connection to the printer.

A single LPS40 is able to accept requests from up to 16 clients. Only one connection is active at any one time, the others being queued up. It is also possible for a single instance of the client software to dispatch requests to multiple print servers.

The LPS40 is only able to accept PostScript input. The client software includes three translators that allow incoming data streams to be in non-PostScript format. ANSI text, ReGIS graphics, and Tektronix 4010/4014 data streams can all be translated into Post-Script. By allowing the client software to perform the translation, the applications software, such as a word processing program, does not have to be reinstalled.

The symbiont which is part of the client software has several parameters available that are peculiar to the LPS environment. First, because this is Ethernet based, the print symbiont supplements the normal accounting information of the number of sheets per job with an indicator of the number of QIO writes over the network per job.

The symbiont is also able to accept parameters that specify the location of a PostScript initialization file. These PostScript preambles are used by many software environments to customize the PostScript environment for their particular needs.

Ethernet-based output servers are becoming increasingly common. Versatec, for example, manufacturers a TCP/IP based Ethernet plot server. Another TCP/IP based print server is the ImageServer XP series from Imagen. These are 20 page per minute laser printers with 5 Mbytes of RAM and a 20-Mbyte hard disk. They use an Excelan TCP/IP Ethernet interface but are also able to accept other connection methods such as RS-232.

Communications servers

Communications servers provide a link to a wide area environment. Examples of communications servers are DNA routers that extend DNA communications from the Ethernet into a wide area environment. This link could be a simple DDCMP link between two VAXs or a more sophisticated network.

This topic is considered more fully in the next chapter on wide area networks.

Compute servers

It's important not to forget the most general type of server, the general-purpose computer! Distributed processing environments, as we have seen, consist of a series of increasingly specialized servers. Terminal servers and print servers are two examples. It is also possible to take a general-purpose computer, such as a VAX or a Sun Workstation, and turn it into a dedicated database server or graphics server or modeling server or any other compute-intensive activity.

General-purpose compute servers can be as simple as a diskless MicroVAX that is used to perform some compute-intensive task. Or it can be a fully configured VAX Cluster with memory, CPUs, and disk resources all offered in a balanced configuration.

An example of the compute server concept is the database management software sold by SyBase. Many of the developers of SyBase also developed the Britton Lee database machine, the IDM 500. The IDM 500 was a special-purpose piece of hardware that was optimized for relational operations. SyBase, by contrast, takes a general-purpose computer and dedicates it to database functions, achieving very high rates of transactions processing. This database server can be as small as a MicroVAX or Sun Workstation or as powerful as a large scale Pyramid or VAX processor.

High-speed, well-integrated networks allow many computers to be distributed throughout the network and dedicated to specific tasks. By dedicating a computer to a specific task, it is possible to optimize the operating system for that task. Operating systems like VMS are capable of being tuned to the specific characteristics of a particular program. Since different programs have different characteristics, dedicating resources allows more careful tuning of the operating system. The network then allows users to treat all these different resources as a single logical computing environment.

Integration of Personal Workstations

A terminal can be thought of as a personal workstation, but only in a very limited sense. Even if the workstation is a PC emulating a terminal, the device is not able to fully participate in the network. This means, for example, that it requires extra steps to transfer a file from a VAX to a PC hard disk. Usually, this requires establishing a terminal session, followed by invoking a file transfer program such as Kermit or Xmodem on each of the two nodes involved.

A PC can alternatively participate fully in a DECnet as a Phase IV end node. This means that the copy operation can be as simple as typing COPY. The PC on an Ethernet is also able to take advantage of the 10-mbps bandwidth instead of the 19.2-kbps typical maximum for a terminal or terminal emulator.

More sophisticated workstations, such as a VAXstation or Sun Workstation, can also be integrated into the network. The multitasking nature of these workstations means that multiple network operations can proceed concurrently. This does not necessarily mean that the user is functioning in "whirling dervish mode." One task might be a user-initiated remote log-in to another node on the network. Another simultaneous network task would be receiving electronic mail. In this case, the network is automatically used by the workstation. In contrast, the PC user must have mail received on a VAX because of the single-tasking nature of the MS-DOS operating system.

IBM PC integration

There are four general ways that two foreign devices such as a DEC VAX and an IBM-compatible PC can be integrated together. First, the PC and the VAX can participate in the same networking environment. An example of this is to have the PC run DECnet-DOS and the VAX run DECnet-VMS. Integration is fairly simple because the two nodes confirm to the same architectures.

A second way is to have the VAX participate in the PC-based networking scheme. An example of this is connecting a VAX to a PC network such as Novell Net using a token ring or Ethernet adapter. The VAX then provides print services, file services, and other facilities to the Novell Net participants. The equivalent services would be provided in the DNA environment using VMS Services for DOS.

A third way is to not use the network but instead to use an asynchronous connection and emulate a terminal. It is possible for a PC to be connected to an IBM token ring and to also have a serial port or modem to connect to a VAX. Most PC/XT or PC/AT systems are not able to simultaneously keep a terminal emulator and networking software active at the same time. Often, the user must reboot the system to switch services.

A fourth solution, if it existed, would be to gateway the two networking environments together. This is possible for DNA and SNA and other combinations such as DNA and TCP/IP. This method is not available between the PC-based networking environments such as IBM Token Ring, Novell, and 3COM, and the DNA environment.

PC integration into the DNA environment can be accomplished using either DEC's DECnet-DOS software or Technology Concepts' CommUnity-DOS. DECnet-DOS uses DEC Ethernet controllers and a few others on a supported equipment list. CommmUnity-DOS uses the EXOS 205 adapter from Excelan.

DEC DOS solutions

DECnet-DOS is part of the DEC's Personal Computing Systems Architecture (PCSA). This consists of DECnet as well as menu and command-driven user interfaces to access the network. Two data access programs, NFT and FAL, are also available as applications in an MS Windows environment.

VAX systems are able to offer virtual disk services for the DECnet nodes using a software package called VMS Services for MS-DOS. The VAX can also offer CTERM- and DAP-based services to the PC. A more detailed discussion of the DECnet-DOS implementation is contained in Chapter 8.

In addition to DECnet, the PC software from DEC includes a VT200 emulator for use in wide area scenarios and a LAT virtual terminal service. The LAT service allows users to have terminal service features such as load balancing and directory listings.

Polygon and several other vendors also offer LAT terminal emulators for PC systems. Polygon allows the LAT terminal emulator to be Ethernet based. It is also possible to connect PCs to a VAX simply as a terminal emulator, either on a terminal server or on a VAX asynchronous communications port.

CommUnity-DOS

CommUnity-DOS provides the basic Phase IV end node functions. This includes the virtual terminal capability, file transfer, task to task communications, and local management. Like other versions of DOS-based DNA, this does not let the PC offer files to other users. Only client-based DAP services are supported.

Built on top of the task-to-task interface on CommUnity-DOS is a virtual disk utility. The virtual disk utility allows user to store files on an F: directory on their PC. The BIOS calls for the F: disk are intercepted and turned into network-based data access instead.

Apple Macintosh integration

Apple Macintosh systems can participate in three different networking environments. Macintosh systems can be DNA end nodes using DECnet implementations from Technology Concepts or from Alisa Systems. Apple systems can also participate in a TCP/IP environment. Finally, the Macintosh can be part of an AppleTalk environment. Of course, there are many other options available such as the TOPS network from Sun or TCP/IP.

An AppleTalk network consists of a 230 kbps network to which computers and printers are connected. This AppleTalk network can be connected to a TCP/IP Ethernet using the FastPath bridge from Kinetics. Macintoshes can also be directly connected to the TCP/IP Ethernet using an Excelan EtherPort controller.

Once the connection to the Ethernet is made, a VAX can provide services using AlisaTalk software for VMS. This software provides a virtual AppleBus (a single segment of an AppleTalk network) which runs under VMS. The VAX is able to offer file services, print spoolers, and virtual terminal access to the rest of the DECnet. Several other vendors offer similar packages.

Terminal emulation can be provided over a variety of connection methods using the MAC240 package from White Pine Software. This includes a utility which can convert MacDraw and MacPaint images into the DEC-compatible ReGIS and SIXEL formats. ReGis is object-oriented and is used for drawings, while SIXEL is a bit-map oriented format used for paintings. Again, several other vendors offer similar packages.

A variety of applications development tools are able to use the services of the VAX to provide a Macintosh oriented user interface. An example of this is CL/1, which was developed by Network Innovations, an Apple subsidiary. This software is an applications development language that allows Macintosh applications developers to access a variety of different data stores such as commercial database systems or RMS files on a VAX.

Network terminals

Although a VAXstation can operate as a multitasking set of protocols, the network services examined in DNA are oriented around a single user on each end. There is no provision for multiple processes to all share a bit-mapped graphics screen. Instead, a single window is opened for each terminal session on the network.

The last part of this book discusses the X Windows protocols that allow multiple applications to share the real estate on a bit-mapped graphics screen. This means that a new window can be opened by the application and that applications can communicate with each other. A database server, for example, might be programmed to send data to a word processing program, which then opens a window to display a formatted document.

With the X Windows System, and an underlying transport mechanism such as DECnet, it is not necessary for each user to have a personal workstation. The workstation is a general-purpose computer that happens to be used as the user interface. Instead, a special-purpose piece of equipment, known as a network terminal, can be put on the users' desks and all computing resources are distributed throughout the network. This network terminal has DECnet (or OSI or TCP/IP) and the X Windows protocols and relies on the network for other resources.

The advantage of the network terminal is very simple. A dedicated piece of hardware like this can be made more cheaply than a general purpose computer system such as a VAX. Since DEC, Sun, and many other vendors have endorsed a common set of protocols including the X Windows System and OSI, the network terminal can be used in any of these computing environments.

There are several vendors that are beginning to specialize in X-compatible terminals. There is some question as to whether these terminals will be able to displace more general-purpose workstations, such as a VAXstation, Sun Workstation, or IBM PS/2 system.

Facilities wiring: DECconnect

The planning of facilities wiring is a crucial aspect of a network's ability to grow in a steady, modular fashion. Poor planning can lead to long delays because of the necessity of tearing up a building to lay new cables.

Several strategies are available, including some formalized ones such as AT&T's Premise Distribution System, IBM's Cabling System, and DEC's DECconnect. All of these strategies provide a method of wiring a facility at one time and then adding nodes to a network without extensive rewiring.

No single methodology is able to meet every situation. It is important to examine a particular facility and mold the wiring strategy to meet the special needs of that environment. A well-planned wiring plan allows for cost-effective wiring and for modular growth of nodes on the network.

Most wiring strategies consist of a mix of different physical media. Some media, such as ThinWire, is cheap and flexible. However, ThinWire is only recommended for horizontal distribution and not as a backbone in places like elevator shafts. In those places, ThickWire or broadband might be more appropriate.

DECconnect is DEC's recommended way to wire buildings for Ethernet-based networks. Like the IBM Cabling System, this is simply one company's view of the proper way to distribute cables in large buildings. Several alternatives strategies are available and may be better suited to particular applications.

DECconnect uses a series of satellite equipment rooms (SER) as distribution points to individual offices. The SERs and the main computing area are all connected together with a baseband Ethernet backbone. Also terminating in the SER are video and voice facilities.

Fig. 6-17   A DECconnect satellite equipment room.

A series of four cables is strung from each office to the SER. Two twisted pair connects are strung, which can be used for terminals, phones, or unshielded twisted pair Ethernet connections. A CATV cable is strung for video and a ThinWire coax cable is strung for workstations and other Ethernet nodes.

Each office then has a faceplate which can accommodate up to four connections consisting of video, voice, terminals, and workstations. The ThinWire port is really the end point of a ThinWire segment. Several ThinWire nodes could be connected to this faceplate, as long as parameters such as maximum cable length, node separation, and number of nodes are not violated. Figure 6-17 and 6-18 show a SER and the standard faceplate.

The SER itself consists of two racks. One rack holds equipment. Typically, this is one DELNI that connects to the backbone cable that

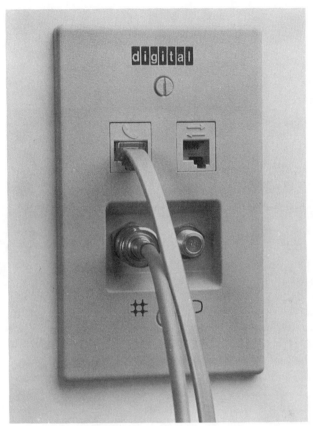

Fig. 6-18 DECConnect face plate.

passes through the SER. The DELNI is then connected to a series of terminal servers and multiport repeaters (DEMPR).

The equipment rack thus serves as a distribution point from the Ethernet backbone. Next to the equipment rack is a patching rack. On the right side of the patching rack is where all the wiring to the offices terminates. On the left side are all the wires leading to the terminal servers and multiport repeaters.

When a user moves into an office, a patch is put in place to connect the users' equipment to a port of the equipment rack. Since all the wiring is done in advance, it becomes easy to connect new users.

The number of users a single SER can support depends greatly on the users' proximity to the SER. The typical SER can support 48 to 64 faceplate connections. Up to 80 connections can be patched in and active at any one time. Needless to say, these DEC-furnished guidelines do not illustrate any physical limitations but are simply advisory.

The DECconnect system is one of several strategies that can be pursued. As can be seen, DECconnect places heavy reliance on the use of DEMPR and ThinWire coax cable, and it is appropriate for most office environments. Other organizations, such as a manufacturing environment with a lot of electrical noise, may wish to base their network strictly on ThickWire. This is because ThickWire, with its larger shielding, is more resistant to outside noise. Fiber or broadband is another possibility for this type of environment.

It should be noted that electrical noise, known as electromagnetic interference (EMI) is rarely a serious problem in most environments. EMI is measured in volts per meter (v/m). ThinWire Ethernet is able to function in environments with EMI ratings as high as 1 v/m. Broadband and ThickWire are able to withstand 5 v/m. A DEC field survey of a variety of industrial networking sites found that even the most exceptional sources of EMI, such as a printing press or other heavy industrial equipment, rarely produced more than 0.013 v/m.

An alternative to placing terminal servers in satellite equipment rooms is to use another form of front-end network as a switching device. The terminal servers are stored in the machine room, and a data PBX is used to switch terminals in an office to a port on the PBX.

Other Media Access Control Options

DEC, one of the pioneers of Ethernet, has chosen to emphasize that type of LAN to the exclusion of others. Token ring and token bus systems are alternatives to Ethernet. DEC has endorsed the token bus for use in MAP networks and the token ring for use in FDDI backbones.

Ethernet serves as a good general purpose LAN protocol but has some limitations for real-time applications. As the number of nodes increases, so does the probability of a collision. There is also an increase in the amount of noise introduced onto the medium by each Ethernet adapter. Despite these problems, the CSMA/CD protocols scale well with the number of nodes on the network. It is not unusual to find an Ethernet with 60 hosts and only 4 percent utilization.

Because of collision detection, CSMA/CD protocols don't scale well with distance, transmission rate, and minimum packet size. All three factors contribute to the amount of time that a packet is active on the Ethernet. If the packet does not reside on the network for a minimum time, a node might not detect a collision with a packet it sent.

An alternative technology to Ethernet is the token bus. A token bus is used for MAP networks using broadband physical media. The token bus scales well with distance. However, as the number of nodes increases, so does the amount of time spent passing the token around. This limits the number of nodes in a token bus.

The last data link protocol used is a token ring. In an IEEE 802.5 token ring, a node does not release its token until the previous data it has sent has gone all the away around the ring. This limits the distance that a token ring can have.

IEEE 802.5 token ring

The token ring standard uses twisted pair wires, like those used in a telephone system, as a physical medium. These networks operate at speeds of 1, 4, or 16 mbps.

Each node on a ring has two neighbors to which it is connected. When the ring is initialized, a token is passed around. Each node that receives a token copies the data to its neighbor on the other side. All data is thus received at one node, copied and sent along to the next node.

If a node has data to send on the ring, it waits until it receives the token. It then fails to send the token back out, thus claiming it. This node can then send a data frame. The frame is copied around the ring. The destination address for that frame makes a copy for itself and then sends it back out into the ring. The sending node receives the frame back, checks it for errors, and then sends the token back out into the ring.

Most implementations of the token ring protocols are centered around IBM PCs and compatibles. Novell and 3Com, for example, both offer PC-based token ring networking products. As of the writing of this manuscript, DEC had not announced any support for IEEE 802.5 token ring networks as a data link layer of DECnet.

Incorporation of token ring as a data link layer of DECnet would allow a large homogeneous network. This would be useful because in many corporations individual departments make individual purchasing decisions on departmental networks. Later, there is an attempt to integrate these disparate systems into a single coherent network.

There are several alternatives that provide different levels of connectivity. An inelegant solution is to connect PCs to both a token ring and an Ethernet. A computer such as a PC/AT would have to reboot when choosing between the two environments and only one environment could be active at a time.

Another solution is to connect a VAX to both a token ring and a DECnet/Ethernet. The VAX would have a token ring adapter and provide virtual disk and file services to the PC network. That VAX could also serve as a gateway to the larger DECnet environment. Both 3Com and Novell provide these types of solutions.

FDDI token ring

The Fiber Distributed Data Interface is a standard developed by the ANSI committee. FDDI uses the same token passing concepts that the IEEE 802.5 standard does. However, FDDI operates at a speed of 100 mbps and has several other characteristics that make it suitable as a high-bandwidth data backbone.

The first difference between FDDI and the IEEE token ring is that FDDI sends the token out immediately after transmitting the frame. This allows the medium to be used to capacity instead of requiring the original data to circle the ring completely before sending the token out again.

A second major difference between FDDI and the IEEE token ring is the FDDI capacity management scheme. An FDDI frame has a maximum size of 4500 bytes. FDDI allows single frames (asynchronous mode) or a series of frames (synchronous mode) to be transmitted.

The nodes on an FDDI network agree on a target token rotation time (TTRT). This number is the amount of time, on average, that should pass before a node on the network sees a token again. Note that although the TTRT is a measure of expected delay, it also serves as a measure of the number of bits that can be transmitted during that delay and thus serves as a measure of capacity. The TTRT thus serves as a limit on how much data any one node may transmit at one time.

Setting the TTRT is usually done when the network intializes. Each node transmits a continuous stream of CLAIM frames that contains its target TTRT. If a node notices that the neighbor it receives tokens from has a lower claimed TTRT, it defers to that neighbor. Eventually, every node will defer to the one with the lowest TTRT.

To begin with, all the capacity on an FDDI network is allocated to asynchronous mode. If a node wishes to transmit synchronous data (multiple frames to a single destination), it requests a synchronous allotment using a Station Management Protocol. The sum of these synchronous allotments must be less than the TTRT.

When a node receives the token, it may transmit synchronously for the time of its synchronous allotment. It may then transmit

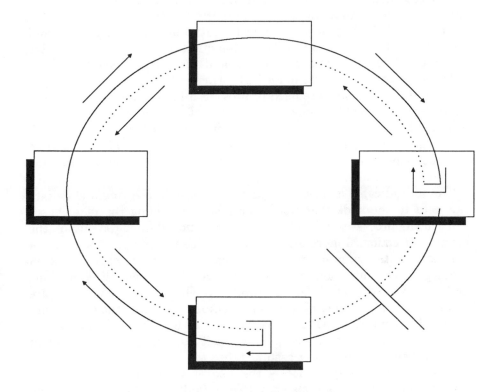

Fig. 6-19 Dual cable FDDI token ring operation.

asynchronously so long as the next node still sees a token within the TTRT period.

Asynchronous data is put into eight different priority levels. Data of each priority has a parameter for the amount of data that can be sent. Typically, small amounts of high-priority data might be sent followed by larger amounts of lower-priority data for user applications. Finally, the timer would expire and the node would have to give up the token.

To establish a high-bandwidth dialog with a partner, there is a special form of token called the restricted token. Only the partner of a particular node can grab the restricted token, thus allowing request-response traffic on the network. The asynchronous bandwidth of the capacity can be used for restricted transfer.

At the physical layer, FDDI is based on optical fiber. A single piece of fiber can be used to form a ring between all nodes on the FDDI network. A second piece of cable can be used for increased reliability on selected nodes. Class B stations are connected only to the primary cable, whereas class A stations are connected to both.

Because of the high capacity and low attenuation of fiber, the total path of the fiber ring can be 200 kilometers (km). The distance between any two nodes can be 2 km without the use of repeaters. Up to 1000 nodes can participate in an FDDI ring.

Several mechanisms are used to provide a high degree of reliability. First, the dual cables provide a degree of reliability (assuming, of course, that you put your cables on different paths). Normally, all traffic goes on the primary cable. If the there is a break in the ring, the node closest to the break will loop data back in the other direction on the second cable.

The second cable is used to bypass the break in the ring and deliver the data to the node that would have been receiving the token next. That node processes all data and then sends data back out in the original direction. Figure 6-19 illustrates this process.

Breaks in the ring are detected using a BEACON message. BEACON messages are sent when no data is received for a long period of time, or if a claim arbitration fails to resolve itself. BEACON messages are always copied by receiving nodes immediately, even if they were continuously sending CLAIM messages. A node can expect to see a BEACON message back fairly quickly. If it doesn't see the message at the other side of the ring, it assumes that the cable is broken.

A second reliability device is the use of wiring concentrators. A wiring concentrator is somewhat like a multiport transceiver on an Ethernet. One or several devices can be connected to the concentrator. Usually, the devices are Class B devices, whereas the concentrator can be a Class A device.

Finally, bad stations on an FDDI ring can be circumvented by using an optical bypass switch. This means that a station that is powered off or malfunctioning doesn't bring the whole network down by causing a break in the ring.

FDDI has been endorsed by several vendors, including DEC, for use as a backbone network. Most nodes would be connected to an Ethernet system, in the DEC scheme of things. Routers or bridges would then be used to connect FDDI and Ethernet-based systems. Of course, there is no reason why FDDI can't also serve as a backbone for SNA and token ring networks as well as Ethernets.

Token Bus: Hyperchannel and MAP

A token bus is usually implemented on a broadband physical medium. Instead of a ring technology, the token and data are broadcast on a broadband cable, much like Ethernet packets are broadcast on a broadband cable. In contrast to the random access nature of the Ethernet, however, the token bus technology allows a node to transmit only when in possession of the token.

Hyperchannel is a 50 to 80-mbps token bus implementation used in environments with high-bandwidth data transfer requirements. Often, Cray supercomputers are connected to a Hyperchannel network along with series of VAXs that serve as front-end processors for the Cray. The case study of the San Diego Supercomputer Center in the next chapter illustrates such an application.

A second application of token bus technology is in manufacturing environments that use the MAP protocol suite to direct the activities of robots and intelligent programmable controllers. The MAP protocol suite is discussed in more detail in Chapter 12 on the OSI upper-layer services.

Summary

This chapter discussed a variety of different methods of configuring Ethernet networks, ranging from single segment to multisegment to extended Ethernets. All of these different configurations appear to the routing layer or other data link service user as a single logical bus. The next chapter discusses technologies that serve the same purpose in a wide-area environment: ISDN and X.25.

Ethernets allow multiple devices to be connected to a single system at high speeds. Because of this functionality, as well as the upper-layer users of the Ethernet, it is possible to distribute processing among multiple computers. Terminal, database, communications, and compute servers all participate in the network. This approach permits specialized computers to be added to the network in a modular fashion without necessarily affecting the view of the network that the user sees. In fact, with the LAT protocols, the users don't see computers—they see services.

For Further Reading

Digital Equipment Corporation, "DECconnect System Requirements Evaluation Workbook," EK-DECSY-EG-002, September 1987.

——, "DECconnect System General Description," EK-DECSY-GD-001, January 1986.

——, "DECconnect System, Planning and Configuration Guide," EK-DECSY-CG-001, April 1986

——, "Network and Communications Buyers Guide," quarterly publication.

Cooper, Edward, "Broadband Network Technology," Prentice Hall, Englewood Cliffs, NJ, 1986.

Hawe, et al., "The Extended Local Area Network Architecture and LANBridge 100," *Digital Technical Journal*, vol. 1, no. 3, September 1986, p. 54.

Mann, et al., "Terminal Servers on Ethernet Local Area Networks," *Digital Technical Journal*, vol. 1, no. 3, September 1986, p. 73.

Stallings, et al., *Handbook of Computer-Communications Standards: Local Network Standards*, Macmillan Books, New York, 1988.

7

Wide Area Networks

Overview of Wide Area Networks

This chapter begins with a discussion of how to connect remote devices together using a dedicated point-to-point link. In the DEC environment, this link usually uses the DDCMP protocols. The link might be a remote terminal connected to a computer, two computers connected together, or two LANs connected together.

An alternative to using DDCMP for a point-to-point link is to use an extended Ethernet. The extended Ethernet uses the same bridge technology examined in the previous chapter, but it is extended to a wide area environment. The extended Ethernet, because it is protocol-transparent, can be used to carry non-DNA traffic such as LAT, TCP/IP, or any other user of the Ethernet.

The Ethernet is an example of a technology that makes every node appear to be a single hop away from the users of the Ethernet, such as the DNA routing layer. Another form of subnet is X.25. Internally, X.25 can be a complex topology, but the X.25 protocols mask this internal structure from the user of the subnet.

A third form of subnet is the Integrated Services Digital Network. ISDN is protocol independent to the extent of being able to carry voice, video, data, or any other form of information. Like X.25, the ISDN permits a virtual point-to-point link to be formed between two processors. Unlike X.25, ISDN is able to provide both circuit-switched and packet-switched bandwidth and greatly increased control over communications.

Point-to-Point Connections

Point-to-point connections can be as simple as two VAX systems connected with DDCMP lines or a terminal talking to a remote computer using a 300 bps modem. More sophisticated point-to-point connections are used to connect Ethernets together, using dedicated routers or extended Ethernets.

Original implementations of DECnets consisted exclusively of point-to-point connections. These point-to-point connections were used even in a local area networking environment. Increasingly, point-to-point connections are used as a method of connecting separate LANs together. Individual workstations are part of the LAN, and connected to the LAN is a dedicated server that processes internet communications.

Asynchronous connections

Asynchronous wide area links are used in two types of situations. First, they are used to connect remote asynchronous terminals to a terminal port. Second, they can be used to connect PCs to an Ethernet using the asychronous version of DDCMP.

Remote terminals (or a PC emulating a terminal) can be connected to any device that would normally have a locally connected RS-232 cable. Modems have been standardized and can use the services of the dial-up telephone network at speeds of up to 19.2 kbps. Several modem standards exist, however, so it is important that the modems on either end of a connection share a common set of protocols.

The remote end of the connection from the terminal, or terminal emulator, can be any device that would expect to see a terminal. This could be an asynchronous communications terminal on a VAX. It could also be a port of a terminal server. Either of the two ports would have a modem attached to it.

It is important that the host controller have modem control enabled on it. This allows the port to detect when the signal has been terminated. Otherwise, users will hang up the phone when they are done without properly logging out. This leaves an open session on the system which is taken over without authentication by the next user to reach that port. This is especially a problem when the discontinued session had high levels of privilege and the user was cut off because of some technical difficulty.

Asynchronous traffic, in the form of the DDCMP protocols in asynchronous mode, is also used to connect remote DECnet nodes together. This is frequently used for connecting a PC to a remote VAX for limited periods of time.

One of the features of DECnet/DOS is that it allows a port on an asynchronous communications controller on the VAX to dynamically switch over from being a terminal port to being a DDCMP data link port.

The VAX device driver has two pieces. One piece is the user-dependent part, known as a class driver. In this case, there is a terminal driver and a DECnet driver. The lower part of the device driver, known as a port driver, is the device-dependent part. In this case, this is an asynchronous communications controller.

The dynamic connection is established because the VAX has been programmed to detect a special escape sequence from the incoming terminal session. This signals the VAX to switch from using the terminal driver for that port to using the DNA driver instead.

Instead of a VAX, a dedicated asynchronous router may be used. DEC sells the DECrouter 200 which consist of eight asynchronous ports. The router also has an Ethernet connection. This allows eight direct connections or eight modems to be placed on the router. This also allows non-Ethernet PCs to participate in the DECnet environment. Of course, the line speed of each port on this DECrouter is only 19.2 kbps which is significantly less than the 10 mbps that is used for Ethernet-based PC systems.

The DECrouter 200 can participate on the Ethernet as a level 1 router and is even able to become the designated router on the Ethernet. In fact, it is possible to disable all eight serial ports and use the device strictly as an Ethernet router. In this case, the device is able to forward up to 600 packets per second.

With the lines enabled, the router usually is only able to forward less than 170 packets per second. This is an aggregate metric under optimistic loading conditions.

A DECrouter 200 can be connected to any form of Ethernet connection. It uses a standard transceiver cable and can be connected to an H4000 (baseband), DELNI (multiport transceiver), DESTA (ThinWire), or DECOM (broadband) transceiver.

The DECrouter is a full member of the DNA routing configuration, with support for out-of-order packet caching and path splitting. Path splitting allows a manager to configure two lines of the DECnet Router going to the same location with the same cost. DNA routing algorithms send packets down both paths (if they are both up), thus acting as a form of load balancing.

Often a VAX needs to provide outgoing asynchronous calls which are used to connect to online information services such as the Dow Jones News/Retrieval system. If modems are connected to a VAX, this

Courtesy of Digital Equipment Corporation

Fig. 7-1 Rackmounted DF100 modems.

can be accomplished using some VMS software from DEC called the VAX Public Access Communications.

This software works with the DF series of modems as well as the Hayes series made by Hayes Microcomputer Products, Inc. The software is able to register phone numbers and then autodial them for users. DF series modems from DEC can be rackmounted in a machine room environment (see Figure 7-1).

The software has built-in support for the Kermit protocols developed by Henson Associates, Inc., and distributed by Columbia University. Most online information services support downloading using Kermit as a file transfer protocol.

Public Access Communications is also able to support session logging, which can be enabled or disabled using a special hot key. The information logged can be sent directly to a printer or can be put into a file.

If several dial-out ports are available, the modems can be configured in a rotary, connecting the server to the next available port. The manager can restrict the use of connection features and can preconfigure numbers for users.

Later in this chapter, we will examine the use of the X.28 and X.29 protocols as an alternative to point-to-point connections between the host and the terminal. X.28 connects an asynchronous terminal to a Packet Assembler/Disassember on an X.25 packet switched network. The PAD then communicates using the X.29 protocols to a host also connected to the X.25 synchronous network.

It is possible to use Public Access Communications to allow a host to emulate a terminal. This is then fed into the local point of access for an X.25 network, such as Telenet or Tymnet, which passes the connection through to the remote end.

This strategy is often used as an alternative to placing long distance calls directly to online information services. Hosts are able to access their local point of access for the X.25 network which provides a cheaper way of connecting to these remote services.

Synchronous Connections

Point-to-point links between two VAXs are usually done with a synchronous form of DDCMP. This requires a synchronous communications controller in each VAX that supports the DDCMP protocols. These controllers are available from DEC as well as many other vendors. The controller needs to match the peripheral bus type of the VAX being configured. For example, a DMB-32 is a DEC controller that is BI-bus compatible and can thus be used on any of the 8000 series of VAX computers (See Fig. 7-2).

A DMB32 is a general-purpose synchronous device able to support different synchronous data link protocols. This controller can perform a many of the transmission, reception, and framing tasks of the data link layer as well as calculate the FCS. It is important to remember that any device controller will consume a portion of the CPU's resources. A DMB32 is able to process synchronous data at rates ranging from 4800 bps to 64 kbps.

Depending on the speed that the DMB32 is run at, it uses a portion of a VAX's resources. DEC has a metric called a load unit that is supposed to represent "average" use of resources. Each device operating at a certain speed represents a number of load units. A particular size VAX also has a capacity expressed in load units. For example, the DMB32 has the following load unit table:

DEVICE: DMB32

SPEED	4.8	9.6	19.2	48.0	64.0
LOAD UNITS	9	18	36	90	120

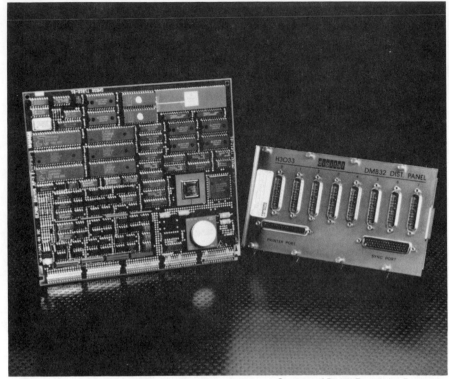

Courtesy of Digital Equipment Corporation

Fig. 7-2   A DMB32 and distribution panel.

A VAX 8250 has a maximum capacity of 125 load units, while an 8700 has a capacity of 700 units. Using this metric, only one 64 kbps processor could be used on an 8250 without using all the capacity.

It is important that this metric represents average packet sizes, average loads, and a variety of other averages. A true measurement of usage is very application specific and can usually only be measured based on historical data.

For MicroVAX systems, the DSV11 provides synchronous services analogous to the DMB32. The DSV11 is a general-purpose synchronous communications controller. It can be used for SNA connectivity using the SDLC protocols or X.25 connectivity using the LAP B data link protocols. In a DDCMP environment, the board can be configured to operate with a single line at 256 kbps, or two lines at 64 kbps.

It is not unusual to configure a MicroVAX as a dedicated routing node on an Ethernet. This configuration would have a DEQNA Ethernet adapter and a DSV11 DDCMP board. Ethernet nodes, such as

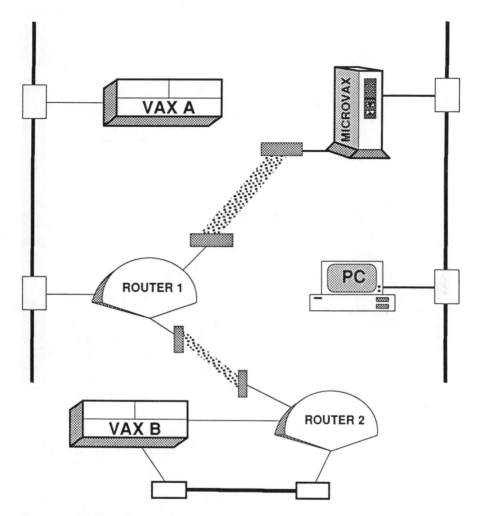

Fig. 7-3 Ethernet-based routers.

PCs or other VAXs, can then use the dedicated MicroVAX to reach other areas of the DECnet. The advantage of this approach over the dedicated gateway is that the MicroVAX can then be used for other functions. Figures 7-3 and 7-4 illustrate various routing configurations.

Synchronous terminal links

A second use of point-to-point links is for terminal traffic. When many terminals are all located at one site, it does not make sense to have a

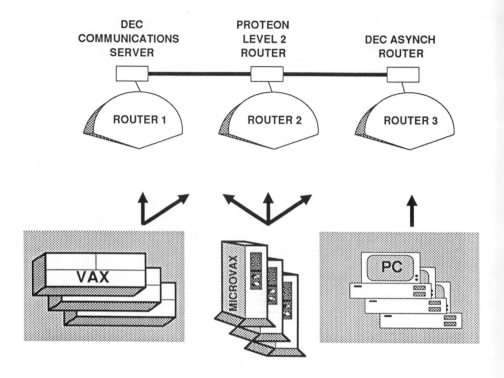

Fig. 7-4 Three types of routers.

separate dial-up line for each device. Instead, a multiplexer is used to concentrate all the traffic onto one line. This line might still be dial up, or it could be a leased line.

At the other end of the connection, another multiplexer demultiplexes the traffic back out into separate data streams. The lines are then fed into an asynchronous communications controller. It is possible for the multiplexer and the communications controller to be built into a single device.

An example of a combination of a multiplexer and an asynchronous communications controller is the MUXserver 100. The MUXserver 100 is a combination of a DEC DFM series multiplexer and a 16-port terminal server. Remote traffic is concentrated onto a DDCMP synchronous line and is then demuxed by the MUXserver 100.

Network-to-network connections

Dedicated routers are devices used to bridge a particular local area network to a wide area environment. The DECrouter 200 is an example of such a device which was able to provide an asynchronous DDCMP service. This is suitable for connecting a PC or MicroVAX to an Ethernet for occasional traffic.

For more demanding situations, synchronous routers are needed. The DEC Communications Server (DECSA) is an Ethernet-based device that is able to provide synchronous routing services (See Figure 7-5). The routing could be to another Ethernet or to a host that can support synchronous data transmission.

The DECSA communications server uses a modular approach. Up to 16 line cards can be put in the device. Aggregate throughput on the device is limited to 512 kbps. It could thus have a single 512 kbps V.35 connection or dual 256 kbps V.35 connections. Another option is 32 V.28 connections (2 per card), each operating at 19.2 kbps.

Protocol Assist Modules (PAMs) are used to boost the performance of synchronous line cards. A single PAM can support up to 16 line cards and there can up to 2 PAMs per DECSA.

The 512 kbps total throughput of the DECSA is a metric based on average data. Several factors can change these throughput estimates. First, the router can be configured as a level 1 or level 2 router. If configured as a level 2 router, aggregate throughput will be less than 500 kbps. Another factor is whether the DECSA functions as the designated router for an Ethernet segment.

A successor to the DECSA is the DECrouter 2000, also known as a MicroServer or DEMSA. While the DECSA is based on a PDP architecture, the DEMSA is based on the 32-bit MicroVAX II chip set. Like the DECSA, this same device can also be used for X.25 or SNA traffic. For SNA applications, the device must be dedicated. X.25 and DNA traffic, however, can be mixed on a single DEMSA processor.

While the DECSA is able to support packet-forwarding rates of 150 packets per second in a DNA environment, the DEMSA provides the potential for up to 1500 packets per second. Also, because it is based on the more general MicroVAX architecture, upgrades to communications functionality can be accomplished more easily.

The initial release of the DEMSA supports an aggregate bandwidth of 256 kbps links configured in any combination of one to four synchronous lines. There is no reason why this basic configuration

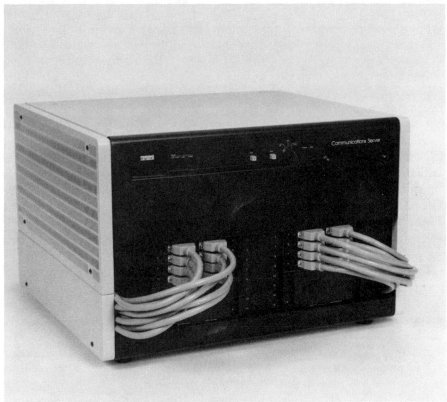

Courtesy of Digital Equipment Corporation

Fig. 7-5   A DEC communications server.

cannot be upgraded in successor models for higher bandwidths by sub-
stituting higher-performance communications controllers.

General purpose communications servers

The same DECSA communications server can be used for a variety of
purposes. The use of a single hardware platform as a general purpose
communications server is an important development. It allows the
network manager to add bandwidth and protocol suites as needed
using the same piece of hardware.

Many other vendors are also working to provide a general-purpose
communications utility. This allows a series of routers to form a
general-purpose communications backbone for many different types of
subnets. It would not be unreasonable to see the same MicroVAX II-

based system process and route data for different networking environments, such as X.25, SNA, TCP/IP, and DNA.

Another example of such a general-purpose communications utility is the Sun Microsystems SunLink product. SunLink is a synchronous communications utility that can downline load various protocol suites, including OSI, SNA, X.25, TCP/IP, MAP, and others. Because the protocols are stored in software and then downline loaded at run time, the same board can serve different users as needed.

What makes the SunLink products especially useful is that a Sun Workstation supports all three major upper-level protocols used on Ethernet: DNA, TCP/IP, and XNS. This one workstation is thus able to route through traffic on behalf of any local area users to any of the various wide area protocol suites that are supported.

A similar multipurpose solution is provided by the Proteon p4200 router series. These routers are able to connect to Ethernet systems as well as to 4-mbps token rings and their own proprietary 80-mbps token rings. All three subnetworks are then connected together with the p4200 router series.

In contrast to wide area bridges, the Proteon routers are able to accept routing information from upper-level protocol users. The same device, for example, is able to process Internet Protocol traffic at the same time as it processes DNA packets. Each packet is forwarded based on the network architecture that it uses.

There are a few limitations on these routing capabilities. For the TCP/IP environment, the routing update protocols are RIP for interior gateway protocols and EGP for the external protocol. For DNA, the p4200 series can only function as a level 2 router. This makes sense as both DNA level 2 and IP use static routing tables.

Many sites combine a variety of different types of equipment to form a flexible link between their LAN and wide area facilities. The different types of equipment have complementary capabilities and together are able to form a general-purpose routing interface.

Wide area bridges

An alternative to using routers for wide area communications is to use an extended Ethernet that supports wide area communications. Routers provide a great deal of control over forwarding decisions but do so at a performance cost. This is because each packet must be examined for all of the functions of the routing layer.

Bridges allow a packet to be forwarded at the data link layer. This allows the routing layer to treat the extended Ethernet as a single subnetwork in which every node is one hop away. Wide area bridges thus perform the same function as LAN-based bridges, but they extend that functionality to wide area links.

One of the most popular wide area bridges is the TransLAN device manufactured by Vitalink. DEC makes extensive use of Vitalink products, both internally and by remarketing the products. The basic TransLAN device consists of an Ethernet controller and a series of synchronous line interfaces.

The TransLAN device consists of a single Ethernet connection and eight wide area synchronous data links. Up to nine networks can thus be connected to a single bridge. This is a marked difference from the one-to-one connections supported by LAN bridges. Wide area bridges, because they are able to make routing decisions among multiple networks, introduce a new level of complexity. For this reason, these devices are called "brouters" in marketing-speak, signifying that the layer 2 bridges are able to make some layer 3 routing decisions.

The eight wide area links on the TransLAN can go to eight separate networks, or can provide multiple paths to a single network. By having multiple paths to a network, it is possible to provide redundancy in case of a line failure. Needless to say, it is recommended that the common carrier provider be instructed to route these two lines through different paths. Otherwise, a single backhoe can easily destroy any fault tolerance by destroying both the main and the alternate connection with one poorly placed trench. Remember, not everybody calls the telephone company before they dig.

Extended Ethernets allow connectivity, but at the expense of bandwidth. While a local bridge can supports speeds of 10 mbps, the wide area bridge is not usually connected at speeds of more than 1.544 mbps. Often, 19.2 or 56 kbps lines are used for the connection.

The implication of the significantly lower bandwidth is that extensive internet traffic can quickly swamp the buffers in a bridge. Vitalink provides a series of filtering mechanisms used to implement policies that segregate certain types of traffic to local networking environments.

Filters are set up on the basis of network groups. A network group consists of all lines from one bridge terminating in the same remote bridge. Filtering is accomplished when the packet is received, followed by the decision to route the packet among a particular line in a network group.

Filters are set up based on the packet contents. Usually, this consists of excluding traffic based on protocol types. It is also possible to establish filters based on incoming or outgoing addresses. Finally, arbitrary filters can be set up based on a template that examines arbitrary fields in the packet.

Filters are most commonly used as a method of including or excluding certain types of traffic from a certain network group. Filters can also be used as a method of measuring types of traffic. An additional filtering feature is the low-priority queue. If this option is selected, received traffic is put into a special queue. Only after the queue for normal priority traffic is forwarded is this queue sent.

An important feature of Vitalink bridges is that they are not necessarily limited to the Ethernet Media Access Control (MAC) protocols. Vitalink bridges exist for bridging token ring networks together. The IEEE MAC Bridge standard makes provisions for interconnecting different MAC layers together into a single extended LAN.

A multi-MAC LAN is only useful if the clients of the local area network speak the same network language. If, for example, TCP/IP is running in both environments, the multi-MAC LAN provides a significant level of connectivity.

Using an extended Ethernet for LAT traffic

One example of an extended Ethernet is DEC's Easynet network used for internal data communications. A more extensive study of Easynet is provided at the conclusion of this chapter.

Extended Ethernets are used by DEC in almost all of their sales regions as a way of connecting different subnetworks together. While the extended Ethernet could be used to carry DNA traffic, a policy decision has been to limit wide area extended Ethernet links to LAT traffic only.

This decision was based on control and performance considerations. Routers provide a higher level of control and security than a bridge. A parallel wide-area routing network is provided to carry DNA traffic.

The extended Ethernet serves as an extended terminal network. Figure 7-6 illustrates one of the extended Ethernets used by DEC in the mid-Atlantic region. A series of T1 and 56 kbps links are used to connect remote locations. In addition, the Washington area hub includes a variety of fiber-based bridges. Not shown on the diagram are a large number of local bridges. Also not shown is the parallel Easynet routing network for DNA traffic.

Performance is one of the major reasons for segregating traffic. The LAT protocols are designed to operate in a very short time frame, typically 80 ms. Most of the wide area bridge links provide a link of 56 kbps between different sites. If a DNA file transfer begins, it is easily possible for the bandwidth to be eaten up by DNA protocols, leading to late or undelivered LAT packets. This of course results in NAK mes-

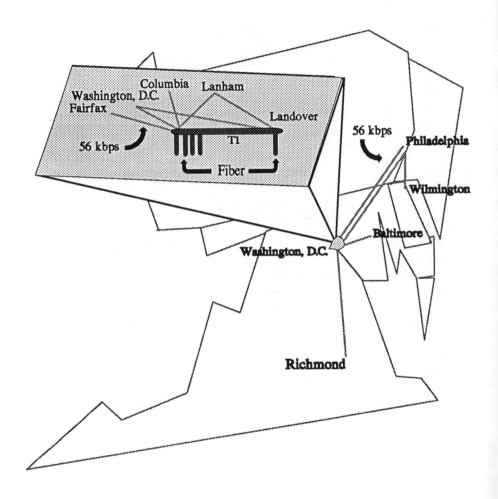

Figure 7-6   A DEC extended Ethernet used for LAT fraffic.

sages, which generate even more LAT traffic, which further aggravates the situation.

Using an extended Ethernet for general traffic

A more general use of extended Ethernets is provided in a network maintained by VLSI Technology, Inc., of San Jose, California. VLSI makes application-specific integrated circuits. These are custom made for clients and manufactured in small quantities.

VLSI maintains a series of design centers throughout the country, each of which is staffed by engineers and other design specialists who work with clients. Each design center consists of a variety of different workstations that use TCP/IP protocols. Design centers also have VAX computers and LAT-based terminal servers, using LAT and DNA protocols. Finally, Ungermann-Bass terminal servers use the XNS protocols.

All of these design centers make extensive use of the computing facilities located at corporate headquarters in San Jose. Headquarters computing resources include the Elxsi 6400 superminicomputer, VAX 11/785 and 8650 processors, HP 3000 systems, and a wide variety of other systems. Figure 7-7 illustrates a portion of the network.

Links to headquarters are used for electronic mail, order entry, accounting, and other administrative tasks. In addition, computer-aided manufacturing information frequently flows between design centers and corporate headquarters. This large volume of traffic requires a high amount of bandwidth that can operate in a protocol-independent fashion.

VLSI chose to use Vitalink bridges as a common connectivity solution. Some of these bridges use 19.2 kbps leased lines. The large design centers are all connected together using a satellite link. The satellite link provides 56 kbps between headquarters and design centers and 19.2 kbps in the other direction. In addition, another TransLAN bridge is used with a T1 microwave connection to the San Jose Design Center.

Establishing a general purpose routing interface

Many organizations prefer to isolate routing traffic from general-purpose processing for a number of reasons. First, they want incoming connections to be concentrated in one area to allow for greater control over them. Second, a lot of routing control information is exchanged

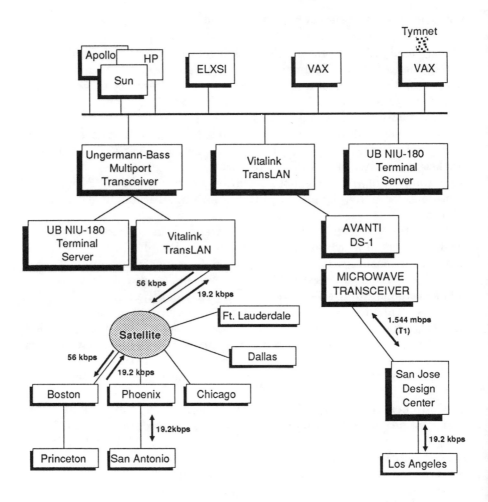

Fig. 7-7 VLSI Technology, Inc., extended LAN.

between these devices. It often makes sense to segment that traffic onto a single front end network.

The San Diego Supercomputer Center is an example of such a general-purpose front-end system. The Supercomputer Center serves a variety of remote users, ranging from networks such as NSFnet and

Arpanet to dedicated network connections for affiliates of the center. Figure 7-8 illustrates the SDSC network configuration.

The San Diego Supercomputer Center is one of five supercomputer centers that were financed by the National Science Foundation. Because the Center is involved with NSF, it makes extensive use of wide area communications to provide access to supercomputing facilities to researchers located throughout the nation.

Computing resources at the center are focused around a Cray X-MP/48 and a minisupercomputer made by Scientific Computer Systems. Online storage is very expensive for both of these computing environments, so an extensive file management system was built around an IBM 4381 running the MVS/XA operating system.

All three of these resources are connected together using a dual-cable Hyperchannel network. Each cable runs at 50 mbps. Running on the Hyperchannel is a proprietary network called SDSCnet.

A Cray does not provide very useful interactive computing facilities, so the user interface to the computation servers is handled by a series of front-end VAX computers. These computers provide a wide variety of communications functions.

The VAXs begin by providing print services to users. Large-scale laser printers from Imagen and Xerox are connected to a VAX 11/785. There is also a film recording unit made by DICOMED. The Cray and the DICOMED film recording unit are used by Disney Studios for some of their animation.

VAXs are also used to connect dial-in terminal users. A 32-port rotary is connected to one of the VAXs. Users within the facilities of the SDSC can also connect directly to the VAX using a M/A COM data switch.

The primary use of the VAXs is to provide a programming environment for users to prepare jobs. All of the VAX systems share a common file system in a VAX Cluster. In addition, all of the VAXs are on the SDSCnet system so they can access compute resources on the IBM, SCS, or CRAY environments.

One of the VAXs has an additional high-speed link directly to the Cray I/O Subsystem (IOS). This allows for data transfer rates of up to 4 Mbps from the 8350 memory up to the IOS. This direct link also bypasses the overhead of SDSCnet.

Incoming remote users are connected to a front-end Ethernet. All of the VAX systems are also connected to the Ethernet. Note that this means that the 8350 is a member of four different networks: Ethernet, the CI bus cluster, the Cray link, and the SDSCnet Hyperchannel.

Users access the front end network through a wide variety of remote communications devices. A series of Proteon and DEC routers provide dedicated links for 56 kbps and T1 lines. These lines could connect to

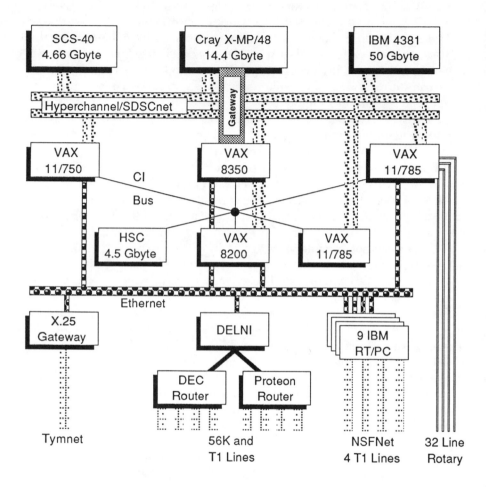

Fig. 7-8 San Diego Supercomputer Center.

an individual host or to another router on a remote Ethernet. The Proteon devices are able to accept both TCP/IP and DNA traffic.

This modular approach to remote wide area lines, separated on a front-end network, was not the first solution used by SDSC. The system began by using a series of PDP computers as front-end processors. These systems accepted a wide variety of leased-line and satellite links. The advantage of the separate front-end network in the current configuration is that it is conceptually much clearer and easier to implement. When the center started, however, dedicated routers were not advanced enough to handle the volume of traffic expected.

Tymnet users originally accessed the center using a 9.6 kbps link with a Packet Assembler/Disassembler which was then connected directly to one of the 11/785 VAX systems. The software used is DEC's Packet Switch Interface (PSI). The migration path used was to install an X.25 server and thus off-load that functionality from that VAX.

NSFnet is used to provide a link to the Internet environment. This in turn gives access to most major national laboratories, universities, and corporate computing networks. This means that NSFnet makes the resources of the SDSC available to most of the country. Needless to say, financial considerations serve to limit this potential user population to those who have sent in checks.

The original link to the NSFnet backbone used PDP 11/73 processors connected to two 56 kbps lines. This is being replaced by nine RT/PC systems linked to four T1 lines. The switch to the RT/PC is part of the revamping of NSFnet by the MERIT consortium, which includes IBM, MCI, and the University of Michigan.

X.25 Networks

X.25, like Ethernet, is an example of a subnetwork. To the user of X.25, every node on the subnetwork is one hop away. X.25 is a three-layer network architecture based on CCITT standards. These standards provide a common method of transmitting data across national boundaries.

X.25 is actually a family of protocols that define how a user of the network, known as a Data Terminal Equipment (DTE), communicates with the boundary of the network, known as a Data Circuit-Terminating Equipment (DCE). Once a packet of information is presented to the DCE, the X.25 network routes the information to the DCE closest to the destination DTE. Figure 7-9 shows the basic components of an X.25 network.

Internally, the X.25 network can be a complex routing topology. The details of this routing are outside of the scope of the X.25 standards. X.25 details how information is presented to the boundary of the network. Routing within the network is up to the X.25 implementor. Because the routing is not visible to the user, the X.25 network is usually represented as a cloud.

X.25 has some similarities with the local area networks discussed in the previous chapter. Both Ethernet and X.25 allow multiple devices to be connected to a subnetwork. Both Ethernet and X.25 allow the user of the service to treat all nodes as though they were one hop away.

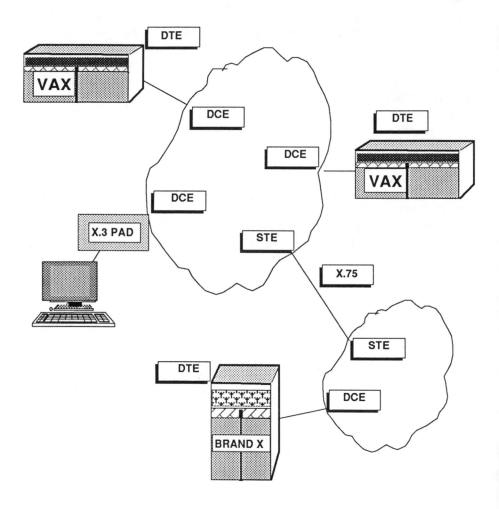

Fig. 7-9   X25 subnet components.

In X.25, service is performed by establishing a connection. This is in contrast to Ethernet which is a connectionless-oriented datagram service. An X.25 connection can either be a permanent logical connection or can be established dynamically. These dynamic connections last only for the length of the session and are known as switched virtual circuits.

Two other sets of protocols supplement the basic X.25 model. The X.75 protocols are used to route traffic between X.25 networks. The boundary of the two networks is a Signaling Terminal Exchange (STE). The X.75 protocols define how traffic is routed between two STEs on the boundary of two X.25 networks.

The last set of protocols are for asynchronous terminal access to an X.25 environment. X.25 is a synchronous environment—data is sent in packets. An X.3 Packet Assembler/Disassembler (PAD) is used to connect the asynchronous terminal to the synchronous network.

Communication between the X.3 PAD and the terminal is defined by the X.28 protocols. Communication between the X.3 PAD and a synchronous DTE such as a host is defined by the X.29 protocol suite. The basic function of these protocols is to prevent each character from traveling in a separate packet.

The X.3 PAD is able to hold data from the terminal until a packet is full or a special character, such as a carriage return, is encountered. The X.3 PAD thus functions as multiplexer/demultiplexer for the network, much like the LAT architecture does in an Ethernet environment.

X.25 layers

X.25 defines three different levels of operation:

- The network layer
- The frame level (a data link)
- A physical level

The frame level uses the LAP B protocols, which are a subset of the OSI HDLC data link protocols discussed later. At the physical level, X.25 uses the X.21 and X.21bis interface standards.

At the packet level, X.25 provides a series of logical channels that are available to the DTE. During X.25 operation, these logical channels are mapped to a virtual circuit, which can be either permanent or switched. X.25 thus provides a connection-oriented subnetwork service, in contrast to the connectionless Ethernet service.

Flow control in this environment is independent for each of the two directions of the circuit. This allows different flow control buffer sizes for different capacity devices. Each direction has a window size established which determines the number of unacknowledged packets that may be outstanding. Each time a packet is received, the current available window is opened up to the maximum allowed. Every time a packet is sent, the window is closed by one.

In addition to establishing window sizes, the two sides can establish maximum packet sizes. This process of determining the window and packet sizes is known as flow control parameter negotiation.

X.25 and DNA

Support for the X.25 protocols is provided either with a dedicated X.25 gateway or by using the services of a general-purpose VAX. Dedicated X.25 gateways are based on either the DECSA or DEMSA architectures discussed in the routing section.

A general-purpose VAX can use an X.25 network as well. The VAX needs a synchronous communications board that can support the LAP B protocols. On a MicroVAX, for example, this might be a DSV11 communications controller. On a larger system with a BI bus, this might be a DMB32 communications controller.

Access to the X.25 environment is provided through the Packet Switch Interface (PSI) software. PSI drives the communications board and provides packet layer control for establishing virtual circuits. Remote nodes on the DECnet can also access the services of PSI using the PSI Access software. PSI Access establishes a DECnet logical link to the PSI node, which in turn sets up an X.25 virtual circuit and maps that to the DECnet logical link.

The X.25 gateway node runs an X.25 Server Module, which is a DNA application, just like DAP or CTERM. DNA hosts that access these services run another program called the X.25 gateway access module. The server and access modules communicate with each other using the Gateway Access Protocol (GAP). The PSI Access software contains the X.25 gateway access modules.

The purpose of the PSI Access software is to allow a program to be shielded from the intricacies of X.25. Generic calls to the access module, such as OPEN PORT, are then mapped into a series of GAP commands that can open virtual circuits, make calls, accept or reject calls, and transfer data.

X.25 can be used three different ways in the DEC environment:

- As a DNA service provider
- To allow DNA users to access remote hosts
- To allow remote terminals to access DNA hosts

As a DNA service provider, X.25 functions as a subnetwork accessible to the DNA routing layer. This allows X.25 to provide a link between two points, just like DDCMP or Ethernet. This line has a cost associated with it and the routing layer would choose to route certain packets down this line based on factors such as congestion, cost, and availability of hosts.

This true integration of X.25 into the DNA architecture has some limitations in Phase IV. In Phase IV, only permanent virtual circuits can be used as a data link service provider to the DECnet routing layer. In Phase V of DECnet, there will be a definition for a dynamically established data link (DED). This will allow a switched virtual X.25 circuit to be established upon demand. Note that this DED facility will also allow dynamically established DDCMP links to be established, including support in the architecture for the commands needed to activate a modems and dial a number.

The second way to use X.25 in the DNA environment is as a tool for establishing a connection to a heterogeneous environment. In this case, the X.25 connection is not used to carry DNA traffic. Rather, the X.25 connection is used as a way of connecting a local user on the DECnet to some non-DNA host. X.25 really just serves as the equivalent of dialing up the host with a modem.

A third use of X.25 is as a method of connecting remote terminals on the X.25 subnetwork to DNA hosts. The terminals are connected to an X.3 PAD, such as DEC's DFM X.25 Packet Assembler/Disassembler. A VAX or X.25 gateway is then connected to the subnetwork. The PAD is able to establish a switched virtual circuit to the gateway node, which then passes the user through to other nodes on the DECnet that have the PSI Access software.

X.25 optional facilities

Several facilities that are specified as optional in the X.25 standards are supported by DEC on their gateway facilities. These options include:

- Closed user groups
- Call redirection
- Security and charging options

User groups provide a measure of security. A closed user group (CUG) limits either outgoing or incoming access to a DTE to a specific group of users. This allows the manager to limit the users on the local network that may place outgoing calls. It also allows the ability to limit remote users.

A special type of closed user group is the bilateral CUG. This allows pairs of DTEs to connect but limits calls from DTEs that have not formed this bilateral arrangement.

Call redirection is used when a DTE is out of order busy, or just plain antisocial. The call redirection facility allows calls to be redirected to a single target DTE or can provide suggestions of alternative DTEs to try. Note that this doesn't mean that the suggested DTE will accept the call. The standard allows calls to be continually redirected until the calling user gives up and slams the phone down in disgust.

A network user ID allows a DTE to provide authentication information with a call. When an incoming call is received, it is possible that the DCE will reject it based on unsatisfactory information. This prevents an undesirable user from gaining access to the system (unless of course they are able to impersonate a valid user).

Call charging allows charges to be imposed on the network. A reverse charging acceptance facility allows a DTE to specify that it will accept collect calls. A local charging prevention facility prevents the user of a DTE from initiating a call that will be locally charged.

Most charges on an X.25 network are a function of the amount of data that was transferred, both the number of bytes and the number of packets. Often, this information is not presented to host DTEs until the end of a billing cycle. If the host DTE wishes to use this information for billing purposes, it needs some estimate of the amount of traffic. The charging information facility allows a DCE to give the DTE using this facility information it needs to calculate bills.

ISDN

The Integrated Services Digital Network is another example of a subnetwork. Like X.25, connection oriented services can be set up between any two points on the boundary of the network.

ISDN, like X.25, defines the access protocol to the edge of the wide area network. Within the network, a related set of protocols, Signalling System 7, are used to allocate bandwidth, manage internal signalling, and recover for a digital network.

This book uses the term ISDN fairly loosely to refer to both the ISDN access protocols and the internal SS7-based communications network. Users on both ends of this network see the ISDN protocols, even though another protocol is being used inside of the network.

ISDN provides greatly enhanced capabilities over more traditional subnetworks such as X.25. The basic principle of ISDN is to allow users to share a common transmission media for different functions. Voice, video, and data all can be transmitted on the same digital lines. These lines are available in increments of 64 kbps and are known as B channels.

Signaling and management in the ISDN environment is done over a separate line called the D channel, which operates at 16 kbps. In addition to providing out-of-band signaling, the D channel is able to accept X.25 packets and telemetry information. An example of a telemetry application is a remote alarm for a security system.

An end user of the ISDN network will typically have a Basic Rate Interface (BRI) to the network. This consists of one D channel and two B channels (2B+D). The entire BRI interface can run on four wires. The ISDN protocols define a time division multiplexing protocol so the B and D channels are all able to access the physicial medium.

Larger organizations will have a Primary Rate Interface. This consists of 24B+D in North America and 30B+2 in the Europe. 24B+D corresponds to the T1 standard of 1.544 mbps in the United States, while the 30B+D corresponds to the other standard bandwidth allocation in the world of 1.984 mbps.

In both the BRI and PRI interfaces, the D channel is used to control the bandwidth on the B channels. The B channel is totally transparant and appears as a physical wire to the user. On top of the B channel, the data communications user might run DDCMP, SDLC, LAP B, or any other data link protocols, as well as voice or other nondata traffic.

ISDN defines two protocols that run on the D channel. LAP D is a data link protocol that provides multiplexing support. Protocol D corresponds to the network layer of the protocol stack and allows connections to be established and other control information to be exchanged.

An important way that ISDN differs from X.25 is that the internal routing of the network is defined. The LAP D and Protocol D define the interface to the edge of the network from the ISDN terminal. Another protocol, Signaling System 7 (SS7) defines how traffic is routed within an ISDN network. A common signaling system allows seperately administered ISDN environments to provide a unified communications environment.

LAP D protocols

The D channel in ISDN is crucial because it provides the signaling mechanism available for multiple different connections. Note that the B channels do not have any data link or network layer protocols defined. This is because they provide transparent bandwidth for use by different types of applications, such as voice traffic.

The D channel defines both a data link and network layer. The data link layer uses the LAP D subset of the HDLC protocols. Access to this D channel is based on a variant of the CSMA access protocols used in Ethernet. Like Ethernet, multiple nodes can access a common D channel and can sense if others are using the network. Rather than waiting for a random period of time after a collision, HDLC uses a contention resolution mechanism similar to that used in the CI bus on a VAX Cluster.

Then, each node wishing to transmit listens for a consecutive number of free line indicators. Different nodes can have a different parameter for this free line indicator (i.e. eight consecutive 1s on the line instead of nine). After a node has transmitted, it ups its free line indicator to allow others to access the network.

Note that the D channel is actually sharing the physical medium with the B channels so the term "line" is somewhat of a misnomer. The access method to the physical medium makes the D channel appear as though it were the sole owner of a physical wire, but in reality it is sharing time slots with the other channels.

The LAP D protocols add several important functions to the LAP B protocols used in X.25. Most importantly, LAP D allows several different data links to be multiplexed on a single D channel. This moves the multiple access function down from the network layer into the data link layer. This also allows a broadcast mode to be supported between the multiple data link users. Another important improvement is the addition of a permanent supervisory function on the channel.

A LAP D frame begins with a flag indicating the beginning of a new packet. This same flag is appended at the end of the LAP D packet. After the beginning flag is an indicator of the type of packet (signaling, information, control) being sent. This is followed by an address field and some control information.

The content of the control field depends on the type of frame being sent. For a normal data (information) frame, the control field contains two sequence numbers. The first sequence number is the number of the frame being sent out. The second sequence number is that of the last frame received from the other side of the connection. This prevents unnecessary acknowledgment frames from being sent through the network.

Error control is done through the use of acknowledgments. Normally, returning data would contain the acknowledgment. Otherwise, a special supervisory frame can be sent which contains a sequence number of the next frame expected. If no acknowledgment is received before a timer elapses, the frame is resent. After several consecutive transmissions, the data link layer gives up and sends a notification up to the network layer user.

Idle nodes periodically send out **RECEIVE READY** frames on the data link. This is because multiple users can share a LAP D channel, and therefore it is impossible to tell at the physical level if a node is still active. These RR frames contain a sequence number of the next frame expected. A special management function is used to identify every user of the D channel. This is done by requesting an identity when a new user joins the channel.

Protocol D

Protocol D is a network layer protocol that runs on top of the LAP D data link protocols. In OSI terms, Protocol D is a subnetwork access procedure. Higher sublevels of the network layer would provide routing and other traditional network layer functionality.

An important consequence of separating the subnetwork access routines from the rest of the network layer is that multiple entities can now access this subnetwork. Thus, the OSI data communications environment might use Protocol D to set up X.25-like virtual links on the D channel or to allocate B channel bandwidth. Another user might be a voice telephone user, who would request a B channel circuit for voice transmissions.

Protocol D is used to set up and manage a call over the D channel. It is then used to supervise message transfer and detect faults on the underlying subnet. The call setup in Protocol D is very similar to that on a telephone system.

The call begins by a user notifying the ISDN network that they wish to communicate with some foreign address. The ISDN addressing scheme is very similar to the current telephone numbering system. SS7 would then be used to establish a virtual circuit to the destination side of the ISDN network.

The destination edge of the ISDN network would then ring a particular user of the D channel. This results in a call proceeding message on one side of the connection and a ring to the other side. During the call setup procedure, the network may send ring-back indications to the initiating user to indicate that setup is proceeding but the other side has not answered. Once the other side "answers" the call, a connect message is sent back through the network.

During the call setup procedure, it is possible to have up to four user information messages sent in each direction. This allows the call setup procedure to include personalized welcome or authentication services. A typical use of the ISDN is thus to send the calling number in with the call setup procedure, as well as some supplementary information. The receiving end can process this information and route it to several users of the D channel. For example, an incoming call can be routed to the user's voice telephone as well as notifying the user's database server of the incoming caller's identity so the computer automatically pulls up a profile of the caller.

Signaling system 7

SS7 is the protocol used within the network for supervisory and control functions. The SS7 protocols run on a 64 kbps data channel and uses the HDLC protocols discussed earlier. SS7 also includes a variety of upper layer functions such as security functions.

The SS7 network architecture is divided into two parts. The network layer provides for connections among different signaling points in the network. The ISDN and public telephone networks can both use SS7 as a method of allocating bandwidth. Upper layer SS7 functions also use the SS7 network layer to exchange security and management data among signaling points.

The network layer of SS7, known as the message transfer part, offers a set of services to the different upper-layer users. The network layer module is the manager of resources at a particular signaling point in the network. One of the prime functions of the network layer of SS7 is to monitor error rates on all lines currently in service and to terminate any lines with unsatisfactory performance.

If the user of SS7 is a telephone user port, this will usually be used for a call setup function by sending an initial address message through the network. An enhanced version of the Telephone User Port definition allows user information to be transmitted with the call setup request. This information might include the extension of a calling party on a private PBX. It might also be used to directly specify the extension of the user who is being called. Finally, this user to user information may include authorization information.

SS7, by providing a common signaling method, allows different common carrier providers to easily communicate with each other. The impact of SS7 is that users of the ISDN see one common subnetwork. SS7 handles allocation of bandwidth, routing decisions, security functions, and other internal matters on the network. Protocol D and LAP D then define how the user interacts with the access device on the edge of this network.

Use of ISDN

ISDN provides many important enhancements to the present system of voice analog lines and the potpourri of data transmission facilities. Most important is the unification of voice, data and video onto a common transmission medium. This allows a common terminal to be used for a variety of functions, include FAX transmission, teletex, voice, data, television, and videotex.

Just because the services are integrated doesn't necessarily mean that the user will have a single device for all these functions. What it does allow is the coordination of the different types of resources. For example, when a telephone call is received, it may include the phone number of the called party. The receiving PBX would then perform two signaling operations.

First, the call would be routed to a particular voice telephone. The telephone would automatically ring and display the phone number of the calling party. Call redirection could be performed or call waiting notifications sent if the terminal is already occupied.

A second set of signals could then be sent to the user's computer. This signal would contain the name of the calling user. The computer would then automatically call up the available information on that user and display it on the screen as the phone is ringing.

Another application of ISDN is to allow the user facility to perform extended accounting. Calls received can be routed directly to the user's terminal. In addition, an accounting computer can be notified and can log the call.

Because multiple calls can be multiplexed, it is possible for a user to use an ISDN terminal to switch between multiple communications contexts. An example of this is putting one person on hold while handling another call. This allows the possibility of a new generation of telephone/data sets to become available.

AT&T provides an impressive demonstration of this multiplexing capability. They provide an ISDN terminal which consists of an ISDN interface board for a PC and an ISDN-compatible telephone. A BRI interface is then provided to a 5ESS central office switch. The user is able to establish a voice call on one B channel and a 64 kbps connection to a host computer on the second B channel.

The D channel is then used to route X.25 traffic over to several other hosts. A single PC is able to have five or six different simultaneous connections, including one 64 kbps high-bandwidth connection, in addition to the 64 kbps voice connection. The X.25 support on the D channel is an example of a value-added service from the ISDN provider (in this case, AT&T).

It is important not to overlook one of the simplest advantages of ISDN—tremendous bandwidth. Emerging fiber optic standards are providing gigabits of transmission capability between signaling points in the wide area network. ISDN allows users to quickly take advantage of that bandwidth. For example, fax systems usually transmit at 2400 to 4800 bps. A 64 kbps line could be used instead to transmit at significantly higher speeds.

DEC's CIT program

DEC's Computer Integrated Telephony is an architecture for integrating PBX systems with the data network. While it does not assume the availability of an ISDN network, it does allow a smooth transition into that environment as facilities become available.

CIT allows a CIT server to be connected to selected PBX systems that support CIT. The CIT server (a VAX) is connected at speeds of up to 64 kbps using the LAP B protocols to the PBX. CIT functions allow the server to make and answer calls, disconnect, and do other operations typically available to the telephone system.

A CIT client module then makes the services of the PBX available to an application program. An incoming call would thus go to the server module, which would then send that information to the appropriate client module on the DECnet. The client module would notify the application program, which in turn might look the incoming number up in a database. Figure 7-10 shows a basic CIT configuration.

Most of the functionality available depends on which vendor is implementing CIT support on their system. A function like BARGE IN for example, might not be available on each type of PBX. Likewise, RING BACK, which allows a connection to proceed as soon as the destination is free, is not necessarily available on each PBX or enabled for each user.

A typical CIT system in an ISDN environment would have calls first routed to a central switching station, possibly with an attendant to answer the phone calls. Phone calls received would then be routed to the user's telephone. At the same time as the call is routed to the telephone, the number of the calling party would be sent to the CIT server. The CIT server would notify an applications program, which would in turn pull up data on the incoming caller and send it to the user's terminal.

Wide Area Implementation: DEC's Easynet

A fairly amazing example of a wide area network integrating DEC equipment is the internal network for DEC employees. The network reached 25,000 nodes in 1987 and is continuing to grow. The network is used extensively for internal functions. Applications range from

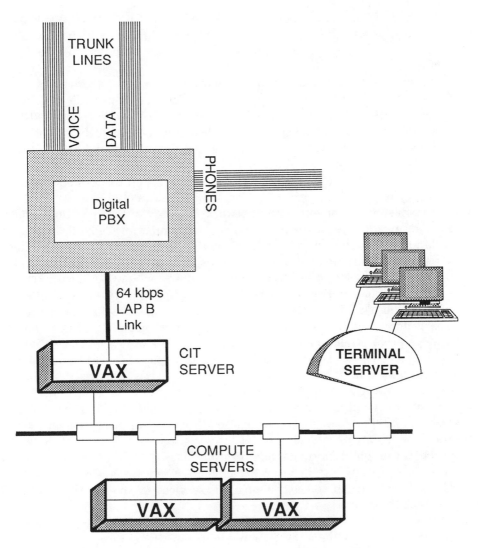

Fig. 7-10 A CIT configuration.

electronic mail for 80,000 users to videotex for distributing new sales information to file transfer for publications applications.

The wide area portion of the network is a backbone utility that is available to a wide variety of different applications. The same backbone is able to service voice traffic, video traffic, terminal access, and various DECnet routing traffic. The overall backbone bandwidth is manually allocated to accommodate the various demands.

The core of the network is located in northern New England where most of DEC's corporate facilities are located. The backbone in this arena is a 200-mile fiber optic network connecting major facilities. Between any two facilities there is a minimum available bandwidth of 45 to 90 mbps. This bandwidth is allocated in standard T1 to T3 modules.

Fanning out from the corporate facilities is a general mesh of T1 lines. Over 200 T1 lines span the United States and provide multiple paths to different locations in case of failure. T1 switches from Network Equipment Technologies, Timeplex, and several other vendors are used to allocate the T1 bandwidth to different applications. Compression on the switches allow more traffic to be accommodated. A T1 line can be allocated as a single data path, or it can be divided among multiple 32 kbps voice or 56, 128, or 256 kbps data channels.

The European portion of the network is a mix of 64 kbps lines and the European T1 equivalent of 2.048 mbps. Hubs in England, France, Ireland, and Switzerland link the individual countries to the backbone system. Satellite links of 64 kbps are used to connect Puerto Rico and the Orient. A series of 9.6 kbps lines are used for South America.

The backbone network is used primarily for four types of applications, although bandwidth can be allocated as needed for other uses. The primary applications are a terminal access network, a video network, a private telephone network, and of course the Easynet DECnet.

The private telephone network is used to bypass the local telephone companies. The day that this network was activated, Bell Atlantic saw a significant drop in the volume of traffic on their network. The hub of the Digital Telephone Network is a series of four Northern Telecom SL-100 PBX systems. These PBX systems in Massachusetts and New Hampshire each have a total configured capacity of 30,000 ports, although a normal configuration uses less than half of the potential capacity to allow for expansion. The PBX systems connect together in a mesh topology using the services of the backbone fiber optic facilities.

The video network is used typically as a one-way video channel with two-way audio. This is used for presentations by senior management to multiple facilities. The network also has the capability to provide two-way video or teleconferencing. The video network is also used for new product announcements, press briefings, and training classes.

The terminal access network is based on X.25. DEC uses a combination of the Tymnet public X.25 network and a private X.25 network built on top of the Tymnet facilities. Hosts connected to the network use DEC's PSI software for connection. Terminals are connected to X.3 PADs. Over 300 X.25 nodes are used to transmit 7 billion characters per month.

The data network uses a series of dedicated DEMSA systems as dedicated routers. The DEC network consists of multiple DNA areas.

In the United States, regions are separate areas. In most of Europe, single countries or groups of countries constitute areas. In northern New England, several areas exist. Each area has one or several of the DEMSA systems as level 2 routers.

A standard hardware configuration is used in most area routing sites. These "towers" consist of a machine rack that has several DEMSA DECnet Routers. The tower also has two MicroVAXs that function as the load hosts for downline loading software to the DEMSAs. Two MicroVAX systems are provided so that there is a backup load host.

The areas tend to be Ethernets or extended Ethernets using the Vitalink TransLAN bridges. Over 250 separate Ethernets are set up on the Easynet. Each of the areas is separately administered by a regional network manager.

Overall administration of the Easynet is through a central Network Control Center. This group monitors the Easynet backbone using the NMCC software and several custom programs that interface to the Network Control Program. NMCC and NCP are both discussed in the next chapter.

The Network Control Center regularly collects DNA counters from nodes on the network. Circuit statistics are also monitored using devices such as modem control systems. The Network Control Center also monitors the number of user calls as a high-level indicator of network performance—loud users are an indicator of network problems.

The data network also has several gateways to other facilities. AT&T and DEC, for example, share a gateway for mail interchange. Several other organizations are also able to interact with DEC for purposes of electronic data interchange. DEC also has several computers that provide online access to customers for purchases.

Needless to say, most of the generally available network nodes such as the DEC Store for customers are carefully segregated from the rest of the network. Even then, security on the network is still a difficult chore.

This network is able to link 432 DEC facilities and 15,000 additional home connections into one unified network. During the annual DECworld show, DEC adds an additional area that has 500 nodes for a period of 2 weeks. During that time, Email users goes from the normal 80,000 to add another 20,000 DECworld attendees.

The Easynet system has become crucial for DEC. A corporate official estimated at one DECworld that the corporation would loose 2 to 5 million dollars per day if the network were not available. An estimated 3 million minutes was shaved off the DEC phone bill in a 6-year period because of the wide availability of Email facilities.

Summary

Wide area networks are increasingly shifting from a focus on connecting terminals to computers or computers to computers toward being a subnetwork access protocol. This could be a dedicated link between two subnetworks, as in the case of the Vitalink TransLAN bridges.

A more general method is to connect the local subnetwork (the Ethernet) to a wide area subnetwork. Examples of wide area subnetworks are ISDN or X.25 implementations. This approach allows the user to decide who to communicate with. The network manager is not forced to predetermine the user populations that will be reachable through the use of dedicated lines.

ISDN provides an order of magnitude increase in performance and flexibility for wide area networks. Bandwidth in increments of 64 kbps is available using software commands. This bandwidth is flexible and can be used for voice, video, data, or any other purpose. Value-added services in an ISDN subnetwork provide gateways to more traditional environments, such as an X.25 packet switched data network.

For Further Reading

Black, *Computer Networks: Protocols, Standards and Interfaces*, Prentice Hall, Englewood Cliffs, NJ, 1987.

CCITT, "Data Communication Networks Interfaces," vol. VIII, fascicle VIII.2 and VIII.3, *CCITT Red Book*, CCITT Plenary Assembly, October 8-19, 1984.

G. Dicenet, *Design and Prospects for the ISDN*, Artech House, Boston and London, 1987.

Hall and McCauley, "Planning and Managing a Corporate Network Utility," 1987 *Society for Information Mananagement Juried Papers Competition* (first place winner), copies available from DEC.

Rose, "Wide Area Network: Sewing a Patchwork of Pieces Together," *Data Communications*, May 1988, (VLSI Case Study).

8

DNA Implementation and Management

Overview of This Chapter

This chapter discusses two distinct types of issues. First, the details of implementing DECnet on particular operating systems are discussed. VMS, Ultrix, and DOS all pose unique problems in implementing the functionality that was discussed in Parts 1 and 2 on network architectures. Although DECnet is heavily oriented toward the three DEC-supported operating systems, there are several third-party implementations of DNA on other operating systems.

The second section of this chapter considers the problem of managing the network. Most network management products use the VMS operating system as the basis for providing a user interface to network management capabilities. Network management involves two distinct types of issues.

First, there must be a general model of the entities involved in network management. An entity might be a DDCMP module or a routing layer module or a DAP-speaking process. The network management architecture details the type of interface presented by entities to the network manager.

Second, there needs to be a user interface able to interpret the information that is received from these various network management entities. As will be seen, Phase IV network management involves a variety of different interfaces for the different types of architectures. One program is used for monitoring DECnet nodes, another is used for monitoring a LAT server, and a third is used for managing bridges in an extended Ethernet.

Phase V of DECnet is able to unify all these different types of architectures into a single user interface. This is because network management has been generalized beyond the issues of DECnet to include multiple architectures, including systems that are not traditionally network based, such as databases or operating systems. In addition, the Phase V network management protocols have been extended to provide greater functionality.

Implementation of DNA on VMS

The VMS implementation of DECnet is closely tied into the other parts of the operating system. Most network services are part of the VMS source code and are compiled in with the operating system. Of course it takes the proper authorization code and software license to use the software.

Most operations in a DECnet operation are identical to those used locally. QIO calls are used to read and write from the network as well as for local file and clustered file operations. The ASSIGN and DASSGN calls are used to assign channels in the network, in a similar way to their function in the file system.

A node name in VMS can be used to signify a variety of different types of network access. The full specification for the nodename can contain access information or use the default access on the remote node:

> nodename::filespec
> nodename"username password account"::filespec

Each VMS node contains a proxy log-in database. This is a one-to-one mapping between network users and a proxy account on the local system. Any logical link request that does not contain explicit control information is run in the proxy account's authorization context. Several network services, such as FAL data access, also have default accounts used if there is not a proxy log-in. Note that proxy log-ins can seriously compromise network security, particularly in the case of proxy log-ins on privileged accounts.

An interesting feature in VMS is that a file specification can refer to a foreign task. This allows the same user interface to be used for file access and for remote task execution. The three different forms of a "filename" are:

> nodename::"file_specification"
> nodename::"task=task_spec"
> nodename::"n=object_number"

A task specification is equivalent to an object number 0. As discussed in the session control layer, this information is passed to the session control module on the remote node so that it knows which higher level service to notify for incoming requests.

Since the network and a file system both use a QIO interface, the user can make direct calls to either service. Another option is to use the Record Management Services (RMS) which can work with both types of services, network and local. RMS network file services include the ability to access remote files in record or block mode as well as in sequential, relative, and ISAM files.

Since a filename also can include a task specification, the RMS services can be used to communicate with a task as though reading and writing to a sequential file. All remote input and output from the task are assigned to a local logical name called SYS$NET. Thus to run a foreign task and display the results locally, the user would first open a file, then read the results:

> open node::"task=taskspec"
> type sys$net

There are several ways that a task can become known to the network. The most frequent way is that the image is registered in a local database. NETACP will create a process in the appropriate context and run the task when it receives an incoming request. If an entity is not registered, NETACP assumes that the task is a command procedure and that the task is located in a default account.

The VMS kernel has two components that do most of the network access. NETDRIVER is a pseudo device driver that receives QIO calls for reads and writes to the network. The second process, NETACP, is used for more compute intensive tasks such as start-up or shut-down of logical links. Figure 8-1 shows the structure of the VMS implementation of DNA.

In addition to the logical read/write capabilities, NETDRIVER also contains the bulk of the routing layer software for DECnet. NETDRIVER is a high priority process and stays resident to avoid process start-up times.

NETACP is used to define and provide access to the volatile database, which is part of the virtual address space for the process. NETACP controls state transitions for the data link layer, the routing software, and for logical links. NETACP is also used to create the

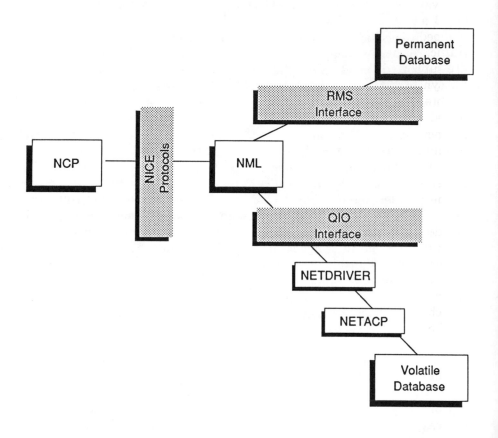

Fig. 8-1   VMS DECnet processes.

process for incoming logical links with no declared task. Finally, NETACP provides a mapping between DECnet and X.25 data links.

Two other process are also implemented in VMS, both for network management. A Network Management Listener (NML) is a server that also maintains the permanent database for network management. The NML then uses the NICE protocols to communicate with a user interface process, usually the Network Control Program (NCP). If the Network Control Program needs access to volatile data, it still communicates with the NML process. However, rather than providing direct access to the volatile database, the NML process communicates with the NETACP process.

A variety of data links are supported in a DECnet, including both 802.3 and Ethernet Level 2. X.25 permanent virtual circuits can be mapped to a DNA data link. The CI bus can also be used for DECnet traffic. Finally, asynchronous and synchronous versions of DDCMP are supported.

Asynchronous DDCMP is often used for PCs accessing a VAX as a remote DECnet node. This could pose a problem when DECnet use is mixed with non-DECnet (i.e., simple terminal emulation). VMS allows an incoming PC to dynamically convert an asynchronous line from a terminal line into a remote DECnet (asynchronous DDCMP) line. This is possible because DEC separates device drivers into a class driver and a port driver.

The port driver is the portion that actually works with the physical line. The class driver provides the interface to the services that use the device. Multiple users of a port driver is similar to multiple networking services (LAT, TCP/IP, DECnet) sharing the Ethernet class driver.

To convert the line, VMS first sends an escape sequence to the PC which tells the PC to convert itself into a DECnet node. VMS then switches to the class driver used for that session. At that point, the VAX and the PC exchange routing layer initialization information.

DECnet/VAX performance

Performance of DECnet on a VAX is a function of the communications devices and the size of the CPU. DEC publishes a series of guidelines based on load units. Each device operating at a particular speed using average data is worth a certain number of load units. Each VAX has a capacity measured in load units.

Three classes of devices are considered for DECnet on the VAX. The worst in terms of performance are non-DMA devices that require software to perform all functions. When a new character is received, an interrupt is generated by the communications device. The VMS system must stop processing and receive the character, place it in memory, echo the character back, then go back to the original job.

It is very rare that a site would depend on a non-DMA device for more than a few incidental terminals. In a DECnet scenario, a non-DMA device might be used for an asynchronous DDCMP connection to a PC. It should be stressed that the same type of connection could also be made with a communications controller that does have DMA capabilities.

Direct memory access allows the controller to receive several pieces of data and then place them all into a portion of memory. This allows the controller to buffer the information and only call on the CPU when its attention is really needed.

DMA devices fall into two classes. Some devices are able to access a portion of memory but still require the use of the CPU device driver to process the information at the data link level. A DMB32 is an example of such a device.

The second, more advanced type of DMA device is one where the data link level is built into the firmware. An Ethernet controller is an example of a DMA device of this sort. Encoding and decoding packets can all be done at the controller level, only requiring CPU attention when the data is ready to be presented to the client of the Ethernet.

The load units for each class of device (operating at various speeds) is as follows:

Load Units as a function of Line speed (kbps)

Device Class	9.6	19.2	56	>56
DMA (DQNA)	8	16	45	100
DMA (DMB32)	10	20	NA	NA
non-DMA	13	26	NA	NA

A VAX 8800 or 8700 both have total load unit capacities of 1200. A MicroVAX II has a capacity of 280, while an 11/780 has a capacity of 240. Once again, it is important to stress that these metrics are very application dependent and are simply based on hypothetical average data transmission requirements. These numbers should be taken as firm only by families with 2.2 children and a dog named Spot.

Implementation on Ultrix

The Ultrix implementation of DECnet includes several modifications to the socket mechanism that is present in the 4.3BSD implementation of Unix. Sockets are virtual ports on a Unix system that can communicate with other sockets. Sockets are organized into domains, such as INTERNET, UNIX, and DECNET. Domains are families of sockets that can talk to each other.

The original 4.2BSD implementation of sockets didn't allow for programs to pass data or other access control information along with a connection request. It also didn't allow a server to reject a requested connection with a reason. Both of these changes were made, as were extensions to the network management interface that allow circuits to be turned on and off, multicast broadcasts to be switched on and off, and counters to be gathered on various devices.

The DECnet domain has two interfaces to the Ultrix socket interface. A stream socket interface does not sequence data and requires all data to be self-describing. This interface is not used by DEC-provided services but is implemented to allow user programs to be easily ported from other domains. The other interface is the sequenced packet interface which provides an ordered delivery of data.

DEC made two types of changes to Unix. First, several changes were made to the kernel to support the new domain. Two system calls were changed to increase the maximum data length from 112 to 1024 bytes to allow the passing of connect information. The network device drivers were also extended to support counters and multicasting addresses.

The second major change was the addition of an object spawner. The 4.2 socket interface requires all possible targets to be running and listening. An object spawner accepts incoming requests and then either passes them to an existing process or activates (spawns) a process.

In some cases, end-user processes bypass the object spawner. Keeping a process resident decreases the amount of start-up time needed. Also, the object spawner can only connect one process per socket. Thus, multisocket processes also bypass the object spawner.

The Network Control Program is used to declare a server to the spawner. NCP may also notify the spawner of a default user account if no access control information is furnished with the connect request. The spawner then handles authentification, executes the desired process in the context of a user account, sets up the necessary socket connections, and redirects standard input and output streams toward the sockets.

The network management interface had to be changed somewhat from the original Unix implementation. This is because in TCP/IP, the usual network protocols for Unix, there are only two network management files. These ASCII files contain address mappings and are never written to by TCP/IP. Instead, an editor such as VI is used to change these files. In DECnet, the NCP must work with several files and often writes to these files. Access to configuration files must be through NCP because they are stored as sequential binary files rather than ASCII text.

Upper-layer services are fairly similar to the VMS services. The data access protocols, virtual terminal, and mail services are all provided. An Ultrix gateway provides an interface to the TCP/IP environment. This gateway is somewhat transparent, allowing access to destination nodes not on a DECnet as long as the name of the Ultrix gateway is known. The Ultrix gateway participates in both the TCP/IP and DECnet environments. Note that this has frequently been done by end users as a method of interconnecting two different environments. The Ultrix gateway simply eliminates the extra step of manually logging into the Ultrix gateway via DECnet, then using a TCP/IP command to interact with the other environment.

Implementation on MS-DOS

Implementing DECnet on an MS-DOS system is difficult because of the single-tasking nature of the operating system. DECnet makes heavy use of background processes for things like transmitting and receiving periodic routing and line confidence messages as well as for maintaining multiple network connections simultaneously.

To support background processes, DECnet-DOS uses a scheduler. The scheduler is activated by either timer or communications interrupts. When a timer expires, the foreground application is interupted and the background network task is run. Another type is interrupt is when network communications are received, such as the receipt of an Ethernet packet.

An interrupt automatically saves the current CPU state and the interrupt return address. Once the current application has been saved, the scheduler first performs the requested task and then examines a background process list to see if other tasks have registered themselves as runnable. The foreground task is then rerun. For example, to process an incoming Ethernet packet, the system must save the state of the current foreground task. The data is then copied from the controller into a receive buffer. The controller is reset to receive the next message.

With the incoming message processed, the scheduler then looks for immediate work to perform. Since a data link packet has just been received, the routing layer must process the receive buffer. After all immediate work is performed, the foreground task is given control again.

Most of the application layer modules are similar to those of the other operating system implementations. For example, the Network File Transfer (NFT) program is a DAP-speaking utility used to send and receive files on the network. The File Access Listener is a DAP server. If a PC user has the FAL process up and running, that PC can send and receive files to remote users.

DECnet-DOS also includes a virtual disk and printer service in addition to the NFT and FAL utilities. These utilities allow the establishment of a virtual disk volume or printer at a foreign node. A virtual driver is then loaded at boot time in the MS-DOS CONFIG.SYS file. Communication is established in the form of a logical link that uses the DAP protocols. The virtual driver supplements the default driver in MS-DOS. I/O requests are either passed to the standard driver for local I/O or passed to the network disk utility for remote access.

In addition to a single threaded CPU execution, I/O in an MS-DOS environment is also single threaded. This poses a particular problem for receiving mail messages because a mail message could easily contain more bytes than the background network process has memory for. The network process has no knowledge of the context in which the foreground process is executing I/O operations.

Rather than receive a mail message, the PC uses the services of a VAX host as a post office. When an outgoing mail message is processed, the DECnet-DOS mail interface automatically inserts the address of the designated receive node rather than the address for the PC, then sends the message out using the message-handling protocols.

To access the VAX that receives mail messages on behalf of a user, DECnet-DOS users are able to use a VT220 emulator. The terminal emulator allows PCs to emulate an 80- or 132-column terminal. This emulator implements both LAT and CTERM virtual terminal services. The LAT support allows load-balancing and other DECserver features on an Ethernet. The CTERM support allows the DECnet-DOS user to access any host on the DECnet.

Physically, DECnet-DOS supports both DDCMP and Ethernet data link protocols. DDCMP links use the asynchronous version of the protocol at speeds up to 9.6 kbps in AT-based systems and 19.2 kbps in higher-end PS/2 models. Several Ethernet controllers are supported, including those from DEC, 3COM, and MICOM-Interlan.

DNA Clones

Several vendors have provided other implementations of DNA on alternate platforms from the traditional DEC-supported operating systems. Alisa Systems has provided an implementation of DECnet that runs on the Apple Macintosh. Technology Concepts, a Bell Atlantic subsidiary, has provided a variety of different implementations, including MS-DOS, Apple Macintosh, and several Unix-based systems.

Implementations of DNA on general-purpose computers are for Phase IV end nodes. In addition, many of these implementations support only client versions of applications. Thus, Technology Concepts' CommUnity provides a client version of the FAL process for the MS-DOS implementation as well as client versions of CTERM. Other nodes cannot log into or access files from a PC, but the PC can access other nodes. These limitations are understandable given the limited capabilities of the PC.

A related series of products, VMS clones, are provided by Boston Business Computing. The combination of a VMS emulator and a DNA clone often provides a viable alternative to a VAX. An example of such an implementation is the Elxsi 6400 parallel processor.

The Elxsi is a system consisting of up to 12 processor boards operating in parallel. The basic operating system for the Elxsi is EMBOS, the Elxsi Message Based Operating System. This operating system works on a very high-speed bus and is able to address over a gigabyte of real memory.

EMBOS provides the underlying base, on top of which several operating systems are implemented. Both System V and Berkeley versions of Unix can be run, as well as EMS, Elxsi's VMS emulator. Each processor can run a different operating system, and the failure of one processor does not affect other processors.

The VMS emulator allows source code from a VMS system, complete with VMS-dependent system calls and VMS extensions to the Fortran language, to be recompiled on the Elxsi. In addition, a version of the popular EDT editor is provided along with most of the common DCL commands. In other words, the Elxsi looks virtually identical to a VMS system as far as users are concerned.

To supplement the VMS emulation, Elxsi also has an implementation of a Phase IV DECnet node. Users can access the Elxsi using the usual CTERM and FAL processes. If the Elxsi log-in banner is changed to the same as that of a VAX, users won't even know that they are on a non-VMS system in most cases.

Other non-DEC versions of DECnet exist on powerful minisupercomputers such as Alliant or Convex. While VAX computers are suitable in many circumstances, these third-party implementations provide an important degree of flexibility to network managers. If a VAX is unable to provide the appropriate level of performance (at the appropriate price), additional heterogeneous equipment can be added..

DEC is well aware that end users of equipment demand alternatives to DEC computers. This push toward heterogeneous systems has pushed DEC, as well as other vendors, towards the OSI networking protocols. Since OSI is a vendor-independent set of protocols, in theory heterogeneous resources will be able to form a unified network.

Part 4 of this book discusses OSI and the impact of these standards on DEC networking.

Phase IV Network Management

Phase IV network management consists of a variety of products. Several are available to manage the Phase IV components, such as dedicated routers or VMS nodes. In addition, there are a variety of other products that are used for managing other architectures, such as LAT-based terminal servers and extended Ethernet bridges.

This section begins by discussing the Phase IV network management framework. Next, the NMCC/DECnet monitor is discussed as a common interface to Phase IV network management. Finally, the alternative user interfaces are discussed.

The next section of this chapter discusses the Phase V network management architectures as well as EMA, an important new user interface architecture that provides a common user interface for heterogeneous network architectures.

There are several functions that are not present in the DNA network management layer. Accounting in a DECnet is the responsibility of the individual layers. On a VMS node, a file called NETSERVER.LOG supplements the VMS accounting utility to provide accountability for use of resources from remote users.

Automation and protection against malicious use are two other functions that are not part of the network management layer. Some automation is provided at the individual node, particularly with the advent of VMS version 5 and dynamic tuning of sysgen parameters.

Security is also the responsibility of individual nodes on the network. Making security node based instead of network based is a deliberate design decision for DNA. There are no generally accepted methods of securing a network, but security on an individual computer system is a fairly well understood problem.

It is possible to provide encryption over data links. This is in a sense a form of network-based security. However, it is up to the two nodes involved in the exchange to encrypt and decrypt the data.

Management entities

The DNA model is composed of entities and functions that operate on those entities. There are six kinds of entities in the network management model:

- A node is the basic entity in the network and encompasses CPUs as well as routers and other specialized types of computers.
- An area is an entity that consist of groups of nodes.
- Logging entities are used to keep track of a number of counters and events that the network manager may need.
- A line is a physical communication path, such as a leased phone line.
- A circuit is the logical communications path that is on top of a line. Circuits and lines are entities that connect nodes together. In the case of the Ethernet, there may be several circuits on one line.
- A module is a catch-all entity that doesn't fit into the basic five classes of entities. X.25 gateway functions and maintenance modules are both examples.

Functions in the network management model are operations on entities. SET, CLEAR, SHOW, and LOAD are examples of functions. For particular combinations of functions and entities, there are a variety of attributes that are allowed. In the case of a node, for example, the network manager can SHOW the STATE, NAME, or ADDRESS of that node. Figure 8-2 shows selected attributed for a node.

Network management can be distributed throughout the network. For the purpose of any one instance of the network manager, however, the function resides on one particular node. This node is the director node because it is the one executing the network management user interface. Other nodes are agents. Directors communicate with agents using the NICE protocols. There can be several directors communicating with agents in the network.

Because the data link and physical layers are closely coupled in DECnet, lines and circuits are usually considered together even though they are separate entities. A line corresponds to the physical layer of the ISO model and a circuit to the data link layer.

Multipoint DDCMP lines and Ethernet are both cases in which multiple circuits reside on one physical line. X.25 differs slightly because most of the processing for X.25 is accomplished in an X.25 gateway module. Thus, DECnet is not really aware of X.25 lines.

Several user interfaces are available for network management. The two primary ones in DECnet are the Network Control Program (NCP) and the Network Management Control Center (NMCC). NCP is a command-oriented interface and is the original user interface to network management function. A more modern system is the NMCC, which makes more extensive use of graphics. Instead of issuing the NCP SHOW CIRCUIT command, the NMCC user can see a circuit go from green to red on a graphic representation of the network.

SELECTED NODE ATTRIBUTES

COUNTER TIMER	The number of seconds to wait before logging node events and zeroing counters
CPU	CPU type
DIAGNOSTIC FILE	File to read for adjacent node downline loading diagnostics
DUMP ADDRESS	A memory address for up-line loading
HARDWARE ADDRESS	The Ethernet hardware address of adjacent node
LOAD FILE	File containing the operating system for a target system
PHYSICAL ADDRESS	The executor node's Ethernet address
ADDRESS	DECnet address of executor node
NAME	Logical name for the node
MAXIMUM LINKS	Maximum number of active logical links for the executor
BUFFER SIZE	Maximum size of a routing message which is therefore the maximum size of a packet the routing layer will forward

Fig. 8-2   Selected node attributes.

The user interface communicates with the rest of the network management model by issuing calls to the network management access routines. The access routines translate these calls into local and remote access to network management data. Local calls are routed to the node's local network management functions. Remote calls are translated into the NICE protocols and sent to a remote Network Management Listener (NML). The NML will in turn send the request down to the local network management entities on the remote node. Figure 8-3 shows the structure of the network management model.

The local network management functions convert generic requests into operating system-dependent calls. They also provide an interface to several special purpose modules. The maintenance module controls the operation of the MOP protocols for downline loading. The physical and data link modules control their respective layers. The event logger is a sink for data that was requested to be collected by a network manager. The event logger can log data for the local node as well as information received from remote nodes.

Typically, the NCP user will tell the remote Network Management Listener to set certain parameters. These requests are sent down to the local network management functions. Another typical request is to log certain information, where the NCP user specifies the location of a sink node. When information is logged, the remote node sends it back to the local event logger which processes the information.

The Network Control Program user has four major types of functions available:

1. The user can change relevant parameters, such as the circuit ID.
2. The user can gather information through the use of an event logger.
3. The user can control maintenance events such as downline loading, upline dumping, and triggering bootstraps.
4. The user can test links and zero counters.

Local network management functions can receive four types of requests. A local instance of a user interface, such as the NCP, may request information. A NICE request may received from another node via the local instance of the Network Management Listener. The NML may also issue requests on behalf of itself, as in the case of an NML being instructed to regularly collect certain information. Finally, the local network management functions may sense certain types of service functions automatically, such as in the case of a physical link watcher notifying it that a line has gone down.

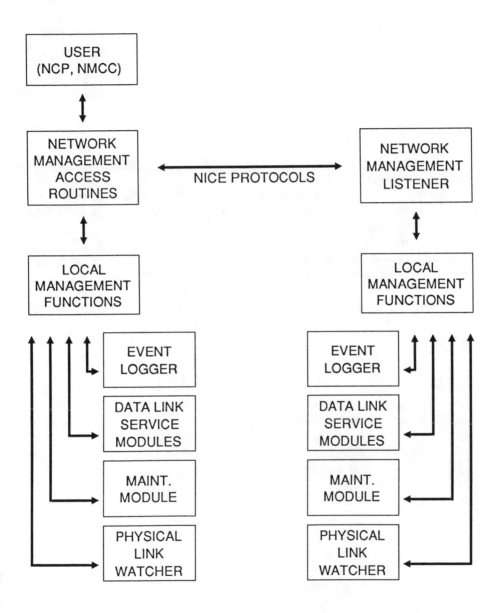

Fig. 8-3 Phase IV network management modules.

Event logging

Events may originate from any node on the network and from any one of the DNA layers. The system manager specifies which nodes to log, and the address of the sink node that will receive that information. A sink node is a place on the network to send an event. NCP would then examine that sink node for a record of past events. It is possible to specify several sink nodes for the receipt of information.

On the sink node, the manager can specify a filter to dispose of certain types of information. The filter allows certain events to be disposed of. Other filters may redirect data of different types to different repositories. Figure 8-4 shows an example of an event log.

The event logger module consists of nine different types of components. This architecture is meant to reduce the possibility of an event logger overrunning the host node, as well as to allow events to be dispatched and processed on multiple nodes.

Event queues are used in several different types of situations depending on the eventual destination of the information. The queues buffer information on a first-in-first-out basis. One module will fill a queue and another, separate, module will empty it.

It would not be practical to require the filling module to hold events if the desired event queue is full. This would make the module fairly complicated for buffer management and error processing functions. On the other hand, it is necessary to take some action to specify that information has been discarded because of a full queue.

If the queue is full, the filling module discards the event. It also makes sure that the last event currently on the queue is an event called EVENTS-LOST with a time stamp. The receiving module will then know the time that the first event was lost.

To avoid overrunning a remote node and because different sinks may process events differently, no processing is done at the event logger. Raw events consist solely of an event code, the event identification, and raw data.

An event processor turns this information into an event with the following fields:

> Event Code
> Source Node ID
> Sink Flags
> Entity Name
> Date/Time Stamp
> Data

DECnet event 4.14, node reachability change
From node 3.921 (PIZAZZ), 20-SEP-1988 11:07:29.05
Node 3.221 (NHTR02), Reachable

DECnet event 4.18, adjacency down
From node 3.921 (PIZAZZ), 20-SEP-1988 11:07:33.49
Circuit UNA-0, Adjacent node listener receive timeout
Adjacent node = 31.248

DECnet event 4.15, adjacency up
From node 3.921 (PIZAZZ), 20-SEP-1988 11:07:36.60
Circuit UNA-0, Adjacent node = 3.341 (PSI)

DECnet event 4.13, init failure, operator initiated
From node 3.921 (PIZAZZ), 20-SEP-1988 11:07:36.60
Circuit UNA-0, Adjacent node block size too small
Packet beginning = 0D020000AA000400550D03AB00000300
Received version = 2.0.0

DECnet event 4.15, adjacency up
From node 3.921 (PIZAZZ), 20-SEP-1988 11:07:51.53
Circuit UNA-0, Adjacent node = 3.341 (PSI)

DECnet event 4.15, adjacency up
From node 3.921 (PIZAZZ), 20-SEP-1988 11:08.15.40
Circuit UNA-0, Adjacent node = 3.218 (BIGE)

DECnet event 4.14, node reachability change
From node 3.921 (PIZAZZ), 20-SEP-1988 11:08:24.76
Node 3.218 (BIGE), Reachable

DECnet event 4.10, circuit up
From node 3.921 (PIZAZZ), 20-SEP-1988 11:08:25.13
Circuit DMC-0, Adjacent node = 3.921 (PIZAZZ)

DECnet event 4.7, circuit down, circuit fault
From node 3.921 (PIZAZZ), 20-SEP-1988 11:08:35.45
Circuit DMC-0, Line synchronization lost

Courtesy of Digital Equipment Corporation

Fig. 8-4   An event log.

Like event processing, event filtering is only done at the sink node. Each sink type, such as a monitor, file, or console, may have different filters. A filter has a two-level structure. A global filter is maintained for each event class. Specific filters are also available for particular entities within an event class. The filtering algorithm first checks the specific filter, then the global filter.

When examining logging, operations can occur on groups of sink sites. An NCP command can refer to all ACTIVE LOGGING to get a list of all sink types that are in the ON or HOLD states. Alternatively, the user can request all SIGNIFICANT LOGGING nodes which only returns a list of sink sites with significant activity. Nodes can also be qualified to only include certain areas, circuits, lines, modules, or nodes.

Events are ranked by classes. A class 0 event is a network management layer event; a class 4 event is a routing layer event. Within the event class, there are event parameters for different entities. Each event is uniquely identified by a type number within the class number. Event classes 480 to 511 are customer specific and can be used for user-written applications.

Downline loading

Downline loading is managed from the network management layer. This layer issues specific MOP commands, which are passed directly to the data link layer. This is different from other DNA functions, which are passed through the other layers of the network.

Several requirements exist for a downline load:

1. The target node must be directly connected to the executor node via a physical link.
2. The primary MOP loader must be resident in the target node in bootstrap ROM.
3. The executor node must have access to the file. The file can be local or remote on a host node via the FAL protocols. The file can be specified by the target node in the load request or can be looked up by the maintenance module.

A load request can be initiated by either the target or executor node. Typically, the initiation is by the target node. The executor node's link watcher would detect a target-initiated load request and pass it through to the network management module.

The ROM of the target node usually contains a primary loader. The next program that is passed through from the executor node is a secondary loader. This may even be followed by a tertiary loader.

Finally, the operating system is passed down to the target node and the MOP operation is completed.

The MOP protocols are also used for an upline dump operation. This is the reverse of the downline operation in that data goes from memory on the target to a file on a host system.

MOP protocols are used by routers, bridges, terminal servers, and other dedicated devices sold by DEC. The MOP protocols are also used by cluster members to boot themselves up. A MicroVAX 2000 is a diskless node and would issue a MOP request over the Ethernet. Large VAX systems booting over a CI bus also use the MOP protocols.

NMCC/DECnet Monitor

The Network Management Control Center (NMCC) provides a more sophisticated presentation environment than the more traditional NCP. NMCC uses the same NICE protocols and event-dispatching techniques used to collect data in NCP. Instead of collecting that information and presenting it to the NCP user, however, a more sophisticated type of processing is invoked.

NMCC consists of two parts, a user interface and a data collection and storage portion. This allows the data (known as a kernel) to be collected by one or more data managers. From there, terminals or nodes located elsewhere on the network are able to access this kernel of information. Figure 8-5 shows the structure of the NMCC software.

The user interface to NMCC allows data to be presented in a variety of graphic formats. For example, a topology of the network can be used to examine the status of different componenets. Lines or nodes that are not operational are shown in red on the map.

Other graphic formats in NMCC allow histograms and tables to be used to examine historical data. One nice feature of NMCC is that several data requests can be outstanding. NMCC will periodically deliver new data to the user for all outstanding requests. The user is able to switch between various displays for the various data requests.

NMCC data model

NMCC defines five types of information that can be collected. The first three are data collected from the network itself. These include characteristic parameters that define the control structure of the network and status parameters that reflect the dynamic nature of it. In addition, counters are used, usually to summarize status parameters. Figure 8-6 shows some counters available on a network.

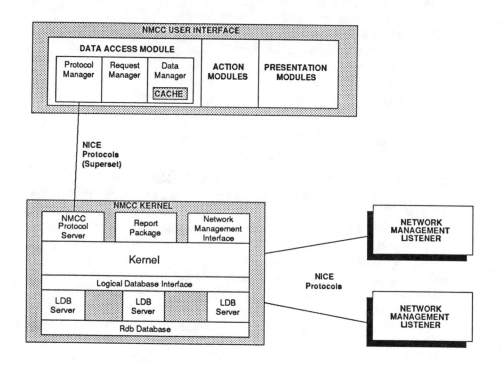

Fig. 8-5 Network Management Control Center structure.

To supplement the three information types collected from the net-work, NMCC adds two more types. First, users can supplement the network information with a variety of user-friendly information known as reference data. For example, a node name can be supplemented with the name and phone number of the system manager of that node.

The last type of data defines the various information available. This last type of information is then processed through the help portion of the user interface to let users know what data they can examine about the network. By providing meta-data, data about data, NMCC allows for easy extensibility.

NODE COUNTERS

Seconds since last zeroed
User bytes received
User bytes sent
User messages received
User messages sent
Total bytes received
Total bytes sent
Total messages received
Total messages sent
Total (NSP) connects received
Total connects sent
Received connect resource areas
Maximum logical links active

Aged packet loss
Node unreachable packet loss
Node out-of-range packet loss
Oversized packet loss
Packet format error
Partial routing update loss

Fig. 8-6   Selected DNA counters.

The five basic types of information are supplemented by three derived databases. Summary data is added to prevent the accumulation of needless details. Statistical and topographical information is also derived from the base data.

Each of these types of information is collected for the different components in a network. Components include systems, circuits, remote nodes, and wires. Wires are the physical instance of a particular line that a system uses.

A particular combination of the different component types and the different types of information form an instance of data collection within the database. Since network management is a dynamic environment, all of these records are further categorized by time of collection.

Time stamps for data are provided upon receipt by the NMCC kernel. This is because there is no provision for network-wide time synchronization in DECnet Phase IV. A special time value for data collected is current. When users request current data, they are given the latest data collected. As new information arrives, it is automatically dispatched. This is known as a news function and allows historical and real-time data both to be presented within the same framework.

NMCC kernel

The data collection portion of the NMCC is known as the kernel information manager (KIM). The kernel is able to respond to requests from multiple user interfaces. The kernel shields the underlying storage format of the data from the user interface and provides a uniform interface for both historical and real-time data.

The actual data for NMCC is kept in an Rdb database. Rdb is DEC's relational database management system. Rdb presents a synchronous interface to users of the system. This means that the beginning of a transaction must be followed by each of the transaction statements and then terminated by an end of transaction. Rdb does not allow a single user to have multiple requests outstanding.

A synchronous interface is not appropriate for a network management environment. A user may have several data requests outstanding and new data requests may be received at any time. To present an asynchronous interface, a software module called the logical database (LDB) is wrapped around Rdb and interacts with the KIM module.

The LDB process is responsible for all transaction-related processing. As such, it is actually several different processes. Each of the LDB processes interacts with the underlying Rdb database. Each processes represents a separate transaction context for data requests.

Three different kinds of modules work with the KIM data kernel. A Network Management Interface (NMI) is responsible for working with Network Management Listeners throughout the network. The NMI module is analogous to a data sink in the network management model.

User interfaces interact with the NMCC protocol server (NPS). This allows the user interface to be located anywhere throughout the network. NPS and user interface processes communicate using an enhanced version of the NICE protocols. The enhanced version is necessary because the NMCC database contains information that supplements the basic event/parameter/counter model of network management that NICE was originally meant to handle.

A report package is used to summarize data in the Rdb database. This information is extracted hourly from the Rdb database and summarized into historical files. The historical files are stored in a standard binary format.

Access to these historical files can be through the NMCC user interface (the DECnet Monitor) or through programs. Datatrieve, for example, could access these historical files as could any program that uses the Record Management Services to access data.

Because the Rdb database is of finite size and because historical information is summarized in flat files, it is necessary periodically to purge the database of historical data. A special program that interacts directly with the Rdb database is available for that function. It is also possible for a database administrator to use all of the normal RdB DBA facilities to backup the database or monitor disk usage and other performance metrics.

NMCC/DECnet Monitor

The DECnet Monitor consists of three different modules. The data access module is responsible for interacting with different NMCC kernels, managing different request contexts, and caching data. The action module is responsible for processing that information into suitable screens of information. The presentation manager works with the different types of terminals available.

The data access module works with the kernel to present a stream of information to the action modules. The protocol interface deciphers incoming data and presents that information to a resource manager.

The resource manager can have multiple requests outstanding and is responsible for matching responses to requests. The resource manager is also able to detect duplicates and cancel old read requests. In case of a disconnection, the request manager will automatically try to reconnect to a kernel. This is important in cases where the DECnet Monitor is running unattended.

The data manager accepts information from the requests and caches it. When users cancel displays, the data manager passes that information on to the request manager. When data arrives in the cache, the data manager sets a flag to notify the users of that information.

The action routines do most of the work in the DECnet Monitor. Incoming information is prepared for presentation to the user. Commands are parsed and then passed along as data requests.

The parser in the action module is context sensitive. This means that commands are parsed in the context of previous interactions. A NEXT command is a prime example of context sensitive execution: it is interpreted by the parser to mean a display of a particular screen (usually the next screen in a list of outstanding requests).

Often an action routine is used to display real-time data. It is possible that the data requested has not arrived in the cache before the first screen is sent to the presentation module. In this case, the action routine uses default values and then updates information as data arrives in the cache.

The parser allows the user to request particular displays based on components in the database, relevant time periods, and information types. Through a combination of averaging and interpolation, it is possible to show data for any arbitrary time period.

A special set of action routines is used to modify data in the kernel. They switch from an asynchronous to a synchronous mode of action, which means that all steps in the modification are processed serially. This prevents the user from issuing a command and, after several intervening actions, receiving an error message.

In addition, the command parser is able to invoke the services of the report writer, exit to the operating system, or connect to different kernels. The command parser also maintains a help system similar to the VMS hierarchical help system.

The presentation modules are used to manage a single screen with multiple display areas. A command area accepts new directives and a message area returns messages from the DECnet Monitor. The actual display consists of a data area and an identification area. The data area holds the screen constructed by an action module. The identification area shows what screen is being displayed, and may contain information on previous or subsequent screens.

The actual format of the displayed data depends on the type of data that is requested. Maps are used for topographies. Forms, tables, and histograms are also available for displaying data. For maps, the parser is able to accept commands to magnify or zoom in the map or to pan to a different location.

Other Management Interfaces

This section will discuss a variety of other management interfaces for working with individual systems and other network architectures and components.

The section begins by discussing two software systems for managing individual nodes on the network remotely. The VAX Cluster Console System allows operator functions to be performed remotely. The Remote System Manager allows system management functions, such as software updates and backups, to be performed remotely.

Next, several packages are discussed for managing the Ethernet, terminal servers, and bridges. The Ethernet managment package, ETHERnim, can be used to examine all traffic on the Ethernet and is protocol independent. Terminal server and bridge management software systems are used to manage those particular types of devices.

VAX Cluster Console System

This software allows a single console to manage a series of different VAX systems. Up to 24 VAXs or HSC controllers may be managed from a single console system. The software uses the remote console capabilities of the MOP protocols to make a MicroVAX appear to the remote system like a locally attached console terminal. Figure 8-7 shows a VAX Cluster Console System configuration.

The VAX Cluster Console System (VCS) runs on a MicroVAX or a VAXstation II/GPX. A fiber link is used to connect to each node. Fiber is used to isolate the traffic. The console system must be configured with at least 5 Mbytes of memory and a 70-Mbyte disk.

Another way of connecting to remote nodes is to use the reverse LAT capability of a terminal server. An RS-232 cable is connected to the console port of the foreign device and to a port on the terminal server. That terminal server port is then connected to the VAX Cluster Console System using a LAT virtual circuit.

Reverse LAT on a terminal server allows foreign devices, such as a Vitalink TransLAN bridge, to be managed from a MicroVAX. The TransLAN is otherwise managed with a local VT220 terminal. This is not terribly convenient if an organization has several bridges located in different portions of a facility.

The software presents four different interfaces. Interactive users use an interface similar to the VMS monitor utility. This allows one or two nodes to be monitored. The interface can also search logs of console data to look for specific strings, such as system diagnostic messages.

To examine a particular node, the VCS can connect itself to the a member of the VAX Cluster system as though it were attached to the console of that node. This allows a single console to appear as though it were actually connected to all the console ports of the different nodes.

A programming or access interface allows specific actions to be taken when an event occurs. When an event arrives, a predefined piece of user software is activated and information about the event is passed in. If a system crashes, for example, the user software might

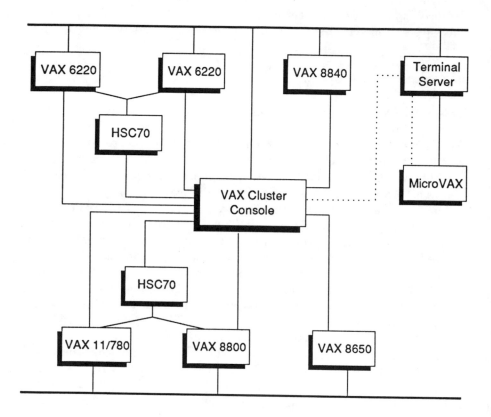

Fig. 8-7   VAX Cluster console.

activate a modem, call the system manager, and use DECtalk to inform the manager that a particular node is sick and needs attention.

The last interface is used to pass information to hard copy console terminals. One or several nodes can have their console logs redirected to a particular hard copy terminal.   When this data is received, it is logged with the time received and the source node, and then it is sent to the appropriate console. In a large machine room, this feature allows a single hard copy console to be monitored by operators, instead of requiring them to wear roller skates to check all consoles periodically.

An interesting feature of the monitor interface is the presence of a scan line file. This file contains a series of text strings. All incoming messages are compared against this scan line file to see if any of the strings occur in the message. If so, they are displayed on the monitor screen. The scan line allows high-priority console messages to be displayed on the screen and lower-priority messages to be routed to the hard copy terminal. A tape mount request by a user, for example, would probably go to the screen.

VCS requires a MicroVAX dedicated substantially to this function. It is possible to have extra CPU cycles available at times (during slow periods for example), but the real-time nature of this activity requires a guarantee of available resources.

Remote System Manager

While the VAX Cluster Console System provides remote operator functions, the Remote System Manager is used for remote system management. Remote management of workstations is particularly important because many VAXstations are used directly by end users with no system management training. RSM allows a single manager to perform backup and update functions for a variety of different clients.

RSM clients can only have one server, and they are usually on the same Ethernet as the server. It would not be unusual to have the Local Area VAX Cluster (LAVC) boot node also function as the RSM server. The RSM software does not consume resources when it is not being used, and hence the boot member can easily function in both roles.

One of the key features of RSM is that it allows backup to be automated among clients. This common backup is then used as an archive for the entire LAVC (or noncluster-based clients). Particular files can then be picked out of the backup set.

A common backup environment makes a lot of sense when all clients share an LAVC. Most of the files will be on an MSCP-served disk on the boot member. In addition, RSM can access disks that are local to RSM client members.

The second key function is a way of automating the software distribution process. These functions do not require clients to be on the same Ethernet as the server. Often, a software update requires an update on the configuration of several RSM client members. RSM allows clients and software to be put into groups. Each group accesses a common subset of software files, and other configuration information.

Files that may be automatically distributed include system information as well as commercial software. For example, every time a new node enters the network, in Phase IV it is necessary to update every other node's session control database. RSM can be used to perform that task for each of the client nodes.

A final function of RSM is the ability to create central print queues and then authorize access to the queues by client groups. This function is complementary with the Distributed Queuing Service (DQS) discussed in Chapter 3.

Terminal Server Manager/VMS

This is the third place that discusses terminal severs. The basic overview of the LAT architecture was in Chapter 4. Use of the terminal server was discussed in the Chapter 6 on local area networks.

Terminal service management can be done with a locally attached terminal or using the Terminal Server Manager/VMS software. Since a local terminal can be used, it is also possible to use the remote carrier console capabilities of the MOP protocols from the NCP user interface. The NCP interface lets a user connect to the terminal server, then type a CTRL/D to disconnect from that port.

The Terminal Server Manager/VMS offers several additional features over a local terminal or the use of NCP and the MOP remote carrier console capabilities. The software allows domains to be defined consisting of multiple terminal servers. A particular operation can be applied to the entire domain.

With domains, wild card operations can be performed. For example, the user could specify that port 1 on all terminal servers be changed to 9.6 kbps. With NCP, this would have to consist of several different operations, possibly driven by a batch file. Another advantage of the Terminal Server Manager/VMS is that a remote test can be initiated on a terminal server to determine if it is operational.

A management directory allows all terminal servers to be given ASCII names. The software can also set up domains of terminal servers. Domains are useful for group operations. In addition to configuring the remote, local, or dynamic characteristic of a port, the manager is able to set many other characteristics. Speed, character size, parity, and terminal type are just of some of the many and wonderfully varied parameters. Figures 8-8 and 8-9 show some terminal server characteristics.

This software can perform operations on both permanent and volatile parameters on remote terminal servers by name. For the DECServer 100 and 200, permanent parameters are stored in non-volatile random access memory (NVRAM). For the DECServer 500 and the Ethernet terminal server, permanent information is instead stored on a Phase IV host which then downline loads an image at initialization time.

Remote Bridge Management Software

Bridges are fairly self-sufficient, given the automatic nature of the initialization, the deterministic spanning tree algorithm, and the automatic learning algorithms. The RBMS software is used to control filtering on a bridge, to test availability, and to disable a port on the bridge as a way of isolating one Ethernet.

To simplify management, each bridge is given an ASCII name which corresponds to a physical address. The RBMS manager can then invoke a self-test on a particular bridge by name. It is also possible to display a variety of different statistics, such as the status of the forwarding database or the current values of traffic counters. Figures 8-10 and 8-11 show some bridge characteristics.

The software allows multiple users to access a single bridge. While this is technically feasible, it is an unusual network manager that would want to have several people simultaneously working on a single bridge. The multiuser interface is useful for multiple data collection activities.

Since bridges are an operational node on the Ethernet, there is really no reason that the bridge should have a separate management interface from, say, a terminal server or a VAX. The Phase V management architecture has the hooks necessary to include these types of devices into the broader DNA management structure. This level of integration allows a single user interface to manage a variety of different related devices.

NMCC/EtherNIM

The NMCC software is an interface to two sources of information. The DECnet Monitor portion of NMCC provides a graphic interface to Network Management Listeners and thus provides an alternative to NCP. The Ethernet Network Integrity Monitor (ETHERnim) provides an interface to the Ethernet subnetwork and thus replaces some of the function of the LAN Traffic Monitor.

ETHERnim provides a graphic representation of network status. Since multiport transceivers and all repeaters are transparent to the network, the software allows the user to manually construct a topology

```
Local> show port

Port 48: ^[

Character Size:          8         Input Speed:        9600
Flow Control:          XON         Output Speed:       9600
Parity:               None         Modem Control:  Disabled

Access:              Local         Local Switch:       None
Backward Switch:     None          Name:           LC-3-16
Break:               Local         Session Limit:         4
Forward Switch:      None          Type:               SOFT

Preferred Service:   None

Authorized Groups:   80-81
(Current) Groups:    80-81

Enabled Characteristics:

Autobaud, Autoprompt, Broadcast, Loss Notification, Message Codes
```

Courtesy of Digital Equipment Corporation

Fig. 8-8   Terminal server port characteristics.

```
Local> show server

DECserver 500 V1.0        LAT V5.1       ROM V1.0.2    Uptime: 45 16:37:;

Address:   08-00-2B-08-16-0A        Name:   zk33cZ    Number:    2

Identification:

Circuit Timer:          80         Password Limit:        3
Inactivity Timer:       30         Queue Limit:           8
Keepalive Timer:        20         Retransmit Limit:     10
Multicast Timer:        60         Session Limit:       256
Node Limit:            100

Service Groups:   None

Backup Hosts:   None

Enabled Characteristics:
```

Courtesy of Digital Equipment Corporation

Fig. 8-9   Terminal server characteristics.

```
                    Bridge Characteristics Display Example


Bridge Characteristics as of 20-Feb-85 12:13:25
Bridge LANZtoLAN5, Address AA-00-00-12-34-11

Bridge id: (priority/address)            128/AA-00-00-12-34-11
Bridge type:                             DEBET
Firmware version:                        2.0
Forwarding entries - max volatile:       8059
Forwarding entries - max non-volatile:  117
Total data line entries:                 2
Current highest line number:             2
```

Fig. 8-10 RBMS screen of bridge characteristics.

```
Known Forwarding Physical Entries as of 20-Feb-85 12:35:55
Bridge LANZtoLAN5, Address AA-00-00-12-34-11

Physical Address     Outbound  Last Seen  Destination    Set by       Auto-
                     Line      On Line                                 Delete

08-00-2B-22-00-00    NONE      N/A        NONE           SELF         NO
AA-00-00-12-34-11    NONE      N/A        NORMAL         SELF         NO
AA-00-00-00-12-34    Line 2    Line 2     NORMAL         MANAGEMENT   NO
AA-00-00-00-12-33    NONE      Line 2     ACTIVE LINES   MANAGEMENT   NO
AA-00-00-00-12-22    Line 1    N/A        NORMAL         LEARNING     YES
08-00-3B-22-00-01    NONE      NONE       NONE           MANAGEMENT   NO
```

Fig. 8-11 Bridge forwarding database.

that includes the different segments. Otherwise, the Ethernet is considered to be a logical bus.

Because ETHERnim operates at the Ethernet level, it is able to work with all devices on the Ethernet regardless of their protocols. The topology can thus include non-DEC devices, and the monitoring commands and statistics can include non-DEC protocols. The reference database in NMCC allows information on all devices to be supplemented with data such as the physical location of the device or the person responsible for it.

Various types of summary data can be examined. The top talkers and listeners on the network can be shown. Data can also be sorted by protocol type. Finally, the top pairs of nodes that communicate with each other can be displayed.

In addition to providing summary information on network status, ETHERnim is able to provide testing of nodes to various levels in the protocol stack. If the remote node is running VMS, the software can perform loopback tests all the way up to the user level. This confirms that all of the different layers of the network necessary for user to user communication are functioning properly.

LAN Traffic Monitor

LAN Traffic Monitor is a combination of a LAN Bridge 100 and some special software that is downloaded to change it from a store-and-forward device into an observation device. This software is known as the LTM Listener and is stored on a Phase IV host and then downloaded.

The LTM Listener periodically sends out datagrams. Those LTM datagrams are received on all VAXs that have the LTM user interface. This software collects the datagrams and summarizes them.

The software is able to summarize the data from the LTM listener and provide information on current, long-term, and peak usage. This information can be presented as a function of protocol types, nodes on the Ethernet, or packet size. The LTM Listener can display a historical graph of use for up to 48 hours.

One useful feature is the ability to display the top 10 talkers on the network. When users notice a slowdown in service, one of the first place to look is to see if some outrageous file transfer is in progress and has caused Ethernet saturation. Often nicknamed as a **LOUD$MOUTH** command, this accompanies the **PIGS** command which display the top CPU users on a particular node. Network managers are not always known for their tact.

PBX/Facilities Management

PBX/Facilities Management (P/FM) provides a management and accounting interface to selected PBX systems. Not surprisingly since DEC owns several, there is an interface to the Northern Telecom SL-1 family. There are also interfaces to the AT&T Dimension and System 85 PBX systems.

The software allows a user to track calls and produce billing reports. The billing reports are produced at the conclusion of each call and can thus be used for chargeback systems, such as those used in hotels.

Call billing is based on standard rate tables. Charge estimates are constructed based on the mileage bands, country codes, and other normal indicators for long-distance communication charges. In addition, bills can include allocated costs such as facilities rental.

As a management tool, the software is able to examine blocked or queued calls as a method of assessing capacity. In addition, calls can be directed by cost or duration or by specific lines. An online directory facility is included.

Phase V Network Management

Network management in Phase V has many similar functions to Phase IV, but the architectures have been generalized to support a more heterogenous environment with different types of management interfaces. The main functions in the network management modules include several important features.

First, the network management function gives the user the ability to configure parameters or fine-tune parameters that have been automatically configured. The user is also able to monitor performance and log relevant data automatically in various kinds of sinks. The network management functions also provide the manager with warnings for failures of network components. Finally, the user is able to start up and shut down components.

There are two main types of objects in the Phase V network management model. Entities are things that are managed. A node is an entity, as is the occurrence of a DDCMP data link module on that node. The director is the program that controls entities. Every entity on the network is required to provide an agent that interacts with the directors. This is in addition to the normal function of that entity which is to provide services to other entities. Figures 8-12 and 8-13 show the structure of the Phase V network management model.

Directors are the set of processes and commands that are used to provide the control. The interface to a director can be either an interactive user, using a user interface program, or a program that automatically provides network management. Management in a DECnet can be either centralized or distributed—each provider of the network management function interacts with a director.

Each entity in the network consists of a unique name and a series of attributes or events. An attribute is a piece of information that the entity maintains, while an event is a state transition that occurs at a particular time. An event might be a log-in failure. An attribute could be a count of log-in failures that occurredafter a particular time.

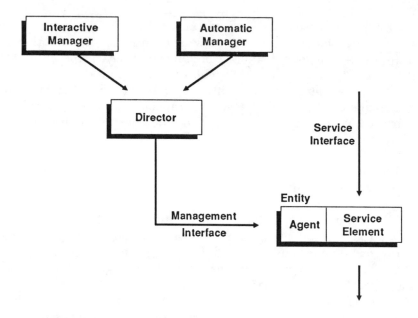

Fig. 8-12 Phase V management structure.

Entity names are unique within the network. The top level component of the namespace is a node, which has a unique name. Each node has a series of modules that have unique names, such as the routing module, the DDCMP module or the OSI transport layer module. Each module may then have a series of subentities. The DDCMP module would have a subentity for each data link that is currently defined.

The information an entity can maintain is quite varied. Each entity has a unique ID. It also has a series of entity specific characteristics such as the polling rate for a DDCMP multipoint link. Entities also have a series of status attributes which change dynamically without intervention. An example of this would be a change in the link state of a DDCMP link.

Another type of attribute is a series of counters. These counters are used for error management, billing, and performance tuning. Each entity in DNA has a series of counters defined. There may also be counters specified for events that are marginally related to the network, such as distributed naming service name changes.

Phase IV network management consists of a Network Information and Control Exchange (NICE) Protocol. This protocol is being replaced by the Common Management Information Protocol (CMIP). CMIP has two subprotocols:

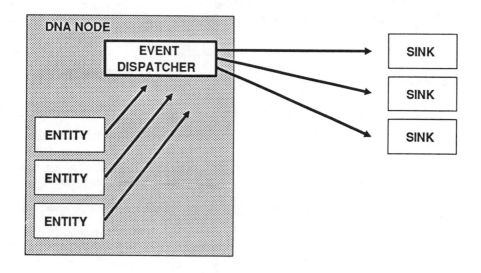

Fig. 8-13   Phase V event dispatching.

■ MICE is the Management Information Control and Exchange protocol which replaces the previous NICE protocol with an equally cute name.
■ The Management Event Notification (MEN) has been added to explicitly deal with the problem of passing events around the network.

In Phase V, there may be an arbitrary number of sinks for events. The MEN protocol is used to communicate between the source of the event and the sink node. Each node on the network provides an event dispatcher. This dispatcher is able to accept events from a variety of events on that node. The dispatcher provides both a buffer for events and the ability to filter particular streams of events to different sinks.

A significant change in Phase V is the replacement of the venerable Network Control Program (NCP) with a series of more modern interfaces. The command language interface replacement is the network control language, which also can issue NCP commands for management of Phase IV environments.

The network control language receives input directions from a terminal. These are then translated into directer commands. The directer then uses the MICE protocol to notify the relevant entities. A significant improvement in NCL is the ability to use a wild card in entity specifications. This would allow a single command to affect all lines in a particular DDCMP module or all nodes on a network. The NCL also allows interaction with a DNS nameserver to register node names.

EMA: Phase V user interface architecture

Accompanying many of the Phase V management advances is a new architecture for the structure of network management user interfaces. This architecture, called the Enterprise Management Architecture (EMA), is meant to handle the problem of directing a complex heterogeneous network.

EMA consists of a management information repository that is similar to the NMCC management database. This is managed by an EMA executive, similar to the NMCC kernel. This kernel presents a common interface to all users of the management tool. Figure 8-14 shows the structure of EMA.

In NMCC, the NICE protocols were the only method of accessing information and adding it to the kernel. EMA moves beyond that by defining a series of access modules. These access modules can access Phase IV networks using the NICE protocols. Another access module is able to access Phase V networks using the CMIP protocols. Yet other protocols can be designed to manage terminal servers, bridges, or any other entity on the network.

A particular protocol family, such as NICE is able to manage a wide variety of different entities. In the DNA/NICE protocol family, DDCMP or routing modules are two of the different types of entities that can be managed.

All entities are registered in the EMA Management Information Repository (MIR) when an access module is assigned. This entity class data defines the management functions available for a particular entity. If the entity is a television set, for example, the ON/OFF management function would be defined for that entity. When the management database sends down an ON command to an access module, it is the responsibility of the access module to form a valid ON message using the protocol for television sets.

Once a series of access modules has been defined and the entity class data loaded into the database, there needs to be a way to activate those functions. Functional modules are used to activate actions on the entities. Because a functional module is separated from the access modules, it is possible to have one functional module perform a single operation on many different kinds of entities. For example, in the television example, a functional command might be to

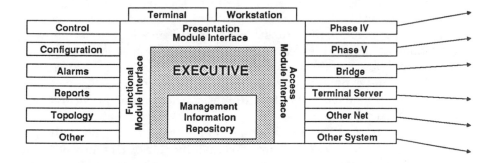

Fig. 8-14   Modular user interface architecture.

turn off all electrical appliances.   It would the responsibility of the television access module to formulate a TELEVISION OFF command and the responsibility of the lighting control access module to broadcast a LIGHTS OFF command.

Functions for an entity can be grouped into five classes, corresponding to the five categories used to classify CMIP data in the OSI network management model:

- Configuration is used to set the original permanent characteristics of a network.
- Fault management is used to cure fault conditions, such as switching to a backup line in the case of circuit failure.
- Performance management is used to control overall performance, such as adjusting window sizes to optimize a transport layer module for a particular transmission media such as satellite.
- Accounting management is used to collect data on usage.
- Security management controls access to the network.

Each of the functions can be incorporated in a set of functional modules that interface to the executive just as access modules do.   If entities all share common classes of entity data, such as an ON/OFF command, a single functional command is able to work on all the different types of accesses required.

Functional models are not necessarily limited to the five OSI clas-ses. A functional module might be used to periodically generate reports on the behalf of users or to form topological maps based on entity locations.

By keeping functional tasks in separate modules, the network management capabilities can grow gracefully. Questions of perfor-mance and fault management, for example, can start with a very simple manual capability of switching to alternate lines. That module can slowly grow to incorporate automatic switching or artificial intel-ligence-based decision making.

The presentation of information on the screen is the responsibility of a third set of modules, called presentation modules. One presentation module can be used to display information on a VT100 terminal, while a second could handle the DECwindows environment of bit-mapped screens. Users could write custom presentation modules for other equipment, such as 3270 terminals.

Many of the functions that were present in NMCC are also present in the new architecture. Instead of fixing the functionality of the sys-tem and limiting protocols to NICE, the new structure allows a modular approach to network management. It would even be possible to manage an IBM network from this product by defining a set of NETVIEW access modules.

What makes the architecture important is that it is not limited just to network management. A database management task can define a series of functions, such as BACKUP DATABASE. An SQL-based access module can then be defined and the database management functions can be integrated into the same user interface as the network manage-ment. Similar access modules could be defined to manage the VMS operating system.

Just because a common tool is used to manage different environ-ments does not mean that the same person will perform both tasks. EMA allows entities to be grouped into domains. Access to domains can then be limited by class of user.

It is possible for a single entity to be part of multiple domains. This allows entities to be available to multiple groups of users. For ex-ample, both the data and the voice manager may need the ability to allocate bandwidth from an application-independent backbone. Both managers, in this case, would need the ability to control bandwidth allocation through T1 switches. Needless to say, abuse of this multi-ple access can easily lead to a policy change to put the T1 switches into a separate, singly managed domain.

Summary

This chapter began with a discussion of the implementation of DNA on various operating systems. DNA is a flexible architecture which permits the same functionality to be implemented in a wide range of operating systems. While VMS still provides the highest level of functionality, even DOS systems are able to participate in a DECnet as a full-featured end node.

Managing the network is potentially a very complex task. Phase IV networks are managed using the NMCC and NCP user interfaces. Other user interfaces are used to manage multiple VAXs, terminal servers, bridges, PBXs, and other components of a distributed network environment.

Phase V of DECnet provides several valuable additions to network management capabilities. First, the DECnet protocols have been expanded to be more flexible and more powerful. More importantly, DEC has developed the EMA architecture which permits a single user interface to manage a wide variety of components. These components can be Phase IV or Phase V entities but can also include other network and nonnetwork components.

For Further Reading

Beck and Krycka, "The DECnet-VAX Product—An Integrated Approach to Networking," *Digital Technical Journal*, vol. 1, no. 3, September 1986, p. 88.

Digital Equipment Corporation, "DNA Phase IV Network Management Functional Specification," AA-X437A-TK, December 1983.

——, "DECnet-DNA Network Management Functional Specification" V4.0, AA-X437A-TK.

Forecast, et al., "The DECnet-Ultrix Software," *Digital Technical Journal*, vol. 1, no. 3, September 1986, p. 100.

Le Pelle et al., "The Evolution of Network Management Products," *Digital Technical Journal*, vol 1, no. 3, September 1986, p. 117.

Mierswa, et al., "The DECnet-DOS System," *Digital Technical Journal*, vol 1., no. 3, September 1986, p. 108.

Sylor, "The NMCC/DECnet Monitor Design," p. 129, *Digital Technical Journal*, Vol. 1, No. 3, September 1986.

——, "Managing Phase V DECnet Networks: The Entity Model," *IEEE Network*, March 1988, vol. 2, no. 2, pp. 30–35.

Part

4

Internets and Open Architectures

9

TCP/IP and the Network File System

Overview of This Chapter

This chapter discusses the TCP/IP networking protocols which are an alternative to the Digital Network Architecture and other DEC-developed networking schemes. One of the features of TCP/IP is that it is a nonproprietary set of networking standards. Because of the open nature of the protocols and the adoption of TCP/IP in the Unix marketplace, a wide variety of vendors support TCP/IP implementations, including DEC on both the VMS and Ultrix operating systems.

The basic TCP/IP protocol suite was sponsored by the Defense Advanced Research Projects Agency (DARPA) for use in Arpanet. The Arpanet is a wide area network that connects different research groups and contractors involved in defense contracting. Although Arpanet has been supplanted by more modern networks, the TCP/IP protocols continue to be used.

TCP/IP provide layers 3 and 4 of the ISO protocol stack. The Internet protocols provide routing among networks and in some cases within a particular network. The Transmission Control Protocol (TCP) and the User Datagram Protocol (UDP) take data delivered by IP to the appropriate node and send it up to various upper-level protocol users.

The original TCP/IP protocols offer only a limited amount of network functionality. Built on top of TCP/IP are three applications built directly on the transport layer that provide file transfer, mail transfer, and a virtual terminal service.

TCP/IP has been supplemented by the Network File System, developed by Sun Microsystems. Sun started out by adding session (RPC) and presentation (XDR) layers to the TCP/IP model and then providing a variety of layer 7 services.

The basic NFS service is a distributed file system. This allows files from one computer to be remotely mounted on another computer. The NFS client sees a series of files as though they were local. The files actually are a combination of local files and remotely files from a variety of NFS servers. This allows diskless nodes to remotely mount an operating system. Another use of NFS is to allow a user to remotely mount their files no matter which machine on the network they log into. This means that users can use a variety of different computers and always see a common file space.

Overview of IP

Internet protocols are used for delivering data between different networks in addition to within one centrally administered system. This is done by connecting groups of autonomous systems, or networks. Each of these networks is connected with a gateway.

The Internet protocols only define how subnetworks or data links are connected together. A subnet might be X.25 or Ethernet or ISDN. The subnet provides a virtual link between any two nodes in the subnet.

IP defines how packets are forwarded from one subnet to the next. This forwarding process is aided by the presence of routing update messages that keep forwarding databases up to date. Several different types of update messages are used, depending on the collection of subnets involved in a management domain.

A related set of services are the domain nameservers. These nameservers are able to translate logical names into internet addresses. While not a part of IP, the nameservers are an important supplement.

The Internet protocols are especially important because they form the basis of the connectionless network service of the Open Systems Interconnect model. The IP is very similar to the level 2 routing in between DNA areas, and some of the original work on IP was done at DEC. DEC will use the IP protocols in Phase V of DECnet as a method of routing data between DECnet areas and between DECnet and non-DECnet administrative domains.

Internet Addresses

The Internet addresses are administered by the Network Information Center (NIC) located at the Stanford Research Institute (SRI). If a locally administered Internet system is not connected to the larger Internet, the address can be arbitrary. However, when the network manager wants to connect to other IP based systems, such as the Arpanet, all local addresses have to be reassigned.

An IP address is a 32-bit number. Usually, each octet of the address is represented by its decimal equivalent. Thus, an Internet address of all 1s would be represented as:

$$256.256.256.256$$

There are three classes of Internet addresses assigned by SRI. If bit 1 is set to 0, this is a class A address, reserved for a very few large networks such as the Arpanet. Class As have the next 7 bits as the network ID, leaving the remaining 24 bits as a host ID. Class A networks are reserved with networks with more than 2^{16}, or 65,636 hosts.

If the first bit of the address is set to 1, the IP address is a class B or class C address. Class B addresses have bit 1 set to 1, bit 2 set to 0, and 14 bits for a network ID. The remaining 16 bits are for the host ID, allowing networks of 256 to 65,000 nodes. Class C networks have a 22 bit network ID and are used with networks with fewer than 256 hosts.

An Internet address represents a connection to the network. It is important to understand that a gateway is connected to two different networks and would thus have addresses on both those networks. There is also a broadcast address with all bits set to 1. Broadcasts are received by every host on that network, but they are not rebroadcast by gateways onto other networks.

Address Resolution

Internet addresses are conceptual addresses assigned by a network administrator. When an IP node wishes to transmit information to another IP node, the IP module dispatches the data to the data link layer. The data link layer sends it across to another data link layer node on that network. In order to send the IP packet, the IP address must be translated into a physical address for that particular transmission medium.

Internet protocols can be implemented over a wide variety of data link mechanisms. In each case, the data link layer makes all other

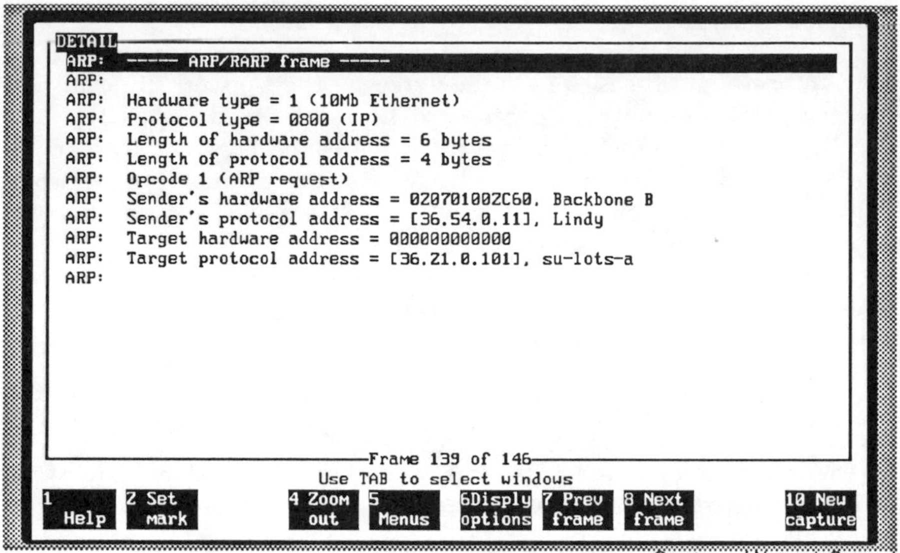

```
┌─────────────────────────────────────────────────────────────────┐
│ DETAIL                                                            │
│ ARP:  ───── ARP/RARP frame ─────                                  │
│ ARP:                                                              │
│ ARP:  Hardware type = 1 (10Mb Ethernet)                           │
│ ARP:  Protocol type = 0800 (IP)                                   │
│ ARP:  Length of hardware address = 6 bytes                        │
│ ARP:  Length of protocol address = 4 bytes                        │
│ ARP:  Opcode 1 (ARP request)                                      │
│ ARP:  Sender's hardware address = 020701002C60, Backbone B        │
│ ARP:  Sender's protocol address = [36.54.0.11], Lindy             │
│ ARP:  Target hardware address = 000000000000                      │
│ ARP:  Target protocol address = [36.21.0.101], su-lots-a          │
│ ARP:                                                              │
│                                                                   │
│                         ─Frame 139 of 146─                        │
│                      Use TAB to select windows                    │
│ 1        2 Set        4 Zoom   5        6Disply 7 Prev  8 Next     10 New │
│  Help     mark         out      Menus   options  frame   frame    capture│
└─────────────────────────────────────────────────────────────────┘
```

Fig. 9-1   An Address Resolution Protocol frame.

nodes on that particular network appear to be one hop away. Ethernet does this using a bus topology and the CSMA/CD protocols, possibly with bridges to form an extended Ethernet.

A token ring also makes all other nodes appear one hop away, through the mechanism of passing a token. Finally, X.25 can also be used as a subnetwork. X.25 allows the creation of switched or permanent virtual circuits. These circuits allow the IP layer to assume that it is directly connected to the host to which it wishes to talk.

In order to map Internet addresses into physical addresses of "adjacent" nodes, the Internet uses an Address Resolution Protocol (ARP). An ARP packet is a special type of broadcast. On the Ethernet, ARP packets are a special packet type, just as IP or LAT or the DNA Routing Protocol have their own packet types. Figure 9-1 shows an ARP packet on the Ethernet.

When a node broadcasts an ARP request, the node also includes its own Internet to physical mapping. Since each node contains a small cache, this minimizes the number of ARP requests broadcast on the network.

One of the Internet design philosophies is to minimize the locality of broadcast requests. If an ARP request was rebroadcast by gateways, this could lead to a tremendous drain on network resources.

The reverse of the Address Resolution Protocol is the Reverse Address Resolution Protocol or RARP. RARP requests are sent by disk-

```
┌DETAIL──────────────────────────────────────────────────────────────
│DLC:  ───── DLC Header ─────
│DLC:
│DLC:  Frame 95 arrived at 13:31:34.9574; frame size is 60 (003C hex)
│DLC:  Destination: Station 02608C063841, Pine C Gtwy
│DLC:  Source      : Station 02608C036310
│DLC:  Ethertype = 0800
│DLC:
│IP:   ───── IP Header ─────
│IP:
│IP:   Version = 4, header length = 20 bytes
│IP:   Type of service = 00
│IP:        000. .... = routine
│IP:        ...0 .... = normal delay
│IP:        .... 0... = normal throughput
│IP:        .... .0.. = normal reliability
│IP:   Total length = 41 bytes
│IP:   Identification = 30718
│IP:   Flags = 0X
│IP:   .0.. .... = may fragment
│IP:   ..0. .... = last fragment
│IP:   Fragment offset = 0
│IP:   Time to live = 15
│IP:   Protocol = 6 (TCP)
│IP:   Header checksum = E9DF (correct)
│IP:   Source address = [36.53.0.181]
│IP:   Destination address = [36.56.0.208]
│IP:   No options
│IP:
│TCP:  ───── TCP header ─────
│TCP:
│TCP:  Source port = 1042
│TCP:  Destination port = 23 (Telnet)
│TCP:  Sequence number = 43117352
│TCP:  Acknowledgment number = 2930105665
│TCP:  Data offset = 20
│TCP:  Flags = 18
│TCP:  ..0. .... = (No urgent pointer)
│TCP:  ...1 .... = Acknowledgment
│TCP:  .... 1... = Push
│TCP:  .... .0.. = (No reset)
└──────────────────────Frame 95 of 97──────────────────
 ┌─────┬─────┐       ┌─────┬─────┐   ┌───────┬──────┬──────┐
 │1    │2 Set│       │4 Zoom│5    │   │6Display│7 Prev│8 Next│
 │Help │mark │       │ out │Menus│   │options│ frame│ frame│
 └─────┴─────┘       └─────┴─────┘   └───────┴──────┴──────┘
```

Fig. 9-2   Contents of an Internet packet on Ethernet.

less nodes to determine their Internet address. Usually, that address is not stored in the ROM of the diskless node, but the RARP protocols are.

IP Packets

The IP protocol offers a connectionless datagram service to deliver data. This means that the service provider sends information one packet at a time. Each packet may or may not get there. Different packets may travel over different routes. Assured delivery, if needed, is provided by the Transmission Control Protocol. Figure 9-2 shows an Internet Protocol packet on the Ethernet.

A packet of information from either an IP control module or an upper-layer user of IP is enclosed within an IP header. The IP datagram is then encapsulated with a subnetwork header, such as Ethernet information. IP is able to take a datagram and segment it into smaller pieces for the data link layer. A design constraint suggested by IP architects is that a data link layer should be capable of handling 576 octets without segmentation. Once an IP datagram is segmented, it usually stays segmented until it reaches its final destination. This occurs even if subsequent data link layers are able to accommodate larger packet sizes. The IP packet format is as follows:

IP version
IP length
Type of service
Total length
Fragmentation control fields
Time to live
High level protocol type
Header checksum
IP source address
IP destination address
Option class and number
Padding
Data

The IP header provides a variety of information in addition to the source and destination addresses. The header begins with the IP version number and the length of the header. The type of service indicates both the service type and the precedence of the data. Precedence is an indicator of delivery priority, ranging from 0 for normal data to 7 for network management data. Service type gives the user a choice of low delay, high throughput, and/or high reliability. Service type can be thought of as a "hint" to routers. High-throughput data might be routed via a satellite, while a low-delay flag might use a low-capacity 9.6-kbps unused line.

Fragmentation fields indicate how to segment and desegment IP messages. A flag can be set in this field indicating that the data should not be fragmented. Another flag indicates if there are more fragments of a message to be sent. An identification field is a unique ID for that message. All fragments of a message contain the same ID field. Finally, the fragmentation offset indicates where in the message this particular fragment is contained.

The TIME TO LIVE field is a number which says how long this particular packet can survive on the network. Each host or gateway that receives this packet decrements the number by 1. If a gateway receives a packet with a time to live of zero, it performs a summary execution.

Option classes determine if the data is normal data or is used for debugging. Within an option class, there are a variety of option numbers. An option class of 0 stands for either a datagram or a network control packet. A number 9 within class 0 indicates that strict source routing, as specified by the source host, must be used. If that route is not available, the gateway should not choose an alternate route.

A number of 7 within class 0 specifies that routes should be traced. Every gateway that is visited has its address stamped in the packet. Option class 2 (debugging) has an option number of 4, which time stamps all stops the packet made on the way. This allows measurement of network performance.

IP Routing

There are two types of routing within an Internet. Within a single network, the IP module need only map the IP to the physical address and send the packet. This, of course, implies that the subnetwork, such as X.25, is able to shield the complexities of the underlying data link from the IP module. Subnet routing, discussed later, allows IP to control routing at the subnetwork layer.

Another IP routing scenario is to route a packet to another network. This is done by consulting an Internet routing table. This table contains a series of pairs of information showing the destination net and the nearest gateway that can access that network. The host then routes the packet to the designated gateway. That gateway, in turn, will consult its routing table for the next gateway. Finally, the data will be delivered to the destination network gateway, which will deliver the packet to the designated host.

An important IP concept is that routing decisions are made on the basis of networks, not by the address of a destination host. A particular destination host is a part of a network, which is accessible by a gateway. A more sophisticated analysis of the location of the host within the target network is not available from the sending node. If we specify the address of a remote host that doesn't exist, an error message will not be generated until the gateway connected to that network is reached.

Since there is no concept of relative costs available in a routing table, there is no capability to do load balancing across multiple paths to a destination host. IP is also not able to segment traffic by type of traffic (i.e., priority) over different data links. One option available is source-specified routing, in which the source node specifies the exact path to take, alleviating the gateways of the responsibility for determining the optimal path.

Two mechanisms will be examined that supplement the relatively unsophisticated routing decision process in IP. Internet control messages are used to allow different IP modules to communicate among each other, and include a REDIRECT DATA request which indicates that data should really be sent to another gateway on the source network that has a better path to the destination host or network. The second mechanism is routing control messages, which allow gateways to communicate among themselves and provide more sophisticated path information.

Internet Control Message Protocol

The Internet Control Message Protocol (ICMP) is used by IP to transmit IP error and control messages. ICMP messages are exchanged between different IP modules. A simple message is the ICMP ECHO REQUEST message, which is used to test whether a destination is reachable. This echo request message can also be used to specify average delay on a line by timing the amount of time it takes to get a reply. Figure 9-3 shows an ICMP packet.

Unreachable destination request messages are sent by gateways when they receive a packet they are unable to forward. The reports sent by the gateway could indicate that the network or host is unreachable or that a particular upper-layer protocol or port is unreachable. If the source host indicated that fragmentation was not allowed, the gateway might also send a report if it would have needed to fragment the data. Finally, a report can be sent if the source specified routing failed.

Unreachable destination reports also include the beginning of the packet data that was originally sent so the source can determine whom to notify about the failure to successfully send the data. A virtual terminal service might use the Transmission Control Protocol, which in turn would use the IP protocols. If, for some reason, the destination is unreachable, the IP module would want to notify the TCP module. The TCP module, in turn, would notify the TELNET virtual terminal service. TELNET would then print a message on the screen to the user.

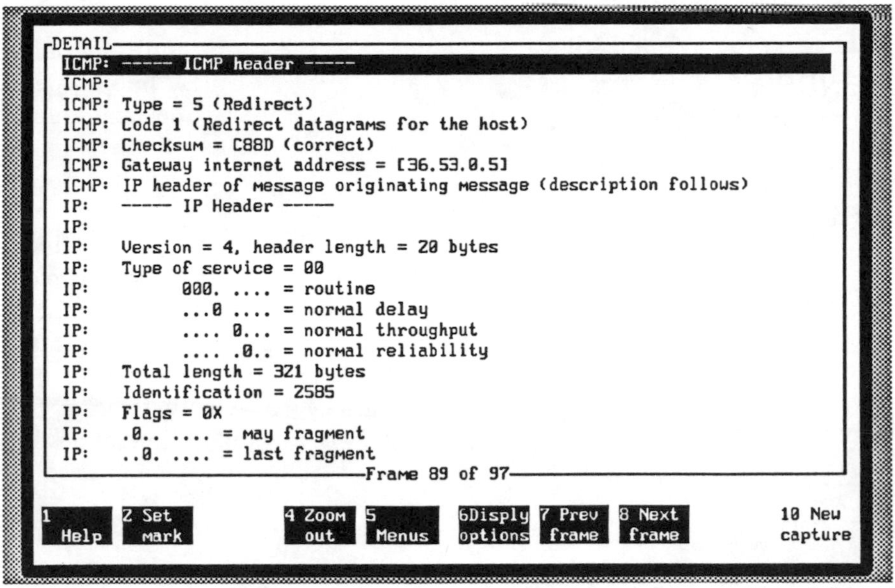

```
┌DETAIL──────────────────────────────────────────────────────────────┐
│ ICMP: ───── ICMP header ─────                                       │
│ ICMP:                                                               │
│ ICMP: Type = 5 (Redirect)                                           │
│ ICMP: Code 1 (Redirect datagrams for the host)                      │
│ ICMP: Checksum = C88D (correct)                                     │
│ ICMP: Gateway internet address = [36.53.0.5]                        │
│ ICMP: IP header of message originating message (description follows)│
│ IP:   ───── IP Header ─────                                         │
│ IP:                                                                 │
│ IP:   Version = 4, header length = 20 bytes                         │
│ IP:   Type of service = 00                                          │
│ IP:        000. .... = routine                                      │
│ IP:        ...0 .... = normal delay                                 │
│ IP:        .... 0... = normal throughput                            │
│ IP:        .... .0.. = normal reliability                           │
│ IP:   Total length = 321 bytes                                      │
│ IP:   Identification = 2585                                         │
│ IP:   Flags = 0X                                                    │
│ IP:   .0.. .... = may fragment                                      │
│ IP:   ..0. .... = last fragment                                     │
│                  ──────────Frame 89 of 97──────────                 │
└─────────────────────────────────────────────────────────────────────┘
┌──────┐┌──────┐    ┌──────┐┌─────┐┌───────┐┌──────┐┌──────┐  ┌────────┐
│1     ││2 Set │    │4 Zoom││5    ││6Display││7 Prev││8 Next│  │10 New  │
│ Help ││ mark │    │ out  ││Menus││options ││ frame││ frame│  │capture │
└──────┘└──────┘    └──────┘└─────┘└───────┘└──────┘└──────┘  └────────┘
```

Courtesy of Network General

Fig. 9-3 An ICMP packet.

A second type of ICMP message is known as a SOURCE QUENCH message. If a host receives more packets than it can handle at the IP layer, it does two things. First, it throws away all the packets, typically in the form of a buffer overflow. Second, the IP module issues a source-quench message which instructs the sending module to reduce the sending rate.

Source-quench messages only operate for a small period of time. The recipient of a source quench message reduces the transmission rate for a period of time. Each time a new source quench message is received, it reduces the transmission rate again. If no more messages are received, the sending module gradually increases its sending rate back to the original.

The third type of ICMP messages are ROUTING CHANGE REQUESTS. A redirect data request is sent by a gateway when it determines that it is not the optimal gateway for a particular destination. The message to the originating host is not broadcast to the network. The message can instruct the host to redirect all datagrams to that destination host to the destination network. The redirect message can also specify that certain types of services be redirected.

A long route notification is sent when a gateway receives a packet with a time to live flag that is about to expire. When the IP module destroys the offending packet, it also sends a message back to the sending host. This is sort of like a telegram sent by the military to

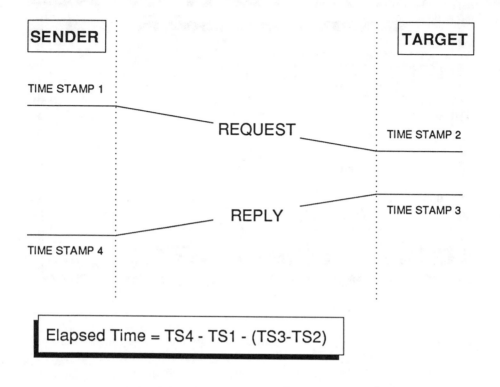

Fig. 9-4   Time stamp sequence.

widows of war victims ("We are sorry to inform you that your packet number ... has expired in the line of duty").

The fourth type of ICMP message is time stamp requests and replies. These messages are used to estimate average delay on the network. Average delay is used to determine the transmission rate to use. Several other timers may also be influenced by average delay. For example, when the beginning fragment of a message is received, a timer is started by the IP module. If all fragments have not been received before the timer occurs, an ICMP FRAGMENTATION REASSEMBLY ERROR message is sent.

To estimate round trip delay, four time stamps are involved (see Figure 9-4). The sender time stamps the request packet. The recipient stamps the packet when it receives it and when it sends back the reply. The original sender time stamps the reply when it receives it. Time stamps 2 and 3 provide an estimate of how long it took the target to process the information. Time stamps 1 and 4 provide the total amount of time on the network. By subtracting the two delay estimates, one can arrive at a delay for the data link. Repeating the sequence several times yields an average delay parameter.

Autonomous Systems and the Internet

The Internet is composed of a series of autonomous systems. An autonomous system is a centrally administered network. For example, the Arpanet is an autonomous system. Each autonomous system offers a series of gateways which are used to connect to other autonomous systems. Note that an autonomous system can be composed of several networks.

A series of core gateways provides the glue that holds all these different networks together to form the Internet. The core gateways are centrally administered and provide a reliable backbone for the Internet and are administered by the Internet Network Operations Center.

The core uses the services of both Arpanet and the National Science Foundation's NSFnet to provide a high-capacity link among core gateways. Core gateways are then connected to a variety of autonomous systems. The gateways on these autonomous systems communicate with each other and the core using an Exterior Gateway Protocol (EGP). Figure 9-5 illustrates this concept of autonomous systems and routing update protocols.

The EGP is used by neighboring gateways. It allows a gateway to acquire (register) a neighbor. Note that the term "neighbor" is misleading; it only implies that the underlying data link, such as X.25, shields the actual location of the node. Note also that gateways don't arbitrarily select neighbor gateways. This is an administrative decision by the network manager.

EGP has two kinds of operational messages. First, gateways periodically test to see if the neighbor is reachable. In the acquisition process, the nodes agree on the interval of these HELLO messages. Presumably, this message will be sent fairly frequently.

A HELLO message must be acknowledged. Even if an ACK is not received, the sending gateway does not immediately assume that the target is not operational. This is important because there is a great deal of overhead involved in a disabled gateway. If several packets are unacknowledged, the host is declared to be dead. Before the host is considered back up again, it must successfully acknowledge several, not just one, HELLO messages.

The second type of message is a routing update message, which will be sent less frequently than the HELLO message. A routing update message is sent in response to a poll request or because of a change in the network configuration. The EGP allows a gateway to advertise

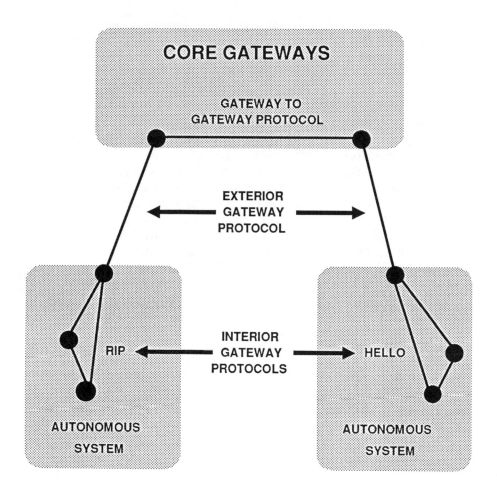

Fig. 9-5   Autonomous regions in the Internet.

the availability of networks only within its own autonomous system. This allows each autonomous system to maintain full control over how it advertises availability.

Interior gateway protocols

Within an autonomous system there may be several gateways since there may be several networks. The gateways within an autonomous system communicate with each other using an interior gateway protocols. There are several interior gateway protocols available, including the Routing Information Protocol (RIP). The core can also be considered to be an autonomous system and has its own interior protocol called the Gateway-to-Gateway Protocol (GGP).

The GGP consists of a series of advertisements within the core. Each core gateway advertises which nets it can reach and the cost to reach that network. Cost is usually measured as hops, although the number can be artificially adjusted to take into account slow networks.

The core gateways that use the GGP have a list of all possible routes to a destination network. The core thus provides alternative routing in case of routing failures. Also, by using the cost metric, they offer a form of least-cost routing. Note that the sending host must first send the data to a gateway, which then determines the optimal route.

The Routing Information Protocol (RIP) is frequently used as an IGP, particularly within Unix implementations of the Internet Protocol. This is because the Berkeley versions of Unix have implemented RIP in a route daemon called **routed**. "Daemon" is a Unix term for a program that functions without user intervention.

RIP is used between neighbors. Note that the EGP advertised the existence of all gateways it knew about. RIP is used only to broadcast destinations it can reach, not those reachable by other nodes. RIP advertises the existence of a network and the cost of reaching that network where cost is the number of hops to that network. Each RIP neighbor thus periodically transmits its routing table to its neighbors.

An alternative to RIP is the HELLO protocol. Unlike RIP, HELLO uses delay as a metric for cost, not just the number of hops. HELLO is used as an interior gateway protocol within the NSFnet. Each node keeps an estimate of the roundtrip delay to various hosts it can reach. It then transmits that information, along with its own time stamp, as a HELLO packet to neighboring nodes. This allows the neighbor to keep an estimate of the time of its neighbors, and so on.

Subnet Routing

Official Internet addresses fall within the three classes outlined earlier in the chapter. Within a network, there are no alternative paths because the IP assumes that it is one hop away from all nodes on the network. Subnets allow a network to be partitioned into a series of subnetworks, each connected by gateways. Thus, although the exterior gateway knows about only one gateway, that gateway can further transmit information to a series of subnet gateways.

One technique for providing subnets is called the transparent gateway mechanism. Only a certain number of hosts are available on the Arpanet. Frequently a site has one officially connected host on the Arpanet but wishes to have other local hosts access the Arpanet also.

The official host is the destination for all packets from the Arpanet. However, an Arpanet address only uses three of the octets in the address (See Figure 9-6). By adding bits in the unused portion of the Arpanet address, the target host can really be a network.

Subnets are another mechanism. A class B network can have between 256 and 16,535 hosts on the network. If a network has significantly fewer than 16,000 nodes, it can allocate a portion of the HOSTID field in the Internet address to be a subnetwork identification.

When subnet routing is used, the routing tables are typically supplemented with a subnet mask. The mask specifies which bits of the total Internet address should be considered as a specific network. A network mask of all 1s is really a way to identify a specific host. For other network masks, this specifies which gateway handles that particular subnet. For true Internet routing, the subnet mask is set to the bits specified for that particular class of Internet address. See Figures 9-7 and 9-8 for an illustration of the two methods of providing access to routing within a network.

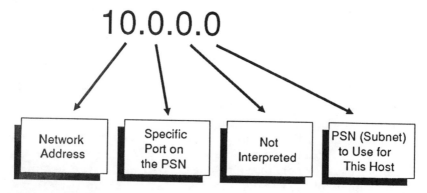

Fig. 9-6 Subdivisions of an ArPANET address.

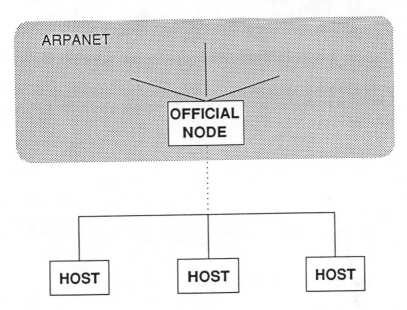

Fig. 9-7 Extending host addresses.

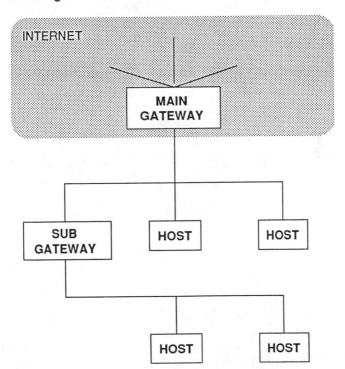

Fig. 9-8 Using subnet routing tables.

In the routing table, a network mask of all 0s means that none of the network address should be considered. What this means is a default rule. If a particular address does not match, this is the gateway to use for all remaining addresses.

The Domain Naming System

The ARP protocols are used to translate Internet addresses into physical addresses for a particular data link. One more level of translation is necessary for users of the network. This allows names to be formed that use alphanumeric characters and have semantic content, as opposed to the 32-bit Internet number.

Names in the Internet are formed in a hierarchy of domains. The name of a machine has the form:

machine.suborganization.organization.domain

Common domains include commercial (COM), educational (EDU), governmental (GOV), military (MIL), the Arpanet (ARPA), and foreign countries (the name of the country).

Each level of the domain naming system has authority over the subdomains it controls. Thus the COM domain can cede authority to the General Motors (GM) organization. GM, in turn, can cede authority to suborganizations, which finally have control over individual host names.

Nameservers are used to map domain names into Internet addresses and are considered to be the authority within their subdomain. Nameservers form a hierarchy, finally reaching a root nameserver which is considered to be the authority for a root domain.

Requests for translation of a name into an Internet address are sent to a nameserver. The server can either respond with the complete translation or with the name of another server to contact. In a recursive translation, the local server provides the interaction with the rest of the network. For nonrecursive translation, the client must then contact each of the servers. Figure 9-9 shows a DNS query on the Ethernet.

Servers cache recently resolved names to reduce the amount of DNS traffic. If the server was not the authority for a translation, it is possible that the cache is out of data. When a server gives out cache information for which it is not the authority, this is considered to be a nonauthoritative binding. The server then provides the address of the server that provided the initial binding of domain to Internet name translation.

```
┌DETAIL────────────────────────────────────────────────────────────────
│ DNS:  ───── Internet Domain Name Service header ─────
│ DNS:
│ DNS:  ID = 166
│ DNS:  Flags = 84
│ DNS:  1... .... = Response
│ DNS:  .... .1.. = authoritative answer
│ DNS:  .... ..0. = not truncated
│ DNS:  Flags = 8X
│ DNS:  1... .... = recursion available
│ DNS:  Response code = OK (0)
│ DNS:  Question count = 1, Answer count = 9
│ DNS:  Authority count = 0, Additional record count = 0
│ DNS:
│ DNS:  Question section:
│ DNS:      Name = sail.stanford.edu
│ DNS:      Type = All records (×,255)
│ DNS:      Class = Internet (IN,1)
│ DNS:  Answer section 1:
│ DNS:      Name = sail.stanford.edu
│ DNS:      Type = Host information (HINFO,13)
│ DNS:      Class = Internet (IN,1)
│ DNS:      Time-to-live = 43200 (seconds)
│ DNS:      CPU = DEC-1080
│ DNS:      OS = WAITS
│ DNS:  Answer section 2:
│ DNS:      Name = sail.stanford.edu
│ DNS:      Type = Well-known service descriptor (WKS,11)
│ DNS:      Class = Internet (IN,1)
│ DNS:      Time-to-live = 43200 (seconds)
│ DNS:      Address = [10.0.0.11]
│ DNS:      Protocol = TCP (6)
│ DNS:      Services = Echo (7), Discard (9), Daytime (13), Quote (17)
│ DNS:               = SMTP (25), Time (37), Finger (79), Supdup (95)
│ DNS:  Answer section 3:
│ DNS:      Name = sail.stanford.edu
│ DNS:      Type = Well-known service descriptor (WKS,11)
│ DNS:      Class = Internet (IN,1)
│ DNS:      Time-to-live = 43200 (seconds)
│ DNS:      Address = [10.0.0.11]
│ DNS:      Protocol = UDP (17)

│ DNS:  Answer section 7:
│ DNS:      Name = sail.stanford.edu
│ DNS:      Type = Host address (A,1)
│ DNS:      Class = Internet (IN,1)
│ DNS:      Time-to-live = 43200 (seconds)
│ DNS:      Address = [10.0.0.11]
│ DNS:  Answer section 8:
│ DNS:      Name = sail.stanford.edu
│ DNS:      Type = Mail transfer (MX,15)
│ DNS:      Class = Internet (IN,1)
│ DNS:      Time-to-live = 43200 (seconds)
│ DNS:      Preference = 10
│ DNS:      Mail domain name = Sail.Stanford.EDU
│ DNS:  Answer section 9:
│ DNS:      Name = sail.stanford.edu
│                        ─────Frame 48 of 97─────
│ 1       2 Set              4 Zoom  5         6Display 7 Prev  8 Next
│ Help    mark               out     Menus     options  frame   frame
└──────────────────────────────────────────────────────────────────────
```

Courtesy of Network General

Fig. 9-9   Domain name service query results.

One of the parameters on a DNS translation is a time to live parameter which specifies how long the translation should remain good. On static networks, this parameter is set very high.

DNS queries can ask several questions within one packet. The domain nameservers are able to handle a variety of classes of names, not just Internet host addresses. Within the Internet class of DNS queries, there is also a provision for mail address translation as well as host translation.

One frequent use of a DNS server is to provide an alias service. This allows the names of hosts to be abbreviated. The DNS server than provides the complete Internet translation. A user might send mail to **joe@pentagon** which would then be translated into an address such as **jmiller@host99876.Army.Pentagon.Mil**

Transport Layer Services

There are two different options available for the transport layer in TCP/IP:

- The User Datagram Protocol (UDP) is fairly efficient but offers a low level of service.
- The Transmission Control Protocol (TCP) offers assured delivery but at the price of more overhead.

The User Datagram Protocol accepts data from the Internet modules that implement IP and forwards the data to different processes on the system. UDP adds to the network service by serving as a multiplexer for several application programs using one routing level module. Figure 9-10 shows a UDP packet on the Ethernet.

Each user of UDP is assigned a port number. Incoming data contains a 17 in the **PROTOCOL TYPE** field of the IP header. This signals the IP module that the data should be given to the UDP module instead of to some other user of the network service.

The UDP header contains both a source and a destination port. Some ports are registered and can be found on many TCP/IP implementations. Some examples of well-known port numbers are:

5	RJE Service
7	Echo Service
11	USERS—Show all users on remote system
15	NETSTAT—Show network statistics
17	Quote of the day service
53	Domain name server

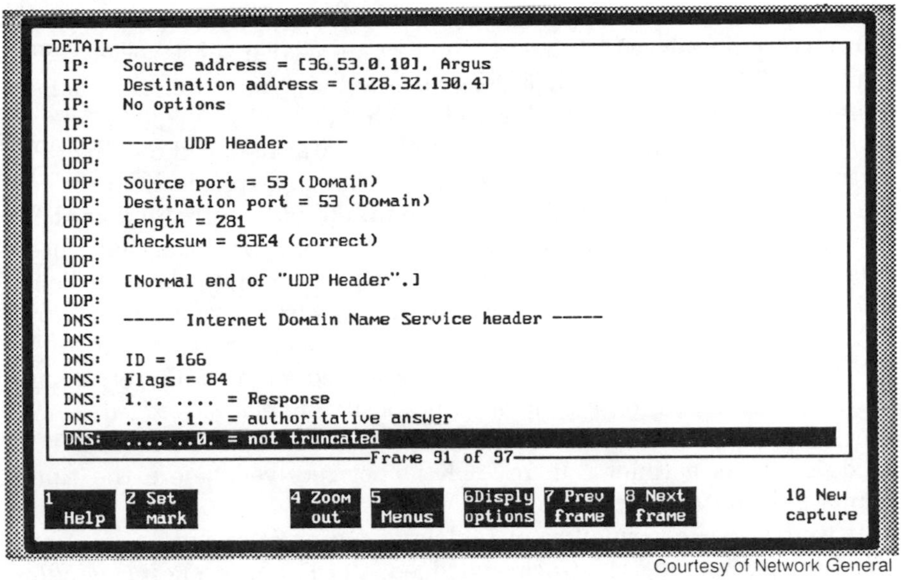

```
┌DETAIL────────────────────────────────────────────────────────┐
│ IP:    Source address = [36.53.0.10], Argus                   │
│ IP:    Destination address = [128.32.130.4]                   │
│ IP:    No options                                             │
│ IP:                                                           │
│ UDP:   ───── UDP Header ─────                                 │
│ UDP:                                                          │
│ UDP:   Source port = 53 (Domain)                             │
│ UDP:   Destination port = 53 (Domain)                        │
│ UDP:   Length = 281                                          │
│ UDP:   Checksum = 93E4 (correct)                            │
│ UDP:                                                          │
│ UDP:   [Normal end of "UDP Header".]                         │
│ UDP:                                                          │
│ DNS:   ───── Internet Domain Name Service header ─────       │
│ DNS:                                                          │
│ DNS:   ID = 166                                              │
│ DNS:   Flags = 84                                            │
│ DNS:   1... .... = Response                                  │
│ DNS:   .... .1.. = authoritative answer                      │
│ DNS:   .... ..0. = not truncated                            │
│────────────────────────Frame 91 of 97─────────────────────────│
│                                                               │
│ 1        2 Set       4 Zoom  5        6Disply 7 Prev 8 Next   10 New │
│   Help     mark        out     Menus   options  frame  frame  capture │
```

Courtesy of Network General

Fig. 9-10   A UDP packet.

69   Trivial file transfer protocol

Many ports are registered to both the UDP and TCP transport services allowing users to access the upper-layer services from different transport layers. An implementation of the USERS command on an Ethernet might choose to use the UDP transport service because of the very low error rate on an Ethernet. A wide area implementation of the USERS command might choose to use TCP because of the possibility of lost packets from leased phone lines or public X.25 networks.

In addition to well-known services with reserved port numbers, there are also port numbers available for transient use. These can be assigned by application programs at run time. Other port numbers are also available for registration by local users of the network as permanent services.

In a UDP implementation, there is no assurance that data will arrive at the destination or that different packets of data will not travel by different routes and have their arrival order permuted. Because of this, UDP data must be self-describing. This means that the user of the UDP service must be able to interpret a message in a stand-alone context and determine what to do with it.

The Network File System, discussed later, is a stateless application. This means no connection exists between the client and server and every packet is self-describing. The NFS services are built on top of the UDP protocols which are a connectionless transport service. By contrast, DECs Distributed File Service is built on top of the connection-oriented NSP transport layer of DECnet.

TCP provides a more robust service by guaranteeing the delivery of data in the order received. This means that the application program can process data sequentially as a stream of bytes without regard for the mechanics of delivery of the data. The TCP protocols have been modified and enhanced in the TP4 transport service which is being used in Open Systems Interconnect (OSI) networking software.

Like the NSP end-to-end communications protocols examined in the DNA chapters, TCP use a positive acknowledgment with retransmit (PAR) protocol. All data sent must be positively acknowledged or will be assumed lost. When a packet of data is sent, the sending TCP module begins a timer. If an ACK is not received before the timer expires, the data is retransmitted.

It would not be very efficient to delay sending a second packet until the first packet has been acknowledged. TCP has a sliding window mechanism to provide higher throughput. The receiving module tells the originating TCP modules how many bytes of data it has received and how many more it is willing to receive. At any time, the sending module cannot have more than that number of unacknowledged bytes outstanding.

ACKs can be sent in their own packet or can by piggybacked on to data being sent back to the other module. Each time an ACK is sent, the TCP module also indicates the current size of the window. This allows the window to vary dynamically in response to network or host congestion.

TCP modules are able to respond to congestion on the network by reducing their transmission time. The time-out parameter for data sent is a dynamic number that is a function of the average round-trip delay between two points on the network. As the delay increases, so does the time-out factor. As these delay times are increased, a well-designed TCP module should also reduce the transmission rate. This will alleviate the need for the target Internet module to send a SOURCE QUENCH ICMP message.

Usually, the user of TCP allows the TCP module to decide how to packetize data. Normally, the TCP module will wait for a certain number of bytes to appear in a buffer before packetizing the data and delivering it to the IP module for transmission over the network.

An upper-layer user can modify this behavior by issuing a PUSH DATA command. Thus, a user waiting for a response from a full-screen editor would not be forced to wait for a TCP timer to expire before having the data delivered to the target system.

Another option available to users of the TCP service is to label certain data urgent. All data in the urgent buffer is delivered by TCP before data in the normal buffer. This is typically used by applications programs for out-of-band signalling, such as an abort interrupt.

Upper level TCP/IP services

The basic TCP/IP model includes three simple types of applications. These applications use the transport layer directly rather than using the services of the presentation and session layers like other services examined in this book. The three basic applications include:

- A file transfer protocol
- A virtual terminal service
- A simple mail transfer protocol

DEC has furnished equipment and other support to the National Bureau of Standards in its effort to build gateways between these three basic services and their OSI counterparts. This allows a file to be transferred using FTAM up to the boundary of the OSI network and then transferred using FTP for the remainder of the path into the TCP/IP environment.

File Transfer Protocol

The File Transfer Protocol (FTP) is a program used for the bulk transfer of data from one node to another. The Berkeley Unix equivalent to the Arpanet FTP service is the **rcp** (remote copy) command. In both cases, only entire files can be transferred, not selected records. Figure 9-11 shows an example of an FTP session.

Data in the FTP environment consists of a stream of data followed by an end of file marker. A more sophisticated interface allows data to be transmitted as records, with each record terminated by an end of record marker.

FTP is supposed to transfer any type of data as long as it is composed of bytes and not arbitrary bit patterns. This poses a problem if the data transmitted has an occurrence of the bit pattern that is used to signify the end of record. To handle this and other signaling problems, FTP uses a byte with all bits set to identify a control sequence such as the EOF mark. If the data actually consists of all 1s, the sending FTP module stuffs in an extra bit and the receiving module strips it.

```
ux1.lbl.gov%
ux1.lbl.gov% ftp
ftp> open ux3
Connected to ux3.lbl.gov.
220 ux3.lbl.gov FTP server (Version 4.7 Sun Sep 14 12:44:57 PDT 1986) ready.
Name (ux3.lbl.gov:bob): bob
Password (ux3.lbl.gov:bob):
331 Password required for bob.
230 User bob logged in.
ftp> status
Connected to ux3.lbl.gov.
Mode: stream; Type: ascii; Form: non-print; Structure: file
Verbose: on; Bell: off; Prompting: on; Globbing: on
Hash mark printing: off; Use of PORT cmds: on
ftp> ls *.log
200 PORT command okay.
150 Opening data connection for /bin/ls (128.3.254.19,13311) (0 bytes).
irds.log
226 Transfer complete.
10 bytes received in 0.90 seconds (0.011 Kbytes/s)
ftp> close
221 Goodbye.
ftp> quit
ux1.lbl.gov%
```

Courtesy of Lawrence Berkeley Laboratory

Fig. 9-11   An FTP session on TCP/IP.

A compressed data mode is available in FTP to strip out unnecessary data repetitions. This is again done with a control indicator, followed by a 2-byte code indicating the type of repetition. The first byte is how many occurrences are present; the second byte is for the character to be repeated.

Flow control is accomplished in several ways. First, the underlying TCP environment provides a form of buffering and flow control. Second, a block mode is available that lets files be transferred in a start/stop mode.

An FTP implementation actually consists of two separate TCP connections. One is used for commands and responses. The channel is used for data and acknowledgments. Usually, these two connections have different TCP flow control parameters (window sizes, etc.).

On most systems, TCP/IP services are implemented as part of the kernel functions. This is usually the case for both Unix and VMS. This is because both modules provide services for a variety of different users and interact with low-level device drivers. The FTP module, like the DNA DAP module, executes in user space to avoid violating file access protection by executing in the wrong context.

SMTP mail protocols

The Simple Mail Transfer Protocol (SMTP) is a set of standard commands for exchanging mail messages between systems. SMTP makes no attempt to define the nature of the user interface or the local functionality that is available. SMTP also does not necessarily operate for transfer of mail between users on the same node. A native mail system may be invoked for this function.

SMTP functions by examining a special queue area on the file system. If messages are present on that queue, a TCP connection is activated on port 25 and a remote SMTP module is notified to accept the messages. SMTP receivers either queue the message locally or place it back into an SMTP queue for forwarding to another system.

SMTP sessions consist of a series of commands, each one of which is acknowledged by a reply. Often the reply consists of a simple status code indicating success. Other times, as in the case of expanding a mailing list name into its membership list, the reply is quite extensive.

The session begins with both sides exchanging HELLO messages to identify themselves. This is followed by a series of commands that indicate that a message is to be sent and receipts are needed and by data commands that actually transfer the data. By separating the data message from the address field, SMTP allows a single message to be delivered to multiple users.

Several other SMTP commands help enhance the utility of the program. A TURN command allows the two nodes to switch the roles of sender and receiver, a VERIFY commands allows user names to be verified, and the EXPAND command expands mailing lists.

SMTP modifies every message that it receives and adds a time stamp and a reverse path indicator into each message. This means that a mail message in the SMTP environment usually consists of a fairly long header with information from each node that handled the message. Many user interfaces are able to automatically filter out that information unless users have some bizarre interest in reading it.

TELNET virtual terminal service

The TELNET service is a virtual terminal service. Both user and server components are available, depending on the role and power of a particular machine. PC-DOS systems implement only the user side of TELNET, because of the single-tasking nature of the operating system.

Like the DEC Virtual Terminal Service, TELNET is an attempt to fool an operating system into thinking that a remote terminal is really locally connected. This means that all the software on the computer is able to function without consideration of the location of that terminal. TELNET was designed to work in a wide variety of different operating environments. In some environments, implementation is quite difficult because of the tight integration of physical devices into commands.

In a VMS environment, this is easily accomplished because of the two levels of device drivers. A device driver in VMS consists of a class driver and then a physical device driver. The class driver accepts calls for a general class of service, for example, terminal I/O. The physical device than accepts a call and transmits it to the actual device. Thus in this case, the terminal I/O class driver would send calls to the TELNET process rather than an asynchronous communications controller or a LAT driver.

The TELNET service models a virtual terminal as a bidirectional character device. This typically means a printer or a screen and a keyboard. Some extensions to the model help support more advanced types of terminals (if you can call a VT100 advanced).

Normally, echoing is performed locally. Most TELNET implementations will perform local echoing except on a few special control characters, such as an interrupt, abort ouput, or break signal. There is also an "are you there" key that is used to find out if the host is still active.

TELNET is based on a half-duplex mode of operation. A turnaround signal switches the sending of data to the other side of the connection.

During the TELNET setup phase, the user and server are able to negotiate for the support of expanded capabilities. This allows the specification of the number of lines on a full-screen terminal, for example. It also allows the specification of a specific terminal type, assuming the host is able to support that type. Another possibility is remote echoing. In a 300 bps wide area link this is not a feasible option. However, if TCP/IP is being run over an Ethernet and the user has a full-screen editing program, it would make sense to allow remote echoing.

Network File System

The Network File System is a set of protocols developed by Sun Microsystems to supplement TCP/IP. A session layer protocol, RPC, allows interprocess communication across a network. The presentation layer protocol, XDR, provides for a machine-independent method of representing complex data structures. Finally, NFS itself allows

```
ux1.lbl.gov% df
Filesystem            kbytes    used   avail capacity  Mounted on
/dev/xy0a               7751    6767     208    97%    /
/dev/xy2a               7751    6698     285    96%    /t
/dev/xy3g             270291   95043  148218    39%    /ux1d
/dev/xy1f             225819   83903  119334    41%    /ux1c
/dev/xy2h             238277   84541  129908    39%    /ux1b
/dev/xy2g             238277  170931   43518    80%    /ux1a
/dev/xy0d             119999   78049   29950    72%    /usr
/dev/xy3h             270291   60121  183140    25%    /usr/ux1
/dev/xy1e              44853   28881   11486    72%    /usr/spool
/dev/xy1g             189785  128112   42694    75%    /usr/local
/dev/xy0f             356283  249339   71315    78%    /usr/local/src
/dev/xy1d              14849     238   13126     2%    /tmp
helios:/usr           490640  438310    3266    99%    /usr/helios/usr
ux3.lbl.gov:/usr.MC68020/ux3
                       20209      25   18163     0%    /usr/ux3
ux3.lbl.gov:/ux3c     254483      37  228997     0%    /ux3c
ux3.lbl.gov:/ux3b     253813  158887   69544    70%    /ux3b
```

Courtesy of Lawrence Berkeley Laboratory

Fig. 9-12   File systems mounted with NFS.

file systems to be mounted on remote nodes as though they were local.
Figure 9-12 shows remote file systems mounted on a Unix node using
NFS.

The NFS family of protocols provides services from the session layer
up. It is conceivable that NFS could be implemented on top of other
lower-layer services, such as DECnet or XNS, but in practice it uses
TCP/IP for the network and transport services.

Although the networking portion of NFS is in theory network independent, the NFS service itself is fairly well tied into the Unix file
systems. The Record Management Services on VMS provide many
higher-level services, such as complex file structures, that are missing
from the native Unix file system. Instead, in Unix, individual applications provide that additional level of structure. The complex nature of
the RMS file system makes implementation of the NFS under VMS a
difficult task (although DEC has managed to do it).

One of the factors in the widespread adoption of NFS as a de facto
industry standard is the fact that Sun actively pursued licensing of
the protocols by third-party vendors. As a result, several hundred
vendors have implementations of NFS available. Implementations are
available for most versions of Berkeley Unix, including DEC's Ultrix,
for VAX/VMS, for MS-DOS, and even for IBM large-scale operating
systems such as VM and MVS.

The key characteristic of NFS is that it allows different machines
with different operating systems to share data and computing resources. A PC can store data on a VAX running Ultrix and thus supplement scarce resources on the PC. Access to the data is transparent to

the PC and looks like an additional hard drive. Hosts can also have programs run on foreign hosts, thus supplementing CPU resources.

Session layer services

To provide a base for complex applications, Sun began by supplementing the UDP transport layer services with a session layer interface. This allows remote nodes to execute processes. Note that this was possible before, but both of the programs involved would have had to use the TCP or UDP interfaces directly. The addition of a remote procedure call (RPC) layer allows application programs to refer to remote process by name or number and not worry about preparing information for use by the network.

RPC thus provides an extension of local memory on a system, where functions can be executed by specifying an address location. RPC functions can be executed and the results left in a prearranged local data structure just like a local function or procedure call.

The RPC mechanism specifies which program on a remote node should be executed. The mechanism for returning information across that network is the external data representation (XDR).

RPC can be accessed at three different levels. At the highest level, a series of programs is contained in a library. These programs shield all of the RPC and XDR details from the program and return information to the users. Examples of these services include:

rnusers	Returns the number of users on a node
rusers	Returns information on users on a node
havedisk	Specifies if that node has a disk
rstat	Remote data on kernel

The lower two levels of RPC allow users to provide more detailed control over execution. The library interface is a mid-level interface to RPC. The low-level interface allows users to explicitly manipulate sockets and transmit RPC messages, and it would usually not be used unless special performance considerations dictate its use.

Library interface access to RPC is done through two different service calls. The **registerrpc** call allows a procedure to be registered as available to foreign users. The **callrpc()** allows the execution of a remote call.

Procedures in RPC are grouped into programs, each one consisting of a family of related procedures. Programs can have program numbers associated with them to keep track of versions of a similar library. Finally, each procedure within a program has a procedure number.

A **callrpc** call specifies which remote machine, program, version, and procedure number are desired. Additionally, the call specifies where the arguments to the call are located and the types (data structure) of the argument. There is also a pointer and definition of a data structure used to store the results.

The **rnusers** call discussed earlier provides the highest level of interface to the remote procedure. The **rnusers()** call ends up issuing a library interface call in the form of:

```
if ( callrpc ( argv[1],
        RUSERSPROG,          /* RPC PROGRAM NUMBER */
        RUSERSVERS,          /* RPC VERSION NUMBER */
        RUSERSPROC_NUM,      /* RPC PROCEDURE NUMB */
        xdr_void,            /* Null Data Structure */
        0,                   /* Null Pointer */
        xdr_u_long,          /* Description of Results */
        &nusers              /* Results Area */
            )
        := 0 )
        { exit(1) } ;
```

The data structure definitions are actually XDR routines provided to translate local data into XDR format and vice versa. The **xdr_void** call above specifies that no translation occurs because there are no parameters to translate.

The **callrpc** service uses the UDP protocols at the underlying transport level. The RPC definition at the very lowest level allows tuning of the number of retries that RPC will attempt before returning an error message. It also allows the use of different transport layers (i.e., TCP for reliable transport).

User programs of RPC work through a service daemon on their machines. The analogous VMS concept is a detached process. The service daemon in turn communicates with a service daemon on a remote node. Finally, the remote service daemon communicates with the target program that is to be executed.

Servers in the RPC environment begin by registering all of the RPC calls they plan on handling. The server then goes into an infinite loop and waits for calls from clients.

There are two types of RPC operation. Normal RPC operates in a nonbroadcast network environment. This means that every request results in one answer. Broadcast mode sends the RPC calls out over a broadcast medium (usually Ethernet). Several answers may be returned for a single call. In the case of a program like **netstat**, all of the answers are relevant. Other calls may expect only one answer and throw the others away.

Security is one of the functions that are provided at the RPC level. Three types are provided. No security means that no authentication of calls is provided. A DES-type security and Unix-style scheme are also available.

Presentation layer

The External Data Representation (XDR) allows an implementation-independent way of representing information. This is important because even integers are represented differently on a VAX and on a Sun Workstation. On one system the first bit is considered to be the most important, while on another it is the last bit that is most significant. Thus, even though the machines have the same size words, they interpret them differently.

This phenomenon can be seen by using the **echo** command on a VAX with the Ultrix operating system. This command simply echoes back the character string it receives. The **rsh** command takes the result of this echo and feeds it to a remote machine. There, the **cat** command simply lists the data it receives. Notice that the 1 on a VAX has turned into a very different number on a Sun:

```
vax% echo '0 1 2 3'
0 1 2 3
vax% echo '0 1 2 3' | rsh sun cat
0 16777216 33554432 50331648
```

Portability problems with integers are nothing when compared to more complex data structures. For example, pointers or floating point numbers have very different representations in different environments. XDR is able to translate machine information into the XDR representation and then deserialize the information back into the machine-dependent form.

Standard routines are provided in the XDR library for short and long integers, floating points, and boolean data. Strings and fixed and variable arrays are also defined. A special kind of data is opaque data, which means that the XDR library passes the data through without translation. Opaque data is used in security systems to pass authentification handles. Users are also able to set up their own XDR translation routines, which build more complex structures on top of the basic routines.

NFS services

The Network File System uses the RPC and XDR layers. The main function of NFS is to provide a remote mount of a file system. NFS is very similar to the DEC Distributed File Service discussed earlier. An important difference is that NFS is stateless—no connections are maintained with clients. This means that if a server aborts, the client is not forced to wait indefinitely for the server to recover. Figure 9-13 shows Ethernet traffic on the Ethernet. Figure 9-14 shows an NFS read operation.

Distributed file systems allow certain nodes to specialize in certain tasks. A common use of NFS is to allow user files to be stored on one large machine and then remotely mounted on the workstation that the user is currently logged into. No matter which node of the network the user is physically on, the same file space is seen.

NFS has several features to help performance, including a read-ahead and write-behind cache. The read-ahead cache means that extra information can be cached at both the client and the server, alleviating the need to return to the disk drive to get more information.

The write-behind cache means that information is not immediately added to the disk before the next operation can proceed. Obviously if either the server or the client goes down, the cache can be lost. Frequent flushing of the cache to disk helps prevent lost data.

By itself, NFS has no state. This means no locks or file open commands are provided in the NFS service. A separate locking service is available to provide consistency guarantees. It is up to the individual application to first use the services of the lock manager, then request the data. For this mechanism to provide consistency across multiple users, it is important for all user applications that access the data to first consult with the lock manager.

NFS defines a basic series of file operations, including read, write, create, and destroy directories, files, and file attributes. Once a particular file ID has been retrieved, the user can retrieve data from the file by specifying the starting address and the amount of data requested in bytes.

Special files, a unique mechanism that allows a user to read and write to a device as though it were a file, are unavailable in the NFS environment. Special files are used in Unix to implement locking and other virtual services.

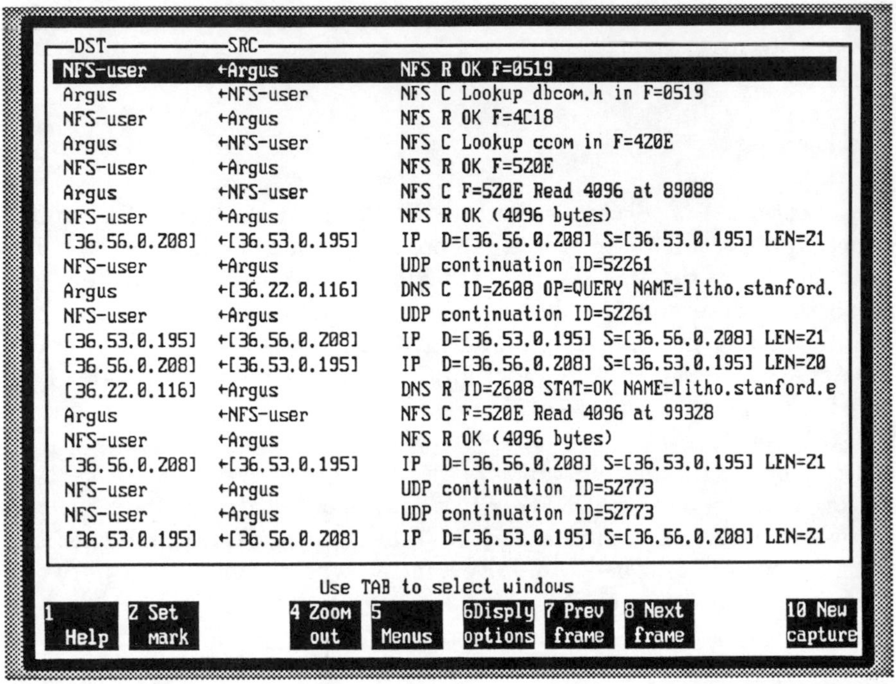

```
 ┌─DST──────────SRC──────────────────────────────────────────────────┐
 │ NFS-user      +Argus        NFS R OK F=0519                        │
 │ Argus         +NFS-user     NFS C Lookup dbcom.h in F=0519         │
 │ NFS-user      +Argus        NFS R OK F=4C18                        │
 │ Argus         +NFS-user     NFS C Lookup ccom in F=420E            │
 │ NFS-user      +Argus        NFS R OK F=520E                        │
 │ Argus         +NFS-user     NFS C F=520E Read 4096 at 89088        │
 │ NFS-user      +Argus        NFS R OK (4096 bytes)                  │
 │ [36.56.0.208] +[36.53.0.195] IP  D=[36.56.0.208] S=[36.53.0.195] LEN=21 │
 │ NFS-user      +Argus        UDP continuation ID=52261             │
 │ Argus         +[36.22.0.116] DNS C ID=2608 OP=QUERY NAME=litho.stanford. │
 │ NFS-user      +Argus        UDP continuation ID=52261             │
 │ [36.53.0.195] +[36.56.0.208] IP  D=[36.53.0.195] S=[36.56.0.208] LEN=21 │
 │ [36.56.0.208] +[36.53.0.195] IP  D=[36.56.0.208] S=[36.53.0.195] LEN=20 │
 │ [36.22.0.116] +Argus        DNS R ID=2608 STAT=OK NAME=litho.stanford.e │
 │ Argus         +NFS-user     NFS C F=520E Read 4096 at 99328        │
 │ NFS-user      +Argus        NFS R OK (4096 bytes)                  │
 │ [36.56.0.208] +[36.53.0.195] IP  D=[36.56.0.208] S=[36.53.0.195] LEN=21 │
 │ NFS-user      +Argus        UDP continuation ID=52773             │
 │ NFS-user      +Argus        UDP continuation ID=52773             │
 │ [36.53.0.195] +[36.56.0.208] IP  D=[36.53.0.195] S=[36.56.0.208] LEN=21 │
 ├────────────────────────────────────────────────────────────────────┤
 │                    Use TAB to select windows                       │
 │ ┌1──────┐┌2 Set──┐┌4 Zoom┐┌5─────┐┌6Disply┐┌7 Prev┐┌8 Next┐┌10 New┐│
 │ │ Help  ││ mark  ││  out ││ Menus││options││ frame││ frame││capture││
 │ └───────┘└───────┘└──────┘└──────┘└───────┘└──────┘└──────┘└───────┘│
 └────────────────────────────────────────────────────────────────────┘
```

Courtesy of Network General

Fig. 9-13   NFS traffic on an Ethernet.

Security in the NFS environment is fairly weak and is based on Unix-style commands. A future NFS enhancement may require an authentication server. Usually, NFS security is built on two levels. When the Unix-style RPC authorization is used, an authorization handle is passed consisting of a group and individual ID. NFS then checks these with the local (Unix-style) group and individual ID protection for the file desired. This implies consistent assignment of IDs across the network, hence the need for the Yellow Pages, discussed in the next section.

A special security case is the Unix superuser account. This privileged account on any Unix account always has a group/user ID of 0. This would imply privileged access on one machine automatically granting privileged access on any other machine of the network. Needless to say, a single security violation on one node can thus compromise the whole network. This defeats one of the purposes of a distributed processing environment, which is to allow distributed management of different nodes on the network. NFS handles this situation by automatically changing superuser IDs to -2 before processing the security check.

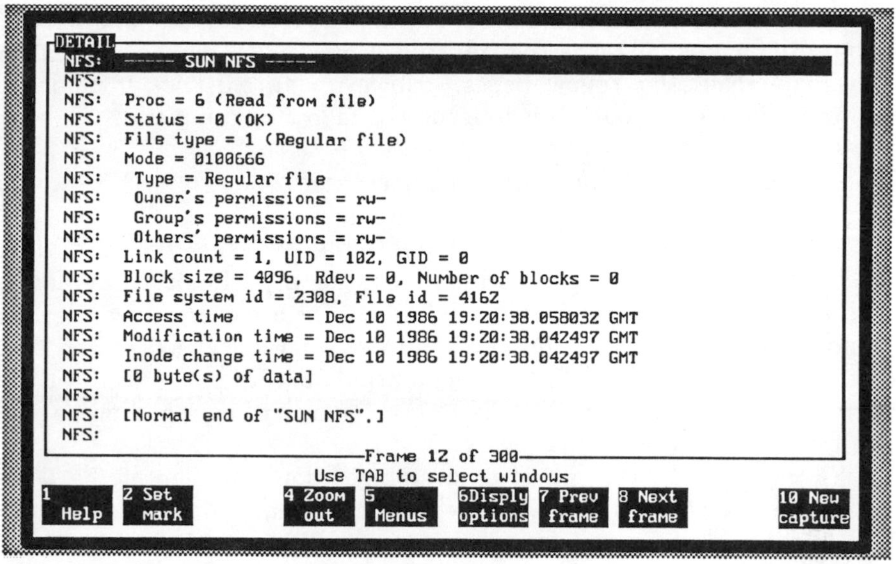

```
┌DETAIL┐
│NFS: ┌─────── SUN NFS ─────
 NFS:
 NFS:  Proc = 6 (Read from file)
 NFS:  Status = 0 (OK)
 NFS:  File type = 1 (Regular file)
 NFS:  Mode = 0100666
 NFS:   Type = Regular file
 NFS:   Owner's permissions = rw-
 NFS:   Group's permissions = rw-
 NFS:   Others' permissions = rw-
 NFS:  Link count = 1, UID = 102, GID = 0
 NFS:  Block size = 4096, Rdev = 0, Number of blocks = 0
 NFS:  File system id = 2308, File id = 4162
 NFS:  Access time      = Dec 10 1986 19:20:38.058032 GMT
 NFS:  Modification time = Dec 10 1986 19:20:38.042497 GMT
 NFS:  Inode change time = Dec 10 1986 19:20:38.042497 GMT
 NFS:  [0 byte(s) of data]
 NFS:
 NFS:  [Normal end of "SUN NFS".]
 NFS:
─────────────────Frame 12 of 300──────
                Use TAB to select windows
 1        2 Set       4 Zoom   5         6Displa 7 Prev  8 Next         10 New
  Help     mark        out     Menus     options  frame   frame         capture
```

Courtesy of Network General

Fig. 9-14   Reading data in an NFS packet.

Yellow Pages

The Yellow Pages (YP) is a set of utilities designed to simplify system administration. It is a set of replicated, read-only databases that contain network information. For example, a Unix password file is usually maintained by using the Yellow Pages. This allows one password space to be maintained for large complex networks. Additionally, each node can have its own customized password file that is not available through the Yellow Pages.

The Yellow Pages consists of a series of maps. A **hosts** map, for example, contains a series of host names and the resulting IP address as values. Standard Unix files that keep track of user passwords, group assignments, hosts on the network, and networks available to this subnet are all candidates for conversion to the Yellow Pages. It is then up to the programs that use these files to know that they are Yellow Pages files.

The Unix **passwd** command thus had to be rewritten to look for the password file on the Yellow Pages. The rewritten command also checks on a local file to see if the local machine has any changes to the network-wide namespace.

One important implication of converting a file to use the Yellow Pages is that the system designer may not know all the different ways that a file is used. In the Unix environment, for example, one user of the /etc/passwd file was the **passwd** command. This was rewritten to know about the Yellow Pages. However, an old trick to find out information about yourself is to issue the following command:

unix% cat /etc/passwd | grep username

The **cat** command says list the /etc/passwd file which is then passed into the **grep** utility which looks for a particular user name. This would be a way to find out default log-in areas or other relevant information. However, the file /etc/passwd no longer exists and this little utility would fail. This is a potentially severe problem in a Unix environment where utilities tend to last for many years and propagate in unexpected forms.

YP can thus be thought of as a stripped-down version of the DNS nameservers which allow a directory (roughly equivalent to a map) to be replicated in several locations. In the YP environment, one YP server is designated as the master for a map. Servers also maintain copies of maps for which another server is the master.

A YP daemon is present on each node that will provide Yellow Pages services to the network. The user program on the client node is usually implemented as a high-level RPC call. Each node has a **ypbind** daemon which links to a particular server for maps. If that server goes down, the **ypbind** daemon on the client is able to broadcast a plea for help and rebind to a new server. The **ypwhich** command shows current binds in the yellow pages environment.

TCP/IP Implementation

Implementation of TCP/IP networks is very similar to that of DNA networks. This is because both architectures incorporate Ethernet and X.25 subnetworks by reference. The differences between the two networks appear in the upper-level services, such as nameservers, distributed file servers, messaging systems, and other network-based applications.

DEC supports TCP/IP for both Ultrix and VMS VAX systems. The same Ethernet board is used as is in a DNA environment but with a different protocol stack implemented in software. DEC also supports the Network File System on both operating systems. The same Ethernet board is able to simultaneously support DNA and TCP/IP protocol stacks. A node with both protocol stacks active serves as a gateway between the two networking environments.

DNA and TCP/IP environments can be loosely connected using the DECnet-Internet gateway which is part of the DECnet/Ultrix implementation. This software allows a mapping between the **rcp** and DAP protocols, between SMTP and DECnet mail, and between the TELNET and CTERM virtual terminal services. Using this gateway, users on a DNA node can establish a DNA link to the Ultrix gateway and then establish a TCP/IP link out to their final destination.

In addition to supporting Ethernet and X.25 as TCP/IP subnetworks, DEC also allows NFS to be used on a CI bus. As in an SCA-based cluster, up to 16 nodes can use the CI bus. These nodes can be HSC controllers or VAX systems. The HSC controllers and VAX systems on the cluster communicate with each other using the NFS protocols.

Equipment for a TCP/IP Ethernet environment is very similar to DNA equipment. An example is TCP/IP based-terminal servers made by Bridge/3Com. These devices use the same modular strcture as the DECserver 500 where several line cards can be installed, each supporting multiple users. As in the case of DEC terminal servers, RS-232 ports or 50 pin connectors are supported for asynchronous terminals.

In addition to asynchronous connections, the bridge terminal servers support synchronous terminals. Instead of a series of RS-232 ports, a synchronous line card has a series of BNC connectors for IBM 3270 terminals. Both types of terminals can be mixed on a single terminal server. Support for synchronous terminals is, of course, not a capability of the network but of this particular piece of hardware.

Like the DECserver 500, the software is downline loaded from a support host. In the case of the bridge terminal server, the support host is the Bridge Network Control Center, which is based on either a dedicated PC/AT or Sun Workstation hardware platform. This differs from the MOP protocols that can use any Phase IV host on the network to downline load boot images. A particular terminal server is able to downline load either TCP/IP, XNS, or the OSI virtual terminal protocol suite.

Although DEC does not make a TCP/IP terminal server, they do support the protocols on their host systems. Standard DEC equipment, such as transceivers, DELNIs, or Ethernet bridges can also be used in a TCP/IP environment. Higher-level services, such as terminal servers or TCP/IP routers, can then be obtained from a wide variety of sources.

It is important to understand that DNA and TCP/IP offer complementary services. It is not unusual to see both networking protocols in a single installation. TCP/IP operates on a wider hardware base than DNA does. However, because DEC focuses on a limited number of hardware platforms, they are generally able to provide specific functionality and performance tailored to their equipment and software.

Summary

TCP/IP, together with the NFS services, provides a valuable alternative to DECnet for heterogeneous networking enviornments. Many research organizations find they are unable to restrict nodes in a network to a certain brand, or even to those that support DECnet. For these organizations, TCP/IP is a viable choice for a networking protocol.

In many organizations, TCP/IP and DECnet coexist to form a common network. The DECnet-Internet gateway, or other nodes that participate in both environments, form a bridge of connectivity. It is not unusual to see both network architectures coexist on a single Ethernet.

NFS provides a de facto standard for distributed data access in a Unix or Internet environment. Although NFS is a de facto standard, it is important to look at the actual implementations from each vendor to make sure they use the same portions of the standard. For example, DEC's VMS implementation of NFS uses the VMS distributed lock manager which was described in the Cluster chapter of this book, while Sun implementations would use another lock manager. Applications that write directly to a lock manager need to take into account these differences. For users who simply wish to read data over the network, these differences are not significant.

Both TCP/IP and DNA are rapidly converging in the form of the OSI protocols. After a brief diversion on SNA, this part will discuss Phase V of DECnet, which is an implementation of the OSI protocols. TCP/IP has been replaced by OSI as the official government-supported networking protocols in the United States. This convergence provides the means for interconnecting previously seperate environments.

For Further Reading

Comer, *Internetworking with TPC/IP: Principles, Protocols, and Architecture*, Prentice Hall, Englewood Cliffs, NJ, 1988.

——, *Operating System Design, Volume II: Networking with XINU*, Prentice Hall, Englewood Cliffs, NJ, 1987.

Stallings, et al., *Handbook of Computer-Communications Standards: Department of Defense (DOD) Protocol Standards*, Macmillan Books, 1988.

Sun Microsystems, "Networking on the Sun Workstation," 800-1324-03, Feb. 1986

——, "Remote Procedure Call Programming Guide," February, 1986.

——. "External Data Representation Protocol Specification," February, 1986.

——, "Remote Procedure Call Protocol Specification," February, 1986.

——, "Network File System Protocol Specification," February, 1986.

——, "Yellow Pages Protocol Specification," February, 1986.

10

System Network Architecture

Overview of This Chapter

Although DEC and IBM computers are usually purchased for different operating requirements, it is very common to find both types of equipment in the same environment. The local area network chapter discussed connection of workstations such as the IBM PC, in the context of connecting the PC to the DNA environment.

This chapter discusses the high end of the IBM environment, using the System Network Architecture. It is also possible for PCs to participate in the SNA environment, using token ring adapters and other LAN technology. However, in discussing DNA-SNA connectivity, we focus on communications between DNA Phase IV end nodes and IBM hosts. Since a PC can be a Phase IV end node, it is possible to connect PCs to the SNA environment using DECnet.

Connecting to the SNA environment can use either a dedicated gateway or the services of a general-purpose VAX. As with X.25 connections or DECnet routers, different speeds are available for these connections. With the high end DECnet/SNA CT gateway, speeds of 1.2 mbps can be achieved. Low-end connections using a stand-alone MicroVAX or BI VAX connections of 9.6 to 64 kbps are also available.

The gateway, whether on a general-purpose VAX or a dedicated gateway, only provides the basic level of connectivity. Services are provided by access routines, which can provide very simple services such as terminal emulation. More advanced services are available to interconnect office and mail systems together or to provide transparent access to databases in the SNA environment.

For high-volume, low-functionality services such as remote job entry or 3270 terminal emulation, there are several alternatives to gateways that will be considered. These include protocol converters and data switches. Often, these direct connectivity methods are supplemented with a gateway to provide more advanced services.

Network Addressable Units

When describing DEC networking architectures, very little thought is given to the type of machines that are connected in a network. With very few exceptions, VAX computers are interchangeable, with only a difference in performance between different types of processors. The only real exception to this rule has been in the limitation against MicroVAX and other Q-bus based processors using the 70-mbps CI bus in clusters. The limitation here was only performance related, because of the ability of Local Area VAX Clusters to provide the same System Communication Architecture functionality across the Ethernet.

In the IBM world, the type of hardware makes a big difference for the different connectivity options available. This is because of the gradual evolution within IBM of different hardware product lines. As will be seen at the end of this chapter, IBM's System Application Architecture (SAA) is an attempt to blur the differences between kinds of hardware.

The basic purpose for IBM's System Network Architecture was originally as a method for connecting many terminals to a System 370 architecture host. This is quite different from DNA's original aim of providing peer-to-peer communication. This is not to say that IBM nodes do not have this capability—only that the capabilities were grafted onto the networking architecture at a later point.

The basic IBM hardware configuration consists of an IBM 370 architecture host, such as the 3090 series. The host provides communications to the rest of the SNA network through channels. These channels provide a maximum throughput of 3 to 5 Mbps, although most devices that connect to the channel operate at T1 speeds or less. A 370 host is known as physical unit type 5 in SNA. Figure 10-1 shows the different physical units in an SNA network.

Attached to the host is a communications controller. The communications controller is PU type 4. Attached to the communications controller are a series of cluster controllers, such as the 3274. The cluster controller is a PU type 2. A series of terminals attach to the cluster controller.

The communications controller is responsible for maintaining communications paths with all the various cluster controllers. In addition,

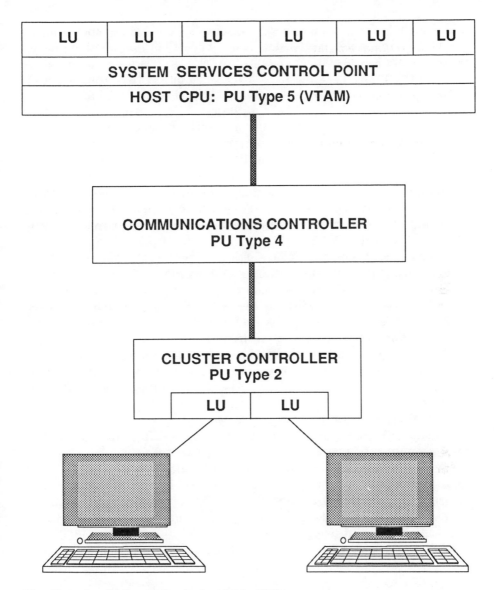

Fig. 10-1 Logical and physical units in SNA.

token ring networks can be attached to newer models of the cluster controller, the 3174.

In the traditional SNA terminal environment, in which terminals are connected to a host, all communications are routed to the mainframe computer. The terminal is represented by software or microcode on the cluster controller. This is known as a logical unit

(LU). Each of these LUs is a part of the SNA network, known as a network addressable unit (NAU). That node then has another NAU, the physical unit, to manage the physical characteristics of the node.

When the terminal connects to a host computer, the terminal's LU initially communicates with a special NAU called the system services control point (SSCP). The SSCP is the central point of control on the host, and it assists in establishing a session between an LU on the host and an LU representing the terminal. To initiate this process, the LU sends a BIND request to the SSCP.

SNA capabilities on the host are funneled through a subsystem on the host called the Virtual Telecommunication Access Method (VTAM). VTAM is the implementation of SNA services for 370 architecture hosts and runs under the various IBM operating systems that support SNA, such as VM or MVS.

Although SNA hosts have a single instance of VTAM, there are several different applications subsystems available for users. In an MVS environment, batch users use the Job Entry Subsystems (JES), while interactive users will use the Time Sharing Option (TSO) or CICS. On the VM operating system, the Conversational Monitor System (CMS) provides interactive services to users.

Different logical units in the IBM environment have different sets of capabilities. A terminal and a printer, for example, have different buffer sizes and operational characteristics, and they support different data streams. An LU type 2 is essentially a terminal session. A more advanced type of LU is the Advanced Program-to-Program Communication (APPC) function, or LU6.2. LU6.2 allows direct peer-to-peer communication between cooperating processes.

As was discussed, traditional SNA communications involve the services of a host processor. In a token ring environment, this is not a very efficient method of providing PC-to-PC communications. A more modern type of PU is the PU type 2.1 which allows peer-to-peer communications without using the services of a PU type 5 or host.

SNA protocol stack

Like DNA, SNA is a layered protocol stack. At the lower layers, SNA supports three types of data link protocols. The basic protocol is the Synchronous Data Link Control (SDLC). This serves the same purpose as DDCMP of providing direct point-to-point connectivity between hosts. SDLC is a subset of the more general HDLC protocol discussed in the next chapter of this book. Figure 10-2 shows the layers of the SNA protocol stack.

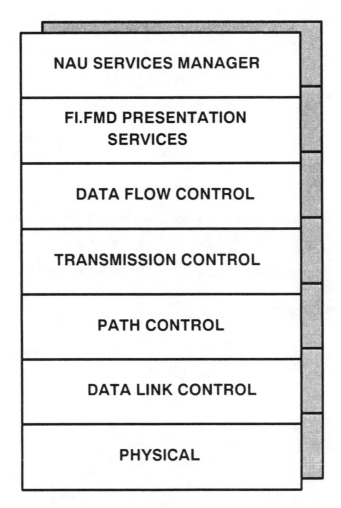

Fig. 10-2   Layers of the SNA protocol stack.

Token rings are another data link protocol supported in the IBM environment. A 9370 host, as well as PC or PS/2 systems can all connect to these token ring systems. The token rings operate at a speed of 4 mbps.

The third connectivity option is to use X.25 as a data link protocol. An X.25 virtual circuit is established between two different SNA systems and SNA protocols are then embedded within the X.25 packet. IBM uses their Network Packet Switching Interface (NPSI) package as a method of using X.25 networks to transport SNA information. Figure 10-3 shows an IBM network using a combination of data link protocols.

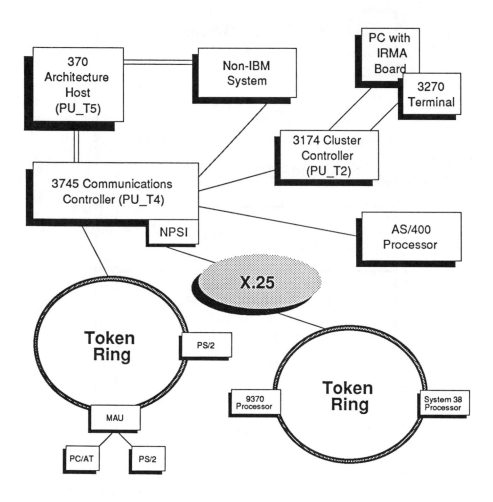

Fig. 10-3 SNA network configuration.

Any of the three data link types sends information to peers using a link header. Embedded within this link header are the higher layers of the protocol stack. The path control layer provides routing functions within the network by embedding a transmission header after the link header.

The primary function of the transmission header is to send data to the eventual destination. This destination could be to a host within this SNA domain or it could be to another domain of the SNA network using the Multiple Systems Network Facilities.

The transmission header is followed by a request header. The request header is then followed by a set of request units (RU). The upper layers of the network communicate with each other using these request units. RUs may indicate presentation layer information (the FI.FMD layer of SNA), or user data.

A packet of SNA thus consists of:

- A link header
- A transmission header
- A request header
- One or several request units

When an LU-to-LU session is initiated, a maximum RU size is defined, which may be smaller than the size of the path control message. Several RUs can be chained together within a single packet. All RUs are chained although often the chain consists of a single RU. Figures 10-4 and 10-5 show different SNA packets on a token ring that illustrate link, transmission, and request headers.

If all the data can be sent as a single chain, the application or other user of the path control layer is able to use a bracketing function. Bracketing allows series of chains that consist of a major unit of work to be bound together as a single logical message. Brackets are similar to major synchronization points in the OSI upper-layer protocols.

In contrast to the DNA environment, it is possible for a session to negotiate throughput parameters and other forms of quality of service indicators on a per-session basis. The IBM Network Control Program, which manages routing functionality, has a series of paths defined in a routing table. These routing tables must be manually defined by the system manager, in contrast to the dynamic routing capabilities of DECnet.

Built on top of the basic SNA architecture are a series of upper-layer architectures used for connecting peer systems. The discussion of DEC connectivity to the SNA environment begins with connection to the basic SNA environment, then goes on to discuss these upper-layer architecture such as those used for office systems connectivity.

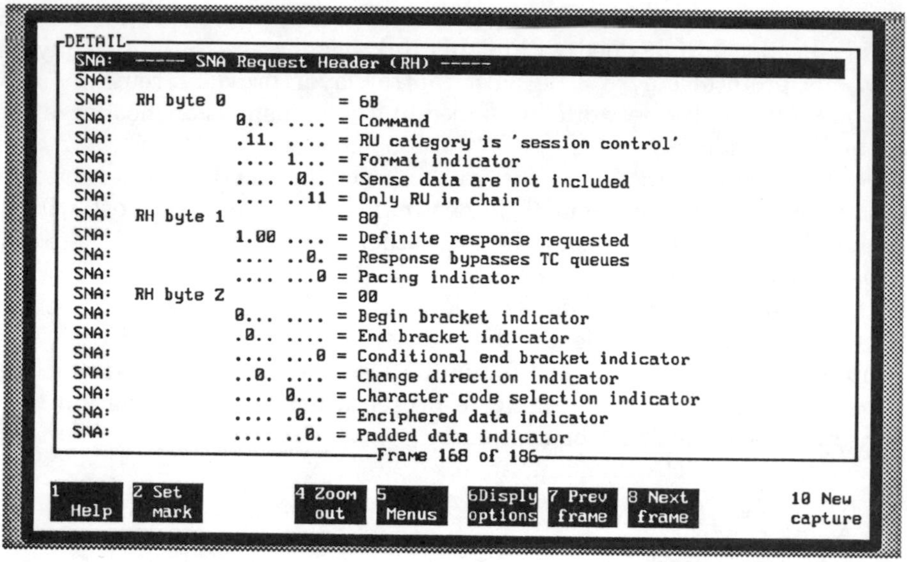

```
┌─DETAIL────────────────────────────────────────────────────────────────
│ SNA:  ───── SNA Request Header (RH) ─────
│ SNA:
│ SNA:  RH byte 0            = 6B
│ SNA:             0... .... = Command
│ SNA:             .11. .... = RU category is 'session control'
│ SNA:             .... 1... = Format indicator
│ SNA:             .... .0.. = Sense data are not included
│ SNA:             .... ..11 = Only RU in chain
│ SNA:  RH byte 1            = 80
│ SNA:             1.00 .... = Definite response requested
│ SNA:             .... ..0. = Response bypasses TC queues
│ SNA:             .... ...0 = Pacing indicator
│ SNA:  RH byte 2            = 00
│ SNA:             0... .... = Begin bracket indicator
│ SNA:             .0.. .... = End bracket indicator
│ SNA:             .... ...0 = Conditional end bracket indicator
│ SNA:             ..0. .... = Change direction indicator
│ SNA:             .... 0... = Character code selection indicator
│ SNA:             .... .0.. = Enciphered data indicator
│ SNA:             .... ..0. = Padded data indicator
│                          ─────Frame 168 of 186─────
│  ┌──┐  ┌─────┐      ┌──────┐ ┌─────┐ ┌───────┐┌──────┐┌──────┐
│  │1 │  │2 Set│      │4 Zoom│ │5    │ │6Display││7 Prev││8 Next│   10 New
│  │Help│ │ mark│      │ out  │ │Menus│ │options ││ frame││ frame│   capture
│  └──┘  └─────┘      └──────┘ └─────┘ └───────┘└──────┘└──────┘
```

Courtesy of Network General

Fig. 10-4 A request header.

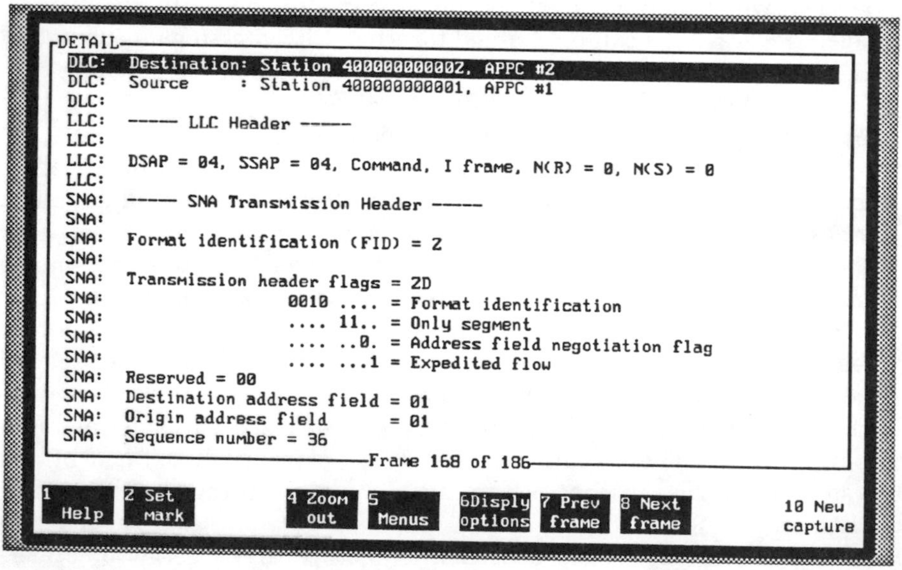

```
┌─DETAIL────────────────────────────────────────────────────────────────
│ DLC:  Destination: Station 400000000002, APPC #2
│ DLC:  Source      : Station 400000000001, APPC #1
│ DLC:
│ LLC:  ───── LLC Header ─────
│ LLC:
│ LLC:  DSAP = 04, SSAP = 04, Command, I frame, N(R) = 0, N(S) = 0
│ LLC:
│ SNA:  ───── SNA Transmission Header ─────
│ SNA:
│ SNA:  Format identification (FID) = 2
│ SNA:
│ SNA:  Transmission header flags = 2D
│ SNA:                 0010 .... = Format identification
│ SNA:                 .... 11.. = Only segment
│ SNA:                 .... ..0. = Address field negotiation flag
│ SNA:                 .... ...1 = Expedited flow
│ SNA:  Reserved = 00
│ SNA:  Destination address field = 01
│ SNA:  Origin address field      = 01
│ SNA:  Sequence number = 36
│                          ─────Frame 168 of 186─────
│  ┌──┐  ┌─────┐      ┌──────┐ ┌─────┐ ┌───────┐┌──────┐┌──────┐
│  │1 │  │2 Set│      │4 Zoom│ │5    │ │6Display││7 Prev││8 Next│   10 New
│  │Help│ │ mark│      │ out  │ │Menus│ │options ││ frame││ frame│   capture
│  └──┘  └─────┘      └──────┘ └─────┘ └───────┘└──────┘└──────┘
```

Courtesy of Network General

Fig. 10-5 Data link and transmission headers.

DNA/SNA Interconnection Strategies

The different types of SNA nodes, corresponding to different physical units, provide a ready format for connection to the IBM environment. Non-IBM environments connect to SNA by emulating a type of physical unit. Emulating a PU type 2 is the usual method for implementing an SNA Gateway. This makes the DEC environment look like a cluster controller with a series of logical units attached to it.

Another option is to emulate a simple terminal. This means that the non-IBM environment does not need to provide the full services of the PU type 2 node. Instead, a PC or VAX can emulate the SDLC protocols and the 3270 data stream. Often, this method of interconnection provides a significantly cheaper and more efficient interconnection method than a fully functional gateway. This is analogous to having a PC emulate a VT100 terminal instead of functioning as a Phase IV end node in DNA.

DECnet/SNA Gateway

The DECnet/SNA Gateway is the same piece of hardware that is used for providing DNA routing and X.25 connectivity services. Like X.25 and DECnet Routers, the DECnet/SNA Gateway uses the PDP and MicroVAX chip sets and supports a variety of transmissions speeds.

It is important to understand that the basic DECnet/SNA Gateway does not provide any functionality for end users. By itself, the gateway does not emulate a terminal or provide print services or any other functions. The gateway instead provides the software routines to map SNA sessions to DNA logical links and to manage all the SNA protocols. A separate access routine is then required to provide the upper layer functionality. The access routine communicates with the gateway over DECnet using a Gateway Access Protocol.

Three types of dedicated gateways are available. The first is the DECnet/SNA Gateway, Version 1.4. This gateway is identical to the DECSA Router and X.25 Gateways and is based on the PDP-11 machine architecture. Up to two 64 kbps connections can be supported on this device with a maximum of 32 simultaneous sessions.

The next level of performance is provided by the DECnet/SNA Gateway for Synchronous Transport. This device, based on the same MicroVAX chip set as the DEMSA Router, is able to support a greatly increased level of connectivity. Up to four 64 kbps connections or a single 256 kbps connection can be supported on this device with a maximum of 128 simultaneous sessions.

The highest level of performance is the DECnet/SNA Gateway for Channel Transport (CT). This system provides a direct channel attached to a System 370 architecture mainframe with potential line speeds of 1.2 mbps and a maximum of 255 simultaneous sessions. Only a single attachment is supported on each CT Gateway. The CT Gateway connects to the IBM channel using standard bus and tag cables.

All three gateways provide the same functionality but have different performance characteristics. It is possible for a single DECnet network to have multiple SNA gateways. These gateways may all go to the same host environment or may go to different SNA networks. The link between SNA gateways can be a local connection or can use the facilities of wide area transmission providers.

Third-party gateways

Interlink provides a gateway to the SNA environment which is built on a platform of DEC equipment. The Interlink Network Controller provides value-added services on two different types of DEC products. PDP-based versions offer throughput up to 50 kbps, while the MicroVAX-based versions offers data transfer rates up to 500 kbps.

Interlink uses a different strategy from DEC to implement gateways. DEC attempts to place almost all of the software on the DEC side, in the form of a SNA gateway manager and access routines. By the time the request has reached the IBM environment, it is in a standard IBM format, such as a 3270 data stream.

Interlink, by contrast, puts a great deal of software on the IBM system. In fact, for file access, no software is needed on DEC client nodes and very little is used on the gateway node. On the IBM system, however, Interlink provides an implementation of the File Access Listener (FAL).

As in the case of DEC's Data Transfer Facility, Interlink allows standard VMS commands such as COPY or TYPE to work with the IBM system just as they would with any other DECnet node. Users on the DEC system refer to IBM files by the same NODE::FILENAME syntax. In order to hide file system differences, the file specification is the one used for "foreign" files on a VMS system:

node"username password account"::"filename/options"

In addition to the standard data access capabilities, the gateway supports a variety of advanced capabilities. Task to task programming is available with a custom library. IBM users are able to access the DEC environment. Bidirectional terminal emulation is also provided. Finally, DEC users have access to MVS JES facilities to access batch and print queues.

IBM users are able to use a series of ISPF panels of a command interface called network file transfer (NFT). ISPF is a mainframe-based dialog manager, a utility that presents users with a standard set of panels used to execute system tasks such as starting up an editor, submitting a batch job, or printing a file. These bidirectional capabilities are very similar to those offered by DEC.

Interlink requires that a single Network Controller be dedicated to an IBM host. The connection is directly into the host and does not offer the option of instead using the services of a communications controller. The direct channel attachment for the Interlink Network Controller provides aggregate maximum speeds of 500 mbps. This capability is similar to the CT version of the DECnet/SNA Gateway.

While the Network Controller can only connect to a single host, it is able to connect to multiple DECnet environments. Any DNA-supported controller is available as long as it is compatible with the Q-bus structure of the Network Controller. For Ethernet data links, a DEQNA Ethernet controller is used. For a DDCMP link to VAX systems or DECnet routers, a DHV11 or DSV11 controller is used. Figure 10-6 illustrates the structure of the MicroVAX-based Network Controller.

Another option is the Flexlink 9750D system based on a dedicated piece of hardware called FastPath from Intel. This is not an SNA gateway in the sense of providing SNA services to the DEC environment. Instead, custom software is provided in both the IBM and DEC environments to communicate with the Fastpath hardware.

Direct host connections

An alternative to using the services of a dedicated gateway is to provide gateway functionality on a general-purpose VAX processor. The decision to use the services of a VAX versus a dedicated gateway is a function of the amount of traffic and the load patterns between the two different environments. If the purpose of an SNA connection is to load batch jobs in the middle of the night, it would make sense to use the existing VAX resources instead of buying a new gateway.

DEC's VMS/SNA package allows a VMS processor to be an SNA gateway. As with the dedicated gateway, this only provides network connectivity. Access routines must be provided separately. These access routines must be on the same VAX that is providing the SNA connectivity. The gateway, by contrast, provides a network-to-network

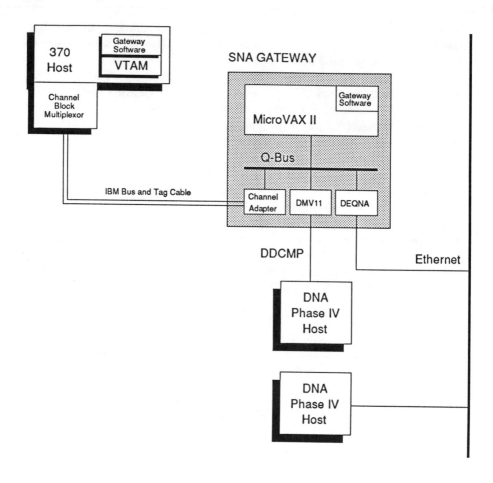

Fig. 10-6 Interlink SNA gateway structure.

connection by allowing access routines to reside anyplace on the DECnet.

VMS/SNA is a software package. It must be supplemented by a synchronous communications board that supports the SDLC data link protocols. On a CI bus system, this would typically be the DMB32 processor, which is capable of supporting a single 64 kbps connection. For MicroVAX processors using the Q-bus, the DSV11 processor provides the same transmission speeds.

As with any communications functions provided on a general-purpose VAX, it is important to understand that a significant portion of CPU resources will be used to provide this functionality. Some access routines, such as Remote Job Entry (RJE) can consume significant portions of a VAX processor. The VMS/SNA package similarly consumes CPU resources. These resources will not be available to other users of the system and thus have a cost attached to them. In deciding between VMS/SNA and a dedicated gateway (or third-party alternatives to the two), it is important to consider VAX-based CPU cycles as one of the cost factors.

Data switches and other front-end alternatives

It is not always cost-effective to use a dedicated gateway or a VAX to provide SNA access. While this may be useful for connecting high-level office systems together, it may be overly expensive for a more basic service such as terminal emulation. It is possible to have both a gateway for machine-to-machine communications and some other form of connection for terminal-to-machine communications.

For simple terminal emulation, there are a wide variety of solutions that do not use the resources of a VAX. Some vendors sell terminals with both a coax and RS-232 connection on the back that can be connected simultaneously to a VAX and an SNA system.

Another solution is to use the services of a protocol converter to make one type of terminal able to speak both low level protocols. Often, both asynchronous and synchronous communications are offered on a PC. This allows a PC to switch between emulating a VT100 terminal and a 3270 terminal. While this is a cheap solution, it should be noted that it makes a fairly intelligent device emulate a fairly unintelligent terminal.

A higher level of functionality is to connect the PC to both types of networks. It is possible for a PC to have both Ethernet adapters for DNA and token ring adapters for SNA. Usually, it is not possible on a single PC to have both facilities available simultaneously. On the PS/2 series, with their more advanced communications functions, this becomes more practical.

Often, terminal emulation is used as a companion to more advanced services. Advanced services are provided on a host-to-host basis using the services of a gateway. Terminal emulation, on the other hand, is provided using a front-end network that switches the PC to the appropriate asynchronous or synchronous communications controller.

A PBX is sometimes used as the front-end switching device. Often, these PBX systems offer protocol conversion services as part of the package. The PBX is connected to PCs as well as telephones. Also connected to the PBX are SNA ports, usually as a series of cables to a cluster controller in the machine room. DNA connections are provided by a series of connections between the PBX and either terminal servers or asynchronous communications ports on a host.

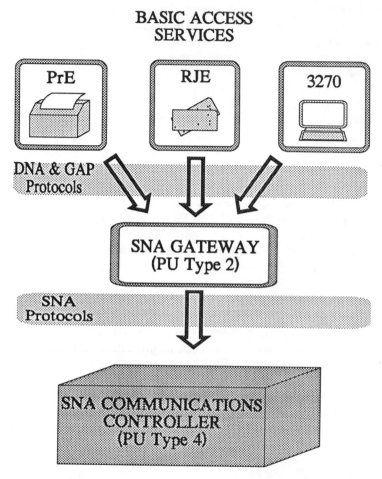

Fig. 10-7   Basic SNA services.

Basic Services Integration

There are three basic services, each offered as a separate access routine by DEC. These services are terminal emulation, printer emulation, and Remote Job Entry (RJE). Terminal emulation allows a VT100 terminal to emulate an IBM 3270 terminal. Printer emulation allows a DEC computer to emulate an IBM printer. Remote Job Entry allows a DEC computer to emulate an IBM RJE station, such as a card reader. Figure 10-7 illustrates the three basic services.

These are termed "basic services" because there are a variety of different solutions on the market. For example, either DEC or Interlink gateways can provide these solutions. There also numerous vendors that sell host-based solutions. These can be software only or a bundling of an SDLC synchronous communication board with software.

As discussed above in the alternative to gateways section, terminal emulation can be accomplished without the use of a host. If the host is to provide that service, as in the case of the 3270 terminal emulator from DEC, it is important to make sure that the gateway has the ability to handle the expected load.

The DECnet/SNA VMS 3270 terminal emulator is an example of a basic service that works on the DECnet/SNA Gateway or VMS/SNA. This access routine uses the Gateway Access Protocol (GAP) to connect to the SNA gateway. The GAP is running on top of a DNA logical link. It is the responsibility of the SNA Gateway to map that logical link into an SNA logical unit.

The 3270 session begins when the logical unit on the SNA side (the applications system) sends a bind request. The terminal LU then accepts the bind request. The 3270 session then consists of the IBM system sending out a series of panels (forms) to the terminal, which responds by filling the form out.

The 3270 software is able to buffer a form in memory and thus make the asynchronous VT100 terminal behave like a synchronous terminal. When the user hits the ENTER key, the buffered form is sent from the access software up to the cooperating SNA application.

The software provides two types of translation services. First, it translates ASCII into EBCDIC character sets. The user can change that mapping for custom applications. The second mapping is from the 3270 keyboard to the VT100 keyboard. It should be noted that this mapping is fairly difficult to accomplish in a way that will please all users because the keyboards are so dissimilar.

The 3270 access routine is the one of the few which runs on a PC with DECnet-DOS. A PC with this access routine is able to directly access a gateway without invoking the services of a host. This method is an alternative to giving the PC an SDLC board or token ring adapter to allow it to connect directly to the SNA environment. Similar terminal emulation software exists for the Ultrix operating system.

A complementary product to the 3270 access routine is the DECnet/SNA VMS Distributed Host Command Facility (DHCF). This access routine cooperates with the IBM Host Command Facility. IBM's software was meant to allow a systems programmer on a 370 architecture host to also control Series/1 and 8100 Information Systems, all from one terminal. DEC emulates one of these foreign systems to allow the IBM software to log onto the VAX that has the access routine.

Once the IBM programmer is logged onto the VAX with the access routine, full access to the rest of DNA resources is available. There are two important limitations to this access. First, the access is of course limited by the VMS security on each node of the network. The second limitation is that the IBM user has only line mode ("glass TTY") access to VMS utilities. VT-100-dependent routines will not function properly. An exception to this is that applications on the VAX that use the Forms Management System (FMS) software are able to provide full-screen access to a 3270 terminal using the DHCF access routine.

The DECnet/SNA VMS printer emulator (PrE) allows a VAX to emulate an IBM 3287 printer that is connected to an IBM 3274 cluster controller. The system with the PrE access routine is able to spool incoming data either to a disk file or to a print symbiont.

PrE is a useful way to integrate VAX-based printers into a large SNA environment. This means that users of RJE services or interactive users of the 3270 service can route information back to a local printer. This is important in areas where the DEC and the SNA environments are connected using a wide area link. A user of a MicroVAX II would be loath to fly to Topeka, Kansas, just to pick up a printout!

Another use of PrE is as a downloading tool. Rather than sending the print job to a VMS print symbiont, the data is spooled to disk. From there, it could be reformatted and used for other disk-based systems such as a home-grown database system.

The third basic access routine from DEC is a Remote Job Entry facility. Assuming that users know JCL (the IBM batch programming language), they can submit jobs that form part of the Job Entry Stream (JES) subsystems. The RJE facility manages a queue of jobs from the VAX and submits them one by one to the JES2 or JES3 subsystems. Output can then be spooled back to a file on the VAX. It is possible to use DAP facilities to spool the output to a different system than the originator.

Programming Libraries

DEC sells three different programming interfaces, each one supporting a different class of logical unit services. These are rarely needed by end users. Instead, they are usually used to build applications by DEC and third-party developers. Most of the advanced services discussed in this chapter are built on these programming interfaces. A variety of similar libraries are available for the Interlink gateway.

The DECnet/SNA VMS 3270 Data Stream Programming Interface is the simplest library. This provides an LU2 interface to the SNA environment. The programming library is able to perform all the actions of starting a session including receiving and interpreting the initial bind request and accepting the bind.

The library also handles many of the flow control features of SNA. To do this, the software maintains a series of state machines for chaining, bracketing, and data flow control. This frees the programmer from dealing with these issues.

The interface can be used at two levels. At the lowest level, data stream mode, the user is responsible for building and interpreting 3270 data streams. This implies a detailed knowledge of the IBM 3270 data stream.

A higher-level interface is provided in field mode. This provides the programmer with assistance in building a screen image. Data can be presented to the interface by fields, and forms can have updated field values processed.

The software is able to process a bind request from the VMS program and terminate an SNA session. The software also is able to respond to an unbind from the SNA session or a failure of either DNA or SNA circuits. The VMS application defines an entry point at run time. In the case of a circuit failure or unbind, the application is notified at that entry point.

A more basic set of routines is provided by the DECnet/SNA VMS Application Programming Interface (API). This provides support for programs in logical unit types 0 through 3. This library consists of a series of useful subroutines. For example, subroutines are provided to accept remote bind requests, send a bind request, or reestablish a connection.

The API routines do help the user by providing low level support for path, data link, and transmission control. The user, however, must process all of the presentation services information such as a 3270 data stream. The user must also respond to all request units, parse bind requests, and perform ASCII/EBCDIC translation.

Programmers using the API will be either writing a cooperating program on the SNA side or cooperating with a previously written program to which they have a very carefully defined interface.

The most advanced interface is the APPC/LU6.2 Programming Interface. This set of routines lets users participate in an LU6.2 conversation with a cooperating process. The interface supports only a single session at a time, limiting somewhat the usefulness of this programming library.

The software is able to respond to incoming requests and thus allow the VMS environment to provide services to SNA nodes. An example of this would be a mail receiver that was able to accept information from the SNA Distribution Services (SNADS). As mentioned earlier, these functions are not normally ones that would be used directly by end users.

The APPC interface has the ability to allocate and deallocate basic and mapped conversations. All the basic verbs are available to allocate and deallocate conversations, wait for data, send error messages, and perform other common APPC functions. Control operator verbs include the ability to activate a session, define remote operations and transactions, and to delete sessions. Nonsupported verbs are special synchronization verbs to backout and set synchronization points in a conversation.

Integrating Data Access

Several advanced routines can make data available across the SNA and DNA environments. These provide more functionality than the simple upload and download capabilities of RJE or printer emulation. These access routines fall into two main categories:

- Integration of database systems
- Integration of file systems

The DECnet/SNA Data Transfer Facility (DTF) is a family of software that integrates MVS file systems with VMS RMS file systems. The software consists of two pieces. On the VAX side, there is a VMS/DTF server. Another component, MVS/DTF is installed on the IBM host. Figure 10-8 illustrates a DTF session from a VAX.

An important characteristic of DTF is that it is a bidirectional gateway. This software allows IBM users to access VMS facilities and DNA users to access the IBM environment. The software is integrated into the operating environments of both types of users so they are able to use familiar syntax to access data resources.

The VMS/DTF server software allows a user to access DTF facilities on other nodes. It includes a checkpoint/recover utility that is used in case of communications failures. The server software also includes routines to perform data translation and to use GAP to access the SNA gateway.

An optional utility, Transfer/DTF allows VAX systems other than DTF server nodes to have access to checkpoint and recovery services directly on their node in the event of a failure during file transfer.

The VMS software has been integrated into the DCL command language. Using a standard DCL COPY command, the user is able to access VSAM and non-VSAM data sets on MVS operating systems.

```
$ Open/write/error=open_error ibmfile DTF$IBMFILE
$ Read/End_of_file=End_of_read sys$input data

  DEC Networks and Architectures
$ Open/read ibmfile DTF$IBMFILE
$ Read/END_OF_FILE=End_of_file ibmfile record
$ Write sys$output 'record'

  DEC Networks and Architectures[0M

$ Close ibmfile
$ DELETE/LOG DTF$IBMFILE

%DELETE-I-FILDEL. ACTVAX"SNADTF"::"TSOVLZ:CINA05.CARL/USER:CINA05/PASSWORD:CINA6
5/SUPERSEDE" deleted (2 blocks)
```

Courtesy of Digital Equipment Corporation

Fig. 10-8   Data transfer facility operations.

The user's request is first parsed by the System Authorization Facility (SAF) which decides if the user is authorized to access the data.

At the DCL level, commands supported include directory commands as well as standard file manipulation commands such as OPEN, CLOSE, READ, TYPE, and DELETE. Alternatively, programmers can access the facility using standard RMS calls or Datatrieve programs. DTF supports all standard RMS sequential I/O capabilities.

The IBM software, MVS/DTF, consists of two parts. First, there is a VTAM application which communicates with the VMS/DTF server software to process requests. The server performs all data translations so the host is not burdened with this task.

Two other components of the MVS/DTF software consist of three user interfaces. One consists of an ISPF dialog panel for use in an interactive session. The second user interface is a TSO command processor which can be accessed from batch facilities. Finally, CLISTS (a concept somewhat like command files on VMS) can be used. Checkpoint and recovery capabilities are supported from MVS/DTF just as they are from the VMS/DTF server.

The session between the VTAM software and the VMS/DTF server software consists of an LU type 0 session. LU type 0 provides very little structure and is essentially a "roll-your-own" SNA implementation—the programmer must process most of the details of interacting with the network. Because the software was written using LU type 0 programming tools, it offers a large increase in performance over standard facilities such as the RJE access routine.

DEC chose to implement this facility using LU type 0 instead of other LU types (such as LU6.2) for a two main reasons. First, it supports a full duplex protocol which provides for an efficient use of SNA resources. Second, LU6.2 implementations require the CICS application subsystem, which many MVS users do not have.

If DTF is run on a 56 kbps line, it is possible for up to 40 kbps of data to be transferred, assuming no other access routines are also using the services of the gateway. With the CT version of the gateway, throughput over 1 mbps can be achieved. Small files reduce throughput because of the setup costs. Running the gateway on VMS/SNA instead of a dedicated gateway can also reduce throughput up to 30 percent. It's important to note that these facilities are not free—the combination of DTF and SNA access can easily use up the better part of a MicroVAX or small BI-bus based VAX.

Database access

The next level of data integration is at the database level. Many vendors are beginning to provide gateways between database systems that run in the two processing environments. The basic goal is to allow a user to continue using a familiar user interface but to be able to access database facilities located in other processing environments. For example, a user of Ingres is able to use the Ingres/Star gateway to access IMS databases in the IBM environment. Users of Oracle's SQL*Star product can access a DB2 database environment from at least one of the different user interfaces that Oracle offers.

DEC has a product called VAXlink, which accesses IMS databases and VSAM files in a transparent fashion. A related product is VIDA, which can access Cullinet IDMS databases. VAXlink and VIDA are part of a broader architecture that allows user interfaces and data repositories to exchange data.

The key to this architecture is called the Digital Standard Relational Interface. DSRI is a standard interface to database systems. A user interface does not store data—it presents and manipulates it. When a user interface needs data, it issues a DSRI call to any database on the system that supports DSRI (see Figure 10-9).

Two DEC-supplied DSRI interfaces are Rally and Teamdata. Teamdata is a spreadsheet-like user interface that spares the user from having to learn data manipulation languages such as SQL. Rally is a slightly more sophisticated utility that allows users to manipulate databases and create simple applications.

A user of Teamdata is able to switch user interfaces and not have to worry about restructuring the database or providing a new interface routine. This also allows the database to move locations since DSRI calls are transparent in a DECnet environment.

The recipient of a DSRI call is responsible for interpreting the call, retrieving data, or doing other data manipulation, and then returning

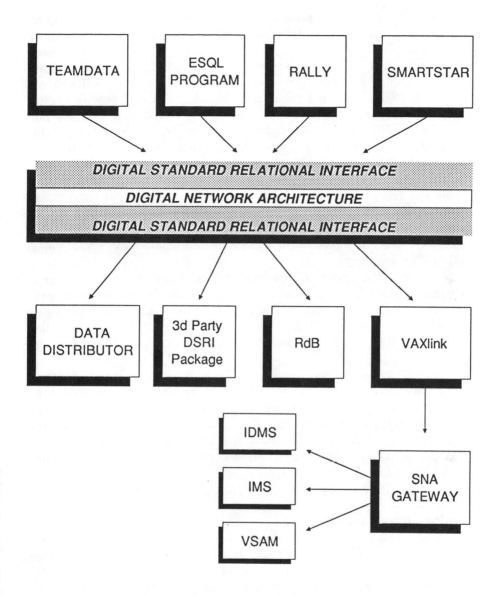

Fig. 10-9 Digital Standard Relational Interface.

the results in DSRI format. The original example of the DSRI recipient was a DEC Rdb database.

Because DSRI is an open architecture, data access is not restricted to DEC-supplied environments. Signal Technology, for example, makes Smartstar, a use interface that is DSRI compatible. Embedded

SQL (ESQL) programs can also be constructed that use the SQL query language to integrate databases with third-generation language programs.

Recipients of DSRI calls are not limited to DEC-supplied software. The Smartstar software can access an Rdb database, but it can also access a DSRI database furnished by Interbase. DSRI provides a very important separation between the use interface and data manipulation functions. This allows data to be distributed across the DNA environment as well as allowing third-party solutions to work smoothly with DEC software.

The VAXlink and VIDA packages are able to accept standard DSRI calls and translate them into the appropriate data access language on the target system. The user of Rally asks for data the same way on an IMS system as they would on an RdB system. Two levels of gateways are provided. In this case a database gateway is built on top of an SNA gateway.

The Data Distributor software is a way of automating the process of extracting data from any DSRI database. Data Distributor can query one or several DSRI systems and extract data. That data is then combined into a single RdB database. Data Distributor can be used to access an IBM-based data repository and make a copy of the information in an Rdb database.

Data Distributor does not provide a true distributed database capability. Rather, it is able to replicate portions of a database at a particular time. This is known as a snapshot of the data. A distributed database allows multiple data sources to all be integrated into one logical database environment. The user is not aware of the location of the data, whereas in Data Distributor, a user has to "point" to where the data is located.

Office Systems Integration

Both DEC and IBM have constructed fairly elaborate office environments. DEC has centered their efforts on the ALL-IN-1 system which integrates word processing, menus, calendars, electronic mail, and other common utilities. It also includes links into the Message Router software which delivers messages in a DECnet environment.

IBM has two different office environments, one for each of their major operating systems. In the MVS environment, IBM has the Distributed Office Support System (DISOSS). This software allows documents to be filed, retrieved by key word, and sent to other DISOSS users. In the VM/CMS operating system, IBM has a functionally equivalent system called PROFS.

IBM office systems are built on several advanced architectures. These architectures supplement the basic SNA functionality and provide higher levels of structure. The two fundamental office architectures are the Document Interchange Architecture and the Document Content Architecture. As will be seen later, these architectures correspond to the envelope and envelope contents that are specified in the X.400 message handling systems.

SNA provides basic data transmission across the network. This has been supplemented by a higher level architecture called SNA Distribution Services which is message based. SNADS consists of a series of distribution service units which accept data for delivery.

Built on top of SNADS is yet another level of abstraction called the Document Interchange Architecture. DIA defines the types of messages and their functionality. DIA is used to distribute documents, search for documents using search criteria, and to retrieve documents. DIA defines two types of nodes. Source/Recipient nodes are able to receive and send messages. They correspond to a user agent in X.400 terminology.

Office System Nodes (OSN) are libraries that hold or forward documents. A typical example of an implementation of the OSN is the Distributed Office Support System (DISOSS). DIA has been widely implemented as DISOSS on MVS nodes and as the Personal Services Series for PCs, PS/38 and OS/2 systems.

The contents of those documents is usually defined by the Document Content Architecture. DCA has two forms, revisable and final. Both RFT (revisable form text) and FFT (Final Form Text) are supported by DEC. RFT consists of a subset of functions found in most modern word processors. FFT is roughly analogous to the capabilities of an Epson dot matrix printer.

For data output, IBM supports both PostScript and their own architecture called the Intelligent Printer Data Stream. IPDS is considered a strategic product and is built on top of an LU6.2 interface. IPDS is used almost exclusively on laser printers, such as the 3820 laser printer. PostScript support is implemented in only a few products.

IPDS requires all layout decisions to be made by the host. In this sense, it is not a full fledged language like Postscript. Instead, it is a language for representing information on the page in a static fashion. The language supports basic multifont text, graphics, images, and bar codes. The graphics primitives include basic items such as lines, circles, boxes, and shading. The image support includes compression algorithms for transmission of data.

DEC has two families of software called Electronic Document Exchange. EDE with IBM DISOSS links to the IBM DIA/DCA environ-

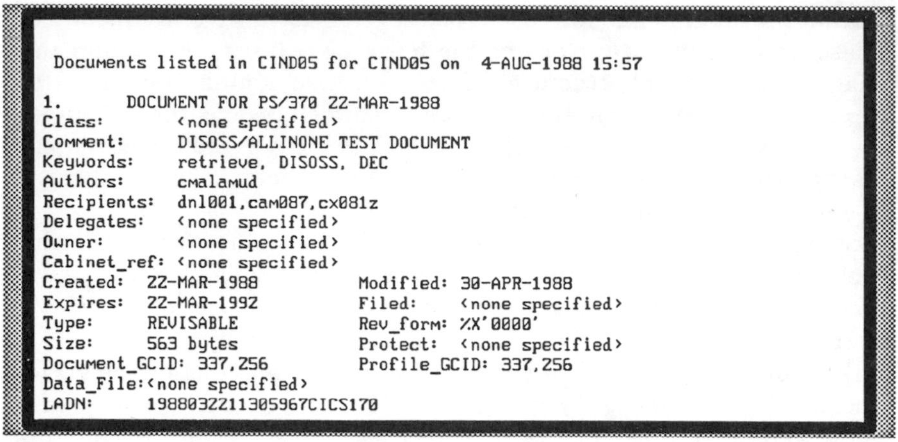

```
Documents listed in CIND05 for CIND05 on  4-AUG-1988 15:57

1.      DOCUMENT FOR PS/370 22-MAR-1988
Class:          <none specified>
Comment:        DISOSS/ALLINONE TEST DOCUMENT
Keywords:       retrieve, DISOSS, DEC
Authors:        cmalamud
Recipients:     dnl001,cam087,cx081z
Delegates:      <none specified>
Owner:          <none specified>
Cabinet_ref: <none specified>
Created:   22-MAR-1988          Modified: 30-APR-1988
Expires:   22-MAR-1992          Filed:    <none specified>
Type:      REVISABLE            Rev_form: %X'0000'
Size:      563 bytes            Protect:  <none specified>
Document_GCID: 337,256          Profile_GCID: 337,256
Data_File:<none specified>
LADN:      198803ZZ11305967CICS170
```

Courtesy of Digital Equipment Corporation

Fig. 10-10 Directory listing of a DISOSS file from VMS.

ments. Similar functionality to the Wang OIS systems is provided with EDE-W. The EDE-W software uses bisynchronous protocols to interface with the Wang environment.

EDE is typically a menu option in the ALL-IN-1 environment. Users are able to use the standard library and distribution services that are part of IBM's DISOSS/370 software. This includes the ability to search, file, retrieve, and delete documents in the library. Users can also send, obtain, show, and cancel document distribution. Figure 10-10 illustrates DISOSS access from a VMS system.

The software allows revisable and final form documents to be transferred both ways. In fact, with a nonrestrictive search command, it is possible to make local copies of DISOSS libraries. It is necessary for the IBM system manager to define all the valid users to the DISOSS environment.

Non-ALL-IN-1 users can access the DISOSS environment using another package called the DISOSS Document Exchange Facility (DDXF). DDXF can only transfer final form documents. DDXF is a prerequisite for the EDE DISOSS package.

Message exchange between the two environments is done using a Message Router gateway, which is discussed in more detail in the OSI upper layer chapter. Message Router allows a variety of different DNA user interfaces to exchange message. For example, users of the native VMS mail package can exchange messages with users of the ALL-IN-1 mail interface.

Message router also includes gateways to other messaging environments. Gateways exist to MCI Mail and Western Union Easylink system, as well as to the TCP/IP SMTP distribution service. Two gateways exist to the IBM environment, one for SNADS (DISOSS) and the other for the PROFS environment. Messaging systems are considered in more detail in the chapter on OSI upper layer services.

Systems Application Architecture

Both DEC and IBM, by their sheer size, have ended up with many different product lines. An early strategic decision by DEC was to emphasize the VAX hardware and VMS operating system. When that decision was made, it was at great cost to the company. Most of the large DEC users at the time of the introduction of the VAX line used the DEC 10 and DEC 20 "mainframes." Reducing support for the DECsystems was estimated to have cost DEC $1 billion in lost revenues.

IBM, because they grew so big so early, was unable to consolidate into one common architecture. Although the 370 machine architecture is the most important one, several different implementations on different machines have resulted in polluted environments. That means that when you want to move from one operating environment to another, you have to learn a whole new set of tools.

Pollution of environments in the IBM world extends significantly beyond the underlying machine architectures. On large 370 architecture machines, there are three different operating systems (MVS, DOS/VSE, and VM). On the MVS operating system there are several different operating environments, including the Job Entry Subsystem, the Time Sharing Option, CICS, and several others.

There have been two serious implications of multiple hardware and software environments. First, IBM has had trouble introducing new products because of backward compatibility issues and the fear of alienating significant customer bases. Perhaps more important, user skills have been very specialized and do not transfer easily to new environments.

Systems Application Architecture is an attempt to bring all the different operating environments together into a common architecture. There are three primary components to SAA: a common user interface, a common program interface, and a common communications interface. Eventually a series of common applications will be developed for the different operating systems.

Because of the magnitude of the differences between the system and the amount of entrenched inertia, transition to SAA is a very long-term activity. Other major operating environments are undergoing similar efforts. These environments include DEC computers and various coalitions of Unix-based systems.

In the Unix environment, AT&T and Sun have joined on a variety of standards that address many similar issues of interchangeability of software and skills. The Open Look standard provides a standard "look and feel" for user interfaces. The System V Interface Definition (SVID) defines a standard operating system as well as some programming interfaces. A binary standard defines a common standard for executable images with an orientation toward the Sun-developed SPARC architecture.

Because the Unix community involves many different companies, it does not have quite the degree of unanimity presented by IBM executives in their discussions of SAA. Splinter groups help form alternative standards which are sometimes incorporated into the consensus set of de facto standards. Unix is often known as "computers by committee" for this reason.

DEC is really in the ideal position when it comes to SAA-type issues. A common operating system and a common programming interface are already in place for most parts of the operating environment. This allows DEC to standardize the user interface. These issues will be considered in more detail in Part 5 of this book.

Common programming interface

The most important impact of SAA is on program development, since programmers see a common interface to the operating system as well as a common user interface development environment. Four sets of standard interfaces have been defined. Associated with each of these programming interfaces are a set of strategic products.

The three key operating systems that programmers will see are the OS/2 extended edition for the PS/2 line, the operating systems on the 370 architectures, and the OS/400 operating system on the AS/400 line. SAA includes an attempt to provide a common operating system interface for all of the 370-based operating systems.

Two sets of graphics interfaces are defined. The OS/2 presentation manager uses an interface such as Microsoft Windows 286. This consists of a session manager, a shell help system, and window and filing capabilities. On 3270 terminals, the graphics interface uses a graphical data display manager which provides similar functionality to presentation managers, but for single terminals.

Dialogs, consisting of sets of objects and actions on those objects, use the ISPF dialog manager for 370 environments and the OS/2 dialog manager for workstations. Defining ISPF as a standard dialog manager means that the software will migrate from the current MVS/TSO environment to include other 370-based operating systems.

Programmers will thus be able to count on a standard dialog with the user.

Both of the dialog managers provide an important extension to the operating system. Dialogs provide generic fill-in-the-blank methods of activating common operating system functions and provide an alternative to the usual command interface. Dialog managers are used for managing libraries, executing compiler, full-screen editing, managing queues, and many other functions.

Data access in SAA consists of two components. Access to files is provided through the use of a distributed data manager. This package allows a single file system to accept data from foreign systems on the network at the record level. As we've seen previously, this is the type of functionality that RMS has provided in the DEC world.

A key part of SAA is that data access is moving from flat files into database structures. SQL is defined as the single method of interacting with database management systems. The SQL may be embedded in programs or can be generated by a user interface such as the Query Management Facility.

Common user interface

The common user interface (CUI) defines a consistent method for individuals to interact with programs. The hope is that if every program uses the F1 key as a help key, users will not have to look that fact up for any new program. Even more importantly, they will not call up the help desk or network manager to obtain that information!

Users are assumed to have a conceptual model of what a computer is and what it does. CUA defines such a conceptual model. For example, the concept that context sensitive help is available at any point may be one of the users' assumptions about the way a computer should work.

CUA emphasizes a consistent interface to users. Consistency in the physical layout of a workstation, in the syntax, and in semantics are all stressed. Physical consistency means that the F1 key is always in the same place on the keyboard. Syntactical consistency means that the F1 key always means HELP.

Semantic consistency means that a command always does the same thing. A common example of semantic inconsistency is the use of EXIT and QUIT commands. In some systems QUIT means to leave the application while EXIT means going back one level. In other systems, the reverse is true. This provides endless opportunities for steering committees to debate semantics. While keeping committees busy may be a desirable goal, it is nice to have the flexibility to have that issue decided in advance.

At the physical level, SAA defines a common keyboard. Many of the keys are predefined in functionality. The F1 key is HELP, the END key moves the cursor to the end of the current line, and the CTRL/END key moves users to the end of data. The mouse is defined as being a one-to-three button mouse. If the last two buttons are missing, the keyboard must have some key sequence that is equivalent to the missing mouse buttons.

Also included in SAA is support for national languages. Three families of languages are defined. Left-to-right languages include English and the Latin languages. Right-to-left languages would include Hebrew. Finally, double-byte character sets are defined which provides supports for large character sets such as Chinese ideograms.

A screen in SAA may consist of a set of panels. The SAA CUA screen presentation is very similar to the Microsoft Windows interface. Although the CUA will run on 3270 terminals, it will only allow a single window at a time. For this reason, most of the efforts on developing the SAA interfaces is oriented around workstations running the OS/2 operating system.

A panel consists of a data area and an action bar. The action bar has a series of verbs that the user can point to. Pointing to an action verb does not initiate any action. Rather, this leads to a pull down menu which then has a series of actions. If there are further choices, a pull-down menu action may lead to a pop-up menu with further choices. Common icons and symbols are used to indicate the presence of further options.

The body of a panel consists of a series of elements, such as entry or selection fields. Selection fields show the user a list and allows them to select a particular item. When the pointer rests on an object it is highlighted. When the select key on the mouse is activated, the object remains highlighted.

Users interact with the screen using an object/action method. This means that users select an object and then select an action against that object. This might mean selecting a file and then selecting the action of EDIT or DELETE. It might mean selecting a username and selecting the action of SEND MESSAGE. The advantage of this method is that the programmer is able to present only the valid actions for that particular object. This means that mixed types of objects can be presented in a single list.

Selection of actions and objects can use a variety of different techniques. Scroll bars, action fields, and other techniques are always available. In addition, advanced users can use fast path interaction techniques. A keyboard accelerator ties a menu item to a key sequence. A mouse accelerator allows specific mouse sequences to accelerate movements.

Common communications support

The CCS portion of the SAA environment allows programmers to see a consistent set of communications facilities across token rings, X.25 networks, and SDLC point-to-point connections. The CCS facilities are primarily for the purpose of allowing OS/2 program developers to get ready access to facilities throughout the IBM network, particularly on 9370, S/370, and AS/400 host systems.

The key advantage for DEC connectivity of the CCS is that it provides a consistent, common interface to non-IBM environments. This allows an architecture-based development environment instead of trying to connect each individual product to its peer in the other environment.

Summary

This chapter considered IBM/DEC connectivity by having DNA-based gateways emulate the SNA environment. This allows SNA applications, such as DISOSS, to communicate with their peers in the DEC world. SAA provides a clear architecture for connectivity through gateways.

Several other options exist for connectivity. These include older protocols such as Bisynch. Another option is to provide virtual terminal services via an X.25 link. Terminal emulation provides a non-SNA based link to the IBM world.

A long term trend for both environments is to use international standards such as ISDN and OSI. These facilities provide a common ground between the two environments. Both DEC and IBM support evolving international standards with various degrees of enthusiasm. Key users of computer technology insist that vendors provide these type of solutions. If both vendors provide the same sets of protocol supports in OSI, connectivity becomes a much simpler issue and a more stable long term solution.

For Further Reading

Cypser, *Communications Architecture for Distributed Systems*, Addison-Wesley, Reading, MA, 1978.

Linnell, *SNA Concepts, Design and Implementation*, Gate Technology, McLean, Virginia, 1987.

Linnell, *IBM Products and Architectures*, Gate Technology, McLean, Virginia, 1987.

Morency, et al., "The DECnet/SNA Gateway Product—A Case Study in Cross Vendor Networking," *Digital Technical Journal*, vol. 1, no. 3, September 1986, p. 35.

11

DECnet/OSI and OSI Lower Layers

Overview of DECnet Phase V

Phase V of DECnet is a significant departure from previous phases of the networking architectures that DEC has developed. DECnet/OSI is based on the Open Systems Interconnect protocols, a nonproprietary architecture, which holds significant promise for multiple vendors being able to interconnect with a very high degree of functionality.

Currently, most systems are able to interconnect. The level of interconnection, however, is very low. Usually, it allows a user of one system to emulate a terminal connected to a remote system. With an OSI environment, advanced services such as record level access become a possibility in a heterogeneous environment.

In addition to the open nature of the new architecture, several important changes have been made. Extremely large networks can be formed in a Phase V environment. In a Phase IV network, "only" 63,000 nodes could be put in the network. In Phase V, the theoretical limit is 10^{48}. Since every node in the world is expected to have a unique OSI address and the number of nodes is proliferating, this large address space is not as unrealistic as it may first seem.

To illustrate the need for billions and billions of nodes (to paraphrase Carl Sagan), think of the evolution of home computer systems. It is not unusual to see multiple nodes in a home environment. In the future, with the proliferation of microprocessor-based technologies, nodes will not be limited to an Apple IIE or PC/AT. Your car computer might communicate with a home central computer system, which in turn requests that your robot make you a daiquiri. Each of these nodes needs a network address.

Other important changes in Phase V include significant changes to the routing layer. The routing layer in Phase V has been expanded to include support for a wider group of data links. The routing algorithms have been enhanced to provide a greater capability for an individual node to determine the state of individual links in the network. The routing layer has also been expanded to support the OSI connectionless network service and addressing methods.

As in previous phases, DECnet will remain N minus 1 compatible. This means that a DECnet network can always coexist with the previous version of DECnet. In this case, Phase IV and Phase V networks will be able to coexist. Phase IV applications, such as the DAP-speaking File Access Listeners will run on Phase V nodes. These applications and other applications based on the OSI applications will be available.

Coexistence will be accomplished through the use of towers. A tower is a set of protocols from either the Phase IV or Phase V architectures. A particular packet may travel part of the way down a Phase IV protocol stack, then use a Phase V network layer and data link. Towers extend from the physical layer all the way up to the application layer, and they allow they various combinations of the two architectures to cooperate. Although a typical tower would splice layers 4 to 7 from one architecture on layers 1 to 3 of the other architecture, it is possible to slice the protocol stack in various places.

Overview of OSI Lower Layers

The lower layers of OSI are an interesting mix of protocols. This is because they build on existing subnetwork technologies running from IEEE 802.3 Ethernet, token rings and token buses to X.25 networks. In X.25, a connection-oriented service is provided with some degree of data integrity checks. In Ethernet, on the other hand, there is only a datagram service with limited error checking. It is the responsibility of higher layers to supplement the Ethernet datagram service to provide the reliable end-to-end communications needed by the time data has passed through the transport layer.

The OSI model integrates this wide variety of different transmission technologies in the network layer. The network layer then provides a common set of services to the upper layers of the OSI model. The network layer itself is split into several sublayers. The upper sublayer, the subnetwork independent functions, provide routing and

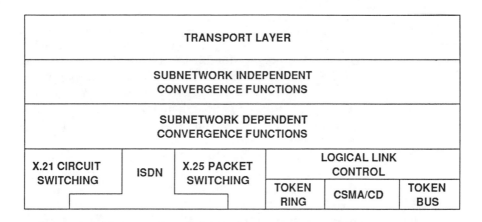

Fig. 11-1   Sublayers of the OSI network layer.

other functions that are needed regardless of the type of subnetwork involved.   A set of subnetwork independent functions allow the routing portion of the network layer to see a common set of network services.

Underneath the subnetwork-independent functions are subnetwork dependent convergence functions. They build on top of the services that the subnetwork is able to provide and add enough functionality to meet the needs of the upper portions of the network layers. Figure 11-1 illustrates the sublayers of the network layer.

The lowest portion of the network layer is the subnetwork access procedures.   These are access routines to the native capabilities of the underlying subnets. In the case of an X.25 subnetwork, this would be the establishment of virtual circuits, clearing calls, and similar functions. In the case of an Ethernet, this would be a simple data transmit or receive function with a specified Ethernet address.

The general model for the OSI network service is thus very similar to the Internet Protocols examined earlier.   Different subnetworks are all connected together to form a common network. In the case of the Internet Protocols, this network service is only a datagram service—no connection-oriented network service is offered. The OSI connectionless network service is actually an adaptation of the TCP/IP Internet Protocols.   In addition to a connectionless network service, the OSI protocols also specify a connection oriented network service.

Physical Layer

DECnet Phase V includes support for all the physical media that are supported in an Ethernet environment such as normal baseband coax, ThinWire coax, twisted pair, broad band, and fiber. In a wide area or point-to-point environment, DNA Phase V has support for the RS-232-D and RS-423 physical interface standards and for the CCITT V.24, V.35 and X.21bis standards.

Phase V also includes support for the X.21 physical interface standard for digital circuit-switched data networks. Although these are not especially prevalent in the United States, X.21 networks are popular in Europe and Japan.

X.21 is a set of protocols used to support leased circuits and circuit-switched networks. Often, an X.21 circuit is used as a physical connection in an X.25 packet switched environment. X.21 support in DNA Phase V includes a call setup facility, which allows outgoing calls to be placed and closed user groups to be established. Criteria can be established on which calls will be accepted. Reverse charging is also available within this facility.

A special type of physical interface standard in Phase V of DECnet is for dynamically established links. The physical interface standard thus includes support for autocall and autoanswer features on modems. This service, known as the modem connect service of the physical layer, has five parts.

The call control function allows the physical layer to make an outgoing call and handle incoming calls. It also allows the ability to clear incoming calls. A data transfer function is used to provide a bit- and byte-oriented service to the data link layer.

A named call reference service is used for network management and control. By naming a call, it is possible to make this a named entity in a Phase V network management environment. This in turns allows counters to be established for the call that can be used for security, performance, or accounting purposes.

The modem connect service for dynamic calls also includes a call-sharing capability. Normally, a user of the data link service on the link would request that the line be cleared upon completion of the tasks. For example, the MOP protocols might be used to downline load an operating system to a remote node. Upon completion of this function, the DDCMP protocols might then need to provide service to another user, the DNA routing layer. The call sharing feature allows a clear line command to be intercepted at the physical layer and effectively ignored.

Data Link Support

Phase V of DECnet supports three different data link protocols. The DDCMP and Ethernet protocols have been previously discussed. The HDLC data link protocols are a more general model that incorporate by reference a variety of subsets including the IEEE logical link control and X.25. HDLC includes a variety of subsets conforming to each of the different types of data links supported in OSI.

The high-level data link control (HDLC) is a general model for data link services. The general model has several subsets that conform to most currently available data links. The LAP B subset corresponds to the X.25 data link level. The LAP D subset corresponds to the ISDN data link layer. All three LLC classes for local area networks are also subsets of HDLC. IBM's SDLC is also a subset of HDLC, although it includes some commands and responses not in the standard. HDLC is thus both a specific protocol and a general model; it uses different subsets for different types of data link technologies.

The model is useful because all the different subsets have a fairly common interface to upper layers of the network. It thus becomes easier to code network layer processes because all the different data links fall into the same general class.

The basic HDLC service is to send a frame from one point to another. Each frame on the line is separated by at least one opening flag that is unique. The flag is a single byte that has a 0, six 1s, and a closing zero. If a string of five 1s is found within the actual data, a 0 bit is inserted. This is known as bit stuffing and allows the HDLC link to provide a transparent data connection while still maintaining the ability to control frames.

A second unique indicator flag in HDLC is the abort flag which consists of seven consecutive 1s. Again, if the actual data contains that information, the HDLC framing process inserts a 0 bit which is removed by the other side.

The actual HDLC packet consists of an address, a control field, data, and a frame check sequence. The contents of these frames depends on what type of frame is being sent. The frame check sequence (FCS) provides error control. It is the responsibility of each HDLC service provider to generate and check the FCS to provide an error-free frame delivery.

The default FCS is based on a 16-bit polynomial, although a 32 bit sequence is also available. The calculation is based on the contents of the address, information, and control fields in the HDLC frame. A separate FCS may be contained in the data portion of the frame. Usually, integrated circuits are used to perform this calculation.

Of course, it is possible for errors to occur at higher levels that HDLC can't find. When a user asks for the wrong file or the session layer swaps 2 bytes, it is unreasonable to expect a data link process to find that error. The FCS is designed to find bit errors that were introduced on the physical medium.

There are two forms of HDLC addressing. A basic address is a single byte. The first bit of the address is set to 1, and the next 7 bits are the address. This limits the number of nodes on a single HDLC link to 128 nodes. This is adequate for X.25 networks, where HDLC is used to communicate between a single DCE and a DTE.

For IEEE or ISDN subnetworks, however, this is not sufficient. With an extended address, the first bit is set to 0. The next 7 bits are then available for addressing. In addition, a second byte of address space can be added. If the first bit of that byte is set to 1, this signifies the end of the address space. The use of the MORE bit allows 14-bit instead of 7-bit addresses.

HDLC has three different kinds of frames. An information (I) frame is used to send sequenced data. A supervisory (S) frame is used to send control information such as acknowledgments between HDLC processes. An unnumbered information (UI) frame is used to send unacknowledged data.

The information frame has a control field that consists of a 0 in the first bit. This indicates that it is an I frame and not an S or UI frame. As in addressing, the I frame control field can be a 1 byte or can use an extended version.

Basic sequence I frames allow up to eight frames to be outstanding at any one time. Each frame is sent with a sequence number. Every I frame must be acknowledged. The last 7 bits of the control field of an I frame have sequence numbers for the outgoing packet and can also include a sequence number for the last packet that was received from the remote node. Piggybacked ACKs remove the need for sending a S frame for every I frame that was sent.

The first bit of the I frame control field signifies that it is an I frame. The next 3 bits are the sequence number of the outgoing packet. The next 3 bits are the sequence number of the last packet that was received. The last bit of the control field is a poll bit. Setting this bit is a way to solicit status information from the remote process.

Extended sequence numbering adds an extra byte for sequence addressing. This allows up to 128 frames to be outstanding each way. Once the 128th frame is sent, the numbering starts back at 0. This modulo 128 sequencing is essential in high-delay environments such as a satellite link.

An S (supervisory) frame is signaled by setting the first 2 bits of the control field to 1 and 0. The next 2 bits of the control field indicate the type of supervisory frame. The last 3 bits can contain a sequence number for a packet it is acknowledging. Extended sequence numbering is available for S frames.

S frames can be used for simple acknowledgment, but they are also used for flow control and error recovery. S frames can request the retransmission of data or can signal that a node is unable to accept more data.

UI frames are used for link establishment and control as well as for unacknowledged information. An example of a UI frame is the exchange ID message which is sent when two nodes are able to initialize a line dynamically. This message is used when a new node enters a LAP D environment. Error reports are also sent using these UI frames.

Two of the main uses for UI frames are for connectionless services and for out of band data. In an connection-oriented data link, UI frames are used to send expedited data. This allows the UI frames to cut in line ahead of a sequence of I frames. UI frames typically carry interrupts that signal the remote process to stop processing.

The other use of the UI frame is in a connectionless environment. Ethernet is an example of this. Using unacknowledged transmission of frames with no acknowledgment or error recovery is an example of the logical link control class 1. LLC 1 corresponds to a minimal subset of HDLC facilities.

The two other LLC classes, as well as LAP B and LAP D, use larger subsets of the HDLC facilities. LAP B for example, uses a connection-oriented subset of HDLC facilities. A link is set up, a series of I frames are exchanged and acknowledged, and the connection is disconnected.

DEC and HDLC

DNA Phase V uses the extended sequence numbering option of HDLC. This extends the number of outstanding frames possible from 7 to 127. In certain wide area links such as satellites, it is important to allow a fairly high window of outstanding frames. DNA uses the 32-bit CRC option of HDLC as a default. The 16-bit option is available as an option when connecting to non-DNA environments.

A special modification to HDLC is used between two DNA stations. In this case, the user data field is segmented into two parts. A user data length field is inserted right before the true user data.

Dynamic line configuration is available in DNA Phase V using an exchange identification (XID) frame. If the other side of a connection does not support the XID frame, the line will have to be manually configured.

Maintenance data in DNA Phase V is not carried in the normal UI packets. This is because these packets are not subject to error correction, sequencing, or flow control. Instead, DEC uses the MOP protocols on top of HDLC to provide this functionality.

OSI Network Layer

OSI in a sense concentrates on providing a different kind of network service than DNA does. OSI concentrates on specifying the upper layers of the model in great detail. In contrast to DNA, the lower layer consists of a general framework that allows a variety of different subnetworks to coexist instead of detailed specifications for operation of a specific subnet.

The subnetwork framework in OSI allows the Phase IV routing protocols to continue to operate in a Phase V OSI network. OSI does not detail how to route information within a subnetwork. Instead, the OSI protocols used in Phase V of a network will be used to forward data from one subnetwork to another. Other parts of the OSI network may be using other routing protocols such as TCP/IP.

While the lower layers of OSI integrate existing protocol suites, the upper layers are a fairly radical departure from networks like DNA. A presentation layer is specified in great detail, and applications consist of a well-defined family of core protocols. File access, virtual terminals, and messaging systems are just a few examples of the types of standardization in the OSI model.

As in DNA, the lowest three layers of the OSI protocol suites allow two end nodes anywhere in a network to communicate. The transport and session layer will then use these network services to begin providing services to individual users.

OSI consists of a series of subnetworks, just like the Internet Protocol. Each subnetwork may use a different subnet protocol, such as ISDN or X.25. A subnetwork makes every node in the subnet look as though they are one hop away. In the case of X.25, there may be many switching nodes in the path between the nodes, but the virtual circuit makes them appear directly connected.

An IEEE data link with Ethernet or token ring MAC layers, provides a similar function. Every node in this LAN environment appear to be one hop away. The data link is responsible for managing its resources to allow multiple users to share the common media. Figure 11-2 shows an ISO network layer packet on an Ethernet subnetwork.

```
┌SUMMARY──Delta t──────DST─────────SRC─────
 M   1                 Host Hello  ←MUZA        ISO_IP Routing Exchange ISH PDU,
     2   14.9229  :Host Hello   ←08001B060561   ISO_IP Routing Exchange ESH PDU,
     3    2.0051   Host Hello   ←08001B06055E   ISO_IP Routing Exchange ESH PDU,
     4    2.0298   Host Hello   ←PC 13          ISO_IP Routing Exchange ESH PDU,
     5   29.1799   Host Hello   ←MUZB           ISO_IP Routing Exchange ESH PDU,
     6    0.0066   Host Hello   ←MUZB           ISO_IP Routing Exchange ESH PDU,
     7   15.0593   Host Hello   ←MUZA           ISO_IP Routing Exchange ISH PDU,
     8   16.8298   Host Hello   ←08001B060561   ISO_IP Routing Exchange ESH PDU,
     9    2.0041   Host Hello   ←08001B06055E   ISO_IP Routing Exchange ESH PDU,

┌DETAIL─────
 ISO_IP: ───── ISO IP Network Layer ─────
 ISO_IP:
 ISO_IP: Protocol ID = 82 (Routing Exchange Protocol)
 ISO_IP: Header length = 25
 ISO_IP: Version / Protocol ID extension = 01
 ISO_IP: PDU type: End System Hello (ESH)
 ISO_IP: Holding time is 210 seconds
 ISO_IP: Checksum = 5C44
 ISO_IP: Number of Source addresses = 13
               ─────Frame 2 of 12─────
               Use TAB to select windows
┌──────────┬──────────┬──────────┬──────────┬──────────┬──────────┬──────────┐
│1          │2 Set     │4 Zoom   │5         │6 Display │7 Prev    │8 Next     │   10 New
│  Help     │  mark    │  In     │  Menus   │ options  │ frame    │ frame     │   capture
└──────────┴──────────┴──────────┴──────────┴──────────┴──────────┴──────────┘
```

Fig. 11-2   Contents of an OSI IP packet on Ethernet

OSI links subnetworks together into one common network. This network layer may offer either connection oriented or connectionless service. If X.25 is the subnetwork, it is very easy to offer a connection-oriented network service. This is because the subnet is already providing that functionality.

In the case of an Ethernet MAC layer, on the other hand, offering a connection-oriented network service would require the software in the network layer to provide sequencing, error detection, and other services. While the network layer could provide those services, another option is to offer a connectionless network service (CLNS). It would then be the responsibility of the transport layer to provide the connection-oriented service.

As can be seen, either the subnet, the network, or the transport service provider can make the connection-oriented link between two processes. If a lower layer cannot provide that service, it is ultimately up to the transport layer to provide it.

When the entire connection-oriented service is provided at a subnetwork layer, as in the case of an X.25-based environment, it is possible for the network and transport layers to be essentially null. All the functionality needed is already provided in the lower layers of the protocol stack.

Other times, the network layer is essentially null. When the subnetwork can provide an end to end data link, there is no need for routing. This is the case when two nodes are connected to a similar or extended Ethernet. In this case, a CLNS service is layered over the Ethernet. The transport layer can provide sequencing and error detection and turn the CLNS into a connection-oriented service.

A connectionless service all the way through the session layer is an optional service in OSI used for request response systems. This might be the case in a network consisting of large numbers of ATM machines communicating to a central bank. Rather than keep circuits open, it might be more efficient to just send self-identifying datagrams through the network.

A connectionless service is also useful for devices that don't have the resources necessary to keep sessions open. A programmable controller in a factory is an example of this. As will be seen, the manufacturing messaging service is an example of an OSI protocol that uses an essentially null session, has transport and network layers, and communicates directly with the subnetwork.

Phase V CLNS Network Service

Routing in Phase V is based on the connectionless network service (CLNS). This provides a datagram service which is similar to the Phase IV routing service. Messages in a CLNS environment can be up to 64 kbytes long. Each routing node in Phase V is responsible for knowing all its neighbors and the cost for each link.

An enhancement to Phase V is the imposition of a further level in the hierarchy. Areas in a DECnet are combined together to form a routing domain. Several routing domains can exist in a single DECnet. It is possible for some of those routing domains to be non-DNA environments.

Routing domains are in turn collected into a single administrative domain. An important feature of Phase V is that other routing domains and administrative domains are all available to other nodes. The CLNS network service, based on the DOD IP protocols, is used to reach other routing domains. That routing domain then uses a domain-specific routing algorithm to reach the final destination.

The routing layer is able to use several different subnetworks. In a broadcast environment, the network layer is able to use Ethernet as a method for getting data between two nodes. In a nonbroadcast environment, the links can be either permanent or dynamic. A permanent link is used as in a Phase IV environment and has a cost associated with it. This permanent link might be a DDCMP data link or it might be a permanent virtual circuit in X.25.

Dynamic links allow a point-to-point configuration to be added on demand. The dynamic link can be static, meaning that it is manually brought up and meant to be permanently available. An example of this would be an X.21 link. Another example is dynamic connection management. The routing layer is able to establish a link upon receipt of traffic. The link is then brought back down when a timer expires.

There are two pieces to the DNA Phase V network layer. A subnetwork independent portion is used to provide much of the logical functionality. These commands include routing decisions, segmentation and reassembly, lifetime control, and congestion control.

Routing decisions are made based on the availability of subnetwork functions. As discussed, the decision within a DNA routing domain is made based on costs and hops. Because of the link state algorithm, this decision can be made in a more sophisticated fashion. Inter-domain routing decisions are made by finding the boundary level 2 router that interacts with the two different environments.

Two kinds of source routing can be specified. Partial source routing gives a list of hosts that must be visited to route the packet. Between any two of the hosts specified, the packet may take any route that is available even if this means visiting unspecified hosts.

Complete source routing specifies exactly which hosts are to be visited. No other hosts may receive the packet if they are not specified in the source routing address. Complete source routing is used for security purposes to only visit trusted hosts. Partial source routing is used to make sure that a packet gets delivered even if intermediate hosts do not know about the location of the final destination address.

Phase V Link State Routing

The Phase IV routing tables consist of a list of nodes that are reachable and the intermediate node to send a packet to for a particular path to the end node. Each path has a cost associated with it. Although the calculation of the number of hops and costs is based on the data links, no information about this is contained in the routing table. The routing table is thus a summary table in Phase IV.

In Phase IV routing control messages, each node transmits its summary table to the next. If one router notifies the next router that it can reach node A with three hops, the next router assumes that it can reach node A with a total of four hops. Because there are alternative paths to each node and because routers summarize the routing information, there may be several different interpretations of how far away a particular node is. It thus takes several messages for the network to stabilize after a configuration change. With a large area and many level 1 routers, it is possible for a significant portion of the network bandwidth to be used on routing control messages until the situation stabilizes.

DNA Phase V has a subnetwork routing algorithm based on link states. This means that each nodes periodically transmits the status of all adjacent links. Nodes thus receive basic routing data instead of summary information. Each node then proceeds to summarize this information for its own routing decisions. Since nodes present basic data on the network instead of their view of what the network looks like, it takes far fewer messages to stabilize a configuration.

An important implication of a link state algorithm is that it lays the groundwork for sophisticated adaptive routing schemes. Since data on each link is available, it is possible for nodes to begin making routing decisions based on link saturation. This is not available in initial Phase V releases, but the basic architectural change permits expansion into these more sophisticated routing environments in the future.

Link state packets are sent out periodically by each routing node to each adjacent neighbor that is also a router. The LSP contains a sequence number. The receiving node compares the LSP it just received to current one it has. If the received one is newer, the node updates its routing database. It then forwards the LSP to all other neighbors. In this fashion, LSPs are quickly propagated among routing nodes.

If the LSP received was older than the one the node currently has, the node sends the newer LSP back out to the receiving line. LSPs contain sequence numbers to help determine the age of each packet. These packets also have an age field which signifies when the information should be deleted from routing databases.

The LSP process occurs simply within the DNA level 1 subdomain. Routing in between areas and in between administrative domains is done using the static CLNS routing scheme based on IP routing tables. The process of determining how to route between these areas is specified in a particular administrative domain but is not necessarily specified in between administrative domains. This is why source routing is provided for packets that are forced to travel extensively over the internet, such as electronic mail messages.

Other Network Layer Functions

The Phase V network layer includes several other functions:

- Segmentation and reassembly
- Lifetime and congestion control

The segmentation and reassembly function is used to reduce a message from the transport layer into segments that are small enough for transmission over the relevant subnetwork. In the case of an Ethernet, the 64,000-byte network message would be segmented into 1500-byte pieces. Segmentation may occur once the packet has already visited several nodes if the next subnetwork has a smaller size. Once a packet has been segmented, it is not reassembled until it reaches its eventual destination.

The lifetime and congestion control functions are used to reduce network saturation and other transient load problems. A time to live field is decremented by 1 for every node the packet visits. Once the time to live field reaches 1, the packet is summarily executed. The assumption behind this function is that once a packet has visited 63 nodes, it is clearly lost. The transport layer at the eventual destination will have surely requested retransmission, and it is therefore more economical of network resources to discard this packet.

The congestion control function is used to inform transport layer users of the network service about network congestion. Presumably, a well-behaved transport service will then reduce its transmissions in the interest of total network throughput. If any node on the network receives a packet and its queue of packets has reached a certain threshold, it sets a congestion experienced bit in the NPDU.

Network Addresses

Addresses in Phase V of DECnet use the ISO addressing scheme which is designed to provide support for world wide addresses. This address space is actually a superset of existing addressing schemes, such as the X.121 public data network addresses (telex) or the E.163 public switched telephone network numbers.

ISO addresses are based on a domain system. The X.121 address space is one example of a domain. The network address consists of an initial domain part and a domain specific part. The initial domain part (IDP) starts with an authority and format identifier which specifies which domain is being referenced. Following the AFI is an initial domain identifier (IDI). The IDI might be a country code or other high-level part of the address space. The domain specific part of the address depends on the type of domain chosen.

The domain-specific part of a DNA routing domain consists of three separate fields. An area designation is contained in the first 2 bytes. This important architectural change allows significantly more than the Phase IV limit of 63 areas in a single DECnet. The area address is followed by a 6-byte local identification.

An important new feature of Phase V is autoconfiguration. Each DNA node has a unique 6-byte node ID. This address is presumed to be unique even across areas. The last byte is a selection ID which indicates who the user of this network service is (i.e., the routing control module or a particular transport layer). End nodes in DNA will automatically find their nearest router and configure themselves to be part of that area. In addition, the selection field is automatically configured.

The automatic configuration feature means that new nodes can be added to the network without manual intervention at the network layer. The distributed naming service allows new logical node names to join the network and register themselves with a nameserver. Together, these two capabilities mean that the only addresses that need be manually configured are routers.

Transport and Network Layer Service Interaction

The network and transport layers are both able to provide connection-oriented services. However, it is the ultimate responsibility of the transport layer to provide reliable end-to-end communications. The transport layer is able to issue facility requests to the network layer that contain queries of the current level of service available.

One type of information the transport layer needs to know is the ability of the network layer to provide congestion control. This influences the need for the transport layer to aggressively monitor transit delay in order to adjust the window of outstanding packets.

Another important type of information is the sequence preservation probability. This is the probability that packets will be preserved in the sequence they were submitted. The transport layer will need a larger holding area buffer if packets frequently arrive out of sequence.

A third facility report the transport layer may request is the maximum lifetime of data units submitted to the network layer. The transport layer will also usually monitor actual round-trip transit delays for packet acknowledgment. Together, these parameters enable the transport layer to adjust expiration timers.

For Further Reading

Digital Equipment Corporation, "DECnet DIGITAL Network Architecture (Phase V) General Description," Digital Equipment Corporation, Maynard, MA, no. EK-DNAPV-GD.

Knightson, Knowles, and Larmouth, *Standards for Open Systems Interconnection*, McGraw-Hill, New York, 1988.

12

OSI Upper-Level Protocols

Overview of OSI Upper Layers

While the OSI lower layers are a mixture of existing protocols, the definitions of the upper layers are more consistent. This is because the network and lower layers need to accommodate a range of existing networks and physical media since the OSI protocol suite was developed after many current technologies were already in place. Many of these existing networks were already standardized and the ISO working groups decided to build on existing technology.

As in DNA Phase IV, the next two layers of the network form a bridge to the upper layers of the network. The session and transport layers provide a reliable end to end delivery service for data and form the bridge to the users of the network.

The OSI model, in contrast to DNA Phase IV, explicitly defines the services of a presentation layer. This is because in an OSI environment there are heterogeneous systems communicating. The presentation layer can handle issues such as transferring the representation of data from ASCII to EBCDIC or encrypting and decrypting data.

The applications layer of OSI defines a series of services. A set of Common Application Service Entities allows two applications to form an association. Services, such as File Transfer Access and Management (FTAM), then use that association to exchange information.

A particularly important set of services is the X.400 message handling protocols. X.400 is similar to other message-handling systems, such as SNADS in the IBM environment. X.400 replaces a variety of different proprietary systems with an international standard for message handling.   X.400 services form the core of DEC's message handling strategy.

Transport Layer Protocols

The Transport Protocols define five types of end-to-end connectivity. The most sophisticated class, TP4, provides end-to-end error detection and recovery.   The TP0 class, on the other hand, is almost a null transport layer. TP0 protocols will only work on top of network layers that provide a connection-oriented service with error detection. Any errors that get by the network layer services have to be dealt with specifically by the application code.

The five classes of service are:

TP class 0: Simple class
TP class 1: Basic error recovery
TP class 2: Multiplexing with limited error recovery
TP class 3: Multiplexing with error recovery
TP class 4: Multiplexing with error detection and recovery

The most basic class, TP0 is provided to give backward compatibility with current Teletex systems and X.400 messaging environments. This class requires a reliable underlying network connection, such as an X.25 virtual circuit. The transport layer data unit size must be smaller than the network layer packet size because TP0 is not able to segment large data units.   Likewise, TP0 is unable to concatenate small data units together before handing them to the network layer to provide higher efficiency.

Because TP0 assumes a reliable underlying network connection, this protocol class makes no provision for reassignment of a network link after failure.   This means that the application software must handle all error recovery mechanisms.   A messaging system, for example, would need to keep a copy of the current message cached in case the transport layer notifies it that message delivery failed.

The next class, TP1, adds a basic error recovery function. The TP1 module assumes that the underlying network will detect errors and signal it when they occur. The TP1 module is then able to reassign the transport session to a different network connection. TP1 also adds an expedited data service, if the underlying network provides that service also. Like TP0, TP1 does not provide any multiplexing capabilities. Only one transport stream may be used. This means that a single X.25 permanent virtual circuit would be dedicated to a single session at a time. This is not a problem if you have many virtual circuits, but a single T1 line might provide more bandwidth than the manager would want to dedicate to a single user.

TP class 2 adds a multiplexing capability to class 1. Class 2 does not provide error recovery capabilities and thus assumes that the network layer provides the functionality to both detect and recover from errors. TP2 then provides a limited notification service to users of the transport service. TP2 is used when bandwidth needs to be shared among multiple users and the underlying network condition is of fairly high quality.

TP class 3 provides both error recovery and multiplexing capability, combining the functionality of classes 1 and 2. Class 4 adds considerably to that functionality by providing an error detection as well as recovery capability. TP4 also allows a single transport connection to be split over multiple lines. Error detection is in the form of out-of-sequence data units or checksum failures. TP4 users are assured of an error-free stream of data. Note that error free is a relative term—the transport layer can only detect bit failures and out of sequence data units. Access to a secure file would be an error that would have to be detected at a higher layer, for example in the validation mechanism of a file access protocol.

DECnet Phase V is built primarily upon the TP4 transport services. TP0 and TP2 are provided in Phase V as a means to interact with non-DNA systems, such as a public X.400 message-handling system. Figures 12-1 and 12-2 show TP4 traffic on an Ethernet.

To begin a session, the user of the transport service specifies the address of the remote user (the remote transport service access point, or TSAP), the need for expedited data, and various QOS targets. The transport service than returns success or rejection indicators. Rejection could be at the local transport service if it is unable to meet the user requirements. Alternatively, the remote transport service user might reject the session because of incompatible QOS requirements or congestion. Finally, the remote TSAP might reject the connection, possibly because of access violations or other security considerations.

A transport connection has three phases. Connection establishment involves negotiating the appropriate transport classes and parameters that meet the transport service users' desired QOS goals. The data transfer phase of a connection provides reliable data transfer, possibly with flow control and expedited data services. Finally, the connection is released.

An addendum to the TP definition provides for a connectionless transport service, although in DNA Phase V, connectionless services can be supported at the network layer and not at the transport layer. A connectionless transport service has only one phase: data transfer. A UNITDATA command is sent down from the TS access point. This

```
┌─DETAIL─────────────────────────────────────────────────────────────
│ ISO_TP: Header length = 33
│ ISO_TP: TPDU type = E (Connection request)
│ ISO_TP: Destination reference = 0000
│ ISO_TP:      Source reference = CA03
│ ISO_TP: Class/options = 40
│ ISO_TP:      0100 .... = Protocol class 4
│ ISO_TP:      .... ..0. = Use extended formats?
│ ISO_TP:      .... ...0 = Use class 2 explicit flow control?
│ ISO_TP: Initial credit allocation = 1
│ ISO_TP: Protocol version number: 1
│ ISO_TP: Maximum TPDU size = 1024 bytes
│ ISO_TP:      Source TSAP: "DGC01"
│ ISO_TP: Destination TSAP: "DGC01"
│ ISO_TP: Additional options = 02
│ ISO_TP:      .... 0... = Use class 1 network expedited?
│ ISO_TP:      .... .0.. = Use class 1 receipt confirmation?
│ ISO_TP:      .... ..1. = Omit class 4 16-bit checksum?
│ ISO_TP:      .... ...0 = Use expedited data transfer?
│ ISO_TP: Header checksum = BE9B
│ ISO_TP:
│─────────────────────────Frame 145 of 162──────────────
            Use TAB to select windows
┌───────┬──────┐       ┌──────┬──────┐ ┌───────┬───────┬───────┐
│1      │2 Set │       │4 Zoom│5     │ │6Displu│7 Prev │8 Next │     10 New
│  Help │  mark│       │  out │ Menus│ │options│ frame │ frame │     capture
└───────┴──────┘       └──────┴──────┘ └───────┴───────┴───────┘
```

Courtesy of Network General

Fig. 12-1   TP4 connection request.

```
┌─SUMMARY──Delta t──────DST──────────SRC──────────────────────────────
│ 145    0.0096  MVZB         +PC 1        ISO_TP Connection request D=0000
│ 146    0.0078  MVZB         +MVZB        ISO_TP Connection request D=0000
│ 147    0.0023  PC 1         +MVZB        ISO_IP Routing Exchange RD PDU, D
│ 148    0.4037  MVZB         +PC 13       ISO_TP Ack  D=0023 NR=5
│ 149    0.0563  MVZB         +PC 13       ISO_TP Disconnect request D=0023
│ 150    0.0195  PC 13        +MVZB        ISO_TP Disconnect confirm D=EE01
│ 151    0.3204  08001B060561 +MVZA        ISO_TP Ack  D=7003 NR=63
│ 152    0.8710  MVZA         +08001B060561 ISO_TP Ack  D=0002 NR=61
│ 153    2.0280  MVZA         +PC 13       ISO_TP Connection request D=0000
├─DETAIL──────────────────────────────────────────────────────────────
│ ISO_TP: ----- ISO Transport Layer -----
│ ISO_TP:
│ ISO_TP: Header length = 33
│ ISO_TP: TPDU type = E (Connection request)
│ ISO_TP: Destination reference = 0000
│ ISO_TP:      Source reference = CA03
│ ISO_TP: Class/options = 40
│ ISO_TP:      0100 .... = Protocol class 4
│ ISO_TP:      .... ..0. = Use extended formats?
│─────────────────────────Frame 145 of 162──────────────
            Use TAB to select windows
┌───────┬──────┐       ┌──────┬──────┐ ┌───────┬───────┬───────┐
│1      │2 Set │       │4 Zoom│5     │ │6Displu│7 Prev │8 Next │     10 New
│  Help │  mark│       │  in  │ Menus│ │options│ frame │ frame │     capture
└───────┴──────┘       └──────┴──────┘ └───────┴───────┴───────┘
```

Courtesy of Network General

Fig. 12-2   TP4 traffic on Ethernet.

UNITDATA data unit specifies an address, data and QOS parameters. QOS indicators include transit delay, a residual error probability, and security protection.

The connectionless transport service definition might use a connection-oriented network service. The transport service might release that connection immediately after sending the connectionless transport data. This means there is a potential for the disconnect command to overtake the data unit at the remote side. The data unit would then be discarded since it belonged to an inoperative network connection. To prevent this situation, CLNS transport services running on a CONS network service are required to let a timer expire before they release the connection.

Quality of service

The transport service user, usually the session layer module, is able to specify a target quality of service for a particular transport connection. Based on these QOS parameters, the transport layer is then able to choose an appropriate network layer over which to route that traffic.

Quality of service can be expressed in terms of goals or in parameters meant to achieve those goals. Example of QOS goals are high throughput, low delay, and low error rates. Note that several of these goals are incompatible. A satellite link might provide very high throughput, but it does so at the expense of a very high delay factor. A low error rate is probably not very compatible with high throughput, since high throughput implies large block sizes which make error recovery more difficult.

Specific parameters can also be specified for a desired quality of service. Line speeds, target bit and block error rates, and data unit or window size are all parameters that help influence the quality of service. A large data unit size might provide higher bandwidth. A large window size means that many data units can be outstanding and un-acknowledged, permitting higher throughput.

A very important quality of service indicator is a security requirement (although this indicator is not provided for in the ISO transport layer specification). A high security requirement objective might require that the network connection use complete source routing to prevent entrusted nodes from receiving sensitive data. A more severe security requirement might require that every data link provide support for data encryption.

Data transfer phase

The data transfer phase begins with the acceptance of a data unit from the transport service access point (TSAP). The transport layer can accept an arbitrary amount of data. If the data size is bigger than the underlying network connection can handle, it is segmented into several pieces. The opposite of segmentation is concatenation where several TSAP data units are concatenated into one transport protocol data unit (TPDU).

Once a TPDU is sent to the network layer, the transport service retains a copy of it. The transport service (TP4) also sets a timer at that time. A TPDU acknowledgment must be received before the data unit is discarded so that the transport service can retransmit the data unit if necessary.

A special kind of data unit is the expedited data unit. Some network service providers have an expedited data facility that has a separate queue from the normal data. Expedited data at this level can only include 16 bytes of user data and only one data unit of expedited data can be outstanding at one time. This service is typically used for interrupts and status messages.

If an acknowledgment of the data unit is not received before the timer expires or if a negative acknowledgment is received, the transport TP4 service retransmits the data unit. It is possible that the TPDU was received at the remote end and that an ACK was sent out but was delayed on route because of congestion. It is important for the timer value to be properly set to avoid overloading an already congested network with unnecessary retransmits. TP4 makes the transport service timer a function of the estimated round-trip delay on the network. This estimate is maintained and updated for each transport connection so that the transport service remains responsive to different users.

Another flow control mechanism employed at the transport layer is a credit mechanism. If the service has 0 credits, it may not send a normal data unit. Expedited data, on the other hand, can always be sent, but only one packet may be unacknowledged at any one time. Credits are established at the beginning of a session and are subject to negotiation during the connection phase.

In some configurations, a transport service provider might provide credits to a large number of different connections under the assumption that they will stay idle. Like a bank, if all users activate at the same time, the transport service cannot meet its obligations. To meet this situation, a transport service may issue a credit reduction, which is somewhat similar to the source quench requests in the Internet Protocol. Immediately after the new policy is announced by the transport service provider, it may be implemented. This means that a foreign node may have transmitted a batch of data assuming it knew the credit policy. The receiving node (the source of the credit reduction) then throws data out that violates the new policy.

DNA Phase V uses two additional algorithms for congestion- avoidance. Some network connections provide a congestion experienced bit. This is used whenever a data unit visits a node that has a queue greater than some architecturally defined number. The transport service then voluntarily reduces the size of its window below the available allotment to help reduce network congestion.

A second voluntary flow control mechanism is employed whenever messages are lost on a connection. It is assumed that message loss is an indicator of serious congestion. The receiving node again voluntarily reduces its credit window below that it is entitled to.

All data sent by the transport service can include a checksum calculation. The use of a checksum is mandatory in all classes of service for connection establishment and termination. The use of a checksum is also optionally used in TP4 sessions. It is assumed that the data link and network layers do some error checking. The checksum is thus not really designed to trap bit errors. On the other hand, missing bytes are easily caught at this level.

DEC transport layer software

The VAX OSI Transport Service (VOTS) provides both the network and transport services of OSI. At the network layer, VOTS provides a CLNS protocol which is equivalent to the TCP/IP Internet Protocol. At the transport layer, VOTS provides the ISO connection-oriented transport service for classes 0, 2, and 4.

The transport interface can be used in both a wide area and a local area environment. In a local area environment, such as the token bus MAP network, the network layer is essentially null because the subnetwork is able to provide the functionality needed.

In a wide area environment, the Internet Protocol is used but only as an end system. This means that the VOTS software cannot be used to route IP traffic through on behalf of other nodes. Even in the wide area environment, the IP service is null when both nodes are part of the same X.25 subnetwork. It is only when going among subnets that the IP software is really activated.

The transport software supports a maximum transport PDU of 8192 bytes in a wide area environment and 2048 bytes in a local area environment. The TPDUs may be sent with or without checksums. The transport layer will work with subnetworks that do not offer expedited data transfer, although this will lead to a sacrifice in performance.

At the network layer, VOTS provides a limited lifetime control function. This means that VOTS does not check the lifetime control over an incoming data unit but is able to properly initialize that value in outgoing data units. Since VOTS is merely a transition vehicle, this is not really a major limitation. Most transition OSI environments will consist of two subnets that are directly connected and there is thus no need to control the behavior of intermediate routing nodes.

Because VOTS provides end system implementation of IP, the routing function is based on a static database. The routing database is entered by the network manager and consists of a list of nodes that are available and which gateway is the next hop needed to reach that node. Users are, of course, free to specify complete or partial source routing to augment the routing database.

Error control functions in VOTS are fairly standard. Checksums can be enabled or disabled. The network manager can specify that outgoing data units have the proper bit field set to inform remote nodes to notify the sender in case of errors. Likewise, VOTS is able to prepare a proper IP error packet in case of incoming errors. Errors generated can be logged.

Session Layer Protocols

The session layer provides a transition from worrying about transferring data on the network to the functions of using that data effectively. The session layer can be a very simple function of setting and releasing a connection.

The user of the session service sets up a session by sending down an S-CONNECT message. This message specifies a session identifier provided by the user. This would be used by a multithreaded application that was providing services to many different users. It might also be used by an application that wished to continue a particular session at a later point in time, possibly because of an error condition.

The session user also specifies the address of the remote user application it wishes to communicate with. Currently, the session layer specification says that a session connection confirmation must be sent by the same application that receives the session connection request. This means that call redirection and generic services are not supported.

The session layer provides two major services to the upper layers: synchronization points and session control tokens. Major synchronization points help identify a particular activity, such as the opening and data transfer of a file within the FTAM service. A minor synchronization point is used to identify particular points in that activity, such as the transfer of a few blocks of data within the file transfer regime.

The purpose of a synchronization point is to "push" all remaining data for an activity through the network. This allows the remote user to finish that particular activity. All data after the synchronization point is thus destined for the new activity. This is important since the next activity might involve a new program or subprocess that is unable to deal with the previous data (or that if it receives data from another context it misinterprets it).

A minor sync point is accomplished by sending sync messages down both logical data channels: normal and expedited. A major sync point ensures that both sides agree by requiring the other side to respond with acknowledgments on both channels. For a major sync point, the sending side does not send any data until both ACKs are received.

Tokens allow several services, including the imposition of a half-duplex mode of operation on a full-duplex transport layer. In order to transmit a message, the session layer must be in possession of the applicable token. There are four kinds of tokens:

1. Data send
2. Connection release
3. Minor synchronization points
4. Major synchronization points

Tokens can be traded with each message or can be permanently in the possession of one side. Expedited data does not need a token to transmit but, as in the lower layers, only one expedited data unit can be outstanding at one time. Although it would be impossible to convince most users, repeatedly pressing the interrupt key on a remote connection does no good if only one data unit of expedited data can be outstanding at one time. This means that the queue of interrupts built up from the user impatiently repeating that sequence takes a good deal of time to clear; 16 interrupts means 16 round-trip sequences before the final one is delivered and normal processing can resume. It should be noted that most OSI implementors would not allow this situation to occur and would only process one interrupt request at a time.

If a node does not posses a token and wishes to send data, it may issue an S-TOKEN-PLEASE request, which may also contain up to 256 bytes of user data. The other side is, of course, free to refuse to give up the token.

The VAX OSI Applications Kernel (VOSAK) consists of a series of procedures contained in a programming library. VOSAK is used by higher-level applications, such as X.400 gateway software. VOSAK consists of a privileged sharable image that can be linked into users' programs. VOSAK assumes the presence of the VOTS service at the transport layer. This is a fairly complete session layer implementation including support for activity management, full-and half-duplex sessions, and expedited data channels.

Presentation Layer

The DNA Phase IV environment has no formal definition of a presentation layer. Each application defines not only the semantics of its operations but the syntax for those operations. DAP, for example, defines a variety of commands for accessing indexed files. This is a semantic operation. DAP also signifies the representation of that data by specifying a particular packet format for that data.

The OSI environment explicitly separates the semantic nature of an operation from the transfer representation of that data. The presentation layer also has some functionality that DNA has in the lower layers. This is the low-level representation of data. Because DNA is a relatively homogeneous environment, issues like bit ordering do not arise. Bit ordering is the issue of whether the least significant bit in a byte is the first or the last bit received. Sun Workstations, for example, use a different bit ordering scheme than VAX workstations. This means that even if both sides agree on ASCII as the data representation for text, they must further agree on the proper bit ordering.

The OSI presentation layer is based on the notion of an abstract syntax. The abstract syntax is a definition of a series of data structures; it defines elements such as booleans or character strings.

Associated with the abstract syntax are a series of available transfer representations. A transfer representation might include encryption or compression options. It could deal with ASCII versus EBCIDIC representations of data. Figure 12-3 illustrates the abstract and transfer representations of data.

The abstract syntax notation (ASN) is a method for representing complex data structures. A file, for example, might be a data structure composed of records. Records are composed of a repeated set of characters terminated by a particular end of record terminator. The application (FTAM in this case) could then send a "files," as opposed to a "records," across the network and the remote FTAM user would know that it was getting a file instead of a record.

The current ASN is ASN.1, which is based on a variety of protocols developed by the CCITT and ISO. ASN.1 is an extremely powerful language, similar to Pascal in notation. Primitive values in ASN.1

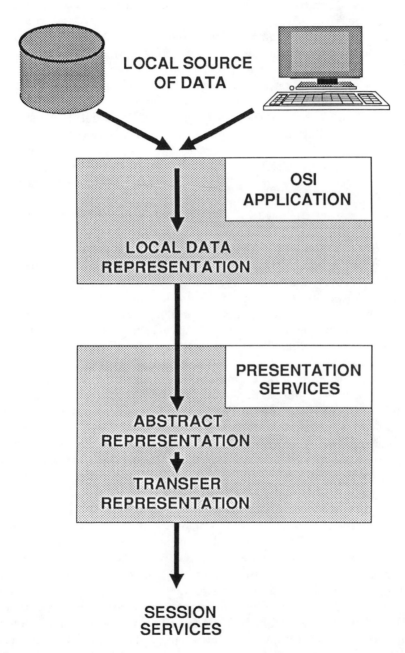

Fig. 12-3 Presentation layer encoding.

include booleans, integers, characters, and other constructs. These primitives may then be combined into data structures using a series of building blocks.

An example of a building block is a sequence. This is an ordered group of lower level structures. We can thus define a protocol data unit in ASN.1 as a data structure. Another building block is a set, which is an unordered set of lower level structures. Finally, a choice is one particular item out of a range of valid choices.

An example of a choice data structure would be to define a priority level in a PDU definition. This might have a definition as follows:

priority CHOICE
{ high (0),
medium (1),
low (2) }
DEFAULT {medium}

This definition has two advantages. The applications can refer to high or low security and not worry about how to represent that value to the other side. It can also not refer to priority levels at all and the other side would know that the default was medium.

ASN.1 also provides a set of built-in structures. Time and date are both defined, for example. This means that an application has only to be able to read time and date using the OSI standard and no longer needs to support 35 different time and date formats Another built-in data type is the visible string—the set of printable characters. An electronic mail message can be defined as a set of characters of type VISIBLE_STRING.

The encoding rules, or transfer representations, specify how to represent abstract syntaxes for transfer over the network. A variety of transfer representations might be defined for use with a particular abstract syntax. Together, the combination of an abstract syntax and a transfer representation form a presentation context.

Once in encoded form, the data sent over the network consists of a 1-byte type identifier, a length indicator, and the actual data. The type identifier includes a type class and a 5-bit ID code. The verbose ASN syntax is thus reduced to a series of low-level information, which is then optionally encrypted or compressed.

The presentation layer allows a set of presentation contexts to be available. One context might be used for the transfer of graphic information (a series of compressed bit strings) while another context would be used for the transfer of textual information (a series of un-compressed values of type VISIBLE_STRING).

Abstract syntax definitions for major applications are named and registered by either the ISO or CCITT. Examples are the syntaxes for message handling and file transfer. Other ASN.1 syntaxes are being developed by other organizations. For example, the American National Standards Institute is developing an ASN syntax for use in transferring standard data dictionary elements between cooperating instances of the Information Resources Dictionary System (IRDS), a data dictionary definition.

Application Layer Overview

The applications layer provides a series of services that will be used by other programs that require open network access. A set of common application facilities, known as the common application service elements, provide an application-to-application association. The CASE facilities can be used by all different types of users of the network, ranging from robots to messaging systems to virtual terminal services.

A series of other services is used for specialized functions. Three basic services give access to files (FTAM), remote processing (JTM), and virtual terminals (VT). Many other services are defined in the OSI model that builds on the basic services. For example, building on top of CASE and other services are remote database access services.

The users of the application layer services are truly user programs. This is in contrast to all the lower layers, where a user is just the next layer up. The user of the network layer is the transport layer, the user of the transport layer, the session layer, and so on. Here, the users of application services are actually programmers. Programmers use these basic services, in the form of library calls, along with other services, such as screen painting utilities or mathematical programming libraries.

CASE Facilities

The application layer defines two types of common application service elements. The association control service elements are used by two applications that wish to establish or terminate an application association. The commitment, concurrency, and recovery facilities are facilities used to allow applications to recover to a previously agreed point.

The ACSE service elements are used to associate, release or abort a session. Level 1 of the ACSE definition allows only a static association. Level 2 allows application switching, so one particular association is used by multiple applications. With a level 1 ACSE definition, multiple semantic contexts require multiple application associations.

The association commands might seem a little wasteful, given the presence of similar functions at the session and transport layers and the establishment of a presentation context (which implies a session). All of these requests are embedded into one message to prevent a wasteful exchange of data units at startup time.

The commitment, concurrency, and recovery (CCR) facilities are similar to the database two-phase commit protocols used in a distributed transaction processing environment. CCR is an optional facility in some applications (such as FTAM) and is required in others (such as JTM).

CCR allows multiple nodes to cooperate in a transaction processing environment. A example of this environment is a distributed banking application. Checking account balances are kept on one MicroVAX (this is a small bank) and saving account balances are kept on a separate one. Users log onto a third MicroVAX, which serves as the automatic teller machine (ATM). When a user asks to have money transferred from savings to checking, the ATM must check to see if the savings balance is adequate, then deduct the amount from savings and add it to checking. If the network goes down after the deduction from savings but before the addition to checking, the user will not be especially enthused about the situation.

CCR ensures consistency by doing distributed transactions in two phases. First, each node is told to PREPARE a particular transaction. This means that the foreign node is prepared to either do that particular transaction or bring the data back to its previous state. The foreign node also guarantees that no other user will perform an incompatible action on that resource. Figure 12-4 illustrates the CCR message exchange.

A node acknowledges a PREPARE request with either a READY or REFUSE message. Once READY messages have been received from all nodes on the network, the ATM would then send out COMMIT messages to all nodes. Once acknowledgments of each of those COMMIT operations is received, the ATM has a fairly high assurance that all transactions occurred.

It is possible that the ATM would issue a ROLLBACK command instead of a COMMIT. Perhaps the checking account would receive a ROLLBACK if a REFUSE message was received from the savings account. It is a responsibility of the CCR remote node to return the resources to their previous state.

One possible situation is that the ATM PREPARES several transactions and then crashes. In that case, it is unreasonable for the remote node to reserve scarce resources indefinitely, and, at some point, it

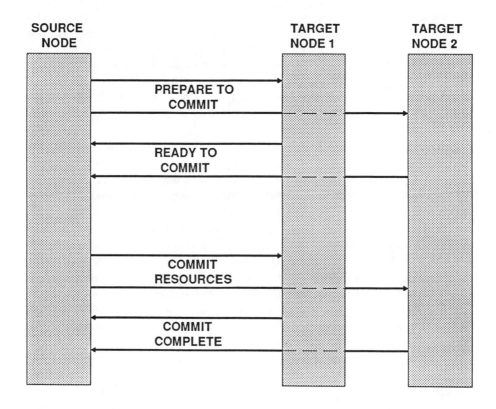

Fig. 12-4 CCR message exchange.

will have to decide whether to commit or roll back that particular transaction. The beginning of a CCR sequence allows the requesting node to specify what to do in case of a node failure. The foreign node is instructed how long to reserve the resources and which action to take upon a time-out. As with most OSI parameters, the two nodes might disagree and then they would need to negotiate these parameters.

File Transfer, Access, and Management

A wide variety of file access mechanisms are available in networks. The FTP service, discussed previously in the chapter on TCP/IP, allows the bulk transfer of data among a large variety of systems. The DNA DAP services provide a high degree of functionality, but at the cost of performance and the support of only a few types of nodes. FTAM is meant to be a highly robust service that supports a wide range of file types and document structures in a highly heterogeneous environment.

FTAM provides an abstract model of different types of file systems using the concept of a virtual filestore. The FTAM implementor needs to map that virtual filestore and operations on the filestore into the particular file system on their implementation. This could be a fairly simple filestore with all files on one level and very few file types. Alternatively, the mapping could be complex as in the case of the Unix filesystem which has a complex directory structure including cross references.

FTAM provides a totally general model of a hierarchical filestore. This means that the file is of a hierarchical nature. Currently, FTAM does not support other file structures, such as the relational model. This should not pose a problem since most implementations of relational databases currently map their data into implementation specific file types, such as an ISAM file. In the future, ISO may define relational or network (cross-referenced) file systems.

The FTAM model also does not currently support a directory structure. All files thus occupy a monolithic filespace. Again, this is not much of a constraint since a hierarchical directory structure can be mapped into a flat file space. This means that the user interface, the user of the FTAM service, needs to be able to reconstruct that hierarchy.

A file in FTAM consists of nodes and data units. A node has a node name and optionally, a data unit (DU). Nodes can have children nodes, which in turn may or may not have children or data units attached to them. A File Access Data Unit consists of a node and all children and data units associated with that FADU. The FADU is the basic unit of operation in FTAM. Figures 12-5 and 12-6 shows data units and file access data units.

A data unit can be of a several different types, each defined in the ASN.1 syntax associated with FTAM. There is no requirement at this level for DUs at the same level to be of the same data type.

To provide a lesser degree of generality, and hence a higher probability of various systems supporting FTAM, ISO has defined a variety of context sets and documentation types. A constraint set is a general

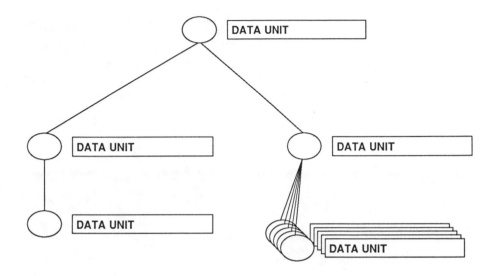

Fig. 12-5 Virtual filestore.

definition imposed on a filestore. For example, the sequential flat constraint set imposes a root node with no data unit and one further level
of nodes with an optional data unit associated with them. Nodes do
not have a node name associated with them.

A more complicated structure is an ordered flat constraint set. In
this set, node names can be used to insert or delete data. An ordered
hierarchical constraint set allows several levels but imposes the requirement that the node names of children of a common parent be
unique.

The next level of definition is a document type. A binary document
type can use the sequential flat constraint set and requires that data
units consist of a series of bytes, as opposed to an arbitrary set of bits.
Another document type is unstructured text. This uses the unstructured constraint set (a root node with a data unit and no children) and
imposes the further structural limitation that data consist of printing
characters and spaces.

The basic FTAM operation is to traverse this hierarchical filestore,
or tree. This is done in preorder traversal sequence. This means you

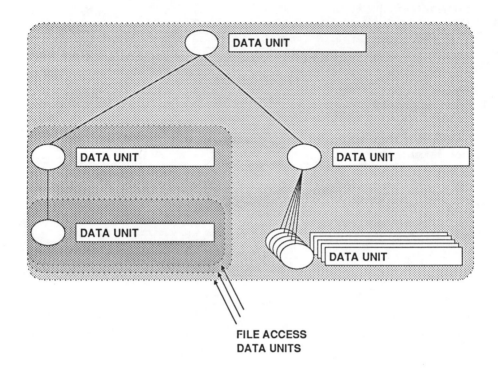

Fig. 12-6   File access data units.

visit every node to your left as far as you can go. Then, you go as short a distance to your right as you can, followed by another traversal to your left. In this way every node is visited. Each node is assigned a sequence number based on the preorder traversal sequence. This mechanism is a way of imposing a linear structure (needed for transmission over the network) on a hierarchical system.

FADUs can be referenced by the unique sequence number or by a FADU name. A list of names can also be used in operations such as erase. A series of logical traversal operations, such as first, last, next and previous, are also available for referencing FADUs.

Once the FADU is located, several operations are associated with that element. Users can erase a data unit or read it. To read a data unit, an access context is specified. This tells the FTAM service whether you want the entire FADU, the root DU, all DUs (with or without node names), or the information content of the FADU. The information content is a series of node names plus a flag indicating the presence or absence of a data unit.

Several other options include the ability to insert a new FADU or to extend the data unit associated with the root of the FADU. Note that all these operations assume your version of FTAM already knows about this particular group of files, usually by specifying a document type. A fully general implementation would allow an FTAM instance to learn about a foreign filestore and its structure during a session. This is the function of data dictionary standard such as the Information Resources Dictionary System (IRDS).

Associated with a filestore are a series of attributes. Operations on these attributes are the management functions of FTAM. One file attribute is the file name. A file name can have directory and subdirectory information implied in the name if the other user of FTAM is aware of this.

Important attributes are permitted actions and access control. Permitted actions refer to the file as a whole. The access control information extends and further limits the permitted actions to individual users. Permitted actions include insert, read, replace, or erase a FADU or they extend a data unit. Another attribute controls the ability to read or change particular attributes or delete the file. A third series of actions limit permitted FADU location methods to forward traversal, forward and reverse traversal, or random access by FADU node names or numbers.

The access control list is based on either a password or an authenticated user name or unauthenticated application titles. Note that any one of these allow the set of permitted applications. If passwords plus the application FTAM$SPECIAL are in the access control list, a user without the password could masquerade as the application name FTAM$SPECIAL and gain access to the data.

Another set of attributes is used for accounting purposes. An account can be established with that pays for storage charges (and this attribute can be read by foreign users assuming they are permitted to). Other attributes contain the date, time, and identity of users who created, last modified, or last read data in the filestore.

A file availability attribute is useful for systems that have large optical disk farms or tape systems. A deferred availability file definition is implementation specific and could mean a 2-second wait or a requirement to send a truck to Iowa to find the data. This allows the filestore to function as a sort of data dictionary.

Attributes can also include a definition of the document type name or of a combination of constraint set and abstract syntax. The last two

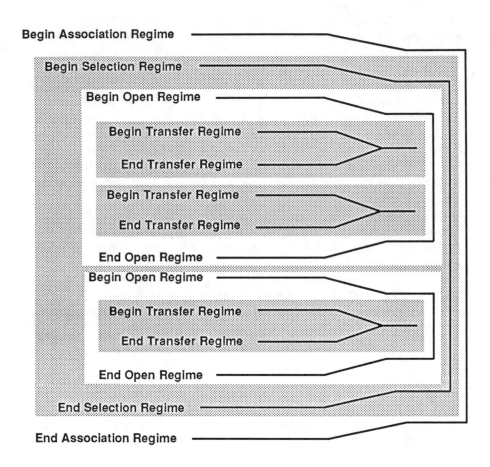

Fig. 12-7   FTAM regimes.

attributes are implementation specific. A legal qualifications attribute is used to inform users of copyright and other legal constraints. A private use attribute is totally undefined (and strongly discouraged) but provides a hook for local attributes.

FTAM operation is based on a series of regimes, which are typically associated with lower level sync points. Regimes are nested, and you can't exit an outer regime without first exiting the inner ones. To begin with, the association regime is used to identify users, set up billing accounts, and negotiate overall capabilities. The conclusion of this regime would probably result in a message identifying charges accrued, although this could also be done in an inner regime. Figure 12-7 shows FTAM regimes.

A file selection regime is the next level. This is used to select or create files and to read or change attributes. This level is also used to apply the first series of concurrency controls or locks on a file.

Next, a particular file is opened. At this time, the user can adjust concurrency controls. Users can also perform operations on FADUs that don't involve data transfer, such as locate or erase operations. Finally, the innermost regime is a data transfer regime used to read, insert, or extend FADUs and data units.

An optional capability of FTAM is to use the services of CCR. This capability, if available, can be associated to particular regimes on a selective basis. The default is to not use CCR since this imposes considerable extra overhead. This means that in the event of a lower-level disconnect (caused by network saturation for example) data can be corrupted. It is up to each individual FTAM environment to decide what to do in these cases.

DEC's FTAM software

DEC supports FTAM on the VAX/VMS operating system. This VAX FTAM software includes an interface to the Digital Command Language. The DCL interface permits the same interface on FTAM files as on native files for file copy and deletion and directory information. Integration into the DCL interface of foreign file systems was also used to make Phase IV distributed data (Distributed File Service) and IBM data (Data Transfer Facility) available.

VAX FTAM supports three of the basic FTAM document types:

- FTAM document type 1 for unstructured ASCII data with stream record formats
- FTAM document type 2 for sequential text files with variable record format and carriage return record attributes
- FTAM document type 3 for unstructured binary data

Job Transfer and Manipulation

A service not present in DNA but included in most other networks is a Remote Job Entry (RJE) service. This allows a batch job to be submitted to a remote site and the results either returned or queued to a remote printer. Unfortunately, most RJE services are based on a very restricted structure of data, usually 80-column records in EBCDIC or ASCII format. Transfer or arbitrary files is not permitted.

The job transfer and manipulation service (JTM) is meant to address RJE-like facilities but in a more general environment. Jobs consist of work specifications and documents. A job may visit several nodes to pick up documents, perform work on several other nodes, and finally return the results to a variety of sink nodes. In addition to job transfer capabilities, several status, reporting, and job control services are offered.

There are two classes of JTM service. The basic class allows operations to be performed only at a single node. The full-class operation allows a deep tree of jobs, including distributed scheduling, the use of FTAM to get documents from other systems, and checkpointing and recovery capabilities.

Both classes of JTM require the use of the commitment, concurrency, and recovery (CCR) facilities. It might be worth noting that unlike the concept of a universal, virtual filestore in FTAM, there is no universal job control language. You are expected to know the relevant commands on each system performing work.

JTM may involve the cooperation of many different nodes. Each node takes on one of several roles. The initiator specifies what work should be done by which node. A source node provides documents that are incorporated into the work specification. In the basic class of operation, the source node and the initiator are usually the same. A more complicated scenario might have a variety of source nodes (plus access to other documents using FTAM).

The two other kinds of nodes are executors and sinks. An executor performs the work specified by the initiator. The results are then shipped to sink nodes. Sink nodes also receive error reports and status messages. Figure 12-8 shows the different types of JTM nodes.

Initiator nodes submit a work specification. The specification includes a list of global parameters that apply to all pieces of the job. There is then a section that specifies what jobs will be spawned off to other executors for completion. Finally, there are a series of subjob specifications.

The fundamental unit of work in JTM is the document. Associated with a document is a particular work specification. A document can be any arbitrary set of information as defined in the accompanying

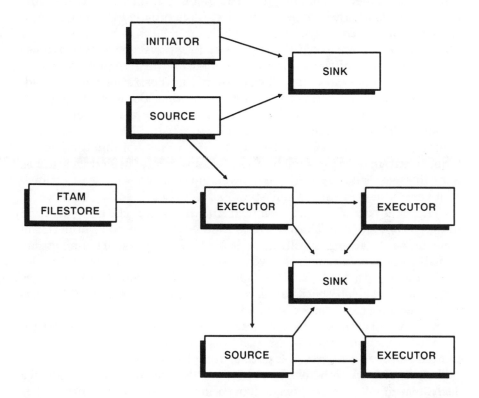

Fig. 12-8 JTM nodes.

abstract syntax. In the basic class of operation, all documents needed must accompany the initial work specification.

In the full operation, documents can be collected in a variety of ways. As before, they may accompany the original job specifications. Alternatively, a remote JTM site may be instructed to use FTAM or a private protocol to retrieve a particular document. Finally, the job may be handed to a JTM relay (a source node) which collects relevant documents, attaches them to the work order, and sends the work order on.

The global parameters for a work order are copied on any clones of the work order that are submitted to multiple executors. These parameters include the system and user ID from the initiator and a unique work order ID for this job. The global parameters also include a trace area that tracks all systems that have handled the work order at a particular time.

The global parameters also include instructions on where to send different portions of the work order as well as warnings and diagnostics. There are also specifications of authorization codes and passwords included for each of the nodes that do work or deliver reports on this particular order. Accounts to charge and security information during transfer are also included.

Subjobs within the work order can be of a variety of different types. A document movement subjob is responsible for transferring a document to a particular site. Report movement subjobs are used to transfer a variety of error and diagnostic reports.

The last type of subjob included in the basic class is a work manipulation subjob. These subjobs request a target node to perform some action on a work specification it already posseses. This might be a modification of a job, a change in status (such as an abort operation), or a request for a particular form of report on job status.

Within the subjob specification are the target nodes as well as any relays needed to collect documents. An urgency field specifies a priority for execution. There are also hold instructions which can be provided which instruct the target system to hold the job until a manual release or a particular date or time has been achieved.

The actual work to be performed is in a list contained in the subjob. Each item on the list is a particular action to take and the name of a document to associate with that action. By the time the action is taken, the document must be present in the work specification.

During the course of a JTM operation, a series of reports may be issued. Three basic class reports are defined. The usual report signals normal or abnormal termination of the job. A second report indicates that some entity has manipulated the job (i.e., killed it). A final basic report is the user message which is used by user applications, such as the operating system, to communicate with remote users.

More advanced reports are available in the full class of operation. Reports can be sent upon acceptance of a document, upon modification of work specifications, or when no progress has occurred for a period of time. Violation attempts by unauthorized users attempting to manipulate the job can also be reported. Finally, accounting information can be sent periodically.

Job manipulations are performed by selecting a series of options, possibly with a wild card specification. These work specifications can then be modified or a status displayed. Two options are available to terminate jobs. A kill operation will abort the action and discard work specifications. A stop operation will stop that particular action but keep the results already obtained for use by future nodes.

Each subjob also includes instructions for error handling. Upon an error, a particular subjob will usually embed diagnostics in place of the output document and continue processing. Other options are to hold the job for a specified time and retry the action. Finally, an option is available to terminate the job and not continue processing future steps.

Virtual Terminal Service

The virtual terminal service is particularly challenging because of the wide variety of different terminal types available. The X.25 solution to this problem is to define a few parameters to use on an X.3 PAD. This provides functionality, but the parameter list keeps on growing in order to accommodate different types of operations.

The VT service intends to solve this problem by developing a general model of terminal operation and then registering profiles of basic types of terminals. These profiles are then available on a negotiation basis between VT users and service providers.

The terminal consists of a variety of objects. These objects may be a screen or a printer. Objects are also defined for mice, joysticks, and any other form of input/output.

The VT model defines a conceptual communications area (CCA). Both parties to the VT session share this CCA and keep it intact. Within the CCA are a variety of objects that represent pieces of the virtual terminal. A data structure definition heads up the CCA and defines the data structures associated with the different types of objects that are operational. Figure 12-9 shows the different parts of a CCA.

The CCA includes a variety of display objects. These display objects are one- to three-dimensional arrays that correspond to some portion of the terminal, such as the screen.

Many devices have a larger memory than they are able to display at one time. Portions of display objects are thus mapped onto a device object which presumably corresponds to some physical device.

A display object can have up to three dimensions. The basic class only applies to characters and character box graphics. A one-dimensional array is thus a single line of text. A two-dimensional array is a screen of text. A three-dimensional array is a multipage terminal device.

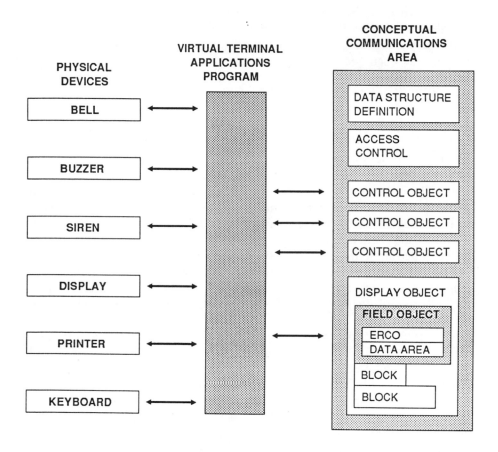

Fig. 12-9   Virtual terminal CCA.

Associated with each element of a display object is a series of attributes. The primary attribute is a representation of a valid character. Secondary attributes include color codes for foreground and background, emphasis (such as reverse video), and a font to use.

Related to display objects are control objects. These are abstract representations of devices such as lamps, buzzers, or bells. A control object has associated with it an information field. This field could be a boolean, as in the case of a lamp being on or off. It could be a scalar as in the case of a lamp with a dimmer switch. It can also be a bit or character string.

Objects can be subject to access control. Access control information is kept in a special access control store of the CCA. This store has a series of tokens which give access rights to any modifiable object in the CCA.

The use of tokens depends on the mode of operation. An asynchronous mode allows only one side to modify the CCA. Asynchronous mode thus has a single token for the display object. An important source of inefficiency in an asynchronous mode is echo control. This allows the local VT, for instance, to perform echoing on behalf of the foreign host, if desired. This can be turned off, as in the case of passwords showing up on the screen

In synchronous mode, users can perform two-way access to objects. Multiple tokens are thus defined which can either remain permanently in the possession of one side or can be passed around.

Because some terminals have local editing capabilities, a variety of delivery control mechanisms are defined. This allows a terminal to modify some object without delivering the data. If quarantine delivery control is in effect, only the net effect of a series of commands is issued when the local virtual terminal service issues a DELIVER command.

A simpler mode is no delivery control which means that delivery of data is at the convenience of the various protocol modules. A form of simple delivery control pushes undelivered data through the model. This might be used to ensure that a function key redefinition occurs simultaneously with the update of the screen display that signals the new definition.

An extended version of the virtual terminal service allows the imposition of additional structure in display objects. The extended mode defines two types of structures. Blocks are portions of the display object that can overlap; fields are portions of the display object that cannot overlap.

In the basic mode, there is a pointer to the current position within the display object array. Extended mode allows further navigation by allowing the user to refer to current blocks and fields, move to the first or last block or field, or move to the next or previous area.

Associated with fields is a series of data entry rules used for validation. Each field has an entry rules control object (ERCO). This ERCO includes a series of rules that specify what to do when correct or incorrect data is retrieved. It also specifies actions to take upon expiration of a timer or when the end of a field is reached. A final rule also specifies what to do upon release of the VT connection.

A variety of profiles has already been registered with the ISO. These include a default asynchronous and synchronous mode. Other profiles include support for multipage color displays and X.3 pads. An important item to be considered is a profile that is compatible with the X Windows System discussed at the end of this book.

Manufacturing Automation Protocol

The Manufacturing Automation Protocol consists of a family of standards that is used to control manufacturing environments. Pioneered by General Motors, the MAP protocol set has been very influential in determining the final specifications of many current ISO standards.

At the lower layers, MAP builds on top of existing technologies. Normally, the MAP network is built on a token bus network that uses a broadband physical media. MAP is used to connect various types of nodes to this media, including computers, programmable computers, robots, and other intelligent manufacturing equipment.

MAP allows two types of nodes. Full MAP end nodes are hosts and cell controllers that form the backbone of the MAP network. Cell controllers, in turn, can control a set of limited functionality devices that need fast response time using the manufacturing messaging services (MMS).

End nodes supplement the MMS services with a variety of other ISO application-level standards. CASE is used to control the association of two application entities. FTAM is used for file transfer. A directory service provides name-to-address resolution to find the location of devices.

Separate MAP networks can be combined together with either bridges and routers. Routers provide a wide area link between two MAP networks. In addition, a router may provide a gateway service to another environment, such as a DECnet Ethernet.

The directory services consists of a series of service agents. A client services agent (CSA) can operate in a standalone fashion or can query a remote directory services agent. DEC's 2.1 MAP product supports a local version of the CSA that queries a local cache of addresses. This local cached directory consists a series of user element names and various addresses used to locate that user element. The directory must contain addresses of all local applications that will accept remote requests and all remote applications.

The manufacturing messaging service consists of a reduced protocol suite for use in a real-time environment. The cell controller, a MAP end system, provides the bridge to the rest of the MAP network. MMS provides a wide variety of services, some of which are somewhat redundant with CASE and FTAM. This is because MMS is optimized for devices that do not have time for data to carefully wend its way through a protocol stack. An example is when a robot is told to lower its arm to put a piece down. At the bottom of the trajectory, it is crucial that the robot receive the next command to stop lowering the arm, release the piece, and then raise the arm.

One of the prime functions of MMS is job and queue management for a variety of devices. Jobs, as in JTM, consists of a series of commands to be executed in order. If the remote device supports queuing, the specifications are immediately sent. Otherwise, they are queued at the initiating device and sent one at a time.

Nodes in an MMS environment can then provide a journaling capability for jobs that are executed. This journal is a series of messages that state what event occurred and provide supporting data. This journaling capability is required in sensitive industries such as pharmaceutical industries to support Federal regulatory activities.

Remote event management provides an even greater degree of control. Remote events can be triggered based on a time limit, the value of a particular variable, or the occurrence of a remote command. Remote operations can also be tied to the occurrence of a remote event.

MMS messages are also used to access remote variables. Remote variables on a device can be defined and typed. Then, the contents can be read or changed. Data can accessed by name or by virtual location. When data is transferred back, it is represented in an independent external representation. It is also possible to group several variables together into one named structure. This allows nodes to treat several data items as though they were contiguous even though they may be located in different parts of the remote memory.

Semaphores are used to control access to data or other resources. Semaphores can be acquired by the event, for a particular time period, or indefinitely. Semaphores are important when a particular device may be controlled by several controllers. A guided vehicle, for example, might provide delivery services for several different cells. This would prevent a vehicle loaded with paint from being diverted to the suede upholstery cell.

An early application of MAP technology was in General Motors' truck and bus division. Jack Rathsburg presented a description of the automation efforts for a series of plants involved in a new series of trucks, known as the GMT400 project at the September 1987 meeting of the MAP/TOP Users Group. The project involved tying together a series of assembly facilities and the supporting fabrication plants.

Assembly facilities in two locations (Pontiac, Michigan and Fort Wayne, Indiana) were both completely wired with broadband cable.

24,000 total tap locations were made available and over 3000 taps actually installed to allow for modular changes to configurations. The broadband cable spans an area of over 5,000,000 square feet of space.

Each plant had a computer that controlled the plant at a system level. Each area of the plant, in turn, had an area manager computer. Area managers communicated with cell controllers, which in turn worked with the intelligent devices on the network. All together, over 1500 intelligent devices communicated with 200 nodes. The plant computers were connected to corporate facilities using a wide area link. Corporate facilities included a variety of SNA and DNA nodes throughout General Motors.

Computer equipment in the installation consists of a series of DEC computers as area managers. HP cell controllers are then used for each individual cell. A variety of different types of robot and programmable logic controllers are used for the different intelligent devices.

If the system support level for the plant is unavailable, area managers are able to function for a period of 8 hours without assistance. Likewise, cell controllers can function for 2 hours without assistance from an area manager.

Automation in the assembly plants includes four main types of areas, including the body shop, paint shop, cab and engine trim areas, and final assembly areas. Programmable guided vehicles are used to deliver materials to their proper locations. An important feature of these vehicles is that they are used within areas to allow trim and assembly operations to occur in a nonserial fashion.

The body shop uses vehicles to deliver parts to the appropriate welding stations. The parts are welded together using either programmable robots or devices that use "hard automation" (nonintelligent devices).

The paint shop is also automated and consists of a series of different paint shops directed by an area manager computer system. Pieces are routed into a particular shop and stopped at a particular location, and a robot is then used to spray paint the part. The part is then routed to an oven which is set to bake the piece to give the paint a hard finish.

The final assembly area includes three different sets of guided vehicles that deliver parts. The engine transmission assemblies are delivered from an off-line assembly area. The truck cab and box trim are delivered by another guided vehicle. Finally, the chassis is delivered by a third vehicle. All three vehicles converge at the final assembly line. A robot is then used to guide assembly, using a vision camera. The vision camera provides feedback to the robot to check for proper alignment of openings, hole patterns, and seams.

X.400 Messaging Services

X.400 consists of a series of message-handling protocols developed by the CCITT. X.400 has been quickly adopted by most major computer vendors as well as most wide area service providers. Versions of X.400 are readily available for most computer systems and for most countries. Some countries, such as France, have adopted X.400 wholeheartedly as a nationwide messaging handle system.

User agents and message transfer agents

X.400 is built on a concept of user and message transfer agents. This split in functionality is very similar to the DTE/DCE split in the X.25 standards. The user agent is responsible for providing a user interface to the ultimate user of the message-handling services. The user agent then takes a message, puts it into an envelope, and submits it the message transfer agent.

The message transfer agent is the edge of the message-handling system. This message-handling system takes a message, enclosed in an envelope, and routes it through the network to a destination MTA. This destination MTA in turn gives the message to a user agent, who presents the message to the end user. Figure 12-10 show the relationship of user agents to MTAs.

Several different sets of protocols help form this environment. The P1 protocols are used for communication between different MTA entities. P3 is the submission and delivery protocol for a user agent to communicate with a remote message transport agent. Note that a user agent commmunicating with a local MTA is able to use its own communication mechanisms.

The combination of P1 and P3 protocols allows a message to be delivered to a final destination. These two protocols thus control the handling of the envelope. Another protocol, P2, controls what is inside of the envelope. This allows a message to be structured in a way to include more than just an arbitrary block of ASCII text.

The protocol between a UA and an ultimate user is not really part of the X.400 protocols. These functions, such as filing messages or editing services, are up to the local implementation. A special case is when Teletex terminals are connected to the message handling system. A special protocol, P5 governs how these telematic access units interact with the network. Figure 12-11 shows the different protocols in an X.400 environment.

Note that the user of the X.400 service may or may not be on the same computer as the software user agent. It is possible for a remote

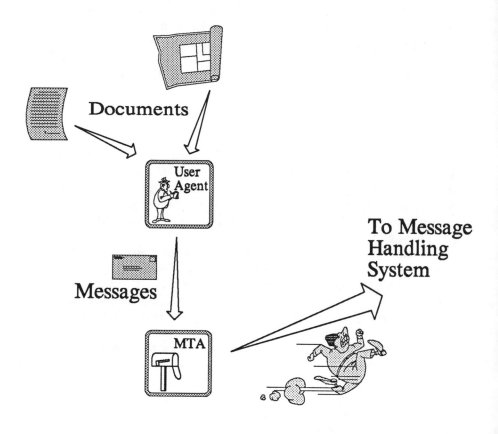

Fig. 12-10   X400 user and message transfer agents.

terminal to be connected to the user agent host using some other protocol, such as the X.29 protocols on a packet-switched network.

Management domains and addresses

X.400 defines a framework for a worldwide messaging environment. Needless to say, the United Nations has not been asked to administer

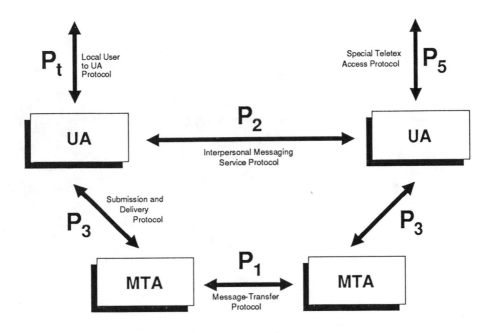

Fig. 12-11   Protocols defined in X.400 model.

this environment. Instead, the message-handling environment is split into a series of management domains.   Each country has one (or several) administration management domain. This ADMD is typically run by the monopoly PTT service provider.

Attached to an ADMD may be a series of private management domains. These would be administered by organizations such as corporations. A PRMD might be connected to two separated ADMDs, but it cannot provide route-through services for the two administration domains. This allows X.400 to guarantee control to each individual

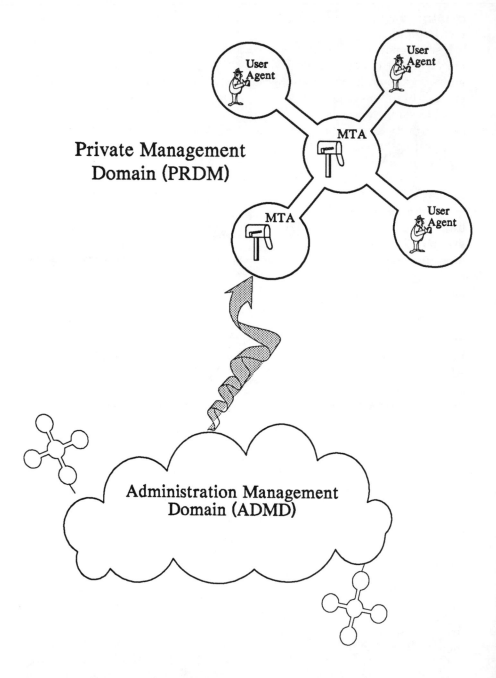

Private Management
Domain (PRDM)

Administration Management
Domain (ADMD)

Fig. 12-12 Management domains in X.400.

country. Figure 12-12 illustrates private and administration management domains.

User agents may be part of either a private or administration management domain. Each user of this system is then given a unique address, known as an originator/recipient address. An O/R address is enough to uniquely identify a particular user.

Addressing proceeds in a hierarchical fashion. The CCITT has ensured that every ADMD has a unique name. It is up to each ADMD to ensure that each PRMD it controls has a unique name. It is then up to each PRMD to ensure that every name it assigns is unique within the domain. A PRMD might cede naming authority to subdomains, but there must still be a unique name for each user.

Names consist of a series of naming attributes that together form a unique name. Attributes fall in four main categories. Personal name attributes include surnames, given names, initials, and a generational qualifier. Geographical attributes include streets, cities, regions, or countries. Organizational attributes could include the name or the organization (or a subunit) but can also include a position or role within the organization.

Special naming attributes are architectural attributes because they are architecturally imposed instead of being derived from some existing naming system. Architectural addresses can include PRMD or ADMD names. They can also include X.121 addresses, which identify a network, plus a unique numeric value that identify a particular user. Domain-specific attributes might include DNA addresses, VMS user names, or other implementation-specific details.

A collection of attributes helps to form a name. The single attribute country name does not uniquely identify a particular user, but the collection of country name, some geographical identifiers, and a personal name might be a sufficient collection of identifiers to uniquely identify a user. A guaranteed collection of attributes that forms a unique name might be a Telex 121 address with a unique numerical identifier for the user of that X.121 address.

OSI has approved two collections of naming attributes that should be supported by each X.400 implementation. This means that any message submitted to this management domain, if it has a properly formed address, can be delivered or relayed. The two approved forms of address are the X.121 form and a "user friendly" collection of addresses that consists of a country name, administration and management domain names, and a unique personal name.

It is up to each management domain to decide how to route messages to the ultimate user. If a management domain has its own unique naming attributes, it may accept supplemental types of names instead of just the ones specified by OSI. A management domain might even accept a badly formed name and route it to a user. For example, mail might be addressed to the GM PRDM in the US ADMD. This is not a complete addresses, but the GM PRDM might specify a location to send poorly formed messages. The other option, of course, is for the GM PRDM to return the message to the originator as undeliverable.

The collection of naming attributes is very similar to partial source routing in the IP and OSI frameworks. Enough information is given so each MTA on the route is able to determine the next MTA to handle the message.

The actual route to be used to deliver a message is not specified in X.400. This is because to specify a routing algorithm implies some issues that are outside of the technical scope of CCITT. Specifying routing might lead to a situation in which a West African node is told to route messages through a neighbor instead of the more traditional use of Paris as a routing hub. Other economic and political issues also influence the choice of routes.

Directories

Directory services become an important issue in a global messaging environment. For the same reason that control is distributed into management domains, directories of users also need to be distributed. Directory services were part of the original X.400 mandate but proved to be difficult enough that they were spun off into a separate X.500 working group.

The prime function of a directory service is to verify the existence of a name or to match a name to a properly formed X.400 address. With the base X.400 specifications, it is possible to specify a probe, which is a message with a null envelope content. The user then receives a delivery confirmation if the address is properly formed and the service elements requested can be supported. One problem with this approach is the delay involved in delivering a message all the way to the ultimate destination. This is definitely not an interactive option.

Directories need to form an environment that allows data to be accessible globally but updated and managed locally. A PRMD might provide a directory of all subdomains it has authorized. The subdomain would then be responsible for updating the list of valid users. This implies that each of the decentralized directory providers is diligent enough to maintain a valid directory. Some organizations, such as military groups, might also make their directories unavailable.

Assuming that a directory is available, several advanced functions are specified as goals of the X.500 specifications. X.500 allows a user to determine if a name is a user or a distribution list. If it is a distribution list, the directory can return a list of names that make up the list (which in turn could be distribution lists).

Users are also able to map a partial name into a possibility list. The partial name "Joe" at "General Motors" might return a large number of names, so it is possible for a particular implementation to limit this capability with users. Remember that directory information gets returned in the form of a message, which carries a charge just like any other message.

Message transfer service

The message transfer service (MTS) specifies how user agents and message transfer agents interact. To begin with, each message formed is assigned a unique ID. This unique ID is used when referring to status messages such as nondelivery notices. The message transfer services are grouped into five basic service groups. The basic message transfer service group includes a set of capabilities common to all MTS interaction.

Included in the basic group of services is the unique message ID, submission and delivery time stamps, and nondelivery notifications. The basic group also allows some control over the types of information that can be delivered.

The message transfer service is mostly independent of the message content. That is a function for the interpersonal messaging protocols which interpret the contents of a message. An exception is the question of encoding information. Encoding specifies things like which character sets are used to encode a message.

As part of the basic MTS, a UA can register the types of valid encoded information it is willing to receive. The UA can also indicate that a particular message it is sending is encoded in a particular way, that conversion is to be performed, or that conversion is prohibited.

The next major set of services defined for the MTS are submission and delivery services. A UA can specify the grade of delivery for a message to be normal, urgent, or nonurgent. The precise meaning of these service levels is up to each domain to decide.

Submission and delivery services also allow the UA to specify if a delivery notification is desired. Note that this means that a receipt is sent when the message is delivered, not when it is read. The UA can also prevent the return of nondelivery notifications. Since nondelivery notifications are a message, they have a cost associated with them. The UA can also specify that in the case of nondelivery the contents of the message be returned.

A final set of submission and delivery services governs the type of delivery. The UA can specify that delivery be deferred and thus not occur before a specific time. Deferred delivery cancellation is available although there is no guarantee that the cancellation order will catch up with the message in time to cancel it. Alternate delivery can be allowed, although there is no guarantee that the receiving end knows who to deliver the message to. If no alternate recipient is available, the message is not delivered.

UAs are allowed to tell their MTA what conditions lead to the assignment of alternate recipients. This function might of course be restricted to certain users. The qualified user would specify what combinations of possibly incomplete attributes to use to select a message and then who the alternate recipient is. A UA may also specify that messages are to be held by the final MTA and not delivered. This is useful for a stand-alone UA, such as a personal workstation, which is not always connected to the message-handling system.

The last groups of service elements in MTS provide a variety of controls over conversion and status. The conversion elements allow a UA to export information to other services agents, such as a Teletex terminal.

Interpersonal messaging service

The IPMS governs the contents of the envelope that is delivered by the message transfer service. The contents of this envelope might be a message from a user agent or might be a status message, such as a return receipt or a nondelivery notification.

The contents of a message is defined using the same ASN.1 syntax used to define other forms of complex documents, such as a file. Figure 12-13 shows a portion of that ASN.1 definition. The message consists of two pieces, a header and a body.

The header of a message consists of a series of service elements. Most of these elements are optional. The basic elements are used to identify the basic MTS options that were picked, as well as the type of IP message that is being delivered. The IP message could be a status message, such as a receipt, or a user-originated message.

Another basic type of information is the type or types of body information that is included. A message could thus consist of a mix of FAX, ASCII text, and other defined formats for the body of a message.

Another set of service elements are called cooperating IPM UA service elements. This is information used by the two IPMs to convey information in addition to that furnished by the message transfer service.

```
IM-UAPDU          :: = SEQUENCE { Heading, Body }

Heading           :: = SET {
                  IPMessageID,
                  originator             [0]    IMPLICIT ORDescriptor OPTIONAL,
                  authorizingUsers       [1]    IMPLICIT SEQUENCE OF ORDescriptor OPTIONAL,
                  primaryRecipients      [2]    IMPLICIT SEQUENCE OF Recipient OPTIONAL,
                  copyRecipients         [3]    IMPLICIT SEQUENCE OF Recipient OPTIONAL.
                  blindCopyRecipients    [4]    IMPLICIT SEQUENCE OF Recipient OPTIONAL,
                  inReplyTo              [5]    IMPLICIT IPMessageId OPTIONAL.
                  obsoletes              [6]    IMPLICIT SEQUENCE OF IPMessageID OPTIONAL,
                  crossReferences        [7]    IMPLICIT SEQUENCE OF IPMessageID OPTIONAL,
                  subject                [8]    CHOICE {T61String} OPTIONAL,
                  expiryDate             [9]    IMPLICIT Time OPTIONAL,
                  replyBy                [10]   IMPLICIT Time OPTIONAL,
                  replyToUsers           [11]   IMPLICIT SEQUENCE OF ORDescriptor OPTIONAL,
                  importance             [12]   IMPLICIT INTEGER {
                                                      low(0).
                                                      normal(1),
                                                      high(2)
                                                      } DEFAULT normal,
                  sensitivity            [13]   IMPLICIT INTEGER {
                                                      personal(1),
                                                      private(2),
                                                      companyConfidential(3)
                                                      } OPTIONAL,
                  autoforwarded          [14]   IMPLICIT BOOLEAN DEFAULT FALSE}

IPMessageID       :: = [APPLICATION 11] IMPLICIT SET {
                  ORName OPTIONAL,
                  PrintableString }

ORName            :: = [APPLICATION 0] IMPLICIT SEQUENCE {
                  StandardAttributeList,
                  DomainDefinedAttributeList OPTIONAL }

ORDescriptor      :: = SET {
                  ORName OPTIONAL,
                  freeformName [0] IMPLICIT T61String OPTIONAL,
                  telephoneNumber [1] IMPLICIT PrintableString OPTIONAL }

Recipient         :: = SET {
                  [0] IMPLICIT ORDescriptor.
                  reportRequest [1] IMPLICIT BIT STRING {
                                          receiptNotification(0).
                                          nonReceiptNotification(1),
                                          returnIPMessage(2)}
                                          DEFAULT {}
                  replyRequest [2] IMPLICIT BOOLEAN DEFAULT FALSE

Body              :: = SEQUENCE OF BodyPart
BodyPart          :: = CHOICE {
                                          [0]    IMPLICIT IA5Text,
                                          [1]    IMPLICIT TLX,
                                          [2]    IMPLICIT Voice.
                                          [3]    IMPLICIT G3Fax,
                                          [4]    IMPLICIT TIF0,
                                          [5]    IMPLICIT TTX,
                                          [6]    IMPLICIT Videotext,
                                          [7]    NationallyDefined.
                                          [8]    IMPLICIT Encrypted,
                                          [9]    IMPLICIT ForwardedIPMessage,
                                          [10]   IMPLICIT SFD,
                                          [11]   IMPLICIT TIF1 }
```

Fig. 12-13   ASN.1 definition of portions of X.400 message format.

An example of this supplemental information is a recipient notification. This indicates that not only was a message delivered as specified by the MTS, but it was read. The recipient notification includes the ID of the message that was read, a time stamp, and an indication of what triggered the receipt. This could be the fact that a user interactively read a message or it could be that the message was printed on a printer.

Another example of cooperating IPM service elements is the autoforwarding indication. This lets the IP user (the user agent) distinguish a message that was delivered direct from one which was originally sent to another user. The UA needs to know this for a variety of reasons, including the fact that it will need to break the body of the forwarded message up into a message header and a body. The UA can also use this information to stop messages from being forwarded more than once, possibly in a loop.

A third set of service elements extend the header provided by the MTS to provide more detailed information. A message can have an expiration date with a time that signifies when it becomes obsolete. It can also have cross references to other message IDs, or sensitivity determinations for data that should be treated carefully. The sensitivity indications might be used by the UA in deciding whether a message can be autoforwarded, or printed on a printer with shared access.

DEC's Messaging Strategy

DEC has always provided network wide messaging services in the DECnet architecture. This has been supplemented with a much more comprehensive architecture based on the MAILbus. The MAILbus consists of a family of protocols that provides a message transport service, a distributed directory service and various mail management services. The MAILbus Message Router, together with the X.400 gateway, provides for a fully compliant X.400 P1 message transport agent. A somewhat similar system is the SNADS architecture in the IBM environment, although SNADS is not X.400 compliant.

The MAILbus is an architecture which is implemented in a Message Router. Users interact with a user interface such as VMSmail or ALL-IN-1, which hands messages off to the Message Router (MR) for delivery. Figure 12-14 illustrates the MAILbus architecture.

Some user interfaces have native Message Router support. The ALL-IN-1 office automation environment, for example, has built in support for the Message Router. Any nodes that have ALL-IN-1 users

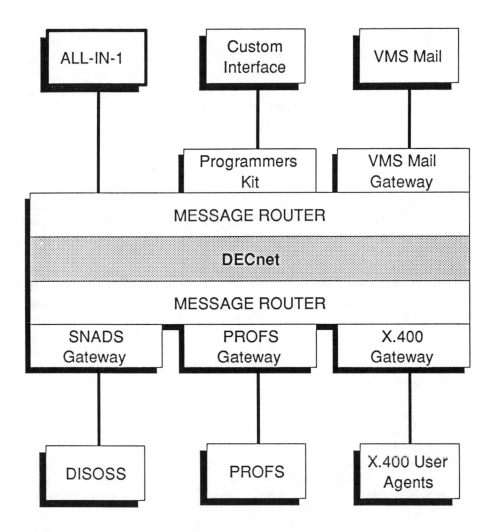

Fig. 12-14 DEC's MAILbus architecture.

also have the MR software running. MR then handles delivery of the messages to other MR modules across the network.

Other user interfaces do not have native MR support. An example of this is the older VMS mail system. This software was designed with another message-routing component known as mail-11. To interact with the MR system, a VMS Mail Gateway is provided. This allows a VMS Mail user interface to hand messages off to the message router software and therefore address ALL-IN-1 users. Prior to

MAILbus, users of the ALL-IN-1 and VMS Mail systems had to manually transfer messages between the two environments.

Mail gateways are used to provide a mapping between noncompliant mail environments and the MAILbus. Each gateway provides three major services:

1. Address conversion between environments
2. Document conversion between environments
3. An interface to the network to provide a cross-environment session.

Gateways can also be constructed using a programmer's kit. The programmer's kit allows a custom environment to participate in the MAILbus architecture. An example would be third-party vendors of integrated office automation packages who wish to integrate their software with the broader DEC environment.

Other gateways are used by the Message Router to hand mail messages off to different types of networks. For example, a Message Router/S gateway is able to use the DECnet/SNA Gateway to hand mail messages off to the SNADS delivery system which in turn delivers the message to a DISOSS user. A PROFS gateway provides the same function for the other major IBM office automation environment.

The SNADS gateway must perform two fairly complex tasks. First, it needs to remove the Message Router header and replace it with a SNADS mail header. This new address along with the original data is then handed off to a SNADS delivery agent.

A second function of the SNADS gateway is to convert the format of documents. The SNADS gateway is able to accept WPS/Plus files, ASCII files, or DX format documents and convert them into IBM's Document Content Architecture. The SNADS gateway is also able to accept MS-DOS files. This feature would be used to send a file between a DECnet/DOS node and an IBM token ring PC.

An X.400 gateway is used to integrate the MAILbus system into an even larger X.400 environment. The gateway software translates the addresses of the messages into the appropriate X.400 address for outgoing messages or DECnet-style addresses for incoming messages.

A directory service is available within the MAILbus architecture. This allows users to maintain directories of name equivalencies for use in addressing. The directory service is also available to gateway packages to perform name translation and validation. The directory services use the facilities of the Distributed Naming Service to maintain distributed name directories.

The Message Router software performs special useful functions in the network. It can log messages and perform forwarding on behalf of intermediate lines and can be configured to accept messages and store them in a queue until off-peak hours, when they are transmitted. The Message Router software runs on every node in the DECnet that has either a gateway or a user agent.

Another gateway that can sit on the Message Router is the VAX Mailgate for MCIMail. This allows ALL-IN-1 (or any other use interface) to access a wide area messaging service operated by MCI. MCI in turn has a gateway to the Telex system. MCI Mail also allows users to address messages to recipients without electronic addresses. Hardcopy is made of the message, and it is sent to a postal address. Users can register corporate stationary for use in printing hardcopy messages.

The VAX Mailgate interacts with the message router to accept messages. It is configured to use standard modems on an asynchronous port. The manager is able to configure the gateway to either dial MCI mail with each new message received or to wait a period of time. The manager can also specify how long messages can be sent in one direction before the direction is reversed and how long to wait after a transfer before dialing MCI Mail again.

Similar to the MCI Mailgate is the Alisa Connection from Alisa Systems. This software connects VAX/VMS mail to Western Union's Easylink system. This system has a variety of electronic mail users and is in turn connect to the Telex system. It can also link to Western Union Mailgram and Telegram services.

This system has the user address all VMS mail to an account called Easylink. The first few lines of the message then contain the address of the user. This is similar to the X.400 method of putting an IP Message envelope inside of a MTS envelope. Here, of course, there are two MTS envelopes. The first MTS is mail-11. The second service is Easylink. There may be a third envelope which has Telex or Mailgram header information.

Voice mail access is provided to the ALL-IN-1 environment using the DECtalk Mail Access Package. DECTalk is an I/O device that is able to "speak" an incoming data stream. DECtalk speaks all words in its dictionary or in a user defined dictionary. Ten different voices are available. This interface allows users to dial into the DECtalk system and have ALL-IN-1 messages read to them.

Summary

As can be seen in this chapter, the OSI protocols provide a highly functional open networking enviornment. The OSI network, transport, and session layers provide a common set of services used by applications in dissimilar environments. The services in OSI allow a variety of sophisticated forms of information exchange to take place among many different types of systems.

DEC's support of OSI in DNA Phase V is a particularly important step in the development of an open network. Other OSI-compliant vendors can integrate with DEC equipment in a tightly integrated network. While previous interconnection might have been limited to remote log-in using a primitive terminal emulator or a file transfer mechanism, OSI networks allow the full range of data access, job control, virtual terminal, and message exchange. As OSI continues to develop, more sophisticated services such as heterogeneous distributed database systems will become available.

DNA Phase V is the continuation of a long-term DEC commitment to sophisticated networking. DNA Phase I was one of the earliest available commercial networks. It allowed simple file transfer between two directly connected PDP systems. In a Phase V network, this has been expanded to provide support for an open, distributed processing environment with both greater performance and greater functionality.

For Further Reading

CCITT, "Data Communication Networks Message Handling Systems Recommendations," vol. VIII, X.400–X.430, Plenary Assembly, Malaga-Torremolinos, 8–19 October 1984 (Red Book).

Rizzardi (ed.), *Understanding MAP*, Society of Maufacturing Engineers, Dearborn, Mich., 1988.

Part

5

User Interface Standards

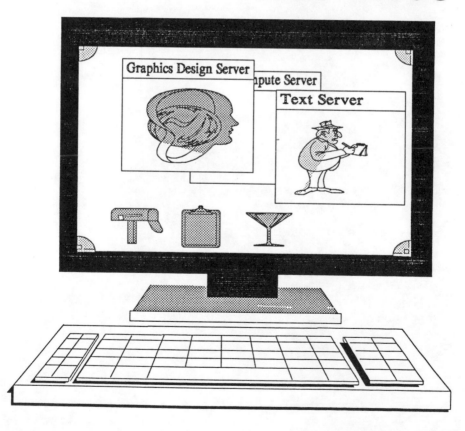

13

X Windows

Overview of X Windows

Several of the protocols examined earlier, particularly DNA CTERM and LAT, were designed to solve the problem of interactive use of remote computers on the network. CTERM is a fairly inefficient solution to a virtual terminal service, but it has the advantage of being able to operate over a wide variety of data links, including wide area links. CTERM provides only a basic terminal emulation function with very few additional functions that would permit more sophisticated actions over the network.

The LAT protocols are a more efficient solution to virtual terminal services because they make direct use of the data link layer and bypass services at layers 4 through 6. The LAT protocols also offer some value added services such as service directories and load balancing based on service ratings.

Neither LAT nor CTERM address problems that are inherent in a workstation environment characterized by bit-map graphics screens. LAT and CTERM assume a fairly low volume of data sent over the data with a low level of graphics complexity. VT240-style ReGIS graphics can be supported, but bit-mapped screens with icons, multiple windows, and sophisticated graphics are not part of the model.

The X Windows System provides support for complex windowing environments that function across a network. Without X, a VAXstation can open a window that serves as a VT100 emulator. The VAXstation can then use the resources of a foreign node through use of the SET HOST command in VMS and the CTERM protocols. A true windowing

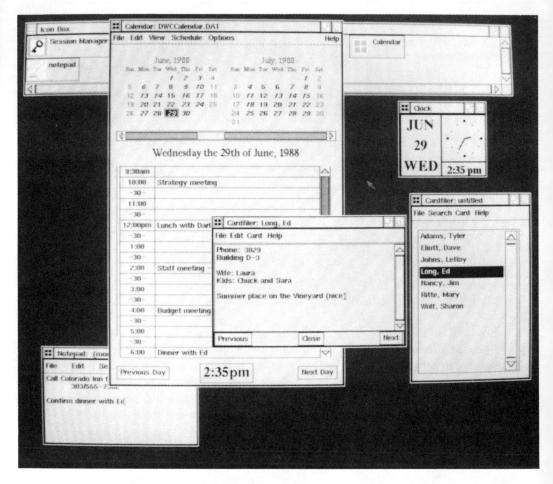

Fig. 13-1   DEC's X Window implementation.

environment differs from this by allowing remote applications to manipulate multiple windows on a display. Multiple processes on multiple remote systems can write information to the screen in a coordinated manner.

Figure 13-1 shows the difference between simple VT100 emulation and a true windowing environment. Notice in the X Windows example the use of special purpose windows, such as icons. An icon is a window that represents another window. When the user selects this icon, the remote program is able to tell the display to remove the icon and replace it with a full-blown window.

The X Windows System is built around the concept of a server. The X server manages a particular bit-mapped display or possibly several bit-mapped displays. Remote programs reside on compute servers.

These servers are clients of the X server for purposes of displaying objects on the screen. Notice that the workstation is in turn a client of the compute server for the purposes of running the program.

Figure 13-2 shows an example of the type of distributed environment made possible by combining sophisticated networking protocols with an open windowing environment like X. The network allows all hosts to be accessible, and the upper layers of the network allow applications to communicate. X helps define the nature, or semantics, of that communication. X can be thought of as a form of presentation protocol. The combination of X and the network allow a true distributed processing environment consisting of a variety of servers. The servers are all accessible from the user's workstation.

Several other window managers also exist, such as MS-Windows for the MS-DOS computing environment. The X Windows System was developed at the Massachusetts Institute of Technology with support by a consortium of companies including DEC, SUN, and IBM. X thus differs from proprietary window managers because of its broad-based support from a heterogeneous group of vendors. If programs and servers built around X windows are developed by a wide variety of vendors and if these vendors also support a common set of networking protocols such as OSI, workstations and compute servers from different vendors easily integrate to form an integrated, transparent network.

A related standard to X windows is PostScript. X provides a very sophisticated method of controlling the windows on a workstation, including pull-down menus and other special purpose windows. X is not particularly sophisticated, however, in the way it represents the content of a window. X allows bit maps to be transmitted across the network, but this can lead to huge amounts of data being transmitted.

PostScript provides a sophisticated language for the description of both printed pages and display screens. PostScript is a de facto standard for page descriptions on laser printers. Using the same language on the screen as on the page offers the ability to have the same output in both environments. PostScript will be discussed in the next chapter.

X Windows System Basic Concepts

An X Windows server consists of three components:

1. A keyboard
2. A pointer, typically a mouse
3. One or several bit-map screens for the display of output

The X Windows System also assumes a set of programs written to use X as the display mechanism. These programs reside on a set of computers on a network. Note that a single workstation can be both the X server and a compute server for a given user.

The foundation of an X computing environment is the X library (Xlib). These are a set of subroutines in a programming library that are used to send messages and receive replies from an X server. Programmers must write code that issues calls to this library to start, resize, and write to a window or other display operations. Presumably, the programmer is also using a set of other libraries, such as database management or mathematical manipulation subroutines. The collection of all the different libraries plus the programmers code consists of an application. An application could be as simple as a clock or as sophisticated as a full-featured desktop publishing system or an integrated circuit design program.

Communication between a program that uses the Xlib and an X Windows server uses a protocol called X Wire. X Wire is built on top of the underlying network, such as DECnet or TCP/IP. Xlib forms the application's interface to the network. In turn, the X server is the interface to the display hardware. Even if some other higher-level language, such as PostScript, is used to describe graphics operations, X Wire is used to transmit the information to the server, and the server performs all direct updates to hardware frame buffers. To simplify the design of the user interface, the X library is supplemented with a series of tools in a toolkit. Tools provide routines that implement a series of widgets. These widgets are predefined menus, command buttons, and other often executed tasks.

A special-purpose tool is a window manager program. Not all X servers have to have a window manager. When one is there, it provides a series of services to the user such as moving or resizing windows, controlling the stacking of windows on a screen, or creating a new terminal emulation window. A program may give a hint to the window manager about the size window it would like, but it is up to the window manager to decide what is allowed.

The reason a window manager is allowed to decide these functions is because of the wide variety of programs that will have to cooperate with different displays. Some workstations have tiled displays that don't allow windows to overlap. A program can tell that window manager it wants a big size, but it is possible that other programs have already used up most of the screen (or tiles). The program must then be prepared to either operate in that small environment or tell the user that it can't operate in that small a space.

All programs must assume the presence of a window manager. It is possible that the X server that the client is communicating with doesn't have a window manager. If there is a window manager there, however, there will be some form of a window layout policy. The client program requests certain sizes or other attributes. Any one of these requests may or may not be granted. Needless to say, this means that an application program needs to be written in a fairly flexible way.

Window Components

A typical window in X actually is composed of three different windows. The main region of the window is one window, and this window is the one written to by the application. Another window is the title bar and this is typically provided by the window manager. Usually, the title bar contains a name furnished by the program or the command used to activate the program.

A third window is the scroll bar. Scroll bars are activated by users to signal that they wish to see a portion of the output not currently displayed. A scroll bar is used in desktop publishing programs to move down the page on a document.

There are many other special-purpose windows which may also be used by programs. Icons are a window used to represent a program that is active but not displayed on the screen. Menus are also windows. Since a menu is a window, many systems allow the menu to be moved to a different place than the current location. These are known as tear-away menus.

A window has five characteristics that are set by both programs and the X server. They are:

1) Window hierarchy
2) Window configuration
3) Depth and visual characteristics
4) Graphics context
5) Window attributes

Window hierarchy

The basic window for any given display is called the root window, which fills the screen. All other windows created on that display are children of the root in the window hierarchy. A child window may in turn have its own child window. Windows sometimes create children with the help of the window manager and sometimes by themselves (a sort of immaculate conception if you will).

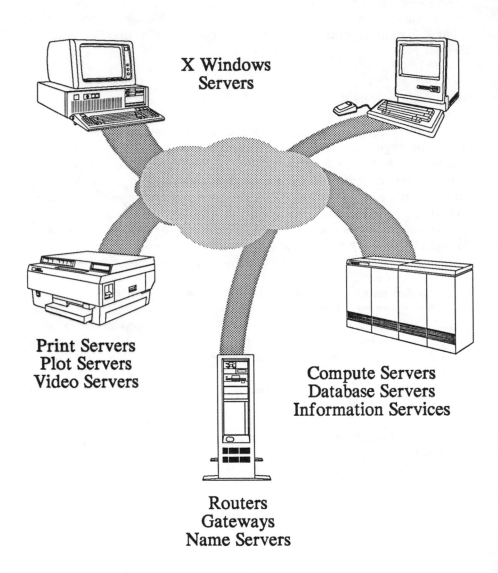

X Windows
Servers

Print Servers
Plot Servers
Video Servers

Compute Servers
Database Servers
Information Services

Routers
Gateways
Name Servers

Fig. 13-2   The world according to X.

Within a window hierarchy, there are several rules that children must obey. A child window cannot display anything outside the boundaries of its parent window. Note that this does allow a child window to open a new window that is not within its own boundaries, as long as it is within the boundaries of the parent. Secondly, a child window cannot receive any input, keyboard, or pointer while the cursor is positioned outside of the parent window.

Window configuration

The window configuration controls the location of the window. Each window has an origin, the upper-left corner, which is relative to the parents origin. If the parent window moves, all the children can be automatically moved with this relative positioning. Each window also has a width and height, measured in pixels. Optionally, a window may also have a border. If it does, the window configuration also contains a border-width parameter which is in addition to the width of the actual window.

The window configuration also contains a stacking order. There may be several child windows for a parent. The stacking order determines which window is visible if they overlap. Usually, a menu would have a stacking order to make it always visible, while data windows might have a lower-priority stacking order.

Depth and visual characteristics

The depth and visual characteristics of a window are used for bitmap graphics. The depth of a window says how many bits of data are used to represent each pixel on the screen. A 1-bit display allows a screen to be either black or white. A 2-bit display has four possible configurations and could thus represent four shades of gray or four different colors. The visual characteristic of a window determines if the bit values of a pixel are actually the color (or gray) value of that pixel. If they are not the actual values, the bit value is looked up in a color map, which translates the value into the actual color.

A color map allows more colors to be in the universe of possible colors than can be simultaneously displayed on the screen. If a 2-bit display value was displayed directly on the screen, the manufacturer of the display would have to predetermine the four colors. Instead, the color map allows the four display colors to be mapped into a range of 16 million possible colors that the screen could display using RGB parameters or some other display technology.

Graphics context

The window graphics context determines how to interpret graphics requests. When a program requests that a piece of text be written into a window, the graphics context determines what font to use for the text. The graphics context also has other default parameters such as what color to use for drawing or what width to use for drawing a line.

Window attributes

The last characteristics of a window are the window attributes. Attributes include which particular color map to use for translating pixels, the border background color and pattern or a window, and what type of cursor that window will have. Attributes also determine if this window can be displayed, moved, or resized without notifying the window manager.

An important type of attribute for a window has to do with event types. Events, such as the cursor being moved, are received by the window manager. The window attributes tell the window manager which types of events this program wants to receive. Events that this window is not interested in are sent up to its parent window. Thus, a desktop publishing program may want to trap mouse buttons 1 and 2 to select menu options. Mouse button number 3, however, may be a signal to the root window to create a new terminal emulator. If the cursor was positioned totally inside the child window, the third mouse button event would be passed up to the parent (root) window.

Graphics Context and Color Maps

The graphics context for a window controls all of the output routines, except for the border and background of a window which are considered to be window attributes. The graphics context sets a variety of parameters which are used by the various output requests. Establishing the context means that the individual request does not have to specify each parameter. A program may define several graphics contexts and rapidly change between them.

A fundamental part of the graphics context is the effect of a graphics request on existing pixels. The pixels could be actually displayed on the screen or could be part of a pixel map that is not being currently displayed. A graphics request is not copied directly to the destination bit map. First, a copy area is constructed. Then, the copy area is moved over to the destination bit map.

Three parameters help determine the effect of a copy area on a destination bit map. A "logical function" specifies how the pixels in the two areas combine. A logical function can add the pixels together (thus forming a new color on the screen), wipe out old pixels, and perform a variety of other boolean operations on the 2 bits of information.

A pixel is represented by a certain number of bits, known as the depth of a bit map, which is related to the number of colors or gray scales that can be on the display. A second parameter in addition to the logical function is a "plane mask." The plane mask says which bits of a pixel representation will be affected by a copy operation. This allows certain planes to be unaffected by operations.

The last parameter that affects the combining of pixels is the "clip mask." A clip mask is a bit mask of depth 1. Any bits set in the clip mask signify that those portions of the destination clip mask are not affected by the copy operation.

The programmer is thus able to filter out planes of bits through a plane mask as well as regions of bits through the clip mask. The remaining bits are combined with the copy area using the logical function that was specified. Figure 13-3 illustrates the effect of a clip mask on a copy area.

Several graphics contexts can be defined. Switching between different contexts is a fairly efficient process. In addition to the mask functions, several other line and fill characteristics help make up the graphics context.

Line characteristics set the default width in pixels for a line. A style can be defined for the line, such as solid or one of the predefined dash patterns. A custom dash list can also be specified. A dash pattern can have fill patterns defined for both the "on" and the "off" portions of the dash.

Cap and join styles are also specified for lines. A cap style defines how a stand-alone line is terminated. Options include round and square caps and the degree of projection. A join style defines how lines meet. Miter or round joins are examples of these options.

File options are another type of characteristic. Areas can be filled with either a solid color, specified by a pixel value or by a tile. A tile is a bit-map pattern which is replicated over the area to be filled. Clip masks are used to prevent a portion of an area from being either filled or tiled.

Color in an X Windows environment is based on series of red, green, and blue (RGB) values. Each of these three basic colors is represented by an 8-bit value. This allows roughly 16 million different hues, or combinations of red, green, and blue.

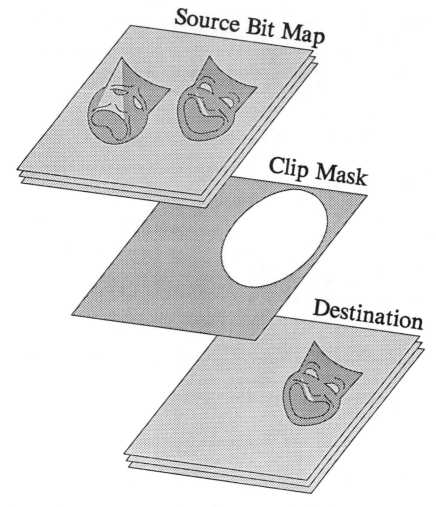

Fig. 13-3 Source, clip, and destination masks.

Some standard combinations of RGB values and their English equivalents include:

R	G	B	Name
234	173	234	Plum
188	143	143	Pink
112	219	147	Aquamarine

Gray scales are derived from these RGB values. A formula is applied to combine the three values into a single value of gray. Note that this means that different shades will end up having the same gray-scale values.

Several kinds of color schemes exist within an X Windows environment. A color map is a mapping between a single pixel value and an associated set of RGB values. When the X server encounters a particular pixel value, it looks up the corresponding RGB values and transmits that information to the hardware.

Color maps use precious resources. Because of that, a client will usually use the default color map defined by the server. The RGB_DEFAULT_MAP contains over 1 million colors, which ought to satisfy most general-purpose applications. A utility named XParse-Color is also available which can parse an English name of a color and map that to the closest approximation of RGB values in a given color map.

Graphics Manipulations

X provides a series of utilities that are used for drawing. An important issue is the degree that the X Windows System provides the drawing capabilities in a windowed environment. PostScript is an accompanying standard that can also provide much of that functionality. One possible implementation is to map Xlib primitives into the corresponding PostScript commands. The PostScript interpreter passes the low-level hardware operations back to the X Server, which performs the actual operation on the screen.

The basic graphics operations available in X Windows are drawing, placing text, using regions, and using images. Basic drawing operations include points, rectangles, and arcs. More sophisticated commands include polylines and disjoint polylines. A rule set in the graphics context determines if a point in a polygon is on the inside or outside of the polygon.

Fonts in X are a series of bit maps. The fonts can either be constant or proportional width. Fonts are defined by a series of font properties that contain information such as the size of the smallest character or a width table to be used for spacing proportional fonts. Font properties also determine display characteristics such as the minimum, normal, and maximum interword spacing or the offset for superscripts and subscripts.

Regions and images

Regions are an arbitrary set of pixels on the screen, identified by a region ID. The region is usually defined by a polygon although it can be defined by a list of points. A given region in X can be moved, shrunk, or increased in size. Regions can be combined as intersections or unions.

Regions are useful because they can have their own graphics context which is independent of the window to which they belong. Region definitions may well define the boundaries of a window. These provide easy ways to change the size or location of a window area. When a window manager allows a user to resize a particular window, it is applying a region command.

Images correspond to an area of the screen or to a particular bit map. Images are used to define pieces within a window. Image operations include the ability to change each pixel in an image by a specified color. This is how clicking on a component of a drawing leads to that image changing in color to signify that it has been selected is accomplished.

Images can be composed of other images and thus help form building blocks within an area. When you add a pixel to the screen, it is typically added to a particular image. That image might then be part of one or several regions. An example of using images is providing an iconic representation of a window to the window manager.

Cursors

Cursors are a special kind of output because they are transient and do not destroy the underlying information as a general rule. The exception to this rule is when the cursor is used in a draw like function. Each window has a cursor defined. If the window does not define a particular cursor, it inherits its parent's cursor.

A cursor has two pieces to it: a mask bit map and a cursor bit map. The mask is the area covered by the cursor. The cursor bit map is the actual shape of the cursor. Thus a cursor bit map might make an arrow that pointed to a particular edge of the mask bit map. The hot spot defines where in this mask the cursor actually points. Figure 13-4 shows the different components of a cursor.

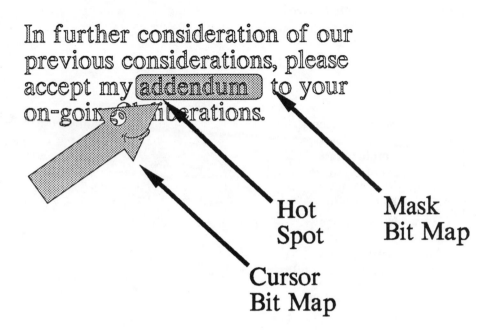

In further consideration of our previous considerations, please accept my addendum to your on-going iberations.

Hot Spot

Mask Bit Map

Cursor Bit Map

Fig. 13-4 Cursor components.

Events

Events are defined as "incidents of importance." A program might receive an event that signals a change in pointer position or a key pressed on the keyboard or any other form of user input. Events are also used to communicate with a window manager or other programs.

Every input event that occurs is trapped by the X server, which then delivers the event to a window that is interested in that event. Windows are in a hierarchy, with the root window at the top and a series of parents and subwindows underneath it. The default delivery for an event is initially the smallest visible window that encloses the pointer at that time.

A particular window indicates what kinds of events it is interested in receiving. Events are selected using an event mask. If a window is

---

Example Types of Masks Available in X Windows

No Events Desired

Key Press
Key Released

Any Mouse Button Pressed
Particular Mouse Button Pressed
Mouse Button Released

Pointer Motion
Pointer Motion While Button Down

Enter Window
Leave Window

Window Exposed
Change in Visibility of Window

Change of Size
Color Map Changes

Fig. 13-5   X Windows system event types.

not interested in an event, it passes the event up to its parent. Eventually, it is presumed that some window will be interested in an event. A special type of selection indicates that the event should not be passed up but should be discarded. Figure 13-5 shows some typical event types that are available for selection.

All events that are selected by a mask are delivered into the event queue for that particular program. It is important to note that a program is free to ignore events and to even ignore the queue. When the program exits, the queue will be destroyed. Figure 13-6 shows the delivery of events to different windows.

There are several general types of masks such as key press events. Within that general category, there are specific events for key press or key release events.

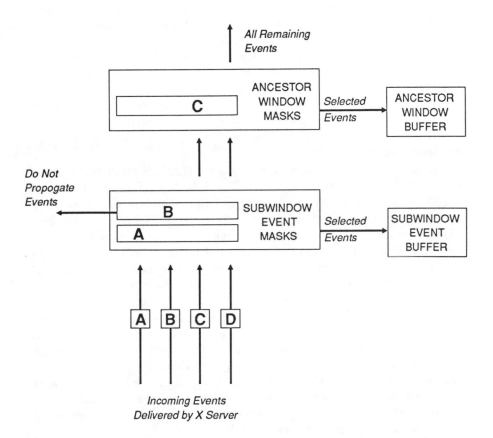

Fig. 13-6 X Window event propagation.

Events in X are asynchronous. They can occur in any order from any number of sources and are queued in the order they are received. This means that programs need to be coded in a fairly general manner and cannot always expect a particular event to occur after another.

Grabbing events is a way of prohibiting the user from acting in an arbitrary way. When the pointer or the keyboard is grabbed, events do not occur in the normal fashion. Grabbing the pointer might allow the program to put a wall around a window and keep the cursor within that wall.

Grabbing the keyboard (or particular keys) prohibits those events from being propagated indiscriminantly. A particular grab can be passive and only take effect when a certain key (i.e., a certain button on the mouse or a function key) is pressed.

Priorities for grabs occur from the top down. This is how a parent window prevents a child from trampling all over input that it shouldn't have. A SHIFT/F1 key, for example, may mean nothing to the word processing program but might be an indicator to the window manager to open a new terminal window. The SHIFT/F1 key would then be passively grabbed by the window manager (which owns the root window).

Exposure events are a special notification that a portion of a window previously hidden is now exposed. The default in X is for the server not to keep track of window contents. When an exposure event is received, it is up to the client program to be able to redraw that area.

Border-crossing events are used to notify a window that the cursor has entered or left its area. A virtual border crossing is when the pointer has crossed from the subwindow of one parent to the subwindow of a second parent. Both of the parents would then receive virtual border-crossing events.

A peculiar type of event is the focus event. If a user is typing on the keyboard and the mouse is bumped by a pet cat, all further input may go to another window. If that's the case, the input may be lost, especially if the cursor now points to the root window. Changing the input focus ensures that certain events are always delivered to the window that owns the input focus or to one of its subwindows. Normally, a window manager has the input focus set to the root window, meaning that all events are delivered as normal.

An event that cannot be masked out is the client message. This allows to client programs to interchange messages. An 8- to 32-bit message type identification is added to client messages, although the X standard makes no attempt to define what these numbers mean.

Properties and Selections

Properties are a way of naming pieces of information. A property is an abstract mechanism and is kept by the server for use by clients, including the window manager and various user programs. A selection is a special kind of property, maintained by the root window but containing application-specific information. Properties and selections use events to notify clients that are interested in the existence or change in either of these.

A property has a name and several attributes associated with it. This includes a type indicator, a data format indicator, and a data area. An example of a property is a default iconic representation for a window that is available to clients that do not supply their own. Other properties might be a set of hints to client programs that specify sizes that are in an acceptable range for use in this environment. A further property is a program name associated with a client. The window manager might use this to display a name in the title bar of the window.

Selections are a property used by clients and passed around. A selection can be acquired and then the current value of a selection can be used by the acquiring program. For example, when text is highlighted and then "cut" to a clipboard, the contents of the highlighted area is passed to the clipboard as the contents of a selection.

Selections are acquired by passing a call to the X Server to acquire that selection and give it a name. Other programs can then send a SELECTION$REQUEST to the owner. The owner takes the request and stores the results as a property. Then, a SELECTION$NOTIFY is sent to the client program that requested it.

One of the important roles of properties is to hold hints for a particular environment. Hints are properties maintained by the window manager that tell client programs of various policies it has. This prevents a client program from attempting an operation that is incompatible with the display. A small display might have a window manager that would hint that windows start up as small entities rather than cover the whole screen. Hints allow civilized programs to communicate in a networked environment and to share a common display.

It is important to note that the X server maintains properties but gives no meaning to the information it stores. It provides a mechanism for keeping the properties and a set of events used to notify other clients of the existence or change in a certain property. The main user of properties is the window manager.

These window manager hints are varied in different manners. Hints are used to tell the window manager if a program wishes to begin life as an icon or as a true window. They tell the window manager how the program expects to receive input, i.e., if it is real estate driven and will only take input when the cursor is in a visible area of the window or if it grabs the input focus and takes all events while active.

Customizing the X Window Environment

Each user is able to set a series of defaults in a file that is automatically read upon startup. This file can include default information that applies to the whole X environment, such as a default border width or a default font. Other types of defaults can be specific to a particular program. For example, a user might specify certain characteristics for a calculator and a mail program in the X default startup file:

```
.font:          fixed
.borderwidth:   2

xcalc.IconStartup:      on

xmail.IconStartup:      on
xmail.notify:           on
xmail.AutoReceipt:      on
```

This file would set fonts as fixed and windows with a thin border. When the X display starts up, the user will see icon representations for mail and a calculator, assuming that the command was issued to start them up on default—otherwise when they do start, they will be icons.

When the mail program is running, it is told to notify the user whenever new mail is received. This would probably occur through a mail delivery program notifying the mail program of new mail or by the mail program scanning the date modified field of a particular file periodically. Using either mechanism, the mail program would then change the iconic representation from a mailbox with the flag down to the mailbox with a flag up.

The X Toolkit

The X library provides a set of primitive routines and makes no attempt to specify the user interface. While this provides a great deal of power in constructing applications, it allows the possibility of trying to reinvent the wheel many, many times. The X toolkit contains a series of routines that can be used by application programs.

There are two main types of tools in the toolkit. First, there is a default window manager available that is used in most implementations of the X server. The second type of tools are used for building and maintaining widgets.

Widgets are predefined tools that programmers can use in their application. For example, a scroll bar is an example of a special purpose window that is used to control scrolling in another window. Rather than initialize this special purpose menu, the programmer is able to use the standard scroll bar widget contained in the toolkit.

There are two levels of interactions with widgets. First, there are a set of intrinsic routines in the toolkit used for maintaining and developing widgets. There are also some predefined widgets maintained in a database.

The intrinsic routines allow widgets to be easily created, managed, and destroyed. Tools are available to define widget initialization, run-time configuration, and the uniform of handling of common events. Over 90 intrinsic routines are available to manage widgets.

There are three important characteristics that make widgets especially powerful. First, widgets can be placed into classes. Second, widgets can bind certain attributes at run time from a database. Third, widgets can be composed of other widgets.

Widgets belong in a class hierarchy. Lower-class widgets inherit selected attributes from widgets higher in the class hierarchy. In addition to attributes, such as border width, widgets can also inherit methods or procedures from higher-class widgets.

Run-time binding allows widgets to have characteristics determined at run time instead of being coded into the widget definition. Input semantics, such as which mouse button activates the widget, can be added at run time. Visual appearance, such as the default font or the color of the widget, can also be defined at run time.

Run-time configuration uses a special tool called the resource manager. The resource manager is a simple database maintained by the X server. The toolkit instructs the X server to load a resource database from the file that it is stored in. There can be several resource databases, possibly one per user.

Composite widgets allow widgets to made of other widgets. It is thus possible for a programmer to use a set of default widgets and some intrinsic routines to define a new composite widget. The composite widget is now treated like a single object by the application program.

Standard widgets

The X toolkit has several predefined widgets that are provided in most X environments. This means that the application programmer can have some assurance of finding these widgets in a heterogeneous environment and can thus depend on their availability. The simplest widgets are primitives, such as buttons or labels.

A label is one of the simplest widgets. It is simply a box with either a text string or a bit map inside of it. The text can be optionally right or left justified or centered. A command widget builds on top of the label. Several actions are defined for this widget, including entering or leaving the label. The user of the widget is also notified when the relevant mouse or keyboard button is set or unset.

Another attribute of the command widget is that when the user's pointing device enters the area, the border of the command becomes automatically thicker. When the SET action is activated, the widget is displayed in reverse video. A further subclass of the command widget is the toggle widget, which stays in reverse video even when the set button is released.

An example of a predefined composite widget is the form. The form widget takes multiple children and arranges them nicely inside of a box. Typically, the child widgets are a series of labels that make up a menu. The form includes definitions of minimal acceptable distances between children of the form. When the form is resized, it can thus rearrange the appearance and order of the children.

Built on top of the form widget is the dialog widget. This combines the general construct of a form with several commands and a label. A dialog box might then be used by an application program to control a series of operations such as scanning in new input. The SCAN dialog box would have commands available to set the resolution of the scanning and the area to be scanned and to start the operation.

The window manager

The second important type of predefined tool in the X toolkit is the window manager. The window manager is a special application that owns the root window and is thus able to redirect input away from client windows. The window manager uses its power to enforce cooperation between different programs. Thus, rather than allowing a single program to take over the entire screen, the program is forced to first ask permission. Presumably, the user has requested this resize operation so the request is granted. Certain hardware, however, does not allow overlapped windows. In this case, the window manager may choose not to grant the request.

DECwindows and X

DEC, along with IBM, Sun, Apollo, and other workstation manufacturers, has wholeheartedly embraced the X Windows System as a standard for windowing in heterogeneous networks. DEC has packaged X Windows along with several other important standard components into DECwindows.

DECwindows runs on all of DEC's major operating platforms, including Ultrix and VMS environments. The development of the same DECwindows environment across VMS and Ultrix environments was the largest single software development project in DEC's history. This includes the development of VMS.

DECwindows includes an implemenation of the X server. Just implementing X servers, however, leaves many ambiguities in the user interface. This is because the MIT standard of X concentrates on providing the means for implementing applications. How they are implemented is a matter of policy and is not dealt with in the MIT standard.

DEC's primary enhancement to X Windows is in providing a standard "look and feel" for applications. This look and feel concept of user interfaces is also present in other standards efforts such as Xerox's Open Look or the SAA Common User Access efforts.

In all three standards efforts the emphasis is on letting the user know in advance how applications work. Things like standardizing which key is the HELP key is a simple example of standardizing the look and feel. Operation of menus and other forms of controlling the dialog are more sophisticated examples.

In addition to standardizing a look and feel, DEC has extended the X graphics model by incorporating additional graphics subsystems. PostScript is the primary imaging subsystem that has been added, and it provides a common representation of graphics on various devices including workstations and printers. PostScript also allows arbitrary transformation of graphics, freeing the user interface from the box-like styles found in X, Macintosh, or MS-Windows environments.

In addition to PostScript, other imaging systems can be added into DECwindows. For example, the PHIGS library for three dimensional graphics is supported in DECwindows as an alternate imaging subsystem. More complex image processing systems can also be added as needed.

The third major enhancement that DEC has done to the X Windows standard is the incorporation of language independent features. These are called user interface language (UIL) files and are read in at run time. The application developer can develop a language independent application, and language specialists can modify the UIL files for different national languages.

The collection of routines that a programmer can use are collected together in a client library called the X User Interface. The X User Interface provides support for all VAX languages that use the standard calling interface. This is an important extension beyond the LISP and C languages supported in the basic MIT standard.

User interface standardization

Standardizing the user interface with a common look and feel requires all the applications programmers to adhere to a common standard. DEC attempts to address this problem by standardizing the look and feel and then providing a set of tools, or widgets, that conform to these policies. This standard look and feel is described in the DECwindows Style Guide. The DECwindows Toolkit supplements the intrinsic widgets that form the basic MIT standard.

Note that providing a standard user interface for all programs is easier said than done—applications programmers typically enjoy the freedom to invent customized interfaces for specific problems. DEC has made the Style Guide mandatory for internally produced software. For externally produced software, DEC hopes that the DECwindows toolkit is easy enough to use that programmers will not want to bother with customizing interfaces by resorting to lower layers.

The common user interface of DECwindows specifies how most aspects of an application operate. This includes the layout of the main window of an application and subareas as well as the operation of dialog panels and the function of the keyboard and pointing devices.

The main window of an application consists of a title bar that identifies the window. The title bar has a shrink-to-icon button and the title of the application. The title bar also includes two other buttons to push the window to the back of a stack and to resize the window.

Below that is a menu bar that lists the actions available to the user. If the application does not have any options for the user, the menu bar can be left off. An example of this is a clock that can only be opened or closed. Opening and closing a window are window manager functions and the application thus does not need any menu options.

Finally, the window has a work area, or main window. The contents of this main window are up to the application to decide.

Several subwindows can also be defined. The most common example of an application subwindow is the scroll bar. Scroll bars allow a user to move the visible portion of the window, or work area, over a larger virtual work space. By providing a scroll bar widget in the tool kit, DEC makes it easier for applications programmers to use the suggested scroll bar actions than it would be to invent a new one.

Scroll bars are actually a fairly complex application in their own right. The scroll bar has a slider, which is a white bar that represents the amount of the virtual file that is currently displayed. The user can drag this slider up and down to scroll through the application. Another motion is to click on the arrows that are on the top and bottom of the scroll bar. This steps the scroll through by a single unit. In a word processor, this unit might be a page of text.

An even more complex scrolling option available in DECwindows is the use of an index window. If the application provides this capability, when the slider bar is dragged up and down, the application also provides a small window that shows the outline of the application. In a word processor, this might be an abbreviated form of the table of contents. The user can thus visually see where they are in the overall document structure.

Another type of subarea is a paned window. Paned windows are formed by dividing a main window either horizontally or vertically. An example of the use of this would be to edit code in one subwindow and show compiler output in another. Note that this could be two separate applications, each with their own menu instead of single application that has multiple subwindows. Those type of design decisions are beyond the scope of DECwindows. Instead, those decisions are made as part of the architecture for a family of applications, in this case program development tools.

Dialog control is one of the most important aspects of the standardized user interface. A dialog is how a user selects actions to take. By standardizing this selection process, a great deal of user training can be avoided.

Many types of dialog management techniques are available. A typical example is a control panel, which consists of a series of boxes. When the user clicks the pointer on that box, an action is taken. Usually, the box contains some iconic representation of the task.

DEC standardizes the types of controls and labels for those controls that are available. A simple type of control is the toggle button—a little square with a text description next to it. The standard user interface specifies that when the mouse button is selected, both the label and the box next to it should visible darken. If the user selects that option, the label should stay darkened and the box color should be inverted.

Several other options are available for signaling that an action has been chosen. For example, an icon can be inverted as in the case of the label selection. Another option is to change the appearance of the icon to indicated that it has been selected. Finally, a further selection area or control panel might appear with more submenu options.

In addition to providing standard menus and other dialog control functions, the user interface standard goes further by recommending how applications should use those capabilities. Matters such as the assignment of HELP keys and other common functions (i.e., next screen, previous screen) are also standardized. Cursor shapes for different functions are also recommended.

The combination of these different levels of definition yields a consistent user interface. One of DEC's strongest selling points in many markets has always been this common user interface. The VT100, Gold-Key style of editing sequences, for example, is fairly standard across the help facility, mail facility, word processor, editors, and other VMS utilities. This has allowed users to easily pick up new program skills without resorting to manuals or extensive online help systems. The DECwindows environment allows the common user interface present in terminal-oriented applications to be extended to a workstation-based environment.

User interface language files

The user interface language (UIL) files are compiled and then loaded in by the resource manager at run-time. UIL files can exist for different languages and even different character sets. It is even possible to have different procedures and widgets supplied for the different languages.

The UIL file for each language lists each of the procedures, widgets, and string labels used by an application that are language dependent. Usually, the string values are different for each file but the procedures and widgets are the same. It is possible, however, to define different procedures for each language.

For example, a "show text on the screen" procedure might be defined differently for Semitic, Latin, and Oriental languages. The Latin procedure lays text left to right going down to a new line after each line is set. The Semitic language procedure would set text from right to left, going down a new line. The Oriental language procedure would set text down the page, moving over after each column is set.

One of the primary users of the UIL feature is the window manager. Different countries have different representations of money, time, and dates. Sorting orders also differ across countries. This information is loaded by the resource manager at run time to customize the Window manager interface.

Summary

The X Windows System provides a sophisticated set of library routines that allow multiple programs to all share a common bitmapped display. These programs can all reside on different hardware platforms throughout the network. The programs communicate with an X server using the X Wire protocols.

Built on top of the X Windows System is DECwindows. DECwindows supplements X by adding several powerful imaging subsystems. One of these imaging systems, PostScript, is discussed in the next chapter. Other imaging subsystems can be used for three-dimensional graphics or other applications.

DECwindows also builds a policy on top of the general capabilities of X. This policy is a Style Guide, which governs how applications present their options to users. This standardized look and feel capability allows a user to work with a new software package without extensive training.

DECwindows provides a common user interface across different application programs and different hardware platforms. While the underlying network, such as DECnet/OSI, provides machine to machine communication in a transparent environment, DECwindows allows applications to communicate in a complex bit-mapped graphics style.

For Further Reading

Nye, *The X Window System, Programming Reference for Version 11*, Release 1, 2 vols., O'Reilly & Associates, Newton, MA, 1987.

Swick and Ackerman, "The X Toolkit: More Bricks for Building User-Interfaces or Widgets for Hire," Conference Proceedings, *USENIX Technical Conference*, February 9–12, 1988, p. 221.

14

PostScript

Overview of PostScript

The X Windows System defined a powerful environment for controlling and manipulating windows in a heterogeneous workstation environment. The X library and toolkit provide a high level language that will work in many different environments. A wide range of different types of information can be manipulated. This generality has some potential drawbacks, however. The chief drawback of X is that it allows for the manipulation of a bit maps but does not provide high level tools for defining the interior of that bit map.

PostScript is a language or, more accurately, an imaging model for describing a page, either printed or on a display. It was developed by Adobe Systems based on work completed at the Xerox Palo Alto Research Center (PARC). The language forms the basis for most laser printers and has been extended to many high end typesetters such as the Linotronic 300, which has a resolution of 2450 dots per inch (dpi).

PostScript has several features that make it especially powerful as an imaging system. First and foremost, it is device independent. That means that a page can be prepared on a device with low resolution and then printed on a high resolution device and look the same (only crisper). The device independence also means portability—any Postscript-speaking application (i.e., a word processor) can communicate with any printer that is PostScript-compatible.

A second set of features in Postscript is the power of the graphics and text languages. The PostScript system is an especially powerful typographic model. Fonts are stored as outlines, allowing them to be displayed at any arbitrary point size. When a region of an X screen is resized, text must be redisplayed at a different point size. The X model stores these each font as a bit map, which means fonts come in fixed sizes. Thus, an X server might choose a font size of 12 or 14 for a resized window, whereas PostScript could pick a size of 11.31.

PostScript was originally developed for use on the printed page. However, the power of the language has led to a version that works on screen displays. PostScript has been adopted by several vendors as an imaging model; they include DEC, Sun Microsystems, and NEXT.

What PostScript has in the power of the imaging system it lacks in the ability to control real estate on a device. X and PostScript thus are complementary standards. It is possible to draw a box in either language. When PostScript and X Windows are combined, there is some choice as to whether to execute a function by a call to the X library or the PostScript interpreter. Many of the widgets defined in the X toolkit could be redefined as PostScript library calls instead of native Xlib calls.

PostScript code usually consists of a set of highly parameterized procedures. These procedures are used by the output module of a program to translate some semantic construction (i.e., a box) into the representation of that object. PostScript performs the same functions as the presentation layer of the OSI model. Instead of encoding text in some arbitrary ASN.1 syntax, code is specified in PostScript. There is no reason, of course, that an ASN.1 definition cannot be developed for both X Windows and PostScript.

Once this presentation layer syntax is defined, a software system is able to communicate with its peer in a high-level fashion. In this case, the peer is a terminal or printer communicating with some software program. What makes this an especially powerful model is that the peers are able to represent complex graphics images without resorting to transmitting large bit maps across the network.

Language Structure

PostScript is an interpreted language. This means that programs are not compiled and then run. Instead, a stream of instructions are sent to the interpreter, which then processes the information and produces the appropriate actions.

Because PostScript is interpreted, it is context sensitive. Any of the commands can be redefined. When a user executes the PostScript command **show** to render text onto a page, that normally prints a string of characters. It is possible for another user to redefine the meaning of the **show** command. The interpreter would then execute the new meaning attached to this command.

In addition to being interpreted, PostScript is a stack-based language, very similar to Forth. The entire function of the interpreter is to manipulate and execute items that are on a series of stacks. These items, known as objects, could be a simple object or a complex object consisting of other simple objects. An integer is a simple object; an array of integers is a complex object.

When an object is received by the PostScript interpreter, it usually deposits that object on an operand stack. An interpreter might receive two objects, 1 and 2, each being an integer. Then, the interpreter would receive another string object "add." The interpreter would look up the string and see that **add** is a PostScript operator, or command. The interpreter would then take the two top items off the operand stack, add them together, and place the results back on the stack.

There are four stacks for each thread of control, or user, of a PostScript interpreter. It is possible that there are several users, each with their own set of stacks. In addition to the operand stack there are dictionary, graphics state, and execution stacks. The graphics state and dictionary are described in subsequent sections.

The execution stack is used to hold executions that are partially suspended. Execution might begin by processing a file object. Within that file, there might be a reference to a procedure to be executed. The object file would then be placed on the execution stack and the procedure would begin. At completion, the file would then be popped off the execution stack and processing would continue.

PostScript data structures

Objects in PostScript can be either simple or composite. Simple objects include integers, characters, and real numbers. A boolean is also a simple object which has a value of true or false. Finally, a name is a simple object.

Composite objects are collections of simple objects. While a simple object is put directly on the operand stack, a composite object consists of a pointer to some portion of real memory. An array consists of one object on the operand stack that points to a portion of virtual memory that holds the individual members of the array.

Arrays in PostScript can be heterogeneous. Each of the elements of an array can be of a different type, including another array. This is how the simple one-dimensional array definition can be expanded to support multidimensional arrays.

A special type of composite object is the string. A string is composed of a series of characters and is thus a special case of the array. Usually, when PostScript encounters a string, it is converted into a name object. The name object is a simple object, usually referred to by a string. The dictionary translates the composite string object into a particular name.

The dictionary data structure

The dictionary consists of a series of key-value pairs. This makes it very easy to redefine the meaning of a command. In fact, the basic PostScript commands are not really commands. They are names which are looked up in the system dictionary which then point to an executable object.

Dictionaries are stacked up in a dictionary stack. Whenever a name is encountered, the interpreter begins searching the first dictionary on the stack, then the next, and so on until it reaches the bottom of the stack. If for some reason a word is encountered that is not in any of the dictionaries, this becomes an error.

The dictionary is really the only way that PostScript directly supports remembering the values of variables. If something is not saved in a dictionary and it is popped off the stacks, it vanishes.

Telling the interpreter to store something in the current dictionary is done with the **def** operator. Thus, when a procedure is defined, it is usually in this form:

```
/name_of_procedure
{

} def
```

The /name_of_procedure signals to the interpreter that a new name is about to be defined or an existing one redefined. The curly braces do not actually get stored; they place marks on the current stack as the data from the procedure is read in. When the **def** operator is reached, the stack is popped down to the mark and the resulting information is stored as a composite object. The dictionary then contains the name of the procedure as well as a pointer to a location in virtual memory that holds the composite object.

The PostScript interpreter stores the definition of all operators in a system dictionary. Rather than define operators directly, they are referenced in a dictionary. The **systemdict** contains a series of key-value pairs consisting of the name of the operator and the procedure to be executed. When an operator is encountered by the scanner, it is popped off the operand stack and the procedure is found and executed.

A default user dictionary holds current definitions. Users can also create new dictionaries for special purposes. Other dictionaries hold errors and procedures to execute when the error is encountered. A second dictionary, **$error** holds information on an error that was actually encountered.

Object attributes

Simple objects, and the pointer part of a complex object, consist of an 8-byte representation. This representation describes the type of the object, its value, and any attributes. Object attributes signify if the object is literal or executable. A literal object is treated as data and is put onto the operand stack for use by a subsequent operator.

An example of a literal object is a literal name. This is signified in PostScript by a / followed by a string of characters. This is then typically followed by some object to be associated with that name (usually in a dictionary). The following code is an example:

/name 2 def

When the scanner encounters /**name**, it converts the string into a name and puts it on the operand stack. It then puts the integer 2 on the operand stack.

The **def** operator is an example of an executable name. The lack of the / signals the scanner that this is an executable name and the action associated with that name should be performed immediately. In this case, the **def** operator pops the 2 and the literal **name** and forms a key-value association in the current dictionary.

The second type of attribute for an object is the access value. Access attributes only apply to arrays, strings, dictionary, or files. All of these have data that could be sharable because the object points to a part of virtual memory. It is possible that another name points to the same composite object in virtual memory, hence the need for access attributes.

The four possible attribute values are unlimited (read, write, or execute the object), read/execute, execute only, or no access. An access value of none is used to prohibit contexts from accessing certain values directly. An example is members of the font dictionary. These can only be accessed by special font operators and not by most other operators. It is possible for one context to have access to a composite object and for another context to have a different level of access.

PostScript structure

Initial input to PostScript goes to a scanner instead of directly to the interpreter. The scanner is responsible for breaking up an arbitrary string of ASCII data into a series of tokens, or objects. Each of the objects, such as integers or booleans, is passed by the scanner to the interpreter, which then executes the object.

The combination of the scanner and the interpreter forms a device-independent kernel. This kernel is prepared by Adobe (or a manufacturer of PostScript clones) and compiled for the OEM vendors that incorporate PostScript in their products. In addition, three device dependent modules are provided to interface with the windowing environment and the operating system.

A front-end adapter provides the interface to incoming data streams. This adapter dispatches incoming data to the various contexts or users of the kernel. Since all input in the X Windows environment is in the form of events, the front end adapter interacts with the X Windows event dispatching service.

An operating system adapter is used to provide operating system dependent functions. These include special provisions for efficient matrix manipulation, a key operation in PostScript. Other operating system hooks include memory manipulation and exception handling.

The display or back-end adapter works with displays on the particular implementation. In a display environment, this access is moderated by the windowing system, which has control over low-level graphics operations. The back-end adapter is used to generate a series of device primitives such as bit-map masks, filled trapezoids, or half tones.

User and Device Space

Every PostScript interpreter presents users with user and device spaces. The device space is device independent—it has the same coordinate system on all PostScript implementations. The device space is then translated by the interpreter into a physical device space.

The user space is used to construct a path, which is then rendered into device state. Exactly how it gets rendered depends on the type of painting operation and various other state variables such as the current transformation matrix (CTM). Figure 14-1 illustrates various transformations of the CTM.

The CTM defines how each point in user space is translated into device space. The CTM is a matrix that can be used to translate, rotate, or scale any path in user space as it is rendered. CTM trans-

Fig. 14-1 Current transformation matrix manipulation.

formations can be accomplished using high level operators such as the **rotate** command.

It also can perform direct operations on the CTM. All of the high-level operations on the CTM, such as **rotate**, have an equivalent direct operation on the matrix.

A **scale** operation can thus be represented two different ways:

3 5 scale

or

[3 0 0 5 0 0] concat

The **concat** operator concatenates the matrix on the stack with the current CTM to produce a new CTM. The **scale** operation allows users to perform the equivalent operation using a single high level operator.

A **rotate** operation could similarly be represented two ways:

angle rotate

or

[angle cos angle sin dup -1 mul angle cos 0 0] concat

The first element is the cosine of the angle. The second is the sine. Since the third element is the negative sine of the angle, the value already on the stack (the sine) is duplicated and then multiplied by -1.

Because PostScript is state based, the order in which operations on the CTM are performed is important. A rotate operation rotates the user space around the point of origin. A translate operation moves the point of origin of the coordinate system. A rotate followed by a translate is not the same as a translate followed by a rotate.

Creating and Rendering Paths

Creating and rendering a path is the basic graphics procedure in the PostScript imaging model. Paths are constructed in user space. The path is then painted onto device space. The painting operation could be a simple fill operation with a given color. It could also outline the current path (known as a stroke operation) using the current linewidth.

Constructing a path and then rendering it is used for font displays as well as graphics. As will be seen in the next section, the font is really just a path. An A is stored as an outline, or path, in the font dictionary. When the **show** operator is executed, the interpreter fills the outline of the character with the current color.

Two clipping paths are defined that limit the impact of rendering a path onto device space. All points in user space that fall outside of the clipping path are not shown on the device space when the rendering operation is executed.

The clip path is the basic clipping path used. Like a user path, this belongs to the current graphics states. When graphics states are switched, a new user path and clip path are introduced.

The second kind of path is a view clip path, which is independent of the graphics state. In a windowing environment, the view clip might correspond to the overall window. Separate graphics states, and thus clip paths, would be defined for each of the components of the window.

A point in user space must fall within both the clip path and the view clip path. The combination of clip paths allows objects to be defined without regard for their ability to fit into the particular space designed. An example of the usefulness of this construct is a procedure that generates a circle. The user may only wish a half circle on user space. However, that is a more complex mathematical formula than that for a whole circle. The user could generate the whole circle and then clip it to end up with the desired object.

Paths are constructed as a series of lines or curves. The path starts at the current point in user space. At the most general level, curves are defined as Bézier curves. A Bézier curve consists of four points in space. The curve itself is a function of the four points. Arcs of circles are a special case of the Bézier curve and separate operators exist for arcs as PostScript path construction operators.

A path can thus be used as a clip path or for painting. If the path is painted, it can be either filled or stroked. Figure 14-2 Illustrates the three uses of a path.

Graphics states

A user path can be rendered in a variety of ways. The current graphics state determines a set of defaults for drawing and painting. The graphics state is very similar to the X Windows graphics state. In a DECwindows environment, the two graphics states are essentially combined.

A graphics state is a data structure that is put on its own stack. This is because a graphics state is accessed frequently and should not be mixed on the same stack as operands or dictionaries. When the user saves a graphics state with the **gsave** operation, the current stack is saved as a special object.

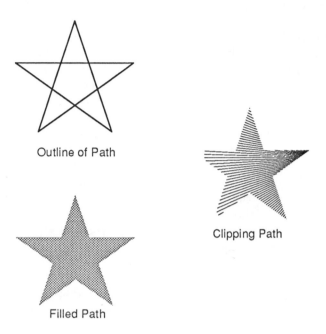

Outline of Path

Clipping Path

Filled Path

Fig. 14-2 Three uses of a path.

Graphics states can be saved as a special type of object known as a **gstate**. These **gstates** are very easy to restore and are thus used for rapid graphics state switching. A window-based application would maintain a variety of different states, corresponding to different objects or subwindows on the screen.

The current transformation matrix is one of the fundamental pieces of a graphics state. A current position, clipping path, and font and several device specific parameters are also part of the graphics state.

The graphics state also includes several components used for drawing lines. A current line width is defined in terms of user space units. A cap style is defined for capping lines that are not joined to others.

Cap styles can be round or flat. Join styles specify how joined lines are put together.

Current color is also a part of the graphics state. Color can be represented in many different ways, depending on the preference of the programmer and the type of output device. Grays are represented as a percentage number, where 0 equal black and 1 equals white. The translation from this 0 to 1 coordinate system into actual gray-scale values on the device are a function of the PostScript interpreter. As will be seen in the section on images, many devices cannot use gray scales and must instead use half-toning techniques. At this point the issue does not concern us and we can assume that the device will output grays as close as possible to the specified percentage.

Color is supported in PostScript using three different models. A reflectance model represents colors using the three process colors (cyan, magenta, and yellow) and black. This is used in commercial typesetting systems. Another model is the luminance model consisting of hue, saturation, and brightness. Finally, a mix of RGB numbers is available to represent colors. The RGB model is the same as is used in a native X Windows System implementation.

It is fairly simple to process PostScript information and produce color separations. A procedure is downloaded to the PostScript interpreter, which takes away all except one of the basic colors in a given image. This image is then displayed, usually on a typesetter. The same information is printed again with all but one of the other colors removed.

Cached user paths

In an interactive environment, many paths are defined and accessed continually. A special type of object called a user path can be cached for rapid access. This cache, like all others, takes up space in virtual memory. The path cache is thus limited and committing a path to the cache may displace a currently cached path.

A user path is a special kind of procedure which only contains path building operators and nothing else. Since the user path is an object type, it can be easily represented in encoded form. This allows the use repetition counts and other mechanisms for more efficiently representing a path.

When a path is cached, it consists of a combination of the path as well as the rendering operator that was used with that path. In addition, a cached path contains the current values of the current transformation matrix. This is because the same operators may result in very different paths if a different CTM is in effect.

The fact that the user path cache is state dependent is no different than the method used for font caching. In both cases, when the system receives a font or path request, it checks the cache. If the precise one referred to is contained in the cache, it uses it. Otherwise, it reconstructs the object in device space.

Fonts

Fonts are a special case of the path construction and rendering operations. A series of special operators is defined to operate on fonts. In most PostScript fonts, the font is defined as an outline. This outline can then be scaled, rotated, or otherwise transformed. The default operation for rendering a font is usually to fill it with black. By changing colors or gray scale, this default can be easily changed. Figure 14-3 illustrates various operations on text.

A font is actually a special dictionary. This dictionary contains, among other things, a set of procedures used to draw each character in a font. Although fonts are usually used for text characters, a font can be defined that has small pictures in it or corporate logos or any other form that can be represented as a procedure.

To locate a particular font, the **findfont** operator is executed. This takes a fontname and returns a dictionary onto the operand stack. This font can then be scaled to the appropriate size using the **scalefont** operator. One of the key characteristics of PostScript is that outline fonts can be very precisely scaled.

Fonts are defined in a character coordinate space. Scaling a font defines how this character coordinate space is mapped into a user space. A more general transformation of character-to-user space is available with the **makefont** operator, which allows the same type of matrix operations that were present for CTM manipulation.

Once a font has been scaled, it is set as the current font. The current font becomes part of the graphics state. Further manipulations to the CTM will affect the font as well as all other components of the graphics state. Blowing up a graphics image that contains text with a **scale** command would thus have all the fonts evenly scaled in size with the rest of the components.

To simplify setting text, a special operator is available called **show**. This operator takes a string and treats each element of the string as a character code. Each of the characters is then set next to each of the other characters.

The decision of which characters go on which line is typically a policy decision made ahead of time by the program that is using PostScript. This policy decision is then implemented by PostScript. The

Fig. 14-3 Different font transformations.

show operator simplifies implementing this policy by allowing characters to be set as a group instead of individually.

The decision on where to place each of the characters, using the **show** command, is actually a fairly complicated typographical process.

Kerning is used to decide how to space characters. Most typographic programs space characters unevenly to provide a more pleasing appearance to the eye. This means that the space between words is greater than the space between letters on a word. This also means that within a word, there is unequal spacing to reflect the unequal width of characters.

PostScript defines two types of kerning. Pairwise kerning looks at each pair of letters to make spacing decisions. An A and a W would thus be spaced closer together than an A and a B. This is because the slant on the W and the A allow them to be squeezed together more tightly than the straight lines of the A and the B.

AW

AB

Track kerning is used to squeeze or expand whole lines of text. Big fonts, for example, should be squeezed together a little. Small fonts, on the other hand need a little extra room between characters to provide a pleasing appearance. Several variations of the **show** operator allow a considerable amount of control over the types of kerning used. It is even possible, with the **kshow** command, to have a user defined procedure executed between each of the characters in a string.

While the normal operation is to show a character, it is possible to use the character as a path for more general operations. The **stroke** operation strokes a current path using the current line width. It is possible to use the **charpath** operator to render a string as a current path and then to show the path.

Another operation is to fill the insides of text. In this case, the character string is again defined as a path using the **charpath** operator. Then, the **clip** operator is pushed onto the operand stack making the path into a clip path instead of a drawing path. Next, the user would generate a graphic and show it. The only part of the graphic (say a pattern) that would show would be that within the boundaries of the clipping path. Usually, the path would then be stroked to provide a definition of the boundary of the characters.

Bit map fonts

Outline fonts are normally most appropriate, but in very small sizes on low resolution devices, the outlines may not be very attractive. For these small sizes, hand-tuned bit-map fonts are most appropriate. PostScript is able to work with both outline and bit-map fonts, if they are available.

When an interpreter is initialized (or is coded), it obtains a list of fonts that are provided by the hardware or the window system. The window system is responsible for interfacing with the hardware environment and thus provides the list of available bit-map fonts.

Once a list is available, the PostScript interpreter knows that it can efficiently render those fonts by calling the hardware instead of reconstructing the character using an outline and painting operator. These small bit maps are available only in particular font sizes and in a particular orientation. A rotated font, for example, would have to be rendered by PostScript.

Font caches

Rendering a character from an outline can consume 1000 times more resources than using a simple bit map of the character. To avoid reexecuting the character outline, a font cache is established in Post-Script virtual memory. Each rendition of a character is cached, along with the CTM and other graphics state parameters that were in effect. The next time the same character is referenced, it is found from the cache instead of being reexecuted. It is not unusual to devote over a megabyte of memory to font caches. This provides a tremendous efficiency boost in complex text setting environments.

Images

Most of the PostScript operations use raster graphics, which consist of a series of primitives such as lines and curves. This allows an individual component of a picture to be changed without changing all of the associated pixels with that component. For most constructions, this provides a flexible, revisable way of representing graphics operations. Since many devices support raster operations that correspond to the PostScript raster operations, this is also an efficient way to represent graphics primitives.

Images are an example of a bit-map type of graphics component. In an image, each dot is individually defined. PostScript provides a resolution-independent way of rendering images such as photographs. Photographs are usually scanned in with a separate program and then imported into the PostScript environment.

Images can also be generated mathematically in the PostScript environment. An example of a machine-generated image is a fountain. A fountain is a space, such as a rectangle, that gradually changes colors or gray scales.

To render an image, a set of samples are furnished to the PostScript image operators. A sample might be scanned in by a scanner. In that case, the number of samples would be equivalent to the resolution of the scanning device. Each sample of data can have associated with it a color or gray-scale value.

The PostScript image operator is able to take this sample, which is now resolution independent, and transform it into device space. Images can thus be rotated, scaled, or translated or any of the other matrix transformation operations available in PostScript may be performed.

One of the operands to the image operator is a data acquisition procedure. This could be as simple as reading a string from the standard input. Another option is to have the data acquisition procedure actually generate the sample points. In either case, the image operator repeatedly calls the data acquisition procedure until it reaches the end of the data. Each of the samples is then rendered using the current transformation matrix for that image.

A special provision is made in PostScript for images that are already customized for use on a particular device. This allows the imaging system to efficiently move a bit map onto a device and bypass some of the overhead of the image operator.

Halftones

Most devices supported by PostScript can render an individual pixel or dot on the page only as black or white. The **image** operator, on the other hand, supports up to 256 shades of gray for a particular sample of the image. Halftoning is the process by which on/off pixels are manipulated to simulate shades of gray (or color).

When an image is rendered, it is rendered at a particular frequency, usually expressed as lines per inch. This frequency makes a grid, to which the samples in the image are mapped. A grid or screen of 175 lines per inch is considered to be a very high-quality image, which taxes the limits of most modern printing presses.

The device resolution of even low-quality laser printers is significantly greater than the frequency of an image. This means that several pixels make up an individual square in the grid. By turning on a certain number of those pixels, the eye perceives different shades of gray.

The order in which the pixels in a grid square are turned on is known as a spot function. The default spot function starts by turning on pixels closest to the center of the grid square and then moving outward to the perimeter of the square. This means that light grays appear as small dots and dark grays appear as darker or bigger dots. The user is able to specify the type of spot function in PostScript, although this is fairly rarely done.

The halftoning process is unrelated to user space, and it operates directly on device space. It can be thought of as a special type of clipping mask. The reason that halftone screens are applied directly to device space is to make sure that two shades of gray that are applied at different times to contiguous portions of device space do not show a seam.

In a color environment, several different halftones can be defined, one for each of the colors. A halftone definition, consisting of a spot function, angle, and frequency, can be stored in a special halftone dictionary to allow rapid context switching. The angle of a halftone refers to the angle that the grid is rotated from device space. Different angles are used for different colors so that the dots for one color do not overlap with the dots from another color. Because PostScript is an opaque painting model and because color combinations are composed of combinations of the basic color dots, angles are necessary for true color output.

Virtual Memory

Virtual memory management is important in an environment where multiple processes all want to the use the services of one PostScript interpreter. This is the case in DECwindows, where a single X server and PostScript interpreter make their resources available to multiple clients across the network.

Two types of virtual memory (VM) are available in PostScript. Shared virtual memory is available to multiple users. Private virtual memory is restricted to one user. Users have their own execution context (i.e., their own set of stacks). It is possible for several execution contexts to share a private VM area.

Memory reclamation can be performed in several ways. A **restore** or **grestore** operation explicitly restores a previous state of operation and thus automatically reclaims memory. In the case of a page-oriented system, this will automatically occur at the end of each page.

In a display environment, there is no end of page, merely a long set of operations on a region of the screen. It is thus possible for objects to remain in VM that are not referenced anywhere in the stacks. A garbage collector is able to reclaim this VM automatically.

If a region of VM is to be automatically reclaimed, the composite element cannot be on the stack and cannot be referenced by another composite element which is on the stack. It is important to note that a composite object might be referenced by a saved context, in which case the automatic VM reclamation algorithm leaves it in memory.

When a new context starts, a separate portion of VM is allocated for that process. Normally, each context accesses its own private VM as well as the shared VM. Shared VM is typically used to hold font definitions and system-wide macros (i.e., X-specific macros might be stored here). A rule established for memory allocation says that it is illegal to have an object in shared VM point to a composite object in private VM. In order to place a composite object in shared VM, the process must first allocate some shared VM.

Normally, shared font directories, the system dictionary, and a specially defined shared dictionary are kept in shared VM. Private VM contains stacks, the user dictionary, private font directories, and composite elements.

Execution contexts and VM

Each execution context consists of a separate thread of control, which means that it has separate operand, dictionary execution, and graphics states stacks. Each context also has defined a current input and current output file specification. Multiple execution contexts can share private VM but only with special coordination by the processes involved.

When a **fork** operator is executed, this signals to PostScript to create a new context of execution which shares the same VM as the original process. As with the Unix fork operator, the child inherits the same state as the parent. The child can then keep the same state or proceed to modify state information to create a different environment.

To aid in coordination, semaphores have been defined for use in PostScript programs. A mutual exclusion semaphore is a lock on a resource. A condition semaphore is similar to the asynchronous system trap (AST) discussed in the context of the VMS locking mechanism. An example of a condition semaphore is to wait until a context has suspended execution for a period of time. These semaphores, or synchronization primitives as they are known, can be immediately acquired, or the process waits until the resource is available.

A special synchronization primitive allows a context to yield to all other executing jobs. This context only executes when no other processes are operating. An example of this use would be in an implementation of a window manager. A user might specify that the root window has a background consisting of a panorama of the Golden Gate Bridge and San Francisco, complete with moving waves. It makes no sense for the interpreter to be moving waves if a "real" processes has work to do. If nothing is happening on the screen, the intrepter is free to use all available resources to create moving waves or even a hurricane.

Program Interfaces to PostScript

PostScript can be accessed at several different levels. At the highest level, users can send ASCII text to the interpreter (or more accurately, the scanner). Programmers are able to use several other mechanisms to access the interpreter.

Binary encoding is the most efficient method of representing Post-Script operations. Binary encoding is equivalent to the internal representation used in the PostScript kernel. Sending data in a binary object sequence (BOS) is equivalent to a program being compiled. The compiled program takes ASCII text in a high-level language and replaces it with machine code. A BOS is the PostScript equivalent of machine code.

Most programmers will not directly generate binary object sequences. Instead, programmers will use two higher-level libraries. The PostScript client library provides a procedure for each of the basic PostScript operators.

Another level of access is using a PSwrap preprocessor. PSwrap allows the programmer to define a PostScript procedure. That procedure is then called just like any other C language procedure. The call to the procedure returns a status value that indicates success or failure. PSwrap allows PostScript to be treated as any other library of utilities.

Both PSwrap and the PostScript client library allow for more efficient execution of code by replacing ASCII commands with their equivalent binary object sequence. Again, the BOS presents a precompiled version of PostScript code to the interpreter, greatly speeding up execution time.

Binary encoding

Normally, the scanner in PostScript reads all incoming text from the current file and parses that information. This scanner functions as a lexical analyzer, breaking up the input into tokens that the interpreter can recognize. The scanner breaks all incoming data into literal strings, numbers, other names, or procedure bodies. This information is then passed to the interpreter which performs the appropriate stack manipulations and dictionary look-ups.

In addition to recognizing ASCII text, suitable for sending over a nontransparent network connection, the scanner can recognized binary encodings. Binary encodings are what the scanner normally produces when it has finished scanning information. A binary encoding is thus a form of precompiled PostScript code.

The use of binary encoding implies a fully transparent communications channel. The network or communications bus on a machine should not add end of line or end record information or otherwise depend on the absence of some unique character. While this is suitable for a transparent transport mechanism like HDLC, a serial line to a printer would not be able to use it. This is because several characters (i.e., X/ON or X/OFF) have a special meaning to the communications software and could not be included as data values.

The binary encoding mechanism offers several different options for representing information. It is possible to represent floating point in a native format for the target machine or in an IEEE standard for use in a heterogeneous environment. The byte order of incoming data can also be specified.

Every binary token received has an equivalent ASCII representation. The binary encoding thus adds no functionality, only convenience for the programs. There are two ways to perform binary encoding. First, any single command can be represented as a binary token instead of as an ASCII token. This is used as a simple compression mechanism so long ASCII representations of, for example, floating point numbers, are not sent over an expensive communications channel.

Each of the tokens sent consists of a packet of data which has a token type and a data field. Standard token types are registered for native data types in PostScript. In addition, several unassigned and unspecified (i.e., window manager-specific) token types are available for expansion or implementation specific enhancements.

A special type of binary token is called the binary object sequence. This is a single token which describes an executable array of objects. The array of objects described by this binary object sequence is in itself composed of a series of binary tokens, which may in turn be complex binary object sequences.

Normally, the binary object sequence functions as a predefined series of commands that are immediately executed. This would be like defining an executable array (a procedure) and then putting the **exec** operator after it instead of the **def** operator. It is possible to send in a binary object sequence and have it saved for later execution by enclosing it inside of some ASCII procedure definitions as follows:

```
/proc_name
        {
                        [BINARY OBJECT SEQUENCE]
        } def
```

In this example, the scanner would put the object on the operand stack just as it would any other name definition. If the binary object sequence had been received by itself, it would have been pushed directly on the execution stack instead.

The binary object sequence is considered as a whole token by the scanner. It thus processes the entire token before sending it over to the interpreter. All name bindings are immediately performed based on the state of the dictionary stack at the time the BOS is retrieved. Because the entire token is processed, it needs to be placed into virtual memory and thus has to have a finite length.

The BOS itself consists of a BOS header followed by a series of 8-byte representations of binary tokens. This is the same basic representation that is used when a stand-alone binary token is sent over the link.

The header of the BOS indicates that it is a special type of token, followed by the number of objects in the top level of the array. Following that is one token for each object in the top-level array of the BOS. Next are any objects that are part of nested arrays included in the BOS. Finally, there is a space that contains room for all strings (which form a composite object).

Each top-level token in the BOS consists of a 1-byte token type indicator. This is followed by a length and value field, the meaning of which depends on the token type. Simple objects (integers, for example) have the actual value and no length stored. Together, the whole token fits into an 8-byte space.

In composite objects, the length and value fields are really pointers to subsequent tokens contained in the BOS. The length field contains the number of objects in this composite object. The value field contains a pointer, which is an offset from the beginning of the composite object list within this BOS.

Since a name is a composite object, the top-level token is really a pointer to the text data area at the end of the BOS. A special provision for names exist which allows the names to be predefined in a name index maintained by the scanner. Name indexes allow names to be referred to by a small integer instead of a large character string.

Two name indexes are defined. The system name index is provided with the PostScript interpreter and is used internally by the software.

The system name index contains all the standard operator names as well as the names of characters and fonts.

A user name index is also available. To define a name to the index, the user pushes an index value and then a character string onto the stack. This is followed by the **defineusername** operator. It is up to the user to remember what the index values stand for.

Name indexes provide a first level of translation maintained by the scanner. The dictionary structure provides a second level of translation. Once a name has been found, the stack contains an ordinary name object. During normal operation, this name is not looked up in the dictionary until execution time.

It is possible to request that a name be immediately looked up in the dictionary instead of deferring the lookup until the operation is executed. This can be done by setting a special type indicator in the token representation or using double slashes in front of an ASCII representation of a name.

The user name index is part of the private VM. It is possible that multiple execution contexts share a space in virtual memory. In that case, it is up to all the programs that share that VM to coordinate their access to the name index.

Structured output capabilities

In the printer implementation of PostScript, a single input stream was used to download information. Output consisted only of the printed page. In a display-oriented environment, it is important to supplement this with a way for the interpreter to communicate with programs that use its services.

A structured output capability allows information to be written to an arbitrary file as provided by the underlying file system. The implementation of this is flexible enough to allow different syntaxes of file names for different systems. The file system would validate access as in the case of any other file access operation. These details, naming and other file-system specific semantics, are outside the scope of the PostScript imaging model.

Output sent to files can be encoded with the same binary encoding mechanism used for sending information to the interpreter. Type indicators are available for errors as well as for dynamic token-type definitions reserved for use by the application.

Library interfaces

It is possible for programmers to generate ASCII data or binary encodings and communicate directly to the PostScript interpreter. This would involve establishing a connection, generating binary encodings, and doing many other complex tasks. Most programmers will instead use one of two higher-level interfaces.

A PostScript client library is a series of routines which are compiled into the user's program. The form of this client library depends on the languages used. Typically, this would be the C-programming language.

The client library manages all communications with the interpreter. This allows the programmer to treat the connection as a stream interface consisting of simple reads and writes. The second function of the client library is to generate binary encodings on behalf of programs. The client library does as much translation as possible at compile time to speed execution speeds.

All of the standard PostScript operators are available as library calls. Each of these library calls takes as parameters the arguments that the interpreter would expect to find on the operand stack. The **moveto** operator, for example, expects to find an x and y coordinate on the stack. The equivalent client library call would be:

PSmoveto (xcoord, ycoord)

The client library is also able to work with multiple execution contexts. The PS calls, such as **PSmoveto**, always work with the currently defined context. To address multiple contexts, a series of equivalent DPS (display PostScript) calls are available that take an additional argument for the context ID:

DPSmoveto (context, xcoord, ycoord)

The second, higher, level of access is a macro library called PSWrap. This allows PostScript procedures to be treated like any other C-language procedure, complete with a return of status messages. PSWrap is a preprocessor which generates C code. That code is then compiled and linked in with the client library.

The programmer begins by defining a C-language procedure. That procedure is preceded by the **defineps** indicator, which tells the PS-Wrap preprocessor that this is the beginning of some code. The **endps** indicator tells the preprocessor that this is the end of the procedure definition.

An example of PSwrap, taken from the PSwrap reference manual, is to define a procedure that generates a gray circle given an X and Y coordinate and a radius:

```
defineps grayCircle (float x,y,radius)
            newpath
            x y radius 0.0 360.0 arc
            closepath
            0.5 setgray
    endps
```

The programmer could then refer to this procedure in the main body of the program with the following call:

```
status = grayCircle ( X, Y, RADIUS ) ;
```

The same procedure could have been executed by manually setting up communication with the interpreter and sending ASCII text or a BOS. Alternatively, the client library could have been used, but this would have entailed a series of different calls. The client library does have the advantage over direct communication with the interpreter of managing many of the details of establishing contexts and communications paths.

PsWrap also allows programmers to pass complex data structures, such as arrays, into the interpreter. Procedures can also return, as output, complex objects including arrays and character strings.

Summary

PostScript is a full-featured language for specifying the representation of text and graphics on a display or other output device. The language allows a sophisticated user interface to be built on top of a windowing system, such as X.

The combination of the X Windowing System and the PostScript imaging system allow bit-mapped workstations to function over a heterogeneous network. That network can consist of many different vendors' compute and print servers. There can also be many different user workstations. If applications are written using the OSI networking standards and the X and PostScript user interface standards, they become available to all users on the network.

For Further Reading

Adobe Systems Incorporated, *PostScript Language Reference Manual*, Addison Wesley, Reading, MA, 1985.

——, *PostScript Language Tutorial and Cookbook*, Addison Wesley, Reading, MA, 1985.

Reid, *PostScript Language Program Design*, Addison-Wesley, Reading, MA, 1988.

Glossary

2780/3780
A model of remote batch terminals used in IBM bisynchronous environments. Bisync gateways are often referred to as 2780/3780 emulators.

370 architecture
IBM architecture for mainframe computers, including the 3090 processors.

3090
IBM top of the line mainframe, sometimes called Sierra.

3270
A series of terminals used in IBM environments.

3274
A cluster controller for IBM equipment, often called a terminal concentrator.

3480
IBM tape cartridges.

3705
An IBM communications controller. A PU type 4 in SNA, used to connect token ring networks, cluster controllers, non-IBM SNA gateways, and other devices to a PU Type 5 host.

3725
See 3705

3Com
A communications company known for Ethernet controllers and PC-based networking equipment. Merged with Bridge Communications.

4.3BSD   *4.3 Berkeley Software Distribution* The current version of the Berkeley family of Unix products.

4010/4014   A series of Tektronix graphics terminals. A de facto standard for graphics terminals.

4GL   *Fourth-generation language* A group of new languages often linked with database packages such as Ingres or Oracle. Contrast with Fortran and other third-generation languages.

80286   An Intel chip, used in the IBM PC/AT and clones. The 80386 is used in new high-end PS/2s and Compaq computers.

9370   Mid-range IBM processor.

ACK   *Acknowledge* A data communications term for acknowledgment of information (packets) received.

ACL   *Access Control List* A security feature in the VMS operating system that allows security on objects to be specified as a list of permitted actions for particular lists of users.

ACSE   *Association Control Service Elements* Core set of facilities in the OSI application layer which allow application entities to form an association.

ad hoc   Latin phrase meaning "for a specific instance." Used in computing to refer to not previously planned functions.

ADMD   *Administration Management Domain* X.400 message-handling system concept. Countries will typically be an ADMD. They might then cede some management authority to a private management domain (PRMD).

Adobe Systems   The company that makes the PostScript Page Description Language.

AFI   *Authority and Format Identifier* Part of an OSI address which signals what type of address follows the AFI.

Alliant   A manufacturer of mini-supercomputers. These computers are vector processors and compete with DEC in the high-end, computationally intensive markets.

ALL-IN-1   DEC's office automation shell, consisting of a menu driver, a mail user interface, a calendar manager, and a file manager.

ANSI   *American National Standards Institute* A leading standards-setting organization in the United States.

APPC   *Advanced Program-to-Program Communication* Sometimes known as LU6.2, refers to peer-to-peer communication in an IBM SNA network. Many advanced IBM architectures, such as DIA and DCA, build on top of APPC.

Areas   A DECnet term used in the routing layer. Level 1 routers are used to route within a DECnet area. Level 2 routers route between areas. Up to 1023 nodes may be in an area, up to 63 areas in a DECnet.

ARP   *Address resolution protocol* A TCP/IP protocol to translate an IP address into a physical address (i.e., an Ethernet or other subnetwork address).

Arpanet   A Department of Defense sponsored network of military and research organizations. Being replaced by the Defense Data Network.

AS/400   *Application System/400* IBM mid-range computer replacing the System/38 and System/36 product lines.

ASCII   *American Standard Code for Information Interchange* A standard character set which assigns an octal sequence to each letter, number, and selected control characters. The other major encoding standard is EBCDIC.

ASN   *Abstract syntax notation* The language used in the OSI presentation layer to define complex objects.

AST   *Asyncronous system trap* A concept used in the
                    VMS lock manager. An AST is a request to be
                    notified when a certain event occurs. In the case
                    of the lock manager, an AST can be set so that a
                    process holding a lock on a resource is notified if
                    another process tries to take an imcompatible
                    lock on the same resource.

Async   *Asynchronous* A data transmission method that
                    sends one character at a time. Contrasted with
                    synchronous methods which send a packet of
                    data and then resynchronize their clocks. Asyn-
                    chronous also refers to commands, such as in a
                    windowing environment, that may be sent with-
                    out waiting for a response from the previous com-
                    mand.

AT   *Advanced technology* Shorthand for the IBM
                    PC/AT or any other Intel 80286-based processor
                    that runs the DOS operating system.

AT&T   *American Telephone and Telegraph* Provider of
                    long-distance service and computing company
                    known for the Unix operating system.

ATM   *Automated teller machine* Used in banking.

AUTHORIZE   A VMS utility used to add new users and define
                    relevant parameters such as privileges, default
                    log-in directories, etc.

autobaud   The ability of a modem on the receiving end of a
                    call to automatically detect the speed of trans-
                    mission used by the calling modem.

backbone   A networking term used to refer to a piece of
                    cable used to connect different floors or depart-
                    ments together. Contrasted with a departmental
                    network or work area network.

backup   Making a copy of stored information to use in
                    case the original repository (usually a disk drive)
                    becomes corrupted. To be contrasted with the al-
                    ternate meaning of the word, "to overflow," which
                    is usually used in the context of plumbing and
                    sewage.

balun	*balanced/unbalanced* An adapter between two different pieces of physical media that adjusts for the difference in impedence.
baseband	Coax cable implementation of Ethernet. Also known as ThickWire.
baud	A term used with older (slow) modems to refer to each modulation of an analog signal. A 300 baud signal modulates 300 times per second. A more accurate term for faster modems is bits per second, as several bits can now be carried on one modulation of the signal.
BBN	*Bolt, Beranek, and Newman* A company that specializes in communications. Responsible for the Defense Data Network.
BI bus	*Backplane interconnect* A peripheral bus used on DEC's 8000 series VAXs. The BI bus operates at a speed of 13.3 Mbps.
BIND	An SNA term used to establish a session between two logical units.
BIOS	*Basic input/output system* The MS-DOS library of calls for access to data. Shields the application from the different types of physical disks.
Bisync	A synchronous protocol used in older IBM teleprocessing environments. See also BSC.
block	A unit of I/O on VMS computers. 512 bytes.
boot nodes	Used in Local Area Vax Clusters to refer to the node that stores the operating system for other nodes in the cluster.
BOS	*Binary object sequence* The lowest level of access to a Postscript Interpreter. Higher levels are Postscript programming library calls and ASCII interfaces.
bps	*Bits per second* Transmission speed on modems, phone lines, and other data communications devices.

bridge	A device used to connect two separate Ethernet networks into one extended Ethernet. Bridges only forward packets between networks that are destined for the other network.
Britton Lee	Manufacturer of database machines.
broadband	An analog media similar to cable TV. Large bandwidth and very long distances make this media appropriate for campus settings. Used with various data link protocols including Ethernet and token buses.
broadcast	A message that is sent to multiple nodes simultaneously. Ethernet is an example of a broadcast media because all nodes can receive the same message. A message with a broadcast address is processed by every node on the Ethernet.
BSC	*Bisynchronous* See bisync.
BSD	*Berkeley Standard Distribution* See 4.3BSD.
bursty traffic	Data communications term referring to an uneven pattern of data transmission.
bus	The part of a computer that connects devices so that they may communicate. An XMI bus, for example, connects memory cards, CPU cards, and peripheral buses (the BI Bus). The BI bus allows multiple peripheral controllers to be connected.
CAD/CAM	*Computer aided design/computer aided manufacture* Software/hardware combinations for the automation of engineering environments.
CASE	*Computer Aided Software Engineering or Common application service element* A term used to refer to a set of tools that help automate and control programming environments. Examples of CASE tools would be the Module Management System or Code Management System from DEC. Also a term used in the OSI application layer services to refer to a service used by all types of applications.

CATV   *Community Antenna TV* The type of cable used in broadband networks.

CCA   *Conceptual communications area* One common view of the state of a virtual terminal used in the OSI VT service.

CCITT   *Consultative Committee for International Telephone and Telegraph (Comité Consultatif International Télégraphique et Téléphonique)* An international standards-making body consisting of national telecommunications authorities. Recommendations are known by their numbers, i.e., X.25 for packet switched networks, X.400 for message-handling systems.

CCR   *Commitment, concurrency, and recovery* Part of the OSI CASE services that allows the coordination of multiple users access to data on multiple nodes.

CCS   *Common communications support* A portion of IBM's System Application Architecture (SAA).

CDD   *Common Data Dictionary* DEC's software that functions as a common repository for data definitions, forms, database schemas, and other parts of an information system. Part of the VAX Information Architecture.

CD-ROM   *Compact Disk–read only memory* Optical disks that are mastered and then can only be read. Used for read only databases.

channel   An IBM term referring to a direct high-speed connection into the 370 architecture machine. A "channel attach" device operates at speeds of up to 3 Mbps, as opposed to more traditional devices that attach to a communications controller at 56 kbps.

CheaperNet   Another term for ThinWire Ethernet cables.

CHIPCOM   A manufacturer of broadband Ethernet equipment.

CI bus   *Computer-room interconnect* Refers to the 70-mbps bus and controllers used in the VAX Cluster arrangement. To be contrasted with Local Area VAX Clusters that use a 10-mbps Ethernet as the transport mechanism.

CICS   *Customer information control system* An IBM data communications interface used typically with the MVS operating system.

circuit   A term used in networking that refers to a logical stream of data between two users of the network. A single physical link may have several virtual circuits running on it.

CIT   *Computer Integrated Telephony* DEC architecture and products for integrating PBXs into a computer network.

class driver   A term used in VMS. A device driver is used to present data to a particular piece of hardware, such as a terminal. In VMS, there are two levels of device drivers. The class driver is generic, for example, a terminal class driver. Underneath the class driver is a physical driver that accepts commands for a specific type of terminal such as a directly connected terminal or a remote terminal session using the LAT protocols. The class driver shields the user of the device from knowing about the particular physical connection used.

clearinghouse   A collection of names, such as used in DNS. A user would query the clearinghouse (also known as a nameserver) to find the location of a particular resource at that time.

CLNS   *Connectionless network service* One of two options for the OSI network layer. See also CONS.

Clusters   A DEC architecture for VMS nodes only that allows several systems to have a common security/management domain and transparent access to the same disk drives.

CMIP

Common Management Information Protocol OSI network management protocols used in DECnet Phase V.

CMS

Code Management System or Conversational Monitor System Code Management System is a DEC software product used in the VMS environment as a library for program development. Conversational Monitor System is the user interface on IBM's VM/CMS operating system.

coax

coaxial A type of cable, used for IBM 3270 terminals, as well as for baseband and ThinWire Ethernets.

Cobol

Common business-oriented language One of the first standardized computing languages. See CODASYL.

CODASYL

Conference on Data Systems Languages The folks that brought you Cobol as well as the CODASYL standard for databases using the network model of data management.

concurrency

When multiple users attempt to access the same resource. A lock manager addresses the problem of maintaining the integrity of resources in a concurrent environment.

conferencing

A term used for communication software that allows participants to "post" notes. Contrasts with electronic mail in that participants do not have to be explicitly addressed. Also known as a bulletin board.

config.sys

An MS-DOS file read in at boot time which contains the names of additional device drivers, such as a driver for extended memory or a peripheral such as a scanner.

connection manager

A cluster term used to refer to the software component in a VAX Cluster or LAVC that maintains the integrity of the cluster by managing state transitions.

CONS   *Connection oriented network service* One of two options for the OSI network layer. See also CLNS.

Convex   A manufacturer of super mini-computers. See Alliant.

CPU   *Central processing unit* You know—the computer part of the computer.

CRC   *Cyclic redundancy check* A type of error-checking mechanism for data communications. A code is generated based on the values of the data transmitted and the resulting number is tacked onto the end of the data. The receiving end recalculates the CRC and compares it to the CRC received.

CSA   *Client services agent* Part of the Manufacturing Automation Protocol (MAP) Directory Service.

CSMA/CD   *Carrier Sense–Multiple Access / Collision Detect* A control method for a network. Ethernet is an example of a CSMA/CD type of data link protocol.

CT   *Channel transport* An advanced model of DEC's DECnet/SNA Gateway.

CTERM   *Communications Terminal Protocol* Part of the virtual terminal service in layer 6 of the Digital Network Architecture. An alternative to the CTERM services is the Local Area Transport Architecture (LAT).

CTM   *Current transformation matrix* A term used in the PostScript Imaging System to denote the transformation between user space and device space.

CUA   *Common user access* The common user interface component of IBM's System Application Architecture. Similar concepts exist with Xerox's Open Look standard and within the DECwindows environment.

Cullinet Software company that markets the IDMS database package.

Culprit	A Cullinet software package used in the IBM environment that is used to extract data from other DBMS systems such as IMS.
daemon	A Unix term referring to a process that is not connected with a user but performs services, such as a mail daemon. The equivalent VMS term is a detached process.
DAP	*Data Access Protocol* A protocol used in the Digital Network Architecture in layer 6. Provides a rich set of functions used for exchanging data between two nodes of the network. See FAL.
DARPA	*Defense Advanced Research Projects Agency* A Department of Defense agency that has helped fund many computer projects including Arpanet, the Berkeley version of Unix and TCP/IP.
Data Distributor	A DEC software product for extracting portions of DSRI-compatible databases and replicating this data on another node of the network as an Rdb database.
datagram	An unacknowledged packet of data in a network as opposed to packets that require acknowledgment of receipt (also known as reliable communications).
DATAPAC	Canadian public packet switched network.
DB2	An IBM database package based on the relational model and the SQL query language.
DBMS	*Database Management System* Software that allows the centralized storage of data with multiple concurrent users, access control, and the use of a high-level data manipulation language such as SQL.
DCA	*Document Content Architecture or Defense Communications Agency.* Document Content Architecture is an IBM architecture similar in function to DEC's Compound Document Architecture (CDA). The Defense Communication Agency is responsible for the Defense Data Network.

DCE	*Data circuit-terminating equipment* A term in X.25 networks that refers to the interface to the communications network. See also DTE.
DCL	*Digital command language* The user interface in the VMS operating system. Similar to the C shell in the Unix operating system.
DDCMP	*Digital Data Communications Message Protocol* A data link protocol used in the Digital Network Architecture. Used for point-to-point links between nodes, either synchronous or asynchronous. An alternative data link protocol is Ethernet.
DDIF	*Digital Document Interchange Format* The part of DEC's Compound Document Architecture (CDA) that specifies how revisable form documents are to be stored.
DDN	*Defense Data Network* A network for the Department of Defense and its contractors based on the TCP/IP and X.25 networking protocols.
DDXF	*DISOSS Document Exchange Facility* A DEC software product that allows transfer of data between DEC and IBM word processing environments. See also EDE.
deadlock	A term used in a concurrent environment. If one user holds a lock on a resource and is waiting for another resource to free up and a second user has the reverse situation, this is known as a deadlock. The deadlock must be broken by arbitrarily picking one of the users and releasing its current lock. The deadlock is also known as a deadly embrace.
DEBET	Model number for the DEC LAN Bridge 100 used for creating extended Ethernets.
DEC	*Digital Equipment Corporation.*
DECconnect	A DEC cabling architecture used for facilities wiring.

DECmate	A piece of DEC hardware roughly equivalent to a PC, but it only runs the WPS word processing system and a few miscellaneous utilities.
DECnet	An implementation of the Digital Network Architecture by DEC, as opposed to implementations of DNA by other vendors.
DECnet/DOS	The version of DECnet for the PC or MS-DOS operating systems.
DECnet Router	A device that routes data between two portions of a DECnet. Could be a general-purpose computer such as a MicroVAX or a dedicated piece of hardware such as the DECSA.
DECOM	A broadband Ethernet modem made by DEC. A DECOM-AA is a dual-cable modem; the DECOM-BA is a single-cable version.
DECrouter 200	A dedicated router with 8 asynchronous DDCMP ports and one Ethernet connection.
DECSA	*DEC Synchronous Adapter* A general-purpose DECnet Router. The same piece of hardware also forms the basis for X.25 and SNA gateways.
DECserver	DEC terminal servers.
DECtalk	A piece of DEC hardware that can "speak" ASCII files.
DECUS	*Digital Equipment Corporation User Society* DEC user group.
DECwindows	A DEC windowing system based on the Postscript Imaging System and the X Windows System standards.
DED	*Dynamically Established Datalink* A DECnet Phase V feature that allows a data link to be established on demand, such as a dial-up leased line or an X.25 switched virtual circuit.
DEFTR	*DEC Frequency Translator* DEC's frequency translator for single-channel broadband systems.

DELNI   *DEC Local Network Interconnect* "Ethernet in a Can." A multiport transceiver made by DEC.

DELUA   *DEC Local Unibus Adapter* An Ethernet controller made by DEC for UNIBUS processors.

DEMPR   *DEC Multiport Repeater* A piece of DEC networking hardware that can connect up to eight ThinWire Ethernet segments and optionally connect them to a backbone cable or DELNI.

DEMSA   *DEC MicroServer* A new generation of routers and gateways based on the MicroVAX II architecture as opposed to the PDP-based architecture of the DECSA.

DEQNA   *DEC Q-Bus Network Adapter* A DEC Ethernet controller for Q-bus systems.

DEREP   *DEC Repeater* DEC Ethernet repeaters.

DES   *Data Encryption Standard* One type of encryption scheme.

DESTA   *DEC Station Adapter* A type of DEC ThinWire transceiver.

DFM   *DEC Frequency Multiplexor* A series of DEC products including X.25 asynchronous PADs and multiplexors.

DFS   *Distributed File Service (or System)* A DEC product similar to the Network File System (NFS). Both allow remote files to appear as though they were locally mounted on a workstation, allowing diskless nodes. DFS uses the DNS nameserver.

DHCF   *Digital Host Command Facility* A DEC software product that, in conjunction with IBM's Host Command Facility, allows an IBM terminal user to log onto a DEC network.

DHV11   A synchronous communications board for Q-bus (MicroVAX) systems. Less powerful than the DSV11.

DIA	*Document Interchange Architecture* An IBM architecture for the interchange of messages. Usually used in conjunction with the Document Content Architecture (DCA). Implemented in a product called DISOSS.
DISOSS	*Distributed Office Support System* An IBM product that serves as a distributed library of documents. See DIA/DCA.
DLAL	*Dual letter acronym listing* See MLAL.
DMA	*Direct memory access* Allows a device on a computer to access main memory without a CPU interrupt.
DML	*Data manipulation language* A language, such as SQL, used for retrieving and manipulating data in a database system.
DMB32	DEC BI bus-based communications controller.
DMF32	DEC UNIBUS-based communications controller.
DNA	*Digital Network Architecture* Architecture for DECnet.
DNS	*Digital Name Service or Domain nameserver* A part of DECnet Phase V. Provides name translation, such as node name to DECnet address translation. Also used for the location of DFS files. Also a TCP/IP service provider that translates partial names into full names for IP addresses for machines and users.
DoD	*Department of Defense* Makes a $10 billion company like DEC look like your local ACE hardware store.
DOS	*Digital Operating System* Microsoft operating system for IBM/PCs.
DOS/VSE	*Digital Operating System / Virtual Storage Extended* An IBM operating system used on 370 architecture mainframes.
dpi	*Dots per inch* A measure of the resolution of printers or scanners.

DQS   *Distributed Queueing Service* A DEC software product that allows print files submitted to a local queue to be automatically sent to a remote queue.

DSA   *Digital Storage Architecture* DEC architecture for mass storage devices and controllers.

DSRI   *Digital Standard Relational Interface* A DEC standard calling sequence for database applications. Allows any DSRI-compatible user interface to access and DSRI-compatible data repository.

DSRVB   DEC terminal server model number.

DSS   *Distributed system services* A family of DEC software including the Digital Name Service (DNS) and the Distributed File Service (DFS).

DSV11   A high performance Q-bus synchronous communications board.

DTE   *Data terminal equipment* An X.25 term referring to the interface to users' equipment as opposed to the DCE interface to the network.

DTF   *Data transfer facility* DEC software products that run in both VMS and IBM environments and permit the integration of both types of file systems from within the Digital Command Language.

DU   *Data unit* Part of the OSI File Transfer Access and Management (FTAM) protocols.

dX   DEC software product for transfer of WPS documents into other formats.

E.163   CCITT numbering scheme for public switched telephone networks.

Easynet   DEC's internal communications network.

EBCDIC   *Extended Binary Coded Decimal Interchange Code* A character code scheme used in IBM environments. See ASCII.

ECC	*Error-correcting code* Feature of the Digital Storage Architecture used in error detection. Similar to a CRC.
EDE	*Electronic Document Exchange* A DEC product that allows revisable form document transfer with DISOSS libraries. See also DDXF. EDE-W is a similar program for document interchange between Wang and DEC systems.
EDI	*Electronic data interchange* A generic term referring to the communication of information between different organizations by computer instead of paper. For example, submitting a purchase order by modem instead of paper or fax.
EDT	Standard DEC editor on the VMS operating system.
EGP	*Exterior Gateway Protocol* A means for updating routing tables in the Internet environment.
ELK	*External Link Interface* A programming library that allows an application to link to a Videotex (VTX) system on a remote DECnet node.
ELXSI	Manufacturer of a parallel processing minicomputer that has a variety of DEC emulation tools.
EMA	*Enterprise Management Architecture* A DEC architecture for network management user interfaces that can work with multiple displays and protocols.
EMACS	An extensible editor developed at M.I.T. based on the LISP programming language.
Email	*Electronic mail* Software/networks that allow the exchange of messages between users.
EMBOS	*Elxsi message-based Operating System* Operating system for the Elxsi, on top of which a variety of Unix and VMS emulation operating systems can run.
EMS	Elxsi's VMS emulator.

end node   A DECnet term referring to a member of the network that can do everything but route packets through on behalf of other nodes. Ultrix, MS-DOS, and third-party implementations of DECnet are all end nodes.

EOF   *End of file* A mark that tells the file system that it has reached the end of a file.

ERCO   *Entry rules control object* Provides validation checks for the OSI virtual terminal service in field mode.

Ethernet   A data link protocol jointly developed by Intel, Xerox, and DEC and subsequently adopted by the IEEE as a standard. Several upper-layer protocols, including DECnet, TCP/IP, and XNS, use the Ethernet as an underlying transport mechanism. Ethernet is to be contrasted with other data link protocols such as the token ring, DDCMP, or SDLC.

ETHERnim   *Ethernet Network Integrity Monitor* A DEC product for monitoring Ethernets.

F.300   A set of CCITT recommendations for Videotex systems.

FADU   *File access data unit* The unit of access in the OSI FTAM service.

FAL   *File Access Listener* A process invoked across the network by a user trying to access data on nonlocal systems. An FAL is a DAP-speaking process invoked by the Record Management Services on the local node.

FDDI   *Fiber Distributed Data Interface* A 100-mbps fiber optic local area network standard based on the token ring.

FFT   *Final form text* A version of IBM's Document Content Architecture (DCA).

field

A term used in designing forms-based systems such as database applications. A field is a portion of the screen used for data input which is automatically mapped to a variable. The field may have attributes such as reverse video or default values.

FI.FMD

Function Interpreters for Function Management Data IBM's presentation layer protocol for SNA.

frame

A series of bytes of data encapsulated with a header. The data link layer sends frames of data back and forth. "Frame" is often used interchangably with "packet," although technically a packet refers to data from the network layer of the protocol stack. A packet is thus usually contained inside of a frame.

FTAM

File Transfer, Access and Management The OSI application layer service that provides access to virtual file stores on foreign systems. Similar to the DNA DAP protocols in purpose.

FTP

File transfer protocol An upper-layer TCP/IP service used in the Arpanet implementation for the copying of files across the network.

full-duplex

A data communications term that indicates that both ends of a communications link can transmit simultaneously. Contrasted with half-duplex where only one side can transmit at one time.

Gandalf

A manufacturer of communications equipment including data switches.

GAP

Gateway Access Protocol A protocol used by applications software to access DECnet Gateways. The 3270 access routine, for example, would use GAP to access an SNA Gateway.

Gateway

There are two somewhat conflicting definitions of gateway, both used in networking. In the general sense, a gateway is a computer that connects two different networks together. Usually, this means two different kinds of networks such as SNA and DECnet. In TCP/IP terminology, however, a gateway connects two separately administered subnetworks, which may or may not be running the same networking protocols.

Gbytes *Gigabytes* One billion bytes of data.

GGP *Gateway-to-Gateway Protocol* An interior protocol in TCP/IP similar in functionality to RIP.

GM *General Motors* Primary supporter of the Manufacturing Automation Protocol (MAP). They also make cars.

GOSIP *Government OSI Protocols* U.S. government version of the international OSI standards.

granularity A term used in lock managers on an operating system. When the lock manager locks an entire file, this is locking with course granularity. When the lock manager locks a single record, this is fine granularity. Granularity is one of the factors that influence the performance of a particular application, such as a DBMS.

H4000 DEC's baseband Ethernet transceiver.

half-duplex See full-duplex.

HASP *Houston Automatic Spooling Program* One of the original implementations of the remote job entry function on IBM equipment. Still used as a common denominator, in conjunction with bisync, for RJE functions.

Hewlett Packard Makers of a wide range of equipment that competes with or complements the DEC product line, including laser printers and minicomputers.

HDLC *High-level data link control* International Standard Organization's data link protocol. Used in OSI and X.25 networks. Alternative protocols include SDLC in the IBM networks or DDCMP in the DEC networks.

hop	A term used in DECnet routing calculations. A hop is one data link. A path to the final destination on a DECnet is a series of hops away from the origin. Each hop has a cost associated with it, allowing the calculation of the least-cost path.
HSC	*Hierarchical Storage Controller* Stand-alone disk and tape controller used in clusters using the CI bus. The HSC is actually a modified PDP computer that has been optimized as a mass storage controller.
IBM	*International Business Machines Corporation* Big.
ICMP	*Internet Control Message Protocol* Protocol used by the IP layer of TCP/IP for exchanging routing control messages.
IDI	*Initial domain identifier* Part of an OSI address. Goes after the authority and format identifiers. For example, the IDI for a telephone address might be the country code.
IDMS	Cullinet's database management system for IBM systems.
IEEE	*Institute of Electronic and Electrical Engineers* A leading standard-setting group in the United States. IEEE 488 is a popular standard for real-time data collection. IEEE 802 is the standard for various types of local area networks.
IMS	*Information Management System* Database management software from IBM based on the hierarchical data management model.
Ingres	A popular relational database management system that runs on a variety of operating system platforms.
Interleaf	A desktop publishing program that runs on VAXstations and Sun workstations.
Interlink	A manufacturer of SNA gateways.

Internet	A collection of networks with a common routing backbone. Encompasses public networks such as NSFnet and private networks such as those at various universities. Also refers to the Internet Protocols that are part of TCP/IP and are used for routing data in the Internet.
I/O	*Input/output* Generic term for transfer of data from main memory to either a disk drive, terminal, printer, or other device.
IOP	*Input/output processor* Term used by Unix-based minicomputer manufacturers to refer to the I/O subsystems.
IP	*Internet Protocol* Layer 3 of the TCP/IP network protocols.
IPDS	*Intelligent Printer Data Stream* A component of IBM's System Application Architecture (SAA).
IPM	*Interpersonal messaging service* The part of the X.400 protocols that defines what the header of a message looks like. The message transfer service (MTS) then defines what the envelope that the message goes in looks like.
IP/TCP	Software product sold by the Wollongong Group. Allows VMS nodes to participate in TCP/IP networks. A similar product is sold by Excelan.
IRDS	*Information Resources Dictionary System* An ANSI and ISO standard for data dictionaries.
ISAM	*Indexed sequential access method* A file structure that allows random access to data via an index and then sequential access to data after that.
ISDN	*Integrated Services Digital Network* A new international communications standard that allows the integration of voice and data on a common transport mechanism.
ISO	*International Standards Organization* International standard-making body responsible for the OSI network standards and the ISO reference model.

ISPF   *Interactive System Productivity Facility* An IBM product that runs on the TSO and CMS user environments. ISPF provides a series of menus (dialogs) for use on a 3270 terminal that allow the user to bypass a command language interface to the operating system.

JCL   *Job Control Language* Language used for batch processing on IBM mainframes.

JES   *Job Entry Subsystem* Types of processes on IBM mainframes that accept JCL.

JTM   *Job transfer and manipulation* An OSI layer 7 standard similar in function to a remote job entry (RJE) service.

Kbps   *Kilobits per second* Thousands of bits per second.

Kbytes   *Kilobytes* Thousands of bytes of information.

Kermit   A popular file transfer protocol developed by Columbia University. Because Kermit runs in most operating environments, it provides an easy method of file transfer.

kernel   A term used in operating systems. The kernel shields the low-level functioning of the operating system from high-level interfaces, such as user shells.

kerning   A term used in typography which refers to the process of putting variable-size spaces between letters and words to produce an even alignment.

LA100   A DEC dot matrix printer commonly found in machine rooms as console printers.

LAN   *Local area network* Usually refers to Ethernet or token ring networks.

LAP   *Link access protocol* A protocol for accessing a data link. Examples are LAP B used in the X.25 environment and LAP D used in the ISDN environment.

LAT

Local area transport A proprietary DEC architecture for terminal servers on Ethernet networks designed to conserve bandwidth and offload processing from hosts.

LAVC

Local Area VAX Cluster An adaptation of the System Communication Architecture (SCA) to run over the Ethernet instead of a CI bus. Used to enable MicroVAXs to operate as diskless nodes.

LLC

Logical link control A term used in the IEEE local area network model. The logical link control layer presents a uniform interface to the user of the data link service, usually a network layer. Underneath the LLC sublayer of the data link layer is a media access control sublayer. The MAC sublayer is responsible for taking a packet of data from the LLC and submitting it to the particular data link being used (such as Ethernet or token ring).

LN03

DEC's first 8-pages-per-minute laser printer. LN03 is a proprietary language that has been superseded by the Scriptprinter, which uses the same engine and the PostScript page description language.

Logical name

A Digital Command Language feature which allows the logical naming of devices, permitting a layer of separation between the physical configuration of a system and the logical view seen by the user process. Similar to the Unix concept of an environmental variable.

LPS40

DEC's 40-pages-per-minute laser printer. Uses the PostScript page description language.

LSP

Link state packet Routing control information message exchanged in a Phase V DECnet.

LTM

LAN Traffic Monitor DEC software that uses a LAN Bridge 100 to monitor an Ethernet network.

LU	*Logical unit* An IBM term in SNA which refers to a software or microcode program that uses the network. For example, a terminal connected to a 3274 cluster controller is represented by a LU2 on that cluster controller.
LU6.2	See APPC.
MAC	*Media access control* A communications term referring to the method of controlling access to a broadcast media, such as an Ethernet. The Ethernet uses CSMA/CD as a MAC-layer protocol. See also LLC.
mail-11	The original mail routing protocol used on VMS mail. Mailbus is a more modern routing architecture.
mailbox	A VMS concept used for interprocess communication. Processes leave messages for each other in a mailbox.
Mailbus	A DEC architecture which provides a common message-handling system on a DECnet.
MAP	*Manufacturing Automation Protocol* An OSI-related application sponsored by General Motors and endorsed by a great many users and vendors.
MB	*Megabytes* Million bytes of information.
MBps	*million bytes per second*
mbps	*million bits per second*
Mbytes	*Megabytes* million bytes of information.
MC68000	A series of CPU chips manufactured by Motorola. These form the basis for many Unix-based workstations, including the MAC II and the Sun 3 series.
MCI	Long distance telephone company.

MEN	*Management event notification* Part of DECnet Phase V network management. Used for sending information about events across the network. See MICE.
MHS	*Message-handling system* A system of protocols, such as X.400, used to exchange messages, such as electronic mail.
MICE	*Management information, control, and exchange* A DECnet Phase V network management protocol. See MEN.
MicroVAX	A series of DEC processors using the Q-bus and competing in the workstation market with Sun and Apollo.
Minitel	A French terminal used for Videotex applications.
MIPS	*Million instructions per second* A measure of CPU processing power. Different machine architectures use different instruction sets, so comparisons of MIPS across products is highly misleading. MIPS also do not take into account the mix of other resources such as bus speeds, I/O processors, disk drive throughput, main memory, network controllers, and other components of a system.
MLAL	*Multiletter acronym listing.*
MMS	*Manufacturing messaging service* Part of the MAP protocols used for communicating with robots, programmable controllers, and other devices.
Modem	*Modulator / demodulator* A device that takes digital data from a computer and encodes it in analog form for transmission over a phone line. Modems are also used to connect computers to an analog broadband system.
MONITOR	A VMS tool used to examine the current status of a system.

MOP	*Maintenance Operation Protocol* A DECnet protocol used to efficiently download large files. Used for downline loading of the operating system for one component from another system.
MSCP	*Mass Storage Control Protocol* The protocol used by HSC storage controllers to communicate with device drivers on the VAXs in a cluster.
MS-DOS	*Microsoft-Digital Operating System* Microsoft's version of PC-DOS.
MTA	*Message transfer agent* An X.400 term referring to the collections of network members responsible for transferring messages. The final MTA delivers the message to a user agent which is concerned with reading, editing, and other types of interaction with the end user.
MTS	*Message transfer service* The X.400 protocols that govern the exchange of envelopes of information. The IPMS defines the content of the envelope.
Multicasting	A term used in Ethernet addressing. A multicast address is a group address that is meant for a certain subset of users on the Ethernet. LAT nodes communicate their current status with each other using a multicast address. To be contrasted with a broadcast address which is received by all users on the Ethernet.
Multiplex	A software product made by Network Innovations (owned by Apple) that retrieves information from a variety of VAX database packages and translates it into a variety of different PC formats.
multipoint	A data link layer concept in which multiple nodes share a common physical media. In a multipoint situation, a single node is the controller of the line and polls all tributaries periodically to see if they wish to send data. This is in contrast to multiaccess media like Ethernet where any node may send without permission.

MUXserver   A DEC product that combines a multiplexer and a terminal server in one device. Allows remote multiplexed traffic to access LAT-based services.

MVS/TSO   *Multiple virtual storage / time sharing option* MVS is an IBM operating system. TSO is the interactive subsystem, as opposed to a system like JES used for batch processing.

NAK   *Negative acknowledgment* Response to non-receipt or receipt of a corrupt packet of information.

namespace   A term used in DEC's Distibuted Name Server which refers to the collection of all names on the network. The namespace is then distributed among multiple clearinghouses.

NAU   *Network addressable unit* The boundary of an IBM SNA network. Logical and physical units are examples of NAUs.

NCP   *Network Control Program* A DEC user interface to the network management layer of the Digital Network Architecture.

ND   *NetDisk* A Sun protocol for loading a raw disk over the network, similar in function to DEC's MOP protocols.

NETACP   *Network ancillary control process* A type of VMS process that provides the link between the user of the network and the I/O drivers (NETDRIVER).

Netbios   *Network basic input / output system* Used in DOS as the interface to the network for accessing information. Similar in function to the DNA DAP protocols.

NETDRIVER   A VMS process that provides read and write services over the network for DECnet applications. NETDRIVER would then communicate with a physical driver that used Ethernet, DDCMP, CI, or another supported data link protocol.

NeWS	*Network Extensible Window System* A windowing environment from Sun Microsystems based on the Postscript language and a proprietary window control protocol.
NEXT	Computer company founded by Steve Jobs, formerly of Apple.
NFS	*Network File System* An extension to TCP/IP developed by Sun Microsystems and licensed free of charge. NFS allows files on remote nodes of a network to appear locally connected.
NFT	*Network file transfer* An interactive utility that gives access to remote data using the DAP protocols.
NIC	*Network Information Center* A facility located at the Stanford Research Institute that administers Internet addresses.
NICE	*Network Information and Control Exchange* A DECnet protocol used for the exchange of network management information.
NML	*Network Management Listener* A VMS process that communicates with a network management interface on another node to provide information about the local node.
node	A member of a network. A VAX is a node on a DECnet. A PC is sometimes a node on the network and sometimes it just emulates a terminal and thus is not a node.
nonrouting node	See end node.
Novell	Makers of PC-based local area networks.
NPS	*NMCC protocol server* A portion of the NMCC software that interfaces to the network.
NPSI	*Network Packet Switching Interface* A type of IBM software that allows SNA data to be carried over an X.25 network to another SNA environment.

NSFnet	*National Science Foundation Network* An NSF-funded network to link researchers to computing facilities.
NSP	*Network Services Protocol* A protocol used at the end-to-end communication layer of the Digital Network Architecture to assure reliable communications.
NSUID	*Namespace unique identifier* See namespace. It is possible (though somewhat unusual) to have multiple DNS namespaces on a single network.
OA	*Office automation* Whatever's in Datamation this month.
OEM	*Original equipment manufacturer* Company that sells equipment which is embedded in another company's products. The other company is known as a value-added reseller (VAR) of the product.
O/R Address	*Originator/recipient address* A valid X.400 address.
OS/2	IBM's replacement for DOS.
OSAK	*OSI Applications Kernel* A set of program libraries sold by DEC as the interface to layer 5 of the OSI model.
OSI	*Open Systems Interconnect* The International Standards Organization's implementation of the ISO reference model.
packet	A general term used in networking to refer to a message sent to a peer entity in the network.
PAD	*Packet assembler/disassembler* A piece of hardware used in packet switched networks to allow asynchronous terminals to participate in the network.

Paging	A memory management technique in a virtual memory operating system. Only a few parts (pages) of a program are actually in memory. When a new part is needed, it is paged into memory.
PAM	*Protocol assist module* A piece of hardware on a DECSA to provide higher performance for protocol processing.
PAR	*Positive acknowledgment retransmit* A method of assuring reliable communications used by the DDCMP data link protocol.
PBX	*Private branch exchange* A sophisticated switch used to route telephone calls and data from incoming trunk lines to the appropriate user's desk. Value-added functions include call forwarding and voice mail systems.
PC	*Personal computer* IBM series of computers or clones.
PC-DOS	*Personal Computer-Digital Operating System* IBM's version of Microsoft's operating system.
PCSA	*Personal Computing Systems Architecture* DEC Architecture for PC-DOS systems, including the DECnet/DOS software.
PDL	*Page description language* PostScript is an example of a PDL.
PDP	*Programmable data processor* A series of Q-bus-based 16-bit minicomputers manufactured by DEC.
PDS	*Premises Distribution System* AT&T cabling system.
PDU	*Protocol data unit* A packet of information conforming to a protocol, such as a data link protocol (e.g., Ethernet) or a network layer protocol (e.g., Connection Oriented Network Service). Usually used in the context of the OSI architecture but the concept applies to any layered network architecture.

P/FM	*PBX/Facilties Management* DEC software for managing PBX traffic.
Phase IV	The current phase of DECnet.
PHONE	A VMS program that allows interactive two-way conversations over a DECnet.
PID	*Process identification number* Used to identify each process running on an operating system. The VMS lexical function F$PID returns the value of PID.
portal	A term used in Ethernet protocols. There may be several different users of the Ethernet service, such as LAT, DNA, and TCP/IP. Each of these users is given a portal, or identification number, in the portal database. Incoming packets are then distributed to the appropriate portal.
PostScript	A page description language developed by Adobe Systems. Widely adopted by many vendors as a de facto standard.
ppm	*Pages per minute* Rating measure for laser printers.
PrE	*Printer emulation* DEC SNA access routine which allows a VAX to emulate an IBM printer.
PRMD	*Private management domain* An X.400 domain. See ADMD.
PROFS	IBM office automation system that runs on the VM operating system.
PSI	*Packet-switch interface* DEC software to allow a VAX to participate in an X.25 network.
PSN	*Packet switched network* An X.25 network.
PS profiles	*Presentation services profiles* An SNA term used to allow two NAUs to negotiate an acceptable subset of presentation functions they can both support.

PTT *Poste Téléphone et Télégraphe* A government provider of communications functions in most European countries.

PU *Physical unit* An SNA term used to refer to different types of hardware in the network. A 3274 cluster controller is a PU type 2 (PU2).

Q-bus The peripheral bus used on MicroVAX and PDP computers.

QIO *Queue input/output* Device-dependent layer in the VMS operating system. See RMS.

QOS *Quality of service* A series of negotiable parameters in X.25 and OSI network implementations.

RAM *Random access memory* Dynamic memory, sometimes known as main memory or core.

RARP *Reverse Address Resolution Protocol* A TCP/IP protocol which provides the reverse function of ARP. Used by diskless nodes when they first initialize to find their Internet address.

rcp *Remote copy program* An upper layer TCP/IP service found in the Berkeley Unix implementation for copying files. See FTP for the Arpanet equivalent.

Rdb DEC's relational database management system.

ReGis *Remote graphics instruction set* A set of DEC protocols used in the VT240 and 241 graphics terminals.

RFT *Revisable form text* A version of IBM's Document Content Architecture.

RGB *Red, green, blue* A method of representing colors as a mix of the three primary colors.

RIP *Routing Information Protocol* An alternative to EGP used for updating routing tables in the Internet environment.

RISC

Reduced instruction set computer Generic name for CPUs that use a simpler instruction set than more traditional designs. Examples are the IBM PC/RT, Pyramid minicomputers, and the Sun 4 (SPARC) Workstations.

RJ11

Standard modular jack developed by AT&T. Used for telephones and data communications. Being replaced by the RJ45 which is the same size but has more wires.

RJE

Remote job entry Facility for submitting a job to a computer for execution. Card readers were early RJE stations. Usually means software that emulates RJE stations.

rlogin

Remote log-in Berkeley TCP/IP command to log onto a remote node.

RMS

Record management services A common I/O interface for VMS used for access to local data via QIO calls and remote data via the DAP protocol.

root

Unix superuser. The one account on a Unix system that has privileged access.

rotary

An example of a rotary is when several outgoing lines are available for a dial-out service. Rather than make the user ask for each line by name, a rotary service connects the user to the first available line. A rotary is thus multiple instances of an all-accessible service using one address. The service provider intercepts all requests for that address and farms them out to a specific address.

Routers

Dedicated hardware used to route traffic on a network. The alternative is to use a portion of a general-purpose system such as a VAX.

RPC

Remote procedure call Part of the Network File System. This is the layer 5 (session layer) services built on top of TCP/IP.

RS-232-C   A physical interface standard, used frequently for connecting asynchronous devices such as terminals. Developed by the Electronic Industries Association to define the electrical and mechanical link between a DTE and a DCE.

RSM   *Remote Systems Manager* DEC software for managing remote MicroVAX computers.

RSTS   *Resource-sharing timesharing system* PDP-based operating system.

RSX   Yet another PDP-based operating system. VMS systems running in compatibility mode are able to execute RSX-executable images.

RT/PC   IBM 32-bit workstation based on a RISC architecture.

RU   *Request unit* A part of IBM's SNA architecture. A series of request units are sent from one session participant to the other; they are then processed by upper layers of the protocol stack.

SA482   DEC disk cluster with 2.5 Gbyte of capacity.

SAA   *Systems Application Architecture* IBM Architecture to present common user, communications, and programming interfaces across multiple hardware platforms and operating systems.

SAF   *System Authorization Facility* A family of IBM security products.

SASE   *Specific application service element* Application layer concept in the OSI network architecture. Refers to special purpose services such as the job transfer and manipulation (JTM) facility.

SCA   *System Communication Architecture* The DEC architecture for Clusters.

Scriptprinter DEC's Postscript printer. Uses the same engine as the LN03 laser printer but with a different controller board.

SCS
System communication services Software services used in a VAX Cluster to provide internode communication. SCS is the lowest level of the System Communication Architecture.

SCSI
Small computer standard interface Pronounced "scuzzy." A standard for connecting disk drives to disk controllers, used typically in small multiuser computers. Third-party vendors sell SCSI boards for MicroVAXs.

SDLC
Synchronous data link control IBM's data link protocol used in SNA networks.

SER
Satellite Equipment Room One part of the DECconnect cabling system.

session
Networking term used to refer to the logical stream of data flowing between two programs communicating over a network. Note that there are usually many different sessions originating from one particular node of a network.

shell
A term that usually refers to the user interface on an operating system. On Unix systems, the C shell or the Bourne shell are the primary user interfaces. Contrasts with the kernel, which interacts with the computer at low levels.

SIXEL
A standard format used for bit-mapped images. Complements ReGIS, which is a DEC format for line-oriented images.

skulker
A term used in DEC's distributed name service. A skulker is a background process which assures that all replicas of a portion of the namespace are consistent with the master portion.

slot
The upper layer of the Local Area Transport Architecture. A slot holds data from one particular user. Several slots are contained in an LAT packet.

Smartstar
A DSRI-compatible application development environment made by Signal Technology.

SMP	*Symmetric multiprocessor* Term used by DEC for true parallel processing in version V of VMS.
SMTP	*Standard Mail Transfer Protocol* The TCP/IP protocol for a message handling system.
SNA	*Systems Network Architecture* IBM network architecture.
SNADS	*SNA distribution services* An architecture used for transferring messages in an SNA environment, similar to X.400.
Sniffer	A network analyzer made by Network General. The Sniffer was used to produce the screen dumps of network packets in this book.
SOH	*Start of header* The beginning of a DDCMP message.
SPARC	*Scalable Processor Architecture* A reduced instruction set (RISC) processor developed by Sun and licensed by several vendors including AT&T and Texas Instruments. Used in the Sun 4 family of workstations.
SQL	*Structured query language* ANSI standard data manipulation language used in most relational database systems.
SS7	*Signalling System 7* Protocol related to ISDN. Directs how the interior of an ISDN network is managed.
SSCP	*System services control point* A network addressable unit in IBM's SNA architecture. Resides on a mainframe and is the central point for that domain of an SNA network.
star coupler	Device used to connect different nodes of a VAX Cluster that use the CI bus.
STE	*Signalling terminal exchange* Equipment in an X.25 network that forms the boundary of a network. Communication between different X.25 management domains is between STEs using the X.75 protocols.

subnet

A term used to denote any networking technology that makes all nodes connected to it appear to be one hop away. In other words, the user of the subnet can communicate directly to all other nodes on the subnet. A subnet could be X.25, Ethernet, a token ring, ISDN, or a point-to- point link. A collection of subnets, together with a routing or network layer, combine to form a network.

Sun Microsystems

Manufacturer of Unix-based workstations.

SVID

System V interface definition AT&T sponsored definition used to determine the compatibility of different implementations of System V.

Sybase

Manufacturer of a hybrid database system which uses general-purpose hardware such as a VAX or Sun Workstation and optimizes it for relational database operations.

symbiont

Symbiosis is the bringing together of two different worlds. A symbiont is a VMS process that takes disk files and prepares them for a printer.

SYSGEN

A program in VMS used to alter system-wide parameters such as AWSTIME.

SYS$COMMAND

A VMS logical name that points to the device that will be used to input commands for the Digital Command Language. Points to a terminal device (i.e., tta0:) for an interactive session or a command file for a batch job.

SYS$ERROR

A VMS logical name that points to the device used to output error messages for the current user.

SYS$INPUT

A VMS logical name that points to the device used to input data (as opposed to commands) for the current user.

SYS$LOGIN

A VMS logical name that points to the default log-in directory for the current user.

SYS$OUTPUT   A VMS logical name that points to the device used to output results (as opposed to errors) for the current user.

SYS$PRINT   A VMS logical name that points to the default print queue for the current user.

SYS$SYSTEM   A VMS logical name that points to the location of system executable images.

T1   1.544 mbps communications line provided by long-distance common carriers.

TCP/IP   *Transmission Control Protocol / Internet Protocol* Department of Defense sponsored networking protocol, used frequently in Unix environments.

Teamdata   DEC-developed user interface for DSRI compatible relational data bases.

Telenet   Packet switched network service offered by GTE.

TELNET   Upper-layer TCP/IP service for Arpanet implementations. Allows users to log onto remote nodes.

terrabyte   One trillion bytes (1,000,000,000,000).

ThinWire   Thinner, and cheaper, version of baseband coax cable used for Ethernet networks. Also called CheaperNet.

TK50   DEC tape cartridge which holds 95 Mbytes of information.

token bus   An alternative to token ring and Ethernet local area networks. Used in the MAP protocols. The token bus uses a multiple access protocol, but the device that "owns" the token is the only one that can send data.

token ring   A local area network protocol in which computers are connected together in a ring. A node waits until a token is passed around the ring, at which point it may send data. When it has finished sending, it releases the token and passes it to the next node. See FDDI.

TPDU

Transport protocol data unit A packet of information exchanged between two transport layer entities in an OSI network. See PDU.

transceiver

A term used in Ethernet networks. The transceiver is the hardware device that connects to the Ethernet media, often a piece of coax cable. The transceiver is then connected to an Ethernet controller on the host system.

TransLAN

A wide area extended Ethernet bridge manufactured by Vitalink.

TSAP

Transport service access point Each layer of the OSI network has a series of service access points, sometimes known as service primitives, that clearly define the functions that that layer can perform on behalf of clients.

TTRT

Target token rotation time A term used in FDDI to set performance parameters. The TTRT serves as a measure of expected delay and is used, among other things, to set time-out parameters.

TTY

Teletype A line-oriented terminal.

tuple

A term used in relational database systems. A tuple is the equivalent of a record in a file management system and corresonds to one row of data in a table.

twisted pair

A pair of wires (or several pairs of wires) such as is used to connect telephones to distribution panels. Twisted pair is also being used as a physical transmission media for Ethernet, token ring, and other forms of data links.

Tymnet

Public packet-switched network based on X.25 owned by McDonnell Douglas.

UDP

User Datagram Protocol Used in TCP/IP as an alternative to TCP for unacknowledged datagrams.

UIC

User identification code VMS code used to uniquely identify every user on the system.

UIL	*User interface language* A DECwindows concept that allows the user interface to be modified for different countries without modifying the source code of the program.
Ultrix	DEC's version of 4.3BSD Unix.
Unibus	A peripheral bus used on 11/780 and 8600 VAX processors.
Unix	Operating system developed and trademarked by American Telephone and Telegraph. Unix is a pun on the Multics operating system.
Usenet	Network of Unix users. This is a somewhat informal network of loosely coupled nodes that agree to exchange information in the form of electronic mail and a bulletin board.
UUCP	*Unix-to-Unix copy program* The standard Unix utility used to exchange information between any two Unix nodes. Used as the basis for Usenet.
V.24	A CCITT standard for the interconnection of DTE and DCE equipment.
V.29	CCITT standard for 4.8- to 9.6-kbps modems.
V.35	CCITT physical interface standard for high-speed data transmission.
VAR	*Value-added reseller* Company that embeds another company's products into a more sophisticated product.
VAS	*VTX applications service* A library used to develop applications on DEC's VTX software.
VAX	*Virtual address extension* A hardware series made by DEC.
VAX 11/780	A single Vax processing unit processor. Somewhat equivalent to a one MIP computer.
VAX 6200	A series of VAX parallel processors with 1 to 6 CPUs using the XMI bus.
VAX 8600	A 4-VPU computer.

VAX 8700	A 6-VPU computer that forms the basis for the Bi-bus-based VAX computers.
VAX 8840	A parallel processor with four 8700 CPUs. Roughly 24 VPU of power.
VAX Clusters	DEC Clusters that operate on the CI bus rather than over the Ethernet.
VAXeln	DEC real-time operating system.
VAXlink	A family of products that allows access from a DSRI-compatible user interface to a series of IBM-based data repositories.
VAXmate	DEC 80286-based PC/AT clone, with the addition of an Ethernet controller and a different keyboard.
VAXNotes	DEC conferencing software.
VAXstations	MicroVAX workstations with a 15-inch or 19-inch bit-mapped graphic screen and graphics co-processor.
VIDA	DEC DSRI product that allows access to Cullinet IDMS databases using any DSRI user interface.
VIA	*VAX Information Architecture* A related set of software systems sold by DEC for data management systems.
VISTA	*VTX Infobase Structure Tool and Assister* Softw are package for maintaining VTX databases.
Vitalink	Makers of the TransLAN wide area Ethernet bridge.
VM	*Virtual machine* An IBM operating system that permits guest operating systems, such as MVS, to reside on top of it. Usually used in conjunction with the CMS user interface.
VM	*Virtual memory* An operating system concept that refers to the address space of a program. A paging system maps virtual memory to the limited physical memory pages as needed.

VMS	*Virtual memory system* A DEC proprietary operating system for VAX computers.
VMS/SNA	DEC software that allows a VAX with the appropriate synchronous communications board to function as an SNA gateway.
VOSAK	*VAX OSI Applications Kernel* DEC programming library for the OSI session layer.
VOTS	*VAX OSI Transport Services* DEC OSI software that implements layer 4 of the ISO reference model.
VPU	*Vax processing unit* A DEC measure of processing power. The 11/780 is equivalent to one VPU. A VPU is roughly analogous to a MIP although these numbers cannot be compared across product lines because an instruction is different on each computer because of different instruction sets.
VSAM	*Virtual sequential access method* File organization method used in IBM environments for direct access files. Similar to ISAM (indexed sequential access method).
VT	*Virtual terminal* OSI application layer service to allow remote log-in to other nodes. Also a series of terminals, such as the DEC VT100 or VT241.
VT100	A series of DEC terminals. The VT300 series is the current family of DEC terminals. VT100 and VT200 are a de facto industry standard, meaning that most software packages include terminal drivers for these types of terminals.
VTAM	*Virtual Telecommunications Access Method* An IBM software system that provides the interface to an SNA network.
VTX	*Videotex* DEC's Videotex software package.
WAN	*Wide area network* Sometimes also used to mean work area network or a small subnetwork for a work group.

Wollongong Group	Makers of the IP/TCP software for VMS and a Unix emulator for VMS called Eunice.
WORM	*Write once/read many* A type of optical disk that can be written locally, contrasted to CD-ROM disk. Also used for fishing.
WSDEFAULT	A VMS parameter that controls the size of a user working set.
WSEXTENT	A VMS parameter that controls the size of extensions for a user working set.
WSQUOTA	A VMS parameter that controls the quota of a user working set.
X.3	CCITT standard for a packet assembler/disassembler (PAD).
X.21	CCITT standard for circuit-switched networks.
X.21bis	CCITT standard for connecting to public data networks using a V-series modem.
X.25	CCITT standard for packet-switched networks.
X.28	CCITT protocols for an asynchronous terminal to communicate with an X.3 PAD.
X.29	CCITT protocols for a synchronous DTE (a host) to control and communicate with an X.3 PAD.
X.75	CCITT standard for interconnecting separate X.25 networks.
X.121	CCITT numbering plan for public data networks.
X.400	CCITT standard for message-handling systems.
X.500	Emerging CCITT standard for directories for X.400 networks.
XDR	*eXternal Data Representation* A machine independent protocol for representing information used in the network file system (NFS).

XI	IBM product for using X.25 in a heterogeneous environment, as opposed to NPSI which uses X.25 as a transport mechanism for SNA.
XID	*Exchange identification* An HDLC frame used when a new node attaches to the physical medium.
XMI	A 100-Mbps bus used to connect CPUs, BI buses and memory on the VAX 6200 series of parallel processors.
Xmodem	A set of protocols used for error free file transfer over voice grade lines. Similar to Kermit, Xmodem is used to transfer binary and ASCII files from different hosts that are not running a common set of networking protocols.
XNS	*Xerox Network System* A set of upper layer (layers 3 and 4) protocols, typically used in conjunction with Ethernet. An alternative to DECnet or TCP/IP.
XQP	*Extended QIO processor* A VMS process that receives requests for data.
X.3	CCITT standard for interfacing asynchronous devices to X.25 networks.
X.21	CCITT standard for circuit-switched networks. Often, a circuit is established using X.21, followed by X.25 traffic over the circuit.
Yellow Pages	A set of services in the Network File System that propagate information out from masters to recipients. Used for the maintenance of system files on complex networks.

Index